CONTEMPORARY TOURIST BEHAVIOUR

Photograph credits:

Iman Simon (4, 5, 6, 8, 9, 12, 14, 15); Lina Simon (3, 10); Ori Hameiri (7, 13); Dan Hameiri (11); Jackie Clarke (1); David Bowen (2)

Thanks:

We would like to thank the numerous individuals who contributed wittingly or otherwise to Contemporary Tourist Behaviour – from fellow tourists who sparked some ideas and made us relate the theory to the real world; through to tourism workers and managers in many parts of the world; and our students who expected us to use their time well and who asked interesting questions. Also, the CABI team – especially our editor Sarah Hulbert – as well as colleagues in the Marketing Department and Hospitality, Leisure and Tourism Management Department of the Business School, Oxford Brookes University.

And finally, a very special thank-you to our friends and families who we sometimes left behind (or vice versa) in the process of writing this book.

CONTEMPORARY TOURIST BEHAVIOUR

Yourself and Others as Tourists

David Bowen and Jackie Clarke
Oxford Brookes University, UK

www.cabi.org

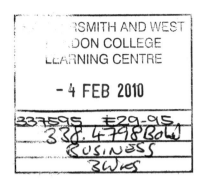
CABI is a trading name of CAB International

CABI Head Office
Nosworthy Way
Wallingford
Oxfordshire OX10 8DE
UK
Tel: +44 (0)1491 832111
Fax: +44 (0)1491 833508
E-mail: cabi@cabi.org
Website: www.cabi.org

CABI North American Office
875 Massachusetts Avenue
7th Floor
Cambridge, MA 02139
USA
Tel: +1 617 395 4056
Fax: +1 617 354 6875
E-mail: cabi-nao@cabi.org

A catalogue record for this book is available from the British Library, London, UK.

Library of Congress Cataloging-in-Publication Data

Bowen, David.
  Contemporary tourist behaviour : yourself and others and tourists / David Bowen and Jackie Clarke.
      p. cm. -- (CABI tourism texts)
    Includes bibliographical references and index.
    ISBN 978-1-84593-520-7 (alk. paper)

  1. Tourism--Social aspects. 2. Tourists--Psychology. 3. Consumer behavior.
I. Clarke, Jackie, 1966- II. Title. III. Title: Contemporary tourist behavior. IV. Series.

  G155.A1B69 2009
  306.4'819--dc22

                                         2009004472

ISBN-13: 978 1 84593 520 7

Typeset by SPi, Pondicherry, India.
Printed and bound in the UK by Cambridge University Press, Cambridge.

The paper used for the text pages in this book is FSC certified. The FSC (Forest Stewardship Council) is an international network to promote responsible management of the world's forests.

CONTENTS

Contents

FIGURES

TABLES

PROLOGUE: YOU THE TOURIST

This is a small book with bold ambitions.

We would like to examine you, the tourist, and others as tourists, from the big picture through to the intricate detail.

We want to dislodge the stereotype of the tourist as 'somebody else'. It is easy to dismiss the camera-wielding incongruously dressed tourist who arrives by charter flight – the cartoon character of the newspapers, anecdotes and postcards, who spends time sightseeing, shopping and sunning themselves on the beach. They are not us, but them.

They have been 'them' in popular culture for a long time. The travel book *Jogging Round Majorca* published in 1929 around the inception of modern-day mass tourism describes how

> [t]hirty open cars, full of people whom we could dimly see through the tornado of dust, roared along the mountain road. Dust obscured the distant sea, obscured the sun, obscured the peaks above from the sight of God and man, and particularly from the sight of the motorists. The valleys threw back the echoing roar of their engines and the hoot of their horns. Sheep on the uplands ceased from browsing, raised startled faces and bolted. Grey lizards flashed up the rocks, shedding their skins as they went, to hide in crevices and holes.…You have guessed correctly: the cars carried rich American tourists. They were 'doing' Majorca.
>
> (West, 1929, pp. 154–155)

In contrast, the author and his wife are walking along the road, taking their time. Later on, they use a local form of transport and travel by mule. Yet, despite the differences and the feelings expressed of 'us' and the American 'them' (perhaps the classic tourist stereotype of the time), the author and his wife are still *touristas*.

You may prefer the term 'traveller', 'backpacker' or 'explorer' to describe yourself. You may buy a safari holiday, a city short break or travel to visit your children who are studying at a university overseas. You may organize a trip yourself using the Internet or buy it pre-prepared from a travel agent. You may travel alone, with your family or with an educational group, local church or mosque. You may ski, sail, study seafood cookery, practise yoga, gamble in casinos, take a short break at a theme park or play golf – you may even do nothing at all but 'escape'. You may go abroad for a gap year, for business or even for an operation. You may go to the densest urban environments or the sparsest of populations. You are likely to search for the aesthetically and spiritually pleasing, but a minority seek out the 'worst' destinations to visit; the dangerous, the polluted, the ugly or abandoned. You may travel 160 km (the minimum distance for a tourist as recommended by the World Tourism Organization) or you may travel to the ends of the earth. One day you will probably be able to go into space.

But – like it or not – you are a tourist.

So we examine you, the tourist, in all your varied forms and outfits and life developments. We use a sweep of examples and a common theme of theoretical explanation. The concepts and ideas contained in this book have generic application as principles for better understanding tourists across the world. We use theory and evidence drawn from academia and industry. Approaches at university have been described as the *indiscipline of tourism* (Tribe, 1997) because study of the subject broadly divides into two, and sometimes opposing, fields: business and non-business studies. For this book, we draw on all the key disciplines that contribute to the better understanding of your behaviour as a tourist. We are interested in contributions from business studies, in particular consumer behaviour and marketing, and from the social sciences such as geography, sociology, anthropology and psychology. So we engage with a range of established and emerging theories from a combination of different disciplines. We also draw on industry material – for example, research studies with a practical agenda by companies, trade associations, special-interest groups and other bodies; newspaper articles and press releases; examples from around the globe that illustrate specific points. We look to unite these disparate sources and so contribute to an understanding of tourist behaviour.

The topic is stimulating. We are now in an era of mass tourism across and between continents in a way unsurpassed by the generations before us. For example, giants like China are truly on the move, driven by the rising middle classes and liberalizing policies to travel. Figures for the World Tourism Organization show that Chinese tourists spent US$30 billion while abroad in 2006 (WTO, 2008). Domestic tourism is also flexing its muscles, with the Chinese taking some 1.6 billion trips in 2006. According to the Hurun Report (a Chinese media and events company specializing in the super-rich), China's newly wealthy now rank travel as their top leisure activity (China Luxury Travel Fair, 2006). Something similar might be said for India, Russia and other former Soviet satellite states, many countries in Southeast Asia and the Gulf States – all have great swathes of population ready to add travel and tourism to their desired lifestyle.

This same era of mass tourism is also one of unprecedented challenges – global equity, distributive justice, poverty alleviation, fuel shortage and climate change. The status, role and behaviour of tourists, both international and domestic, are being questioned and interrogated; what tourists (and tourism) contribute to the problems and what tourists (and tourism) might contribute to possible solutions.

The authors are practising tourists and have been for decades. Between us, we have back-packed in South America and much of Europe, visited friends in Japan and Singapore, participated in conferences in different countries like Poland and China and Australia, climbed volcanoes on the island of Réunion, jazz-danced in Sweden and line-danced in Kentucky, sunbathed in Mallorca and many other places, repaired walls at a heritage site, attended weddings in New York and Israel, and explored the honeypots and less-visited corners of the UK. We say this not to create a list of 'been there, done that' goals to tick off, but to illustrate the infinite variety of accumulated tourist experience that is not atypical to someone of our generation and background in the developed world today. In addition, taken together, we have a tally of around 40 years as professional observers, industry practitioners and academics of tourist behaviour. We coincide in that we both have a background in human geography and currently research and teach tourist and consumer behaviour within business or management studies. We see much of our own tourist behaviour mirrored in the theories and ideas that we explore within this book.

We have structured the chapters into four parts:

- Admiring the panorama
- Focusing the binoculars
- Enjoying the slide show
- Gazing into the crystal ball.

The first part, 'Admiring the Panorama' is all about the sweeping vista of tourist behaviour. It is the big picture of global statistics, patterns of tourist movement and broad determinants, of development as a tourist and life change.

After admiring the panorama, the second part sharpens the focus on to the individual tourist. We consider external influences, motivations, decision making and models that seek to explain an individual tourist's behaviour. We train our binoculars to follow a tourist through their tourism experience, the interactions that they have and the impacts that they make and their resulting judgements of satisfaction – or otherwise.

We then offer a slide show of some tourist behaviour highlights, each selected on merit for its relevance and interest. A few are classic, 'not-to-be-missed' highlights, whereas others are more unexpected. We invite you to sit back and enjoy the show of brands and celebrity, families, fear and gift giving – all as they inform tourist behaviour.

The final part gazes into the crystal ball to see how tourist behaviour might evolve in the future. It garners opinions on the environmental challenges and trends and harnesses the expertise of different tourism industry sectors and governmental and non-governmental bodies.

And to balance our prologue, we have a short epilogue that explains the underpinnings of the methods that lie behind the research on which this book draws.

Whether you read the book from start to finish or dip in and out of chapters as inclination takes you, we hope you gain some intriguing insight into your own behaviour as a tourist and that of others around you.

The Authors

REFERENCES

China Luxury Travel Fair (2006) Australia now the top travel destination for China's richest. Available at: http://www.chinaluxurytravelfair.com/press.asp

Tribe, J. (1997) The indiscipline of tourism. *Annals of Tourism Research* 24(3) 638–657.

West, G. (1929) *Jogging Round Majorca*. Black Swan, London.

World Tourism Organization (WTO) (2008) Emerging tourism markets – the coming economic boom. WTO, Madrid 24 June 2008. Available at: http://www.unwto.org/media/news/en/press_det.php?id=2462&idioma=E

chapter 1

THE TOURIST TODAY

In this chapter, we unravel when you are – and when you are not – a tourist in your travels. You may believe that you instinctively know, but common perceptions often diverge from accepted conceptual and technical definitions. So here we do some groundwork to establish exactly what is and is not included in the term 'tourist'. We could say that this chapter acts as a foundation and orientation exercise for the rest of the book. It is a short chapter and less discursive than the chapters it precedes.

Conceptually, tourism may be conceived as 'the temporary, short-term movement of people to destinations outside the places where they normally live and work and their activities during the stay at these destinations' (Burkart and Medlik, 1981, p. *v*). You the tourist are the principal actor within this movement and activity. As a book that seeks to explore contemporary tourist behaviour, we let the principal actor take centre stage.

SEVEN MISCONCEPTIONS AND REALITIES ABOUT YOU THE TOURIST

There are a number of popular misconceptions about tourists. As memorable tales are often portrayed in sevens, we borrow the magical quality of that number, to highlight for your perusal what we consider to be seven misconceptions about tourists.

Misconception one: Most tourists are international – even long haul. This is not the case. The majority of tourists are domestic, being roughly eight to ten times in magnitude. It is perhaps the aura of glamour that surrounds international travel that props it up on its pedestal. More mundanely, its significance within the household budget as a hefty item of expenditure also contributes to its elevated position.

Misconception two: Most tourists use airplanes to get to their destination. This is not the case. The majority of tourists travel using surface transport, in particular that beacon of personal mobility, the car. Overall, misconceptions one and two are related, for if you believe that most tourists are international (even long haul), then you probably believe in the dominance of air transport.

Misconception three: To be a tourist is to be a leisure tourist. This is only partly the case. To be a tourist, you can be a health tourist, an educational tourist or a business tourist (among others) just as well as being a leisure tourist. We look at 'purpose' as an important defining principle of being a tourist later in the chapter.

Misconception four: 'I am not a tourist because, although I now live in another country, I am a national of the country that I am visiting.' This is not the case. If you have lived abroad for most of the past 12 months or have lived there for a shorter period but intend to continue to do so, you are a resident of that country and therefore a tourist in the country of your birth. It is not your nationality that matters, but your residency. It follows that so-called visiting friends and relatives (VFR) tourism is important in tourist behaviour.

Misconception five: To be a tourist is to take a package tour or inclusive tour with tour operators and other tourism providers such as all-inclusive resorts and hotels. This is only partly the case. If you travel independently, you are also a tourist. In other words, you are not defined as a tourist purely because you buy products from the tourism industry. You could be a tourist and buy no commercial service or product from the tourism industry at all. For example, you could elect to drive to the destination, stay with friends or camp out as the law allows, take picnics, and enjoy walking or swimming in the sea. As a more realistic and less extreme example, you are almost certainly aware of the way that many tourists have adapted to the Internet to make their own travel arrangements with accommodation and transport providers, choosing to bypass tour operators and travel agents in doing so.

Misconception six: To be a tourist is to be on your annual summer holiday. This is only partly the case. You can be a tourist on a second, third or even seventh holiday. You can be a tourist on innumerable short breaks. You can be a tourist in your gap year (as long as you do not exceed 12 months). You can be a tourist at any point in the calendar year. There are many opportunities beyond the traditional holiday pattern – modern-day tourism is fragmented and diverse. And – remember – that is just considering you as a leisure tourist!

Misconception seven: 'I am a traveller/explorer/backpacker/guest (delete as appropriate). It is others who are tourists. I am something else.' This is probably not the case and we hope to convince you of this by the end of this chapter. You are almost certainly a tourist too (if a certain subgroup, type or style). This misconception has much to do with the unenviable reputation of mass tourists built up over the last 50 years or so and the caricatures that abound – for example, the *ridiculous* tourist, the *naive* tourist or the *rich* tourist (Krippendorf, 1987). As a consequence, many individuals try to dissociate themselves from being tourists.

It is the misconception that we highlighted in the prologue.

WHAT, IN ESSENCE, IS A TOURIST?

To distil the essence of a tourist, we need to consider that this form of temporary migration or trip undertaken by an individual has the following characteristics:

- It is a movement outside the *usual environment* or normal place of residence and work. A particular distance is stipulated by some countries – the World Tourism Organization (WTO) recommends 160 km.
- The duration involved (typically referred to as *length of stay*) is from one night to a maximum of 1 year.
- It conforms to one or more of the strict *purpose* of visit categories – for example, recreation, business, educational studies, VFR or health treatment.
- *Remuneration* such as wages, salary and payments-in-kind from within the destination visited is neither received nor sought from the trip (Burkart and Medlik, 1981; Smith, 1995; Cooper *et al.*, 2008).
- Particularly for the leisure tourist, it is a *voluntary* activity undertaken by choice (Cohen, 2004); a *discretionary act* (Beirman, 2003, p. 3).

According to the WTO, we can extend this list of purpose of visit categories to include cultural events, health, active sports, meetings, incentive travel and tourists in transit (when staying overnight). The WTO has invested much over the decades in standardizing tourist definitions and in fostering consistency across different countries for statistical reasons. None the less, Smith's (1995, p. 26) point that operational definitions should be judged on their ability to deal with the vast majority of cases and not the highly unusual circumstance is worth noting.

A BASIC FRAMEWORK FOR CATEGORIZING TOURISTS

We have already mentioned both international tourists and domestic tourists, but we need to broaden the framework to introduce other useful categories. To recapitulate, we have the following:

- International tourists: They travel for one night or more for acceptable purposes outside of their country of residency.
- Domestic tourists: They travel for one night or more for acceptable purposes within their country of residency but outside their usual environment of home and work.

As noted by Cooper *et al.* (2008), the distinctions between international tourists and domestic tourists are blurring for some regions of the world – for example, within the European Union, as borders soften and political jurisdiction widens.

We can develop this further by dividing international tourists into two types (World Tourism Organization, 1991):

- Inbound tourists: They are non-residents of a country visiting a country other than their own. In other words, they are coming into a country, for example, in the case of Argentina, Canadian residents visiting Argentina as tourists.
- Outbound tourists: They are residents of a country visiting a country other than their own. In other words, they are going out of a country, for example, in the case of Argentina, Argentinian residents visiting Canada as tourists.

Of course, governments are also interested in the flows of money that accompany such tourist movements. With our example of Argentina, inbound tourists from Canada bring new money into the country as they spend on accommodation and activities – thus, inbound tourism is a type of export for Argentina. Conversely, outbound tourists from Argentina travelling to Canada take money out of the country – thus, outbound tourism is a type of import for Argentina. To finish the trio, domestic tourists as they redirect money within the one country (say, the different regions of Argentina) could be conceived as aiding import substitution.

To draw the ideas together, we can add the following to this framework:

- International tourists: They comprise inbound and outbound tourists as already stated.
- Internal tourists: They comprise inbound and domestic tourists as they move around the single country of – in our example – Argentina.
- National tourists: They comprise domestic and outbound tourists as residents of a single country – in our example, Argentina – move around their own country and other countries.

The WTO (1991) brought together domestic tourists, outbound tourists, inbound tourists, international tourists, internal tourists and national tourists into one basic framework. We have worked up our simple illustration of Argentina into the diagram to better marry the text with the visual representation (see Fig. 1.1). As you can imagine, this way of thinking about tourists is useful for national governments and international bodies concerned with the monitoring of global tourist flows.

BEWARE THE DISTINCTIONS!

If memorable tales are not portrayed in sevens, then invariably the number three provides the backbone to the storyline. In a similar fashion, we want to draw your attention to three important distinctions over which it is so easy to stumble.

Distinction one: It is between tourists and visitors. We introduce the term 'visitor' because it is an integral component of the WTO definitions for tourists. All tourists are visitors but not all visitors are tourists. The word visitor is used to denote both tourists (who – remember – stay

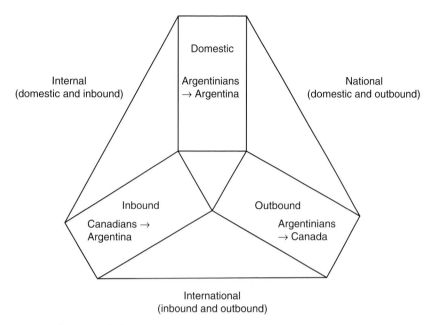

Fig. 1.1. Basic framework for categorizing tourists. (Adapted from World Tourism Organization, 1991.)

for one night or more) and *same-day visitors* (who – not being tourists – do not stay the night). The same-day visitor used to be called excursionist as well. There are permutations of same-day visitors, for they can be domestic or they can be international. Indeed, international same-day visitors can be an important market for countries that encourage duty-free shopping or for neighbouring countries with easy access. And, of course, you can talk of inbound and outbound international same-day visitors.

Distinction two: It is between tourists and travellers. We introduce the term 'traveller' because it is an integral component of the WTO definitions for tourists. All tourists and visitors are travellers, but not all travellers are tourists or visitors. Travellers include diplomats, members of the armed forces, representations of consulates, refugees, transit passengers in the confines of an airport or port, nomads, permanent immigrants, temporary immigrants and border workers – none of these travellers is included in tourist statistics. They are not tourists.

Like all good tales using the number three, there is a certain repetition in the first two sections of the plot. The third differs, and with this at the top of the mind we move on to our third and final distinction.

Distinction three: It is between tourists as numbers of people and tourists as numbers of trips. They are not one and the same. When statistics speak of the number of arrivals, they are referring to individual trips taken and not to individual people. To take a fresh example, one German tourist visiting Australia twice in a single year is measured as two trips or two arrivals. Computed for Australia, over five million international tourist arrivals were measured for the year 2006 (World

Tourism Organization, 2008a). Taken at face value, the unwary might assume that this statistic represents over five million individual tourists. It does not. It represents over five million trips.[1] As a result, those in the know think about the frequency of trips taken by individuals too. As a corollary, if you as an individual visit several countries during a single holiday (sometimes referred to as a multi-centred trip), your arrival in each country is recorded separately (World Tourism Organization, 2008b). So a round-the-world trip may be a seamless holiday of a lifetime to you, but statistically your activity will be measured in accordance with the number of countries that you enter. The upshot is that numbers of tourist arrivals do not necessarily equate to the number of people.

RELATED CONCEPTS

Tourism, leisure and recreation are all related to one another. At an introductory level, leisure is a 'combined measure of time and attitude of mind to create periods of time when other obligations are at a minimum' (Cooper *et al.*, 2008, p. 15). It is discretionary time – that is, time that you have free after the basics of life (eating, sleeping, washing, etc.) and commitments (work, commuting, shopping for food, etc.) have been accounted for. Recreation consists of the activities carried out during leisure time. It is – at an introductory level – a pursuit-based concept.

Tourism – strictly speaking, leisure tourism – requires enough blocks of leisure to allow an overnight stay. But, of course, as you know, not all tourism is leisure-driven. Leisure time can also be spent at home (doing such recreational activities as reading, watching television, playing computer games), in the local environs (going to the cinema, the swimming pool, the bar or coffee shop) or at a distance in the form of a day trip (our same-day visitors visiting a historic attraction, the zoo, participating in an air-balloon experience or whatever).

Changing direction from leisure and recreation, another related concept is you the tourist as a consumer. That is, a consumer of holidays through the right to exercise choice. You can be a consumer of flights, accommodation, hire car services, natural resources, or local cultures and souvenirs. The consumer and the corresponding notion of consumption are dominating forces in many societies today. Thought-provokingly as stated by Gabriel and Lang (2006), by the start of the 21st century

> we had learnt to talk and think of each other and of ourselves less as workers, citizens, parents or teachers, and more as consumers. Our rights and our powers derive from our standing as consumers; our political choices are votes for those promising us the best deal as consumers; our enjoyment of

---

[1] Pause to ponder. Thought through logically, one might expect the actual number of individual German tourists to Australia to be close to the statistic for international tourist arrivals from Germany because: (i) it is a long-haul trip from Germany to Australia probably taken infrequently; and (ii) there are associated high costs in terms of discretionary time and money. The discrepancies would be greater between short-haul or neighbouring countries with strong social and business connections where individual residents are likely to cross the borders on a frequent basis.

life is almost synonymous with the quantities (and to a lesser extent qualities) of what we consume. Our success is measured in terms of how well we are doing as consumers. Consumption is not just a means of fulfilling needs but permeates our social relations, identities, perceptions and images.

(Gabriel and Lang, 2006, p. 1)

The consumer and the tourist collide at the retail outlets and shopping malls that have become tourist attractions in their own right – shopping honeypots where the buying of tangible products and brands is aggressively to the fore as a recreational activity. Some destinations – for example, Hong Kong or New York – are acknowledged for their success as magnets for tourists who love to shop. The rise of consumerism may yet prove a late-20th-century phenomenon to be tempered or terminated by current economic events rocking financial structures and by society demands for environmental constraints to consumption. However, for the purposes of this book, the idea of the tourist as a consumer offers useful theoretical insights into understanding contemporary tourist behaviour. Both, after all, are voluntary behaviours.

THE VITAL STATISTICS OF TOURISTS

There are three key measurements taken for you the tourist, which can be labelled as volume, value and profile (Burkart and Medlik, 1981; Cooper *et al.*, 2008). Volume statistics measure things like the number of trips, number of nights and length of stay. Value statistics measure things like spend per trip, spend per person, spend per day and the breakdown of spend between different product categories such as transport, accommodation, activities, meals and so forth.

Different tourism organizations are interested in different forms of these statistics. For example, length of stay for a national tourism organization is measured in nights. An attraction is more interested in length of stay in the form of 'dwell time' – a consideration of how many hours the visitor spends at the attraction. The tourism section for a city council is interested in both measures – length of stay in nights for tourists and in hours for same-day visitors.

Profile statistics can be thought of as describing both you and the details of the trip that you take. There are many possibilities (see Tables 1.1 and 1.2) that configured together in some form to produce a more rounded and individual picture of the tourist than the vital statistics of volume and expenditure. Hence the term 'profile' is appropriate for it denotes a silhouette that distinguishes you from others. Table 1.1 – person characteristics – relates to the individual unconnected to the trip decision. It would hold equally true for the purchases of breakfast cereals, cars or banking services. Table 1.2 – trip characteristics – relates to the individual within the context of a trip decision. It would not be relevant to other purchases because it describes an interface between the person and that unique trip decision.

Many such profile statistics are captured by different tourism organizations through their market research and market intelligence according to their business needs. They are often used to identify and subsequently target specific groups or segments of tourists that share profile characteristics that are attractive to the organization.

Table 1.1. Tourist profiles: illustrations of person characteristics. (Adapted from Godfrey and Clarke, 2000.)

Age	Gender
Occupation	Income level
Household size	Household composition
Social class	Nationality
Religion	Ethnic origin
Media habits	Car ownership
Attitudes	Opinions
Life stage	Personality
Education level	Marital status
Paid leave entitlement	Country of residence
Rural/urban resident	Lifestyle
Interests/hobbies	Beliefs/values

Table 1.2. Tourist profiles: illustrations of trip characteristics. (Adapted from Godfrey and Clarke, 2000.)

Purpose of trip, e.g. leisure, business, VFR	Benefits sought by tourist
Motivation for trip	Trip duration
Distance travelled	Party size by adults/children
Party composition	Timing of trip, e.g. month, peak, trough
Price sensitivity	Sensitivity to other marketing factors
Information sources used	Method of booking, e.g. online, direct
Timing of booking e.g. advance, last minute	Method of payment
Timing of payment	Usage rate, e.g. heavy, light
Usage status, e.g. first time user, regular	Decision-making roles
Purchase occasion, e.g. honeymoon	Frequency of use
Use of travel organizers, e.g. travel agents	Mode of transport
Social/environmental sensitivity	Satisfaction levels
Loyalty status (to brand)	Decision load/decision environment
Patterns of tourism components used, e.g. accommodation, activities	Trip patterns, e.g. touring, single destination, multi-destination

Do not forget that volume statistics (such as length of stay) and value statistics (such as spend per trip/day/head) also play a part.

Travel propensities

With outbound tourism (as a volume statistic) equating to an import (as a value statistic), countries are apt to calculate the travel propensities of their resident population. There are two types of travel propensity, one being the net travel propensity and the other being the gross travel propensity.

The net travel propensity is the percentage of the population that takes at least one tourist trip in a stated period of time, typically a year. It tells you what proportion of the population participates in tourism. In the 1990s, Medlik (1993) recorded Sweden and Switzerland as having the highest net travel propensities in Europe. Figures for Switzerland in 2007 suggest a net travel propensity of 88%, a significant increase from the mid-1990s (Laesser and Bieger, 2008). However, Cooper *et al.* (2008) suggest that a net travel propensity between 70% and 80% would be the maximum for many Western countries today (after all, not everyone is able or willing to participate in tourism).

The gross travel propensity is the total number of tourist trips in a stated period of time, typically a year, as a percentage of the population. As people take extra holidays, so the gross travel propensity increases. Cooper *et al.* (2008) suggest that a gross travel propensity of nearly 200% has been achieved in some Western countries.

When the gross travel propensity (say, 180%) is divided by the net travel propensity (say, 65%), the average number of trips taken by people participating in tourism over the given time period is calculated – in this case, 2.77 trips. This is the travel frequency for the population of the relevant country.

Behind the travel propensity figures are the broad determinants of demand that operate at the macro or society level. Travel propensity for any country's population is likely to increase with a rise in income levels, greater urbanization, higher educational attainment, smaller family size, greater paid leave entitlement and further spread of car ownership (Cooper *et al.*, 2008; Middleton and Clarke, 2001).

THE GLOBAL TOP SEVEN

Rankings of countries based on vital statistics for tourists give a snapshot of the global picture (see Table 1.3). The table only captures a point in time, in this case 2006, and lacks a sense of dynamism (though we have placed the ranking for 2004 in parentheses where applicable to get a flavour of movement). We have listed the top seven countries for international tourist arrivals (a volume statistic), for outbound international tourists (a volume statistic) and for international tourism receipts (a value statistic).

Governments are interested in those countries that generate international arrivals and tourism receipts for their country. These countries are referred to as generating countries, origin countries or source countries. Of recent interest have been the emerging powerhouses of the 'BRIC' countries – Brazil, Russia, India and China. Both China and Russia feature in the top seven generating countries of the world (see Table 1.3). In the same year (2006), Brazil generated some

Table 1.3. The global top seven. (From World Tourism Organization, 2006, 2008a; international departures compiled from World Tourism Organization, 2008b and rounded to one decimal place.)

International tourist arrivals 2006			International tourism receipts 2006			International departures 2006[b]		
Rank[a]	Country	Million	Rank[a]	Country	Billion (US$)	Rank[a]	Country	Million
1 (1)	France	78.9	1 (1)	USA	85.7	1 (2)	Hong Kong	75.8
2 (2)	Spain	58.2	2 (2)	Spain	51.1	2 (1)	Germany	71.2
3 (3)	USA	51.0	3 (3)	France	46.3	3 (3)	UK	69.5
4 (4)	China	49.9	4 (4)	Italy	38.1	4 (4)	USA	63.7
5 (5)	Italy	41.1	5 (7)	China	33.9	5 (5)	Poland	44.7
6 (6)	UK	30.7	6 (5)	UK	33.7	6 (6)	China	34.5
7 (8)	Germany	23.5	7 (6)	Germany	32.8	7 (7)	Russian Fed.	29.1

[a] The figure in parentheses refers to the rank for that country in 2004.
[b] Figure includes same-day visitors.

4.8 million international tourists and India, around 8.3 million (World Tourism Organization, 2008b). National tourism bodies have been investing where feasible in the BRIC countries to ensure a slice of the international outbound tourism markets as the BRIC economies develop.

SPECULATING THE TOURIST MIX FOR A SPECIFIC COUNTRY

In lieu of statistics, it is possible to guesstimate what the tourist mix for any given country might look like. Other things being equal (e.g. the sufficient development of tourism infrastructure), it is predicated on four key questions:

1. Who are the top generating countries in the world? It is likely that these important sources for international tourist arrivals will figure strongly in the mix (refer to Table 1.3).
2. Who are the neighbouring countries, in particular those that share borders? It is likely that international tourist (and same-day visitor) arrivals from such countries will figure strongly in the mix too. After all, relatively less discretionary time and income are typically the case for short-haul than long-haul travel, and there is usually a choice of transport mode to make the journey. Short-break holidays can be important here.
3. What are the social, cultural, linguistic, historical and economic ties between the given country and another? The closer the ties, the greater the chance that residents from that country are likely to figure strongly in the tourist mix. For example, the Portuguese favour

Latin American countries for tourist trips because of the historical affinity, shared social characteristics and the linguistic connections (Correia *et al.*, 2007) – what is termed the 'cultural distance' is not so great. VFR tourism can be important in such an instance.

4. What is the current political situation between the given country and another and what is the manifestation of this? The smoother the political relationship, the more likely it is that international tourist arrivals will figure strongly in the mix too. The smoothness of visa processes (if any), border controls and security, the absence of political tension (or media interpretation of such tension), the existence of agreements (e.g. the Approved Destination Status system of China or the Schengen Agreement of the European Union), and – at a pinch under the politico-economic banner – the comparative exchange rates[2] are all important features. The business tourist is also likely to thrive alongside the leisure tourist where cordial political relationships between countries exist.

Of course, in the tourist mix for a given country, we should not forget the importance of the domestic tourist. In fact, a healthy number of frequent domestic tourists with a high spend help offset the negative effects that occur when international tourist arrivals stutter or fall. Domestic tourists can prove reliable and robust. As an extreme example, when there is heightened tension between Israel and its neighbours (especially Lebanon and Syria in the north) – so that international tourists delay or abandon trips – the Israeli domestic market often grows in strength because citizens want to support friends and relatives in a time of extra stress.

BUILDING ON THE FOUNDATION

We hope to have convinced you as to when you are – and when you are not – a tourist. We have looked at the notions of usual environment, purpose of visit and duration of stay. We have identified domestic, international, inbound, outbound, internal and national tourists as used by the WTO. We have highlighted the vital statistics of volume, value and profile. And we have given a taster of the importance of you as a tourist to different countries by introducing the global top seven – our chart busters.

Yet, the chapter probably feels a touch impersonal and remote. It addresses you the tourist at a macro level, as part of the ebb and flow of tourism statistics between countries and as an outcome of the major forces that influence these movements. From the foundations now established, our next chapter moves on to elucidate tourist behaviour as exhibited by different nations – for example, how might a German tourist differ from, say, a Chinese tourist? And what explanations can be offered for their respective behaviours? Or, as tourists, do we simply share common patterns and characteristics of behaviour unencumbered by nationality?

---

[2] It is November 2008 and the Icelandic krona has fallen some 65% against the pound at a time when the pound is weakening against the euro and the dollar. As a result, Icelandair has reported that the demand for weekend short-break packages to Iceland from the UK has increased 50% compared with November 2007. In a nutshell, the pound buys more, making Iceland a more attractive destination for price-sensitive markets such as much leisure-based tourism (Lanyado, 2008).

REFERENCES

Beirman, D. (2003) *Restoring Tourism Destinations in Crisis. A Strategic Marketing Approach.* CAB International, Wallingford, UK.

Burkart, A.J. and Medlik, S. (1981) *Tourism Past Present and Future*, 2nd edn. Heinemann, London.

Cohen, E. (2004) *Contemporary Tourism: Diversity and Change*. Elsevier, London.

Cooper, C., Fletcher, J., Fyall, A., Gilbert, D. and Wanhill, S. (2008) *Tourism Principles and Practice*, 4th edn. FT Prentice-Hall, Harlow, UK.

Correia, A., Santos, C.M. and PestanaBarros, C. (2007) Tourism in Latin America. A choice analysis. *Annals of Tourism Research*, 34 (3), 610–629.

Gabriel, Y. and Lang, T. (2006) *The Unmanageable Consumer*, 2nd edn. Sage Publications, London.

Godfrey, K. and Clarke, J. (2000) *The Tourism Development Handbook. A Practical Approach to Planning and Marketing*. Cassell, London.

Krippendorf, J. (1987) *The Holiday Makers. Understanding the Impact of Leisure and Travel*. Heinemann, London.

Laesser, C. and Bieger, T. (2008) *Travel Market Switzerland 2007 Basic Report and Database Specification*. Institute for Public Services and Tourism, University of St Gallen, St Gallen, Switzerland. Available at: www.unisg.ch/hsgweb.nsf/bf9b5a227ab50613c1256a8d003f0349/697be17f222d7486c1257 4ac002896b6/$FILE/Travel%20MarketSwitzerland_2007(Basic%20Report).pdf

Lanyado, B. (2008) Where the pound is still sound. *The Guardian*, 22 November 2008, Money Section, p. 3.

Medlik, S. (1993) *Dictionary of Travel, Tourism and Hospitality*. Butterworth Heinemann, Oxford.

Middleton, V.T.C. and Clarke, J. (2001) *Marketing in Travel and Tourism*, 3rd edn. Butterworth Heinemann, Oxford.

Smith, S.L.J. (1995) *Tourism Analysis. A Handbook*, 2nd edn. Addison-Wesley Longman, Harlow, UK.

World Tourism Organization (WTO) (1991) *International Conference on Travel and Tourism Statistics. Ottawa (Canada), 24–28 June 1991*. World Tourism Organization, Madrid.

World Tourism Organization (WTO) (2006) *Tourism Highlights 2006 Edition*. World Tourism Organization, Madrid.

World Tourism Organization (WTO) (2008a) *Tourism Highlights 2008 Edition*. World Tourism Organization, Madrid.

World Tourism Organization (WTO) (2008b) *Compendium of Tourism Statistics Data 2002–2006*. World Tourism Organization, Madrid.

chapter 2

COUNTRY-FILE: TOURIST NATIONS

In any consideration of tourists from different nations, a number of things should colour our thoughts right from the start.

First, in today's world, the so-called postmodernist world, there is an increasing differentiation in what people want to do in their tourist lives. For example, it is foolhardy to consider that the inclusive tour package of the post-1950s (as developed in the nations of Western Europe) has ceased to be a viable model. But the model has changed and a smaller proportion of the tourist public seek out an inclusive tour with all elements of transport and accommodation and attractions pre-arranged and prepaid. It is unlikely that the old model will be returned to – and far more likely that tourists will seek variety within a less tightly defined inclusive tour. At least in Western Europe – and maybe, too, in a wider Europe now that the West–East division is more subtle – independent and semi-independent travel will most likely increase. So the tourist hordes, to use a pejorative term, will be scurrying around on various and *different* trails rather than *similar* trails. Tourist movements will by default become less strong and defined. The North–South summer flight by most of the nations in Europe will not be concentrated in Spain or Greece or Turkey but will spread throughout the Mediterranean and beyond. Commonality within the broad movements will also be less uniform. Moreover, there will be a break-up of other seemingly entrenched patterns of movement and other behaviour as the successive waves of tourists from newly emergent tourist nations such as China look for similar differentiation in what they do.

Second, we should not assume a continued growth in tourism numbers by all existing tourist nations. Because there has been over half a century of growth in tourism, it is difficult to argue that the trend will come to an end. But all assumptions need to be challenged so that we can be prepared for the unexpected. A blip in tourist numbers related to environmental concerns by individual tourists may be a momentary thing or may develop fast and hard, so that the current tourist way of life becomes as anathema as, say, other previously entrenched social activities in parts of Europe such as organized religious meetings. Or there may be a march forward in regulation on individual movement underscored by government concerns about environmentally unsustainable growth. Or, perhaps more likely, oil and other resources may really start to run out despite our assumed ingenuity to come up with new resource solutions. And finally, notwithstanding a continued growth in tourist numbers – and we speak here of both domestic and international tourists – we should not forget that even in nations whose population has a particularly high propensity to travel there are still significant numbers who are disenfranchised and not part of such movement. The tourist dream is not something within reach of all – tourism is driven by a combination of wealth and free time and other key elements, and one or more such elements are lacking for significant numbers of the population in all nations of the world.

TOURIST CASES

So, what does the global league table of tourist movements look like? Chapter 1, 'The Tourist Today' (this volume), has shown that when all is said and done it is the richer North (and West) of the world that has the most active tourists vis-à-vis the poorer South – even though there are large numbers of people who are not tourists even in the North.

One of the authors of this book well remembers the wry amusement of a group of four students who were provided the opportunity, sometime in the early 1990s, to review travel safety on a country-by-country basis for the Diana Lamplugh Trust in the UK. The Berlin Wall had fallen and it seemed each week that a new country was in the throes of creation within the former Soviet Union and satellites, so that the students' workload grew even as they dutifully worked on their task. Now, skipping forward 20 years or so and with over 200 countries worldwide, it is difficult to choose and highlight specific cases that give a flavour of broad contemporary tourist patterns and behaviours nation by nation. But there is logic in our choice of Germany and China below. Germany has historically been in the vanguard of tourism development through time while China has emerged as a new player.

German tourists

The German tourism industry is closely related to the strength of the German economy. Through most of the second half of the 20th century, there was continuous, strong economic growth up to and beyond the reunification of the East and West of the country. For the first 5 years of the 21st century, the growth was reduced and caused some levelling off or reduction in tourist movement – shown, too, in Chapter 6, 'Economic and Social Influences' (this volume), with specific reference to the influence of the German economy on the Balearics, Spain. But by 2000, the trend of nearly 50 years of growth had established the German tourist as a ubiquitous feature of tourism worldwide. According to Poon and Adams (2000) and as highlighted in Bauer (2002), by the end of the 20th century, the Germans were the world leader in trips taken and nights spent abroad (standard measures used by the World Tourism Organization (WTO) for country-by-country comparison – Chapter 1, 'The Tourist Today', this volume) and also had the highest travel propensity in the world with over three-quarters taking at least one annual 5-day holiday. Poon and Adams (2000) reckoned that the travel propensity would grow to 84% by 2005, although it actually levelled off as a result of economic downturn (Munoz, 2007).

The underlying strong tourist movement through time was based on high vertical integration – that is, tour operators with their own network of travel agents and other distribution outlets coupled with control and/or power over international and local transport and accommodation in destinations worldwide. But tourist movement was based on independent travel too. So much so that by the 21st century the same percentage of tourists organized everything independently as organized through a tour operator. Moreover, tourist motivation and activities matched what Poon (1993) had forecast in her far-seeing text. Tourists seek fulfilment rather than escape and are active rather than passive and also more environmentally aware – themes that we will return to below and also in Chapter 7, 'The Driving Force of Motivation' (this volume). This is not to say that the sun-and-sea model no longer holds for German tourists – after all the European Mediterranean had a market share of German tourists amounting to 26–29% through the early 2000s – and Spain alone had a share of 12–14% with a heavy concentration in the summer season (Munoz, 2007). But Germans are as close to 'new tourists' (Poon, 1993) – or an updated '*new, new tourist*' – as any other nation in the world.

Chinese tourists

While Germany as a tourist nation has a long pedigree, this cannot be claimed of China, one of the newer entrants into the world tourist stage. China as a tourist destination for inbound tourists has evolved with remarkable speed since the high-profile political visits such as that of US President Richard Nixon and the first tentative reopening of the country to Western influence. The faded photographs of the Nixon entourage, still on display at classic tourist destinations in China, can offer an illusion that the tourism development has had a longer period of incubation. But this is not the case. It was only in 1978 that the China International Travel Service (CITS) was allowed to market general tours through foreign operators and work with the operators to design their own China programmes. At the same time, other essential tourism elements such as group tourist visas became easier to obtain (EIU, 1995). But since then the largely uninterrupted move towards a market economy has developed apace, so much so that each day and week seems to bring some new and barely credible statistic about the growth of the domestic market, the outbound Chinese market or the market for inbound tourists. In large measure, the step-increase in tourism worldwide as a major service industry in the late 20th and early 21st centuries has happily coincided with the explosion and diversification of the Chinese economy – with the resultant demand, from its wealthier beneficiaries, for tourist experience.

There is no doubt that Destination China has the potential to become a remarkable overall tourism product – and so a remarkable tourist experience for both international and domestic visitors. China now has the most United Nations Educational, Scientific and Cultural Organization (UNESCO) World Heritage sites of any country in the world. Many areas of China, particularly in the west of the country, still lie comparatively dormant in tourism terms with yet-to-be audited tourism potential – admittedly, with all the environmental dangers so entailed. Indeed in this regard, as Watts (2006) reports,

> conservationists face a losing battle against the 100 tour operators, hotel chains and travel agents in Shangri-La (and other places across China's least developed and most beautiful regions) that are keen to grab a slice of the 50 bn yuan budget allocated to develop tourism (there in Shangri-La) over the next decade.

(Watts, 2006, p. 3)

Zhang *et al.* (1999) identify three distinct periods of tourism policy development in China – 1978–1985, 1986–1991 and 1992–1999. The period since Zhang's 1999 review – 2000 through to the present – coincides with China's accession to the WTO in November 2001, and its success in winning the bid to host the Olympics in Beijing in 2008. Despite such unevenness and difficulty, China certainly appears to have done more than hold steady on tourism growth in the first years of the 21st century. Indeed, it seems to have made long strides through the various planning and development stages outlined by the China National Tourism Administration (CNTA) – the 'foundation stage' (2000–2005); 'upgrading stage' (2006–2010); 'consolidation stage' (2011–2015) and 'stage of perfection' (2015–2020) (Guangrui and Lew, 2003). The maelstrom of projected growth and development in China is dependent on a number of variable elements and although the truly remarkable projections are feasible they are not inevitable – for example, even before the credit crunch in 2008/09, some economists warned that China has many of the characteristics necessary for a serious economic crash, a crash that would reverberate around the world economy (Richter, 2004). Just as in the case of Germany, there is no hiding from economic influence on tourists (outbound and domestic) despite the mainly positive coverage and analysis (Fishman, 2005). And the global character of varied crises – from natural disasters through to pandemics, terrorism and other political instability – can also have an effect on projections (see Chapter 13, 'Of Fear, Flight and Feistiness', this volume). Indeed, China has already experienced the sometimes-fickle character of the international tourist market following the Tiananmen Square incident in 1989 and the severe acute respiratory syndrome (SARS) epidemic in 2002.

In Yangshuo, not far from Guilin on the Li Jiang River, in an area given special status for tourism, it is possible to head away from the daily influx of cruise boats – that travel downstream from Guilin through the tropical karst limestone landscape – and rent bicycles or join trekking groups to the nearby hills. A café in Yangshuo, favoured by independent travellers, is aptly called the 'Red Capitalism Café'. This offers a nod to the communist past even though the emphasis in Yangshuo is much more on the capitalist future, a future that will cater to the tourists of other nations in the Hong Kong–Guilin–Xian–Beijing route, or routes inland and west with further development and diversification (such as Shangri-La); the new outbound groups; and the huge, really huge, numbers of domestic tourists. Inbound, outbound and domestic tourists – the three legs of the tourism table, as Baumgarten states (2003) – are each necessary for the development of a new tourism entity and a new nation of tourists.

But Arlt (2006, p. 82), a current authority on China's tourism, observes that '*the* domestic or *the* outbound tourist does not exist' – China is a large country with a highly diverse population. This is an interesting view and a view that is certainly credible. Ng *et al.* (2007, p. 1500) draw attention to how 'national culture offers only a limited view, as many countries welcome multiculturalism, have strong regional differences and include people of multiple nationalities'. Any suggestion that there is a single Chinese culture or behaviour is an oversimplification – clearly even more so than in countries of similar geographical size such as the USA. Specifically with regard to China, Arlt (2006, p. 92) bluntly states that the 'basic answer to questions about the characteristics and motivations of Chinese outbound travellers can only be: nobody knows'.

But, on the other hand, some things are known. First and foremost, politics has played a key role through time in both the suppression and growth of outbound tourism. For example, while Arlt (2006, p. 22) points out that 'until recently all long distance movements even within the country needed reasons and permissions', he suggests that visiting friends and relatives (VFR) outbound tourism thrived between the fall of Imperial China in 1911 and the rise of the People's Republic in 1949. Then came the Maoist clampdown on movement. But beyond the Maoist period, Arlt charts the progressive setting and breaking of political rules on outbound travel. After 1983, it was encouraged (as part of Chinese strategic foreign and economic policy) to destinations such as Hong Kong, Macao and countries in Asia with strong ethnic ties to China – home to 50 million overseas Chinese. Later, post-1995, in the face of new realities (and the de facto, underground development of private, non-sponsored, outbound tourism), this encouragement extended to the wider range of countries with Approved Destination Status (ADS). So wide, indeed, that Arlt (2006, p. 42) predicts the demise of the ADS system since 'almost all important destinations (are) covered' – a demise called for by the World Travel and Tourism Council (WTTC) (see Baumgarten, 2003).

Because the beneficiaries of the economic and political situation are securely grounded in their own culture, the travel motivations of Mainland Chinese, according to Arlt, are more 'pull' than 'push' (see Chapter 7, 'The Driving Force of Motivation', this volume). And by way of comparison with other outbound tourist nations (even if a misnomer for China) in four of the five cultural dimensions used by Hofstede (2001), China has an extreme position compared to three chosen comparators – the USA, Switzerland and Japan. First, it has the most pronounced 'long-term orientation' – the acceptance of delayed material, social and emotional needs. Second, it has the most pronounced 'power distance' – an acceptance and expectation that power is distributed unequally. This is good for group leaders – except that the group will also place high demands on the leaders' problem solving and knowledge. Third, it has the lowest 'individualism/highest collectivism' – the stress on personal relationships (*guanxi*), personal image and status (*mianzi*) and human obligation (*ren*) that places stress on group integration and harmony. This is a positive thing for the travel group. Fourth, it has the least pronounced 'uncertainty avoidance' – a feeling of discomfort in an unstructured situation. This is good when it comes to the need for flexibility and encounters with new things and is a mantra for any aspiring tourist. As Arlt (2006, p. 106) states, 'encounters with strange, unknown situations or persons are not perceived as a threat but as a reason for curiosity and amusement'.

And what about the domestic tourist? Here, we can make a stark contrast with the German case. Poon and Adams (2000) recorded that close on 70% of tourism movements among Germans are outbound – living in the heart of Europe, Germans need only drive their cars to leave their country south, west and east or even north to Scandinavia. But in the Chinese case, once movement to Hong Kong and Macao are excluded (for they are part of China nowadays despite the way that China currently counts the figures), only a very small percentage has travelled outbound – easily in single figures. The Chinese tourist as a domestic tourist is graphically captured by Watts (2004), who reports government estimates that 1.9 billion journeys were about to be made over the New Year period in the 'Year of the Monkey':

> It promises to be one of the greatest migrations in the history of humanity. Not Muslim pilgrims on the hajj, but record numbers of Chinese holidaymakers heading for their ancestral homes to celebrate the start of the Year of the Monkey....The exodus has already begun. In recent days, long lines have formed outside travel agencies. Stations and airports are packed with holiday makers...the transport ministry forecasts that 1.7 billion journeys will be made by bus, 137 million by train, 26 million by boat and 10.5 million by air.
>
> (Watts, 2004)

The scale of movement really does dwarf what happens, say, in Europe or North America during festival times – even though Watts makes loose use of the term 'migration'. Do not forget the reality on the ground, too. Arlt (2006) tells us that the Chinese word for a fun atmosphere is *renao* (meaning hot and noisy) – and Watts (2004) reports a government education campaign to address tourist habits, especially noticeable outside China, such as chatting on planes, ignoring no-smoking signs and spitting in the street.

The burgeoning development of domestic tourism, seen as wasteful, bourgeois and dangerous under Maoists, has required more than increased tourist time and money. It has also needed a move towards consumerism or at least, as in the case of 'Red tourism', consumerism with Chinese characteristics. Qu *et al.* (2005) observe that the pace of change only really started to accelerate when the principles of a market economy were not seen to conflict with the prevailing political ideology of the 'socialist market economy'. This brings us back to Yangshuo and the 'Red Capitalist Café' – a symbol if ever of a tourist nation, even one as diverse as China.

NATIONAL DIFFERENCE: REAL OR IMAGINED

In everyday experience, it is often a fair assumption that national differences cause variations in knowledge, attitudes, image formation – and actions. In a class of UK students, with English as a first language, the access to knowledge on Australia is far greater than, say, Argentina – the reverse for a class of students in Barcelona, Spain. Indeed, UK students often have far more knowledge of the Australian tourist product than they have of a near European neighbour –

like France. And speaking of tourists to France or maybe to every country, and of national characteristics, we are drawn to the words of the philosopher-tourist Steve Martin, as quoted by Vitello (2007) in the *New York Times* – 'Boy, those French, they have a different word for everything!'

The lack of shared language creates psychological distance between residents of different countries – even neighbours – and native English speakers in particular have a poor reputation for fluency in other languages.

But such difference among nations is not always the case, as shown in exploratory work by Prebensen (2007), who made an interesting experiment with French, German, Swedish and Norwegian tourists (who were visiting the southern French resort of Nice). The tourists were asked to make comments on the associations conveyed by selected words and pictures of Finnmark County, North Norway (deliberately chosen for its relative obscurity). They were also asked to produce a free collage, using pictures and words from magazines, of what they thought represented North Norway. As it turned out the French, along with the Germans and Swedes, have a common image (the cold, the nature, fish, salmon, the fjords and the clean environment). Moreover, even though the Swedes are geographical and linguistic neighbours of Norway, some informants had rather limited knowledge of their neighbour. For an explanation of this, you might need to ask a Swedish or Norwegian acquaintance – such a quirk in an international relationship is best left to insiders.

Other quirks are also worth consideration. On the surface, we outlined above what seemed like a distinctive German tourism industry and distinctive, identifiable, typical German tourist behaviour. But work by Prebensen *et al.* (2003) queried whether German tourists (in Norway) view themselves as typical or non-typical of the group they belong to (i.e. German tourists). So, is there such a thing as a typical German tourist – and by extension, is there such a thing as national German tourist behaviour? In the experienced words of Prebensen *et al.*:

> [I]t was expected that the respondents would view themselves as different from other tourists and that most German tourists would perceive themselves as non-typical. At the same time it was also expected that the respondents would report similar activities during their stay in Norway and that they would report more or less the same motives for their current trip, regardless of their self-allocation to one of the two groups (typical or non-typical).
>
> (Prebensen *et al.*, 2003, p. 417)

No doubt you are familiar with tourists who view themselves as different from other tourists – the sort of tourists who always claim to eat in restaurants 'just where the locals eat' and so on. Prebensen *et al.* find exactly this – 90% of tourists viewed themselves as non-typical German tourists, even though they were similar with regard to motivation, planning and action. But 90% of any given sample cannot be non-typical! So, Prebensen *et al.* connect such a finding to the discrepancy between people's perception of themselves, particularly as regards their negative attributes, and other people's perception of themselves. Other tourists are viewed less favourably than self – indeed as 'typical tourists'. It is a negative thing to be a typical tourist – and so people view themselves as non-typical and even as 'anti-tourists' (Jacobsen, 2000).

Of course, if we hold that self-perception is critical above all else then we can start to disassemble this chapter. We would lose the premise that there is such a thing as a tourist group small or large – including a national grouping. But we introduce this as an idea for thought rather than anything more concrete. Prebensen *et al.* (2003) offer a treatise on individualism but much else that relates to tourist nations offers a different perspective.

TOURIST MOTIVATION ACROSS NATIONALITY (AND SO CULTURE)

Back in the mainstream, we showcase in more depth particular aspects of tourist behaviour (such as motivation) applied across different nationalities. The role of tourist motivations will be dealt with in Chapter 7, 'The Driving Force of Motivation' (this volume). But, it is a useful precursor of what is to come, and serves our purpose here, to delve into tourist motivation across nationality – using nationality, rightly or wrongly, as a convenient shorthand for shared culture.

At a very practical level, specific motivations appear to differ across nationality. From a gamut of possible examples, we take a report from the *Times of India* (2008) on the eve of the Beijing Olympics:

> The Olympic torch might well burn bright on Friday, but the response (of Indian tourists) to the Games has been quite cold from this cricket-crazy nation….Had it been a cricket game held in any part of the world, the interest and excitement from Indians would have been fabulous but the scene with the Olympics is exactly opposite…there are no takers for this event.
>
> (*Times of India*, 2008)

So, in practical tourism terms, cricket motivates sport travel in India far more than the Olympics and so sets India apart. Pearce and Lee (2005) would not find such an observation surprising. At a conceptual, academic level, they point out how the universality of motivation theories is threatened by the difficulty of applying them across cultures – national cultures. Not that many researchers have tried – most studies of motivation still have a western focus with western tourists at the centre of the study. For example, in studies of festival tourism, Kim *et al.* (2006) find just two non-Western examples – the Moslem cultural festival at Jerash, Jordan (Schneider and Backman, 1996) and the Harbin Ice Lantern and Snow Festival in China (Dewar *et al.*, 2001). Hsu *et al.* (2007) add that attempts to apply models of tourist motivation in non-Western countries – such as the typology of push and pull factors – are narrowly confined to developed societies such as Taiwan and Japan.

However, Hsu *et al.* use source material from in-depth free-flow interviews with Chinese seniors living in Beijing and Shanghai to develop a culture-specific Chinese (national) model and set of propositions. These reflect and emphasize external conditions (societal progress, personal finance, time and health) and internal desires (improving well-being, escaping routines, socializing, seeking knowledge, pride and patriotism, personal reward and nostalgia). Hsu *et al.* (2007)

show how learning and knowledge gained through tourism allow the seniors to maintain respect despite the ongoing dramatic changes in the Chinese social and cultural context (Fig. 2.1). They also show how socializing as tourists allows seniors to increase contacts, decrease the chance of disengagement and remain active – the so-called continuity theory (Neugarten and Berkowitz, 1964). And, finally, they show how seniors would sacrifice time and money put aside for tourism to maintain the traditional model of family support and responsibility.

Without malice, many people from within South-east Asia would initially find it difficult to distinguish major differences between the nationals of different European nations – just as many people in Europe would struggle initially to distinguish a Chinese person from a Korean. But Kozak (2002) makes a comparison of British and German tourists in Mallorca (Spain) and Turkey and finds some objective motivational differences. The use of the word 'objective' is particularly important – one normally good-natured pastime among Europeans on vacation in Europe is to highlight national behaviour stereotypes among fellow Europeans (the English drinking tea or,

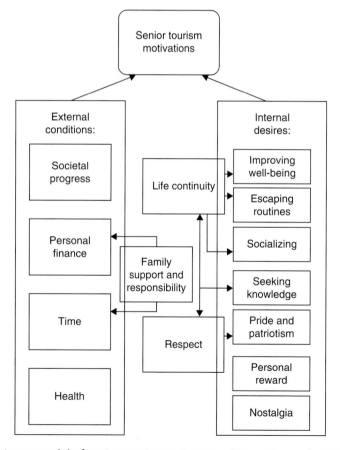

Fig. 2.1. A Chinese model of senior tourist motivations. (From Hsu *et al.*, 2007, p. 126.)

more likely, too much cheap lager and wearing sandals with socks; the Germans crisp and organized; the Italians chaotic and with large families in tow). So Kozak *objectively* generates, through factor analysis of a large-scale questionnaire survey, four types of tourist motivation – 'pleasure-seeking/fantasy', 'culture', 'relaxation' and what he awkwardly calls 'physical motivation' (to engage in sports, to be active and to get close to nature). And what about the result? Compared to the British, the Germans have higher scores in all but the first category. While not conclusive, by any means, and while different people from the same country can clearly have different motivations, Kozak (2002) at least points the way for further study and replication.

Maoz (2007) also shows the role of culture and nationality. She analyses backpacker motivations of her own nationality – Israelis – compared to backpackers from other countries. Maoz suggests that Israeli backpackers are highly cohesive and collective among themselves in 'a subculture, a kind of community with geographical boundaries and shared territory, language, rituals, dress, a sense of belonging, and mutual support' (Maoz, 2007, p. 131). At the same time, the Israeli backpackers emphasize the need for a purposeless existence and 'spend most of their time eating, drinking, smoking drugs and talking' (Maoz, 2007, p. 128). Escape is stronger as a motive than seeking – escape after military service and escape from family – and unlike the case with backpackers from other nationalities, escape is a communal thing, a group thing rather than an individual thing. Other studies of other backpackers, even from Israel, do not replicate Maoz's distinct findings but one cannot doubt the validity of her work, squarely based on in-depth qualitative study – and as a single and perhaps extreme case it dramatically illustrates national difference in tourist motivation. We broaden our thoughts on national (cultural) distance – beyond motivation – in Chapter 6, 'Economic and Social Influences' (this volume).

MARTIN-LIKE TRUISMS

So what can we conclude if, indeed, it is ever wise to conclude too much with regard to any aspect of tourist behaviour? Vitello (2007) in his piece of popular journalism, not only reminds us of quips from Steve Martin but also the truisms that we carry around with us in our travels – or that we use as we host other tourists:

> That people from different countries observe different customs – not only of speaking, but of eating, sleeping, gesturing, counting change, observing boundaries of personal behaviours, tipping cab drivers, standing in lines, avoiding certain topics of conversation at dinnertime as unbearably disgusting – is a truism one probably can never be reminded of too often.
>
> (Vitello, 2007)

We do not deal in depth with the sort of micro-tourist behaviours listed above – although they are instantly recognizable as sometimes very important in determining our tourist experience. But for all the academic debate around tourist difference or similarity by nationality group, the truism that Vitello describes does affect tourist behaviours because we often rely on truisms in our immediate host–guest (or guest–host) dealings. This is why we need to be reminded of such truisms and the stereotypes that can develop as a result.

Our search for nation differences in tourist behaviour has a spatial hue as we selected examples from around the world for closer inspection. Our next chapter focuses on the individual tourist but with a temporal theme – a study of how the holidays that you take and the decisions you make evolve through your own life.

REFERENCES

Arlt, G. (2006) *China's Outbound Tourism*. Routledge, Oxford, UK.

Bauer, T.G. (2002) How Germans will travel 2005. *Annals of Tourism Research* 29(1), 279–281.

Baumgarten, J.-C. (2003) WTTC China policy recommendations. WTTC, 13 October 2003.

Dewar, K., Meyer, D. and Li, W.L. (2001) Harbin, lanterns of ice, sculptures of snow. *Tourism Management* 22, 523–532.

EIU (1995) *International Tourism Reports 1*. Economist Intelligence Unit, London, pp. 19–37.

Fishman, T.C. (2005) *China Inc*. Simon & Schuster, London.

Guangrui, Z. and Lew, A.A. (2003) Introduction: China's tourist boom. In: Lew, A.A., Yu, L., Ap, J. and Guangrui, Z. (eds) *Tourism in China*. Haworth Press, Binghampton, New York, pp. 3–12.

Hofstede, G. (2001) *Culture's Consequences. Comparing Values, Behaviors, Institutions and Organizations Across Nations*. 2nd edn. Sage, Thousand Oaks, California.

Hsu, C.H.C., Cai, L.A. and Wong, K.K.F. (2007) A model of senior tourism motivations – anecdotes from Beijing and Shanghai. *Tourism Management* 28, 1262–1273.

Jacobsen, J.K.S. (2000) Anti-tourist attitudes. *Annals of Tourism Research* (27) 2, 284–300.

Kim, H., Borges, M.C. and Chon, J. (2006) Impacts of environmental values on tourism motivation: the case of FICA, Brazil. *Tourism Management* 27, 957–967.

Kozak, M. (2002) Comparative analysis of tourist motivations by nationality and destinations. *Tourism Management* 22, 221–232.

Maoz, D. (2007) Backpackers' motivations: the role of culture and nationality. *Annals of Tourism Research* 34(1), 122–140.

Munoz, T.G. (2007) German demand for tourism in Spain. *Tourism Management* 28, 12–22.

Neugarten, B. and Berkowitz, H. (1964) *Personality in Middle and Late Life*. Atherton, New York.

Ng, S.I., Lee, J.A. and Soutar, G.N. (2007) Tourists' intention to visit a country: the impact of cultural distance. *Tourism Management* 28, 1497–1506.

Pearce, P.L. and Lee, U.-I. (2005) Developing the travel career approach to tourist motivation. *Journal of Travel Research* 43 (February), 226–237.

Poon, A. (1993) *Tourism, Technology and Competitive Strategies*. CAB International, Wallingford, UK.

Poon, A. and Adams, E. (2000) *How Germans Will Travel 2005*. Tourism Intelligence International, Bielefeld, Germany.

Prebensen, N.K. (2007) Exploring tourists' images of a distant destination. *Tourism Management* 28, 747–756.

Prebensen, N.K., Larsen, S. and Abelsen, B. (2003) I'm not a typical tourist: German tourists self-perception, activities and motivations. *Journal of Travel Research* 41, 416–420.

Qu, R., Ennew, C. and Sinclair, M.T. (2005) The impact of regulation and ownership structure on market orientation in the tourism industry in China. *Tourism Management* 26(6), 939–950.

Richter, R. (2004) When the lights went out in Xinjiang. *The Times*, 3 August 2004, p. 24.

Schneider, I.E. and Backman, S.J. (1996) Cross-cultural equivalence of festival motivations: a study in Jordan. *Festival Management and Event Tourism* 4, 139–144.

Times of India (2008) Olympics fail to excite Indian tourists. *The Times of India*, 9 August 2008.

Vitello, P. (2007) They came, they toured, they offended. *New York Times*, 27 May 2007.

Watts, J. (2004) China's long holiday march. *The Guardian*, 17 January 2004.

Watts, J. (2006) Welcome to Shangri-La. By order of the state council of the Chinese government. *The Guardian*, 1 June 2006.

Zhang, H.Q., Chong, K. and Ap, J. (1999) An analysis of tourism policy development in modern China. *Tourism Management* 20, 471–485.

chapter 3

A LIFE IN TRAVEL

The previous chapter had a spatial flavour to its content. It is complemented by this chapter, which has a temporal theme. After all, tourism consumption involves both space and time. However, this is not a temporal theme in terms of an individual's decision-making process or length of stay at a destination, but one in terms of an individual's lifespan. It is a kind of longitudinal contemplation of your career as a tourist. How might you expect to evolve as a tourist as you progress through life? And what are the concepts and theories that might help to explain the changes that you see?

At a recent Economic and Social Research Council (ESRC) conference – the ESRC being the UK's leading research funding and training agency concerned with economic and social issues – time was conceived of as biographical, generational and historical (Neale, 2008). Biographical time captures the idea of an individual's life as it flows from birth to death and is shaped by a multitude of personal, relational and historical events and circumstances – in short, the biography or story of a person. Generational time places the individual as part of an age or generational convoy that proceeds collectively through time, relating to the generation 'above' (parents, grandparents, other older relatives and friends, and contemporaries of these relatives and friends) and to the generation 'below' (children, grandchildren, other younger relatives and friends, and contemporaries of these relatives and friends). Historical time relates to the individual located within a particular epoch with its characteristic socio-economic conditions and political landscapes.

To pick up on the notion of historical time, tourism academics Burkart and Medlik (1981), writing in the 1980s, detailed three principal *epochs* of tourism, devoting a chapter of their seminal textbook to each. Alongside the socio-economic conditions and political landscapes, the authors highlighted the emergence of technology with a strong focus on the role played by transport. The first of these epochs, 'the beginnings of tourism to 1840', swept through pilgrimages, the Grand Tours of the elite and the rise of the spa and seaside resort. The second epoch, titled 'the age of coal and steam to 1914', was temporally bounded by the emergence of the railway and the onset of World War I, and witnessed the dominance of the railway and the steamship and the arrival of the tour operator in the guise of Thomas Cook's first excursion train from Leicester to Loughborough in 1841. The third of Burkart and Medlik's epochs was 'the modern world 1919–1979', with the growth of the private car and the dominance of air travel and chartered package tours making international tourism available for all sectors of society.

If we were to add to this third epoch to reflect post-1979, we would expand concern for the tourist environment and the rise of environmentalism, the questioning of the role of travel and tourism in global warming, and the rise of computer technology and the widespread use of the Internet and the mobile phone. It may be that mankind's quest for an alternative energy source to fossil fuels will eventually mark the cusp between the third and fourth epochs, with a future focus on the emergence of a new form of transport technology. Overall, this historical notion of time is important in tourism behaviour as it maps out the parameters of possible travel behaviour for any particular individual. It sets a context for our own life journey in tourism.

In this chapter, we start by examining the idea of the family life cycle from a tourism perspective, move on to life course theory, consider period and cohort effects, comment on transition events and rites of passage and introduce the travel career ladder and its reincarnation as the travel career pattern. We indicate something of the rapidity with which certain tourists in society today accumulate tourist experiences (through an illustration of Londoners) before moving on to two cameos crafted from industry information (the youth tourist and the elder tourist). The cameos are drawn from what are likely to be opposing ends of a tourist's lifetime – and so neatly close out a chapter that deals with a *Life in Travel*.

THE INFLUENCE OF LIFE CYCLE

The life cycle is a well-known and established concept that helps to better understand consumer behaviour at both an individual and collective level. Its roots date back to the 1930s (Murphy and Staples, 1979) and it perhaps bears most resemblance to the biographical notion of time. In essence, the life cycle concept is all about how an individual's needs and resources change as he/she moves through different stages of life. It traces the human lifespan. Priorities change as key events (such as birth of a child, divorce or retirement) trigger a transfer to a new life stage with fresh challenges. This longitudinal development results in a given individual desiring different types of products and services as he/she progresses through these life stages. Neale (2008) describes the life cycle as consisting of structured, predefined stages, which are typically seen as benchmarks against which to compare development and behaviour.

As we know, tourism is dependent on both discretionary time and discretionary income, and these two precious resources fluctuate according to life stage. For example, a young couple with no children are likely to have a greater propensity to travel than someone of exactly the same age but with young children to care for. All other things being equal, they do not have the same discretionary time or discretionary income and there are other priorities for them that might take precedence over holidays. When they do take a holiday break, the product is likely to be quite different in style to a young individual who is comparatively free from responsibility.

You can probably think of tourism brands that specifically target a particular stage in an individual's life, for example, the youth package tour operators (such as Club 18–30, Escapades and 2twentys in the UK or TravelCuts in Canada) with a primary focus on the young and single tourist, or Sandals Resorts with its traditional reputation for couples, or Disney with its strong young family orientation or perhaps Saga Holidays in the UK with a dedicated focus on the older consumer (defined by the company as 50 years and older, which admittedly covers a selection of later life stages). On the surface, these brands might be seen as primarily about the chronological age of their consumers. But if they were, then a brand like Club 18–30 would be as popular with young couples between 18 and 25 as they are with singles aged 18–25. And they are blatantly not. Disney theme parks are not about the age of the adults, but about a young family experience. In reality, these tourism brands are concentrating on life stages – age-related, yes, but blended with characteristics associated with life stages, such as marital status, the presence or otherwise of children, the age of children, employment status and so forth.

The life cycle concept is best known in its guise as the family life cycle. As you would expect, the family moves through a series of stages from formation to dissolution, with each stage characterized by variations in available resources. Implicit within the concept is the idea that levels of income will increase over the family life cycle until retirement. The periods of relative want and plenty are largely determined by the arrival and eventual dispersal of children and later by retirement and old age. In other words, each phase embraces a different family circumstance with different opportunities and constraints. Although the concept pre-dates the 1960s with roots firmly in the discipline of sociology (Lawson, 1988), one of the earliest and probably best established of the family life cycle models is that of American academics Wells and Gubar (1966) who applied the concept to the marketing discipline. They conducted a literature review of research on the family life cycle up until that date, believing that the concept was a better indicator of a family's financial situation than simple chronological age.

They proposed an 'overview of the life cycle' consisting of nine stages (see Table 3.1). They even related their work to tourism habits. According to Wells and Gubar (1966), the family life cycle stages most conducive to heavy tourism and leisure spending were the following:

- bachelor stage (young, single, not living in the family home);
- newly married couples (young, no children);
- full nest 3 (older, married couples with dependent children);
- empty nest 1 (older, married couples, no children living in the family home, head of household in labour force).

Table 3.1. The established family life cycle model of Wells and Gubar (1966). (Adapted from Wells and Gubar, 1966.)

Life cycle stage	Stage characteristics
Bachelor	Young, single, not living in the family home. Few financial commitments. Recreation-oriented
Newly married couples	Young, no children. Better off financially than they will be in the near future
Full nest 1	Youngest child under 6. Home purchasing at its peak, liquid assets low
Full nest 11	Youngest child 6 and over. Financial position better, some wives work.
Full nest 111	Older, married couples with dependent children. Financial position better than FN11, more wives work, some children get jobs
Empty nest 1	Older, married couples, no children living in the family home, head of household in labour force. Home ownership at peak, most satisfied with financial position and money saved
Empty nest 11	Older, married couples, no children living in the family home, head of household retired. Drastic cut in income
Solitary survivor 1	In labour force. Income still good but likely to sell home
Solitary survivor 11	Retired. Drastic cut in income

Even 50 or so years ago, Wells and Gubar highlighted a problem with the family life cycle as a concept that still holds true today. In their words, 'no two investigators have yet agreed on just how to categorise the life cycle' (Wells and Gubar, 1966, p. 360), which makes comparison across different studies and through time a taxing task. They also indicated one of the antecedents to this problem, namely the fact that not all people can be successfully categorized into the life cycle stages (e.g. older, single people who never married). In the 21st century, there are alternative portrayals of the modern family life cycle that try to steer round any American bias in family structure and adapt to social trends such as the changing role of women in the workforce, the influence of alternative lifestyles, childless and delayed-child marriages, single-parent families, divorce and remarriage, the re-emergence of the extended family, and other influences on family composition. In fact, a 'modernized' family life cycle which incorporated divorce to build 13 life cycle stages was proposed as far back as the 1970s (Murphy and Staples, 1979).

Today, a number of consumer behaviour and marketing texts present updated versions of the family life cycle for the reader. For example, Brassington and Pettitt (2000) offer a modern interpretation that includes such family life stages as 'married/cohabiting', 'divorced/living apart', 'remarried/new partner', 'empty nest' and 'alone'. The stage 'alone' incorporates those who have always been single. It is important to note the trend of the 'singleton' as a more widespread and more durable life stage (Yeoman, 2008) than its traditional reference to pre-marriage young adulthood. As a second example, Solomon (2006) offers the 'childless couple', the 'single parent 1, 2 or 3' (according to age) and the 'delayed full nest'. A final and tourism-centred example refers to the 'younger single' and the 'older single', as well as the 'single-parent family' among the various life stages (Decrop, 2006).

Some of the detail of the types of products bought in the original Wells and Gubar family life cycle might look out of date now. Take our modern-day grey panther or silver surfer – our elder tourist in the cameo at the end of the chapter – enjoying the improvement over the decades in living standards. The rise in healthy life expectancy alongside actual life expectancy means that many people today in empty nest 11 or solitary survivor 11 may be spending more time and money in leisure and tourism, at least while they remain healthy and mobile. In a sense, this is what a specialist company like Saga Holidays has exploited. A look at the company's holiday products quickly confirms that great swathes of their consumers are physically active and raring to go. Wildlife trips to Namibia, Nepal and Borneo or tours to Mongolia and the Gobi desert or following the ancient Silk Route – these holidays do not seem to belong to the original incumbents of the empty nest 11 and solitary survivor 11 as envisaged by Wells and Gubar. Over forty years ago, the Wells and Gubar (1966) model emphasized the purchase of medical appliances, medical care and other products to aid health for individuals in these life stages. Not untrue today, but there is perhaps a shift in emphasis and a greater appreciation of variation between older people regarding their behaviour. We will look in more detail at the older tourist later in the chapter. None the less, the basic underpinnings of the family life cycle have proved durable in seeking to better understand tourist behaviour at the macro level.

Because tourism is so reliant on discretionary income expenditure, Lawson (1991, 1999) suggests that it should be an example of where consumer behaviour is strongly related to family life stage. Lawson (1991) examined inbound tourists to New Zealand by family life cycle stage using data from the National Tourism Organization's official survey of international visitors to New Zealand. Essentially based on the Wells and Gubar (1966) model with several justified adjustments (e.g. youngest child age under 5 rather than under 6 to more accurately reflect school starting age), Lawson identified eight family life cycle stages. The results suggested the following:

- Young singles (under 25) exhibit a longer length of stay in New Zealand than average, are highly active and are generally lower spenders with a high visiting friends and relatives (VFR) dependency.
- Young couples (no children) show a shorter length of stay than average and are active – although a large Japanese honeymoon market might have swayed the results.

- Full nest 1 (pre-school children) are oriented to VFR and lacking in activities; Lawson summarizes this as a 'relax with granny' vacation (Lawson, 1991, p. 17) due to the constraints imposed by very young children. Another, and very different, study from Denmark captures the feel of this life stage and holiday habits as 'small children, small experiences' (Blichfeldt, 2007, p. 157). When creating a holiday, parents focus on the little things that fall within a very young child's capabilities.
- Full nest 11 (school-age children) is similar to full nest 1, but not as marked as children are less of a constraint. The stage is summarized as a 'keep granny busy' vacation (Lawson, 1991, p. 17).
- Full nest 111 (older children, possibly non-dependent) shows still fewer constraints but with few distinctive traits; perhaps best characterized as 'busy holiday people'? (Lawson, 1991, p. 17).
- Empty nest 1 (still working, no children) exhibits a shorter length of stay than average, but takes a large number of tours and makes use of taxis, hire cars and hotels in a way that reflects their strong financial position. A leaning towards cultural activities contributes to their *comfortable* holiday status.
- Empty nest 11 (retired) displays a length of stay fairly close to the average and tends to visit more locations than other life cycle stages. However, the financial position is weaker when judged by use of hire cars and hotels, and activities are more sedentary and cultural, earning them a *relaxing* holiday nomenclature.
- Solitary survivors (retired) show a length of stay longer than average but visit fewer locations than those in the preceding life cycle stage. There is a tendency towards VFR with generally low activity levels – the 'relaxation with the grandchildren' (Lawson, 1991, p. 17) style of holiday.

Of course, these New Zealand findings are to some degree a stereotyped view of tourists within a given life cycle stage. There is variation within any of the stages, and, as we can see by the example of Japanese tourists, nationality with its implications of culture and other variables play a part.

Around the same time, a study of the overseas tourism behaviour of US residents when classified by family life cycle (Bojanic, 1992) also demonstrated behavioural patterns by life stage. Moving on from the 1990s, an analysis of the turn-of-the-century data from the US government's Consumer Expenditure Survey used a development of Bojanic's modernized eight life stages as the basis of the model (Hong *et al.*, 2005). The study used 'singles' as a reference point against which the other life stages were compared for leisure tourism expenditure patterns. 'Married without children' were the most active leisure tourism group, spending substantially more than 'singles' on transport, accommodation, food and entertainment. 'Full nest 11' and 'empty nest' also spent more on leisure tourism than 'singles'; not unexpectedly, the 'solitary survivors' did not. When the likelihood of leisure tourism spend was assessed, 'married without children' were deemed more likely to spend discretionary income on leisure tourism than 'singles', whereas 'single parents' and 'solitary survivors' were less likely to spend on leisure tourism than 'singles'

(Hong *et al.*, 2005). In essence, the broad pattern of findings tallies with the older work on family life cycle stages of Lawson (1991), Bojanic (1992) and Hong *et al.* (2005).

In conclusion, what can we say about the merits or otherwise of the family life cycle? We would like to highlight the following points:

- The family life cycle provides a well-recognized structure from which to study an individual's changes in tourism habits throughout their journey through life.
- It allows tourism purchases to be set in the context of competing alternatives – that is, those other products vying for the family's available monetary and temporal resources. This is a theme also picked up in Chapter 6, 'Economic and Social Influences' (this volume).
- It appears to offer some applicability across different cultures.
- It contributes to our understanding of how couples and families might fluctuate in their tourism decision processes (for more about this, see Chapter 12, 'The Importance of Family', this volume).

Like most ideas, the family life cycle has its faults and its detractors. For example, Kelly (1997, p. 133) argues that the focus on the family life cycle distracts research attention away from the transitions that occur in an individual's 'unpredictable zigzag life course'. The argument is that we need to focus research on the disruptions that happen in life on the premise that 'real life consists of sequential and cumulative disruptions, traumas, tragedies, and projects of putting things back together' (Kelly, 1997, p. 133). Indeed, some forms of end-of-life tourism can be brought about by the disruption of terminal illness combined with the desire to revisit an ancestral homeland, visit far-off friends or engage in final activities – a final tourist trip that need not be suicide tourism as the term 'end-of-life' initially implies (MacPherson *et al.*, 2007). Neale (2008) criticizes the life cycle concept as being outdated, and highlights the idea of a life course, a more flexible construct that involves an individual in the negotiation of a passage through an unpredictable and changing environment. Thus, the life course brings together the biological processes with the social processes of growing up, establishing relationships, bearing and rearing children, growing older and eventually dying. The life cycle is merely one, or the most conventional, way of expressing this life course.

Oppermann (1995a,b,c) points out the difficulties of separating out the family life cycle from other influences, and in particular, from 'period' and 'cohort' effects. The argument here is that we need to focus research on period and cohort effects – and perhaps examine life stages across different cohorts to pinpoint similarities and differences. It is to such period and cohort effects that we now briefly direct the spotlight.

PERIOD EFFECTS AND COHORT EFFECTS

Zimmermann (1982) referred to a triad of effects, of which the family life cycle was but one. The other two were period effects and cohort effects. Period effects and cohort effects influence us all. Period effects refer to annual changes and specific events in the external environment that, in this case, influence tourism behaviour (Oppermann, 1995b). They affect everybody, regardless of cohort or life stage, to a similar degree. From headline events such as the Gulf War, fuel crises or the tsunami disaster through to the impact of inflation, credit crunch or government adjustment of visa requirements, all influence travel behaviour across the cohorts and life stages. So – you could say – a period effect is something experienced by potential tourists in all the cohort categories present at the time. It is akin to the notion of historical time, as described in the introduction to the chapter.

Cohort effects, sometimes known as generation effects (see generational time in the introduction to the chapter), relate to behaviour patterns that are influenced by the unique characteristics of a given cohort or convoy. These characteristics often relate to the historical background of that cohort – if you like, to the accumulated memory of period effects. For example, young adults from the West in the early 1960s would be influenced in their travel behaviour by their shared childhood experiences of family life during World War II (and its aftermath of rationing and reconstruction), by East–West relations, the Iron Curtain and the Cold War, by society's fear of communism, by the spread of the motor car and television and by the rapid growth of the all-inclusive package industry and its supporting structures. In contrast, young adults from the West in the first decade of the 21st century are influenced in their travel behaviour by being 'natives' of the Internet revolution, by society's fear of climate change and of the 'war on terror', by the shifting balances of global power and so forth. So you have two very different cohorts with two very different historical profiles. And although, say, both these generations are experiencing the Internet revolution, the younger cohort has been brought up within it (hence the term 'native') while the older cohort has had to adapt and learn and change to keep pace, altogether a harder prospect (hence the term 'immigrant'). Following through on this idea, research by Oppermann (1995b) on German residents showed that successive generations display different travel behaviour patterns. If you stop to reflect on your own tourist behaviour patterns as against that of your parents or perhaps your grandparents, we are sure you will find your own personal anecdotal confirmation.

TRANSITION EVENTS AND RITES OF PASSAGE

As we are concerned in this chapter with understanding an individual's tourism choices across their lifespan – that is, across decades of travel – it is also useful to think about the transition between the different life stages, rather than accepting a sole focus on the life stage itself. When someone becomes an adult, marries, has a first child, experiences divorce, retirement or bereavement, these are all transition events that mark a change from one life stage to another. Such events are associated with social rituals that serve to mark the person's change in status. But how do these key events impact on tourist behaviour?

These major life transitions may involve a tourism experience that is an essential part of the transformation. Because the tourist returns to a new status or life stage, anthropologists refer to this phenomenon as 'rites of passage' tourism after the work of Van Gennep at the beginning of the 20th century (Graburn, 1983). Such tourism is generally self-imposed and often personally meaningful to the individual. It often involves a more prolonged period of absence than the standard vacation, and is likely to be characterized by its arduous or challenging nature (Graburn, 1983). It can be thought of as a type of self-test, allowing individuals to prove to themselves that they are capable of making the required life changes (Graburn, 1983). Under this guise, backpacking is a classic 'rites of passage' type of tourism. For example, young adults test themselves as they emerge from school or university prior to the rigours of the workplace, or older adults backpack as a career break or in response to a relationship breakdown. When they return, they enter a new and different phase of their life. Of course, not all backpacking can be classified as 'rites of passage' or life change tourism; Mohsin and Ryan (2003) in a study of backpackers in the Northern Territory of Australia found that only one-third fitted this description. None the less, it is a useful illustrative example that many readers can readily identify with.

The gap year and backpacking are well-recognized examples. For a more unusual example, the tourism industry has recently spotted what could be described as an opportunity arising from the transition in life stages between married couples without children to the 'full nest 1'. The World Travel Market (2007) highlighted the trend reaching Europe from America of 'procreation vacations' – in other words, holidays specifically designed to help a couple conceive a child (thus, hopefully marking the transition from married couple to 'full nest 1'). Such procreation vacations include elements like romantic dinners, food and drinks traditionally associated with fertility or rich in vitamins to help conception, aromatherapy sessions, massages and so forth. Inventively, at Marco Island in Florida, the procreation vacations are tied with the arrival of mating sea turtles. Procreation packages are typically targeted at slightly older couples who have the financial means to afford an upmarket break; that is, those who have delayed child birth in order to establish their careers and a firm financial future (World Travel Market, 2007). Within Western countries there is a general trend towards older parenting and this favours the growth of the procreation vacation.

THE TRAVEL CAREER LADDER AND TRAVEL CAREER PATTERNS

According to the *Oxford English Dictionary*, a 'career' is 'a person's course or progress through life (or a distinct portion of life) especially when publicly conspicuous or abounding in remarkable incidents' and in modern parlance is frequently used for 'a course of professional life or employment, which affords opportunity for progress or advancement in the world'. We probably refer more naturally to the second definition – yet you can see that both link up well with the subject matter in this chapter. Here, of course, we are concerned with your 'career' as a tourist – be it publicly conspicuous (of course), rich with incident and detail (of course) or providing opportunity for self-development (of course) – rather than with your conventional professional career in the workplace.

So what is your 'travel career'? Pearce and Lee (2005, p. 228) describe the 'travel career' as 'a dynamic concept arguing that tourists have identifiable phases or stages in their holiday taking. A pattern of travel motives characterizes or reflects one's travel career. The state of one's travel career, like a career at work, is influenced by previous travel experiences and life stage or contingency factors.'

Pearce and others developed the original 'travel career ladder' during the 1980s and early 1990s. Essentially a travel motivation theory, it brought together two strands of thought – Maslow's needs hierarchy theory of motivation and the concept of a career in tourism (Pearce and Lee, 2005). The travel career ladder uses five levels of motivation – relaxation needs, stimulation needs, relationships needs, self-esteem and development needs, and self-actualization/fulfilment needs (see Chapter 7, 'The Driving Force of Motivation', this volume). These five form a hierarchy or ladder with relaxation on the lowest rung and self-actualization on the highest (see Fig. 3.1). A tourist may have a mix of these motivations, but

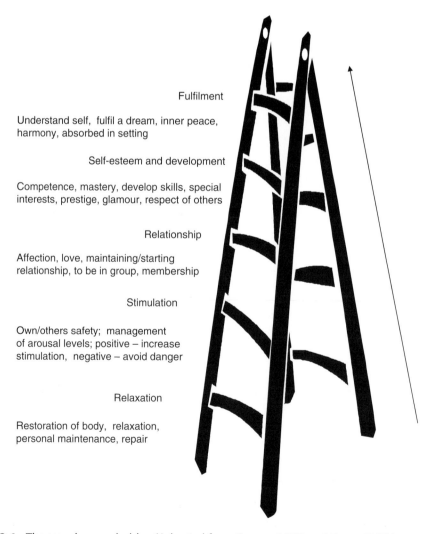

Fulfilment

Understand self, fulfil a dream, inner peace, harmony, absorbed in setting

Self-esteem and development

Competence, mastery, develop skills, special interests, prestige, glamour, respect of others

Relationship

Affection, love, maintaining/starting relationship, to be in group, membership

Stimulation

Own/others safety; management of arousal levels; positive – increase stimulation, negative – avoid danger

Relaxation

Restoration of body, relaxation, personal maintenance, repair

Fig. 3.1. The travel career ladder. (Adapted from Pearce, 1993 and Ryan, 1998.)

one set of motivations or rung of the ladder is likely to dominate. The core idea of the career is that an individual's motivation changes with their accumulation of travel experience. If you are holidaying abroad for the first time you may choose the security (stimulation) of a package tour with a brand you trust. But some years later and with accumulated experience, you may opt for a special-interest trip making the arrangements independently. Thus, it may be said that you have a tourism career with a pattern of motives that change according to lifespan and personal build-up of vacation experiences. Broadly speaking, the travel career ladder suggests that people climb up the ladder through the different rungs of motivation as they gather tourism experiences. Just as in work, they can start their career at different levels. However, some people may remain on a given rung, perhaps due to health or financial limitations – or, indeed, even retire from it (Pearce, 1993).

In essence what we have is 'a theoretical model describing travel motivation through five hierarchical levels of needs and motives in relation to travel career levels' (Pearce and Lee, 2005, p. 228) – the travel career ladder. Ryan (1998) contends that the key contribution of the travel career ladder to better understanding tourist motivation is the idea that there exists a developmental, psychological motivation of tourists that results from past tourism experiences, and that this is discernible and causes changes in patterns of travel behaviour over time. Ryan (1998) also indicates some use of the concept by the tourism industry in Australia. However, the travel career ladder has also been criticized on a number of counts. Pearce and Lee (2005) contend that the use of the term 'ladder' has drawn too much attention to the analogy of the physical ladder with its emphasis on ascending the rungs and being on only one rung at a time. Thus, the travel career ladder has been modified to a 'travel career pattern' which 'emphasises the pattern of motivations and their structure rather than steps on a ladder or hierarchy' (Pearce and Lee, 2005, p. 228). Still, the concept of the travel career with its changing motivational patterns according to accumulated experience remains central to the more recent travel career pattern.

In deciding for yourself how useful or otherwise the travel career ladder and travel career pattern might be, try tracing through your own tourism biography. Of course, in retrofitting your motivations to a particular tourism experience, errors seep in and, as you will find out in Chapter 7, 'The Driving Force of Motivation' (this volume), motivations cannot always be articulated or even necessarily recognized. But you will still get an anecdotal feeling for the framework and its applicability from your own perspective. At least one of the authors feels that it has relevance in understanding their own development as a tourist through the decades that they have been travelling.

A swift comment on the speed of travel accumulation

You should be under no illusion about just how quickly some tourists today are accumulating their travel experiences. For example, survey research by *TNT Magazine* (Chesshyre, 2005; *Evening Standard*, 2005), a publication designed to inspire independent tourists and popular with young Australians, New Zealanders and South Africans in the UK, sampled 2500 people in London (around 75% of whom were in their 20s). The research found that nearly 50% took 11 or more trips – to Europe or within the UK – each year. Around 25% took between seven and ten trips a year and a further 20% between four and six trips a year. Weekend breaks were especially popular according to the survey, with over 80% booking one such trip every month. These figures excluded long-haul holidays – the focus was on domestic and European travel. While the reliability and validity of this survey work cannot be verified, its findings at least provoke some thought as to the frequency with which some people are consuming tourist experiences today. Londoners might be expected to show a high propensity to travel, being in a high population density urban environment. Young people pre-child rearing might be more inclined to purchase trips – think back to the family life cycle earlier in this chapter. And easy access to the London airports and the low-cost airlines might also be a factor.

CAMEOS OF TOURISTS

We finish the chapter by etching out detailed but small portraits of the youth tourist and the elder tourist. We have kept the cameos small and made use of industry information in creating them. At opposite ends of the travel spectrum, they illustrate something of the modern tourist and how a lifetime in travel presents itself.

Cameo of the youth tourist

Around 20 years ago, industry data from a leading UK youth tour operator specializing in sun and sea package tours indicated as follows:

> [C]onsumers are first likely to purchase a downmarket sun product as either a late offer or special deal or by word of mouth recommendation…[then] they are inclined to trade upwards through the middle range of products such as Greece and the Canary Islands, to long haul products such as Florida.
>
> (Clarke, 1992, p. 324)

Young people buying the 'downmarket' sun product were likely to be younger than their counterparts buying the upmarket product, bought fewer holidays a year and were often a first-time purchaser of a package tour (Clarke, 1992).

Wind forward to the present day and to the youth independent tourist.

> There is also some evidence that young people construct a 'travel career', starting out in the 'easier' destinations with the most well developed independent travel infrastructure, and later striking out for more 'adventurous' destinations. In 2007, destinations which tended to attract more experienced travellers included Vietnam, Morocco, South Africa, India and Argentina, whereas less experienced travellers tended to be found in European destinations.
>
> (World Youth Student and Educational (WYSE) Travel Confederation, 2007, p. 23)

The youth tourist market is composed of any number of segments. One basic division is indicated above – the package tourist versus the independent tourist. There is also the group travel segment travelling under the auspices of a school, church or scouting group. Then there is the division between the adolescent (under 20 years old) and the young adult (20–25 or even 30 years old) – a separation of the teen from the young adult market. Adolescence involves an important search for personal identity and is characterized by experimentation with fads and fashions, sociability (partially fuelled by the fear of exclusion) and a rebellion against authority – coupled with a search for close relationships with peers outside the family unit (Rapoport and Rapoport, 1975). To define the youth tourist, the WTO uses the boundaries 16–25 years old, and the Youth Tourism Consortium of Canada sets the upper limit at 30 years old (Youth Tourism Consortium of Canada, 2004). And then there is an industry interpretation according to product sectors – for example, traditional youth tourism products such as language schools and courses, working holidays, volunteering, backpacking (which for the older young might include 'flashpacking') or gap years.

A survey of over 8500 respondents across Africa, Asia/Pacific, North America, Latin America and Europe highlighted certain details about today's youth independent tourist (World Youth Student and Educational (WYSE) Travel Confederation, 2007):

- These tourists think of themselves as travellers or backpackers, and less so as tourists – not an unexpected finding (see Chapter 1, 'The Tourist Today', this volume).
- The motivation of the trip changes as the tourists get older. The youngest (under 20) are motivated more by relaxation and fun, and those aged 26–30 more by exploration.
- On average, respondents had taken over seven major trips outside their region of residence during their travel career to date – possibly indicating a growing frequency or accumulation of travel among the young.
- Again relating to the travel career, it is apparent that fairly inexperienced tourists are likely to visit the major 'gateway' cities, while those young people with more accumulated travel experience travel into the regions.
- Youth tourists are information hungry and use a wide range of information sources pre-departure. The Internet is the main tool for information gathering, although family and friends (word of mouth) remain important. Price comparison features and destination information are valued most in Internet searches. Of those youth tourists pre-booking, around half are purchasing air travel online and over 60% are booking accommodation through the Internet.
- As a proportion of total income, youth tourists spend more on international tourism than other types of tourists (a behaviour that echoes with their stage in the family life cycle).
- The Internet is the most popular means for communicating with friends and family at home during the trip. Those keeping in touch every day are likely to use text messages. More than half still send postcards by the postal system, if infrequently. However, of those away for at least 1 month, one-third never make contact with people at home.

- Over 80% felt their trip had changed their lifestyle in some way; around three-quarters had re-evaluated career goals and career paths as a result of their travel.
- And closing with the travel career perspective in mind, the research showed that the main result from experiencing tourism was a thirst for more tourism; 'once young people start travelling, they find it difficult to stop' (World Youth Student and Educational (WYSE) Travel Confederation, 2007, p. 32).

Some of these youth tourism characteristics can be traced back to the search for personal identity, the temporary separation from family ties and an assertion of independence, and the forging of influential peer relationships.

Cameo of the elder tourist

Age no barrier to silver surfers. Women surfers may have been celebrated in Polynesian legend but only recently has the sport begun to be portrayed as anything other than a male preserve. But two Cornish women, who have over 70 years of surfing experience between them, are proof that female involvement in the sport is nothing new. And neither Sally Foster, 59, nor Gwyn Haslock, 62, has any intention of giving up any time soon.

(Laing, BBC News South West, 2007)

We have used the above quotation to emphasize two points about the elder tourist. First, that many older tourists are active and adventurous, particularly in their fifties and sixties. They have certain expectations regarding their quality of life – hence our 'silver surfers' above who take to the sea and the waves to literally surf on a regular basis. The second point is that the term 'silver surfers' is more normally used within business to describe people aged over 55 who are confident on the Web. Research by Great Britain Target Group Index (GB TGI) suggests that the number of these Internet-savvy 'silver surfers' in the UK is increasing (*Travel Trade Gazette*, 2006) – a trend that is recognized in many other countries too.

As well as the 'silver surfer', the elder tourist may also be known as the 'mature tourist' or as the 'grey panther'. The tourism industry likes to attract these segments for their perceived characteristics of high discretionary income (no dependent children, mortgage paid off, etc.) and flexibility in holiday timing – which means that they may prefer shoulder and off-season months when other sources of business are quiet. We like the term 'elder tourist' for its more traditional connotations of implied wisdom, self-confidence and experience but we also like the dynamism conveyed in the terms 'grey panther' and 'silver surfer'.

UK-based Saga Holidays, which specializes in the elder tourist, sets the age boundary for the elder tourist as 50 years plus; conversely, some national tourism organizations set the boundary at 55 years plus. Confusingly, the term 'third agers' refers to those between 40 or 45 and 65, and therefore overlaps with the elder tourist. Saga Holidays point out that there are different, principally age-based, segments within the elder tourist market. It is interesting to note that Saga Holidays too (just like Club 18–30) has some evidence of a travel career with their clients;

younger Saga tourists gravitate towards the long-haul adventure-inclusive tours and older Saga tourists towards the cruise products.

Some cameo details of the elder tourist suggest the following:

- A growth in demand for tourist products not typically associated with the elder tourist, for example, gap years, volunteering holidays, long-haul adventure trips, and a rise in very active behaviour again not typically associated with the elder tourist. Research into the over-sixties by the British Chiropractic Association found that almost 25% had been horse riding, 20% mountain biking and 16% rock climbing while on holiday (Health Club Management, 2006); research by the Future Foundation found that 'older people are living younger – ever more involved in sport and exercise, ever more sociable, ever more adventurous and in search of new experiences. In many ways their lifestyles have come to resemble those of younger people fifty years ago' (Future Foundation, 2007); and research for the Association of British Insurers found an increasing number of over-55 tourists ignoring health risks and taking part in extreme sports, including bungee-jumping with 20% of respondents taking risks while on holiday abroad they claim they would not con-template at home (*Daily Mail*, 2008a).
- A willingness to arrange trips independently; the GB TGI research indicated that 4.2 million holidaymakers over the age of 55 were happy to make their own independent arrangements (*Travel Trade Gazette*, 2006).
- A willingness to engage with computer technology to organize holidays (silver surfers); the same GB TGI research (a sample of about 25,000 people) found of those making their own holiday arrangements, 32% used web sites and 31% booked their last holiday online (*Travel Trade Gazette*, 2006).
- An appreciation of visiting friends and relatives as a tourist purpose; around 44% of all inbound visits to the UK by tourists aged over 55 involve seeing friends or relatives (VisitBritain, 2006), while in Australia, around 40% of domestic tourists aged 55 plus tend to stay with friends or relatives and around 56% of international tourists aged 55 plus (Tourism Australia, 2007).
- A tendency among domestic and international elder tourists to travel as an adult couple rather than as part of a family group – a finding from the same Australian research into the elder or mature age tourist market (Tourism Australia, 2007).

There is a flip side to this upbeat portrait of the elder and energetic tourist. The increase in overall life expectancy is not quite matched by the increase in healthy life expectancy – not all people over 50 are well enough to partake in such exuberant holidays. Alongside the health split, there is also the split between those with the financial wherewithal and those without. In 2008, in the UK, a report by Help the Aged indicated that one in five pensioners had been unable to afford a holiday for at least 5 years (*Daily Mail*, 2008b) – a sobering thought not often highlighted in tourism industry reports. Then there is the future. With the pensions crisis looming in the developed world because of an increasingly ageing population, it may be that today's silver surfer is riding a wave that will have crashed for the generation coming up behind it. A report by VisitBritain (2003) examines the possible responses, suggesting a rise in the state retirement age, more part-time working by elders to supplement income, and use of 'equity-release scheme' type products to unlock money tied up in the home in order to fund the desired lifestyle.

But to leave our elder tourist cameo on a positive note, we use the refreshing words attributed to mystery author, Agatha Christie (1890–1976), so strongly associated with the popular holiday destination of Cornwall in South-west England:

> I have greatly enjoyed the second blooming…suddenly you find – at the age of 50, say – that a whole new life has opened before you.
>
> (Agatha Christie)

DEVELOPING ON…

Throughout this chapter, we have looked at ideas that help to explain how you evolve as a tourist throughout your lifetime. We have been particularly concerned with ideas of time, the family life cycle as a progression of stages, life course theory, period and cohort effects, transition events and rites of passage, and the travel career as both ladder and pattern. As we mentioned in the introduction, the chapter is a kind of longitudinal contemplation of your career as a tourist. The next chapter builds on this and digs deeper – just how far can tourist experiences change your life?

REFERENCES

Blichfeldt, B.S. (2007) A nice vacation: variations in experience aspirations and travel careers. *Journal of Vacation Marketing* 13(2), 149–164.

Bojanic, D.C. (1992) A look at a modernized family life cycle and overseas travel. *Journal of Travel and Tourism Research* 1(1), 61–79.

Brassington, F. and Pettitt, S. (2000) *Principles of Marketing*, 2nd edn. Prentice-Hall Financial Times, Harlow, UK.

Burkart, A.J. and Medlik, S. (1981) *Tourism. Past, Present and Future*, 2nd edn. Heinemann, London.

Chesshyre, T. (2005) A perfect ten. *The Times*, 26 February 2005, p. 2.

Clarke, J. (1992) A marketing spotlight on the youth 'four S's' consumer'. *Tourism Management* 13(3), 321–327.

Daily Mail (2008a) Thrill-seeking over-55s. *Daily Mail*, 3 March 2008.

Daily Mail (2008b) Pensioners unable to afford a holiday. *Daily Mail*, 18 January 2008.

Decrop, A. (2006) *Vacation Decision Making*. CAB International, Wallingford, UK.

Evening Standard (2005) How we all love to take a mini break. *The Evening Standard*, 8 March 2005.

Future Foundation (2007) *Forever Young*. Future Foundation, London.

Graburn, N.H.H. (1983) The anthropology of tourism. *Annals of Tourism Research* 10(1), 9–34.

Health Club Management (2006) Over-60s more adventurous than ever before. *Health Club Management*, 26 January.

Hong, G.-S., Fan, J.X., Palmer, L. and Bhargava, V. (2005) Leisure travel expenditure patterns by family life cycle stages. *Journal of Travel and Tourism Marketing* 18(2), 15–30.

Kelly, J.R. (1997) Changing issues in leisure-family research – again. *Journal of Leisure Research* 29(1), 132–134.

Laing, J. (2007) Age no barrier to silver surfers. *BBC News South West*, Friday, 30 November. Available at: www.news.bbc.co.uk/1/hi/england/cornwall/7094544.stm

Lawson, R.W. (1999) Patterns of tourist expenditure and types of vacation across the family life cycle. In: Pizam, A. and Mansfield, Y. (eds) *Consumer Behaviour in Travel and Tourism*. The Haworth Hospitality Press, New York, pp. 431–447.

Lawson, R.W. (1988) The family life cycle: a demographic analysis. *Journal of Marketing Management* 4(1), 13–32.

Lawson, R.W. (1991) Patterns of tourist expenditure and types of vacation across the family life cycle. *Journal of Travel Research* 29(4), 12–18.

MacPherson, D.W., Gushulak, B.D. and Sandhu, J. (2007) Death and international travel – the Canadian experience: 1996 to 2004. *Journal of Travel Medicine* 14(2), 77–84.

Mohsin, A. and Ryan, C. (2003) Backpackers in the Northern Territory of Australia – motives, behaviours and satisfactions. *International Journal of Tourism Research* 5(2), 113–131.

Murphy, P.E. and Staples, W.A. (1979) A modernized family life cycle. *Journal of Consumer Research* 6, 12–22.

Neale, B. (2008) The timescapes study and archive: thinking through time. 3rd ESRC Research Methods Festival 2008, St Catherine's College Oxford, 30 June – 3 July 2008.

Oppermann, M. (1995a) Family life cycle and cohort effects: a study of travel patterns of German residents. *Journal of Travel and Tourism Marketing* 4(1), 23–42.

Oppermann, M. (1995b) Travel life cycle. *Annals of Tourism Research* 22(3), 535–552.

Oppermann, M. (1995c) Travel life cycles – a multitemporal perspective of changing travel patterns. *Journal of Travel and Tourism Marketing* 4(3), 101–109.

Pearce, P.L. (1993) Fundamentals of tourist motivation. In: Pearce, D.G. and Butler, R.W. (eds) *Tourism Research. Critiques and Challenges*. Routledge, London, pp. 111–134.

Pearce, P.L. and Lee, U.-I. (2005) Developing the travel career approach to motivation. *Journal of Travel Research* 43(3), 226–237.

Rapoport, R. and Rapoport, R.N. (1975) *Leisure and the Family Life Cycle*. Routledge and Kegan Paul, London.

Ryan, C. (1998) The travel career ladder. An appraisal. *Annals of Tourism Research* 25(1), 936–957.

Solomon, M.R. (2006) *Consumer Behaviour: Buying, Selling, and Being*, 7th edn. Pearson Prentice-Hall, New Jersey.

Tourism Australia (2007) *Mature Age Visitors in Australia 2007*. Tourism Research Australia, Belconnen, Australia.

Travel Trade Gazette (2006) Silver surfers catch the wave. *Travel Trade Gazette*, 1 July 2006.

VisitBritain (2003) Issue of the month. Implications of an ageing population in Britain...*Foresight*, Issue 1 November 2003. VisitBritain Strategy and Insight Division, London.

VisitBritain (2006) Market focus – inbound visits by the over 55's. *Foresight*, Issue 37 November 2006. VisitBritain Strategy and Communications Division, London.

Wells, W.D. and Gubar, G. (1966) Life cycle concept in marketing research. *Journal of Marketing Research* 3, 355–363.

World Travel Market (2007) Pregnant pauses. Available at: www.wtmlondon.com/page.cfm/link=47

World Youth Student and Educational (WYSE) Travel Confederation (2007) *New Horizons 11 The Young Independent Traveller 2007*. WSYE Travel Confederation, Amsterdam.

Yeoman, I. (2008) *Bridget Jones goes on Holiday*, 9 May 2008. Available at: www.hospitalitynet.org/news/4035872.html

Youth Tourism Consortium of Canada (2004) *Youth Tourism in Canada. A Situational Analysis of an Overlooked Market*. Youth Tourism Consortium of Canada, Ottawa.

Zimmermann, C.A. (1982) The life cycle concept as a tool for travel research. *Transportation* 11, 51–69.

chapter 4

LIFE CHANGE: TOURIST EXPERIENCE AND BEYOND

What lies beyond tourism for the tourist? Can the tourist experience lead on to life change – in the pleasures we have, the way we see ourselves, the people we live with, the places we live, the work we do and so the lives we lead? What are the implications of answering 'yes' to each of these questions? In this chapter, we project a life that is somehow influenced, if not moulded, on tourist experience.

TOURISM–LEISURE CONVERGENCE

It is interesting to consider whether day-to-day life beyond the sometimes fantasy life of the tourist experience is influenced by that experience. As a starting point, before moving on to other aspects of life that on the surface seem more removed from tourism, it seems worthwhile exploring the influence of tourist behaviour on leisure behaviour.

Just as one example, consider eating out as a leisure experience. A plethora of world food is now available in the eating places of most towns and cities in the developed 'North'. There are variations, of course, from country to country but in many of the big cities in Europe, the USA, Canada, Australia and New Zealand you do not have to go far to taste the food, of, say, Thailand or Lebanon or Mexico – even if it is adapted to local taste. The Thai government, indeed, with its certification scheme for authentic Thai cuisine outside its borders sees Thai restaurants as a promotional arm for the country and especially for the tourism industry. All of this is a far cry from the case of the early, post-World War II northern European tourists in, say, Spain or Italy who were confronted with the delights of paella or fresh spaghetti and pizza for the first time and who would largely have to contain their appetites until another trip and another year. After 50 years of tourism growth, there is an argument that we no longer have to go anywhere other than our own local, urban-social environment in order to taste the food of the world. Food for pleasure is only part of life and not even a major part for many. But the postmodern world is one of diversified cultural experience (including the food experience) and tourism has played its role in promoting such diversity. For better or for worse the world may be at our local doorstep – and part of the reason is the demand that is generated from returning tourists. Their lives have been changed by their tourist experience and they want to retain that experience in the leisure part of their day-to-day living.

But consider, too, the flip side of such tourism influence on leisure – that is, leisure that influences tourism. So, if you are a keen swimmer in your everyday life does that make you any more or less likely to seek out the sea in your tourist life?

There are differences between tourism and leisure in the temporal side of things (especially if we use the standard definition of tourism that classifies it as involving an overnight stay). There are also likely to be spatial differences (insomuch as tourism normally involves movement over a greater distance). And there are also likely to be differences in the richness and diversity of experience. But there are also similarities. Ryan and Robertson (1997, p. 134) state that 'holidays (are) an extension of time for behaviours similar to those engaged upon at weekends when the main motivations (are) ones of relaxation, having fun, and being with "mates"'. In other words, tourist behaviour is an extension of leisure behaviour. Brey and Lehto (2007) pick this up and explain a relationship between daily and destination-bound behaviours based on individual involvement with a leisure pursuit – and also the extent of participant specialization. A very large sample of over 6000 usable responses contained in a survey of travel activities and motivation by American tourists in Canada, carried out by the Canadian Tourism Commission, show some clear results:

> The general tendency is that the higher the daily participation, the more likely the respondents will participate in the same activity when on vacation. For instance, among destination golfers, the frequent daily players did more while on vacation (52.6%) then those who occasionally golf (28.4%), and (those who) rarely or never do so at home (19.3%). The more golfing one does on a daily basis, the more likely the individual will golf occasionally (52%) or stay at a golf resort (65%) or purchase a package golf tour (75%) during vacation....Highly involved bikers (who bike frequently near home) tend to participate in recreational biking (49.4%) or mountain biking (59%) or overnight biking (63%) on a vacation trip.
>
> (Brey and Lehto, 2007, p. 168)

This general tendency also applies to rather more sedate activities – such as dining, theatre and concerts (classical, jazz and rock) – and not just outdoor, sport and fitness activities. By contrast, team-based activities (such as ice hockey and basketball) showed a negative correlation (daily activity predicts non-activity at a destination).

Actually, at a conceptual level the convergence (or not) between tourism and leisure has been at the heart of some excited thinking by tourism and leisure academics. Mannell and

Iso-Ahola (1987) were critical of the state of tourism research compared to leisure research – according to them leisure research was much more advanced in its understanding. As they concluded:

> All of this leaves the information about the relationship between leisure experience and tourist experience inconclusive. In spite of some intuitively obvious similarities between the two (tourism and leisure), at present it is not possible to conclude when and under what conditions tourist experience becomes leisure experience.
>
> (Mannell and Iso-Ahola, 1987, pp. 328–329)

But, after due consideration, admittedly with further years of thought and debate, Carr (2002) identifies a range of researchers who have suggested an overlap between tourism and leisure (and so between tourists and leisure-seekers) with regard to the definitions of the two fields, the facilities they create, the motivations and psychological requirements of individuals and geography. So, at a conceptual level, while tourism and leisure were for the most part thought of as separate areas of research, study and experience, the differences are not now invariably emphasized. Indeed, Carr (2002, p. 976; Fig. 4.1) produces a model of the 'tourism-leisure continuum' – and so more than hints towards a relationship between the two concepts.

As Carr states:

> At one end of this continuum there is the leisure behaviour exhibited by people within their home environments that is influenced by the residual culture. At the opposite end of the continuum is tourist behaviour, influenced by the tourist culture. In between these two extremes the tourist and residual cultures both influence behaviours to varying degrees.
>
> (Carr, 2002, p. 976)

Moving beyond establishing a link between leisure and tourism and vice versa, Gilbert and Abdullah (2004) suggest that being a tourist creates a general 'subjective well-being' (SWB) after the experience – when back in the home environment. This really is big picture thinking. They refer to theories that attempt to explain the variance in SWB within

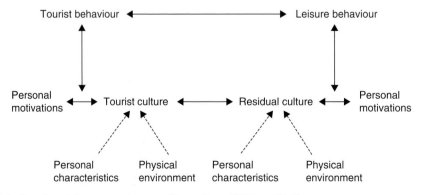

Fig. 4.1. Tourism leisure continuum. (From Carr, 2002, p. 976.)

society – such as theories that link happiness with the attainment of a goal or need. While their findings are not unequivocal (and can be considered narrow insomuch as they are based on an on-street survey in a medium-sized town in England), they are able to state that:

> holidaytaking did alter or impact on the subjective or sense of well-being of the holidaymakers: respondents experienced a higher amount of pleasant feelings after their holidays…the SWB of the holidaytaking group when compared to the other group indicated the former experienced a higher sense of well-being before and after the vacations.
>
> (Gilbert and Abdullah, 2004, p. 117)

We all have most probably felt this from our own holiday taking. As expressed by Gilbert and Abdullah (2004, p. 111) 'respondents are generally happier with their life-as-a-whole after their holidays'. It is interesting to muse on whether the replication of the tourist experience in subsequent leisure experience can help maintain the SWB. Our own experience would say 'yes' – your leisure experience in the form of your favourite local Thai restaurant or mid-winter salsa class can stimulate recollections of the good times and so recreate or reinforce SWB that stems from holiday taking. Through the opportunity for relived experience, the tourism–leisure convergence creates a happier society!

SELF-CHANGE

So it seems that tourist experience can influence day-to-day life through linkage with leisure activity – and vice versa. It can also lead to self-change. Marketers know it – and make use of it in their promotion. Tourists certainly know it, too, because it is the reality of their experience. Tourism can generate the 'fateful moment' (Giddens, 1991) in the self-identity and biography of the tourist person. Many baby boomers with the privilege of a university education, and multiple vacations, can recall tourist events and experiences that propelled them down a life path that they would not have otherwise mapped for themselves. The tourist can deliberately and self-consciously remove normal day-to-day identity and be exposed to new circumstances and experience – and so construct a new identity or at least challenge the existing identity.

In this respect, the work of Jafari (1987, p. 151) still shines brightly. He conceptualized a model of the tourist experience using a visual metaphor – a springboard – such that 'the player (the tourist) sinks into the board, only to emerge to the surface, to rise above it, to suspend in the air, to manoeuvre, and to return to the base'. Life breeds the need or desire to leave the springboard (the ordinary world) behind; departure gives a sense of freedom; the tourist does tourism and leaves the ordinary time and space behind; and then returns to the ordinary mainstream.

Over a decade later the empirical work of Desforges (2000) draws on material from in-depth interviews to look at the uses of long-haul travel in the identities of tourists from the UK. With echoes of Jafari he picks up two key moments – setting off and homecoming – 'when travel is given a particular depth of meaning in the lives of the respondents' (Desforges, 2000, p. 933). He is careful to explain that his emphasis is on individualistic identity – a 'sense of person-hood…(that) would normally be qualified with adjectives such as a moral person, an educated person or a fulfilled person' (Desforges, 2000, p. 930) – rather than identity that connects the individual with a wider social group, such as a class or a region (or country). For one respond-ent the decision to travel (and so set off) was 'like somebody opening a big window and letting all the air in' and it allowed her to 'define herself according to her individual experiences of the world rather than by her position in the institution of the family' (Desforges, 2000, p. 935). And as regards homecoming, tourists formulate the identity they desire through the construc-tion of a travel narrative – telling stories – in which they 'select certain parts of their experi-ences, cut them up, exaggerate for effect, make connections among different places; in short, use a whole host of narrative devices to communicate some kind of story to others' (Desforges, 2000, p. 939). Such an identity sets the tourist apart (if that is their desire) or lines the tourist up alongside like-minded friends, peers and employers (if that is their desire).

The recent outpouring of research work based around backpacker tourism has picked up on such 'formative' or 'transformative' experience – although in reality such experience is not a new phenomenon, whatever the younger generation would care to believe. Backpacker tour-ism is not nearly as far from more traditional tourism as many 'on the road' would argue. Indeed, Uriely *et al.* (2002) are clear that contemporary backpackers should be viewed as a variety within, rather than outside, modern mass tourism. The drifter ideal of travel 'without either itinerary or timetable, without a destination or even well defined purpose' (Cohen, 1972, p. 176) is no longer so relevant to many backpackers. Much backpacking according to O'Reilly (2006, p. 1014) might be termed 'backpacker light' – like 'worthy but boring low alcohol beers'. Presumably with Facebook, e-mail account, mobile phone and credit card never too far away, Niggel and Benson (2008, p. 145), indeed, seem to confirm this in their outline of how backpackers can use the 'Baz Bus' in Southern Africa – with its 'door-to-door service between 180 backpacker hostels and lodges around South Africa, and Swaziland, with links to Lesotho and Mozambique'. How much dismay that must bring to the trail-finders of the 1970s!

But, nevertheless, backpacking is worth some consideration as a case to expand on the idea of self-change. Noy (2004, p. 87) recognizes self-change in the discourse of Israeli backpackers even though 'powerful assertions of self, self-change, and identity are located inconspicuously within the (backpackers) narratives'. The backpackers concentrate on the adventure and the authenticity of their trip – but then invariably recognize self-change:

> One of the most striking characteristics of the narratives is that they consistently describe deep and profound personal changes as a result of the trip. These changes are always markedly positive, and are described rhetorically in terms of a significant development and maturation in central personality traits.

(Noy, 2004, p. 86)

Noy suggests that self-change might certainly embrace other tourists – for example, the growing numbers in search of some form of authenticity. Moreover, authenticity is a socially constructed concept – it is perceived and built by tourists themselves – and so may include what some purists would describe as the inauthentic. From such a standpoint, the relevance of Noy's work very much extends beyond the backpacker and includes a much wider range of tourists.

O'Reilly (2006) – also with a focus on backpackers – picks up on the 'social', 'symbolic' and 'cultural' capital that travel accumulates. She based her work on participant observation – 11 months of backpacking in Central America, South-east Asia, Australia and New Zealand – and follow-up interviews. Under 'social capital' she includes social networks and connections between travellers (and potentially with institutions and employers) and intangible shared norms and ideas (tolerance of difference, awareness of global issues or the sense of common humanity). 'Symbolic capital' comes from the prestige and reputation gained through travel – also used in future employment and social circles. She then uses Bourdieu (1991) to base her definition of 'cultural capital' on 'legitimate knowledge…accrued through the legitimating force of experience that travel is thought to provide' (O'Reilly, 2006, p. 1013).

The role of backpacking and self-change is particularly applied to women backpackers in a number of studies. For example, Maoz (2008) – again in a study of Israeli backpackers (this time focused on women in mid-life, travelling to India) – finds that such women seek a reversal of their lives up until that date. That is they seek repose versus (previous) careerism and activity; irresponsibility and rebellion versus conformism and responsibility; an 'everything will be fine' attitude versus anxiety; inward inclination versus outward inclination; simplicity versus comfort and well-to-do lives; a regression to youth rather than moving on to the next stage in life; sexual openness versus conservatism. But Maoz (2008, p. 198) also suggests that the reversal is only temporary: '[T]he women talk about a certain change they brought back from India, but all admit to have returned to their "old self" in most domains…(their) new self is limited to the liminal phase of the journey, which facilitates temporary reversal and moratorium; it cannot last in daily life.'

Likewise, Wilson and Ateljevic (2008) question the neat fit of travel and the acquisition of cultural capital by women. They studied female backpackers and independent travellers in Australia, New Zealand, China and Fiji. On the one hand, they claim that Western *women* travellers are able to relate to non-Western *women* hosts through 'embodied interaction' – the 'being, doing, touch *and* seeing of tourism' (Crouch and Desforges, 2003, p. 7) rather than just the 'tourist gaze'. So much so that the economic, social and political differences are reduced and 'both tourists and local people walk away from their interactions learning something new about each other, or about the way their (not so opposite) worlds operate' (Wilson and Ateljevic, 2008, p. 107) On the other hand, 'rather than feel they could impress and regale others with stories of their trips, many women found those at home were uninterested in their newfound sense of identity or increased sense of awareness' (Wilson and Ateljevic, 2008, p. 103). Telling stories upon return is one key way in which cultural capital (as well as self-identity) can be expressed – but even other women are not interested. Desforges (2000) found similar instances – and also instances in which the travel identity and the professional identity of the tourist did not match. Contested identities required individuals to suppress their stories.

Of course such self-change, even if it is temporary, certainly requires that tourists get outside their 'environmental bubble' (Cohen, 1972) and interact with local people. And Wickens (2002, p. 849) has shown, in her case study of sun, sea and sand tourists in Chalkidiki, Greece, that even 'individual mass tourists' (Cohen, 1972) are able and willing to do this. Specifically, 'despite an individual's commitment to play the part assigned to him/her by the industry…individual mass tourists in Chalkidiki are characterised by a highly diversified pattern of interests and activities'. These extend outside the bubble. So, the chance of that 'fateful moment' is increased, as the tourists are not only interested in the profane but also the richer and deeper sacred parts of a tourist experience.

But in an ethnographic study of hill-tribe trekkers in northern Thailand, Conran (2006, p. 274) finds a hitherto thwarted search for a shared experience with the tourist hosts. The trekkers seek an 'intimate encounter' with the (Karen) hill-tribe people. But for the trekkers and the Karen there is a gap in communication, so that the trekkers do not get beyond a commodified experience. As an aside, such was not the case as detailed to one of the authors of this book (Bowen, 2002) during participant observation of UK tourists in Malaysia. The tour group that the author was researching was joined by 'Robbi' – a tourist who had just travelled down to Malaysia from Thailand and who had spent some days with Thai hill-tribe people as part of a trekking group. It was a major highlight of his tour and the interaction with the hill-tribe people seemed very real and meaningful. Two short extracts from field notes sum up Robbi's thoughts:

> – So, how was the tour?
> – It was just brilliant.
> – What made it for you? Was it the people or what?
> – Well, yes, it was the people but it was everything really.
> [O]n the Thailand tour Robbi danced with the local tribes-people after the other fellow tourists had returned to sleep in the tribal huts; smoked opium that was made from local poppies with the tribes-people; and even had what seemed like a serious proposal of marriage through one of the tribe elders.
>
> (Bowen, 2002, fieldwork extract)

Conran (2006) points to other examples such as the 'interactional experience' or 'cultural exchange' that Taylor (2001) describes among some tourists and New Zealand Maori. The tourist gaze is no longer unidirectional and both sides take something from the party (something that we return to again in a discussion of authenticity in Chapter 5, 'Models of Tourist Behaviour', this volume).

Finally – and conveniently in harder economic times – self-change does not necessarily require the removal to a foreign destination. Nor does it require an approach to travel, as with some backpackers, that runs contrary to their normal pre-travel approach to life. Palmer (2005) outlines the way in which domestic travel in England by English people to three heritage sites – Battle Abbey, Hever Castle and Chartwell – enables domestic tourists to experience their English identity (and so understand something of who they are). Palmer (2005, p. 8) states that 'tourism is one of the defining activities of the modern world, shaping the ways in which one relates to and understands self and other, nation and nation-ness'. Heritage tourism according to Palmer is a mundane taken-for-granted aspect of social life that can nevertheless remind people of the nation's core traditions and stories of nationhood. Outside England, we would imagine that every reader is able to note at least one heritage site that speaks to his or her national identity – one element of self-identity.

Much of the self-change picked up so far in this section might have occurred in a gap year or overseas-experience (OE) period. There is no doubt that 'gap year' tourism can encourage self-change – for better or for worse. And a gap year is no longer the preserve of the student either pre- or post-university. There are a growing number of individuals who take gap years at strategic points throughout their life. And there are a growing number of companies and organizations that facilitate the demand (Dixon and Chesshyre, 2008).

AFFAIRS OF THE HEART

True affairs of the heart, even if not long lasting, are bound to emerge from widening tourist experience. It might be said that it was ever thus. Liaisons leading to longer-term cohabitation or marriage occurred with due frequency when domestic tourism was the norm and tourism was not such an international industry. But as tourism grows in its global scale and reach, it should not be too surprising that there is a concomitant increase in global relationships based initially on a tourist experience. The role of migration as a life-changing step beyond tourism is detailed in the next section of this chapter. However, it is appropriate to point out here that Bowen and Schouten (2008) find numerous examples of tourist affairs of the heart that were catalysts for migration to Mallorca. One informant, 30 years on from migration and assimilated into island life as a high-ranking local government official, recalled:

> I visited Mallorca first for a short holiday – the usual thing – with my girlfriend. I returned to
> Mallorca because my girlfriend met a singer from a local pop-group, and we had made friends, and
> I thought it would be a good chance to have a change after ending a relationship in England. It
> was not long before I, too, had met someone new and so I found a job and continued to live on the
> island even after the relationship ended – and before I met my present partner.
>
> (Bowen and Schouten, 2008, fieldwork extract)

A further respondent, originally a hotel project manager, who had also lived on the island for many years, while changing jobs and partners, commented on the mix of personal relationships and tourist experience. Host–guest contact it seemed often led to the development of important personal relationships. She summed up the situation:

> My experience is not unique – many females from the boom years have the same story:
> holiday – single – drawn to the island – marriage – divorce – stay on.

Two of the five subtypes of tourist that Wickens (2002, pp. 838–839) identifies among the individual mass tourists in Chalkidiki are the 'Raver Type' and 'The Shirley Valentine Type'. The ravers are intent on a casual fling with fellow tourists or with Greeks while the Shirley Valentines are more interested in a romantic experience with a 'Greek God'. Singh (2002) draws on Lee (1976) and distinguishes three types of conjugal love – 'eros' (characterized, for example, by immediate physical attraction, sensuality, close intimacy and rapport); 'ludus' (playful, hedonistic and free of commitment) and 'storge' (affectionate, companionate and devoid of passion). Singh (2002) considers that most mass tourists are likely to be more influenced by 'eros' and 'ludus' rather than 'storge' and there is little in Wickens (2002) that contradicts such a view. Maoz's (2008) research of affairs among Israeli women tourists in mid-life and younger Indian men is in line with Singh's way of thinking. As Maoz states:

> The (tourist) story is usually told as a love story and not just sex, similar to what is termed 'romance tourism' (but) regarded as different from 'sex tourism' – which is attributed mainly to men, and is based on sex only.
>
> (Maoz, 2008, p. 197)

In a Jamaican context, Pruitt and La Font (1995, p. 423) emphasize how Euro-American women tourists hold the same view in their relationships with Jamaican men:

> It is significant that neither actor considers their interaction to be prostitution, even while others may label it so. The actors place an emphasis on courtship rather than the exchange of sex for money.
>
> (Pruitt and La Font, 1995, p. 423)

But there is a life change brought about by such affairs of the heart in Jamaica – on both sides. So, the women tourists explore new gender behaviour free from the constraints of their own society and 'expand their gender repertoires to incorporate practices traditionally reserved for men' (Pruitt and La Font, 1995, p. 425). For at home in their own countries, there are racial, educational and economic differences that constrain the sort of liaison that the tourist women pursue in Jamaica.

And the Jamaican men experience a new gender role, normally a subordinate role – although they naturally exercise local knowledge and so do have some influence over their companion's circumstances.

> Whereas sex tourism serves to perpetuate gender roles and reinforce power relations of male dominance and female subordination, romance tourism in Jamaica provides an arena of change.
>
> (Pruitt and La Font, 1995, p. 423)

But as always things can go awry and while the Jamaican man may gain immediate economic benefit, there are dangers beyond the stage of the romance when the economic dependency becomes more obvious. The man may also lose the respect of the local community for exploiting Rastafarian values.

Finally, although not often developed into an affair of the heart, the burgeoning world of exploitative and usually male sexual behaviour linked to tourism in a myriad of destinations – East or West Africa, South-east Asia, the cities of the former Eastern Europe (now just a low-cost flight from the weekend sex traffic of the wealthier Western Europe) – should also be mentioned. Sex tourism, of whatever kind, is another world from the tourist experience detailed by Wickens (2002), Maoz (2008) or Bowen and Schouten (2008) in Chalkidiki, India and Mallorca. It would be fair to say that in most instances the heart comes far less into the sex equation – if at all. But there is no reason to assume that such encounters do not lead to change beyond the immediate tourist experience.

TOURIST MIGRANTS

We have seen so far that tourism and leisure converge more than was previously thought – such that tourism activity becomes part of the everyday leisure activity and vice versa. We have seen that the tourist experience can lead to a profound change in outlook by an individual. And we have seen that tourism, involving as it invariably does people-to-people interaction, can lead to romantic and sexual involvement and both short- and long-term partnership. Beyond that, and not unrelated in many instances, it is worth considering whether tourism can lead to migration – a major life change, a formative element of change in much of human history and now intuitively influenced by tourism.

The growth of tourism in the second half of the 20th century and beyond into the 21st century has created a new dynamic for migration – migration based on tourist experience with an identifiable tourism destination. It seems possible to recognize a 'tourist migrant' – a migrant who associates a tourist experience, and especially satisfaction with that experience, as a major factor in migratory movement and settlement to an identifiable destination. Tourist migrants, as so defined, are migrants with a primary motivation traceable to a tourist experience or set of experiences – in the words of Oigenblick and Kirschenbaum (2003) tourism is a 'pre-immigrant facilitator'.

It is still notoriously difficult to pin down exactly how many tourist migrants there may be in one place at one time. Government figures are mostly incomplete, as Salva-Tomas (2002) comments with special reference to the Islas Baleares, Spain. Indeed, Casado-Diaz (1999) in a study of residential tourism in Torrevieja, Costa Brava, Spain, says that there is reluctance on the part of the incoming population to register as permanent residents. This relates to a lack of incentive to do so – for example, the public health system can be used by tourists without registering as permanent residents – and so there is an underestimation of the population size. Moreover, definitions of migration are often opposed to definitions of tourism – inclining a researcher, yet alone a statistician, to assume that they cannot be juxtaposed together. Williams *et al.* (2000) in the context of international retirement migration state:

> One of the problems of estimating the size of international retirement migration populations is the inter-weaving of tourism, residence and multi-property ownership in a blurred continuum....This definitional complexity eludes most secondary data sources.
>
> (Williams *et al.*, 2000)

Theoretical discussion and empirical investigation of migration has an especially large literature in the social sciences – although Aranjo (2000) concludes that most contributions prior
to the 1960s are of mainly historical interest. Moreover, Urry (2003) states that much social
science research has been 'a-mobile', ignoring or trivializing the movement of people for leisure
and pleasure as well as work and family but he also refers to a 'mobility turn' that is 'putting the
social into travel'. Also, Williams *et al.* (2000) urge tourism researchers to embrace the research
concerns of migration studies and other branches of social science.

The cause of migration is variously attributed to a range of economic, social, political and
physical-environmental influences (Cohen, 1996a,b; Massey *et al.*, 1996; Skeldon, 1997; Boyle
et al., 1998; Castles and Miller, 1998). Rationally, what common ground exists between such
mainstream theory and the case of the tourist migrant at the beginning of 21st century? Some
commonality might be found with *migration systems theory* (Kritz *et al.*, 1992) – the view that
envisages migration flows as a consequence of economic, cultural, political and military link-
ages between a sending and a receiving country. Many seemingly clear examples might be
cited – such as recent flows from the UK to Australia and New Zealand or from Spain to
Argentina or within the European Union (EU). On the other hand, tourism with its changing
and growing set of new tourism destinations (and consequent migration destinations) might
be seen as one of the elements contributing, through the diversification of migration flows
and paths, to the *breakdown* of established world migration systems. This is especially relevant
given the rapid development of a global tourism system. Migration systems have been shown
to deepen through time – and, here, there may be some further resonance with the case of
tourist migrants. For example, there would seem to be great potential for a deepening of the
historic and present UK migration to Australia and New Zealand, as the backpacker generation of the 1990s and 2000s enters employment and satisfies the migration controls of the
receiving states. Noy (2004) was able to recognize profound self-change among backpackers –
and it is pertinent to ask why such self-change should also not involve migration to a favoured
destination.

As another potential example, Kang and Page (2000); Feng and Page (2000) and others
explore the very active visiting friends and relatives (VFR) tourism flow – between South
Korea and New Zealand and China and New Zealand, respectively. It might seem like a small
step between such a flow of VFR *tourists* (because they are tourists) and, sooner or later, subsequent migration. Oigenblick and Kirschenbaum (2003) seem to confirm this suggestion.
They conclude that migration from the former Soviet Union (FSU) to Israel is strongly linked
to factors identified with both social capital (e.g. level of relatives' economic establishment in
Israel, future residential proximity to relatives, relatives' advice regarding migration) and also
with tourism (e.g. destination image and experience with multiple tourism services). Duval
(2003, p. 303) concludes that there is a richer 'socially significant' meaning in VFR travel than
just visiting friends and relatives. If such deeper meaning can include a consideration of the
whole migration experience then again there is reason to believe that a VFR journey can lead a
new wave of migration among friends and relatives. Migration, consequent on VFR, also illus-

trates the recognized importance of *migration networks* – another strand of migration theory. Aranjo makes the observation that networks

> convey information, provide financial assistance, facilitate employment and accommodation and give support in various forms. In so doing, they reduce the costs and uncertainty of migration and, therefore, facilitate it.
>
> (Aranjo, 2000, p. 292)

Coppock (1977) acknowledged the role of tourism in international lifestyle migration over 30 years ago – a theme that Hall and Muller (2004) develop. But such work did not explore the more specific elements of tourist experience that may generate flows of tourist migrants – especially tourist satisfaction. However, this is addressed in part by Bowen and Schouten (2008) in their research among tourist migrants in Mallorca, Spain. The tourist experience and especially satisfaction was a dominant element in the decision to migrate – even if other considerations were also important. For example, one respondent, now involved in social work, recounted a distant world of pre-package Spain and 4–6 weeks' summer holidays:

> We drove through Spain from north to south (Zaragoza, Bilbao, Madrid) – saw men in peasant clothes and women with flowers in their hair – and on one occasion crossed to Mallorca on the ferry from Barcelona…there was beach after beach, no 'high-rise' buildings, giant turtles and sea, sea, sea.
>
> (Bowen and Schouten, 2008, fieldwork extract)

Later this respondent returned on package holidays as well as on more independent holidays – and initially helped her partner to start a range of (tourism-related) businesses. Through a chronological account of the process and information on life circumstances the respondent described and discussed how the tourist experience and tourist satisfaction was the dominant migration influence in such life change.

Another respondent, now a local government official, who migrated in the early 1970s, commented:

> It was virtually the beginning of the tourist boom, everybody was really friendly and also the island was at that time very economical. I had a naive and unprepared approach to travel – on one occasion I went to Valldemosa by bus where everyone, including tourists, got off and then disappeared. The tourists had gone to see the monastery (I did not know that it existed) and only reappeared after about three hours. I went to a local bar…it was good fun and from such times I caught a feel for the island.
>
> (Bowen and Schouten, 2008, fieldwork extract)

Such a comment, one extract from a three hour conversation, helped indicate (as with the social worker) how tourist experience and tourist satisfaction – and within that tourist and host performance and tourist emotions – were positive catalysts that led eventually to life-changing migration. The findings certainly expose the importance of tourist experience in what Aranjo (2000) calls the 'micro-perspective of individual decision-making'. The tourist migrant is clearly able to recognize tourist satisfaction, with an identifiable tourism destination, as a major factor in their migratory movement and settlement. It acts as a catalyst for migration. Williams and Hall (2000, p. 9) point out that 'there are increasing numbers with experience of living and working abroad, which both increases their search spaces at retirement and removes the barrier of a lack of familiarity with living abroad'. However, it seems that the process can occur not just at retirement (Williams *et al.*, 2000; Rodriquez, 2001; Gustafson, 2000); not just related to tourism-based second-home development (Snepenger *et al.*, 1995); not just related to labour migration in developing countries (Gossling and Schultz, 2005); and not just related to VFR. Tourist experience removes more than a lack of familiarity with living abroad. It can remove a lack of familiarity with a specific destination and also act, following tourist satisfaction, as the key thrust towards major life change in the form of permanent migration.

The case of the tourist migrant in the migration story is different – insomuch as the basis for migration is dissimilar from so many other classic migration stories. But, with the growth in tourism, and a comparative extension of free movement, the 21st century is only likely to see the development of more tourist-migrant flows based on tourist experience with specific destinations. Sheller and Urry (2003, p. 117) view globalization 'in terms of global fluids constituted of waves of people, information, objects, money, images, risks and networks moving across regions in heterogeneous, uneven, unpredictable and often unplanned shapes'. The tourist migrant component of the people wave, however, is not so unpredictable. It seems that tourist experiences and tourist satisfaction will generate subsequent migration flows that are strong enough to downplay more mainstream migratory motivations. Castles (2000, p. 270) states that '[t]he great majority of border crossings do not imply migration: most travelers are tourists or business visitors who have no intention of staying for long'. However, tourist experiences may very well lead, in an increasing number of cases, to migration.

Changes in leisure time and post working lives, demographic ageing of populations, new family structures and new transport and communications systems have increased the scale of migration and also internationalized patterns of mobility (Hall and Muller, 2004). But such changes would not have so much resonance, in many cases, without tourist experience and the drive for life change that it imparts.

JOURNEY'S END

So this journey through life change related to tourist experience has taken us from the day-to-day effect of tourism on leisure and vice versa, through to self-change, affairs of the heart and migration – from adjustments through to major upheaval. Most probably, readers can think of other ways in which their own lives have been affected, in one way or another, by tourist experience. Perhaps we should also not forget the negative – the migration that just did not work out, the broken affairs of the heart, the self-change that only introduced uncertainty and doubt into existence, or a gap-year tourist flirtation with drugs that led to psychological problems and a wistful view of the benefits that stem from tourist experience. Each negative experience can constrain future decision making. Life change beyond the tourist experience may indeed not conform to what we sought at the start of the journey.

REFERENCES

Aranjo, J. (2000) Explaining migration: a critical view, international migration at the beginning of the twenty-first century. *International Social Science Journal* 165, UNESCO: 283–295.

Bourdieu, P. (1991) *Language and Symbolic Power*. Polity Press, Cambridge.

Bowen, D. (2002) Research through participant observation in tourism: a creative solution to the measurement of consumer satisfaction and dissatisfaction among tourists. *Journal of Travel Research* 41(1), 4–14 August.

Bowen, D. and Schouten, A.F. (2008) Tourist satisfaction and beyond: tourist migrants in Mallorca. *International Journal of Tourism Research* 10(2), 141–153.

Boyle, P., Halfacree, K. and Robinson, V. (1998) *Exploring Contemporary Migration*. Longman, Harlow, Essex, UK.

Brey, E.T. and Lehto, X.Y. (2007) The relationship between daily and vacation activities. *Annals of Tourism Research* 34(1), 160–180.

Carr, N. (2002) The tourism-leisure behavioural continuum. *Annals of Tourism Research* 29(4), 972–986.

Casado-Diaz, M.A. (1999) Socio-demographic impacts of residential tourism: a case study of Torrevieja, Spain. *International Journal of Tourism Research* 1, 223–229.

Castles, S. (2000) International migration at the beginning of the twenty-first century: global trends and issues. *International Social Science Journal* 165, UNESCO: 269–281.

Castles, S. and Miller, M.J. (1998) *The Age of Migration: International Population Movements in the Modern World*. Macmillan, London.

Cohen, E. (1972) Toward a sociology of international tourism. *Social Research* 39(1), 164–189.

Cohen, R. (ed.) (1996a) *Theories of Migration*. Elgar Publishing, Cheltenham, UK.

Cohen, R. (ed.) (1996b) *The Sociology of Migration*. Elgar Publishing, Cheltenham, UK.

Conran, M. (2006) Commentary: beyond authenticity: exploring intimacy in the touristic encounter in Thailand. *Tourism Geographies* 8(3), 274–285.

Coppock, J.T. (1977) *Second Homes: Curse or Blessing?* Pergamon, London.

Crouch, D. and Desforges, L. (2003) The sensuous in the tourist encounter: Introduction – the power of the body in tourist studies. *Tourist Studies* 3(1), 5–22.

Desforges, L. (2000) Travelling the world – identity and travel biography. *Annals of Tourism Research* 27(4), 926–945.

Dixon, L. and Chesshyre, T. (2008) Time out for a different generation as thirty somethings take over gap year. *The (London) Times*, 22 November 2008.

Duval, D.T. (2003) When hosts become guests: return visits and diasporic identities in a common-wealth eastern Caribbean community. *Current Issues in Tourism* 6(4), 267–308.

Feng, K. and Page, S. (2000) An exploratory study of the tourism, migration-immigration nexus: travel experiences of Chinese residents in New Zealand. *Current Issues in Tourism* 3(3), 246–281.

Giddens, A. (1991) *Modernity and Self-identity; Self and Society in Late-modernity*. Polity Press, Cambridge.

Gilbert, D. and Abdullah, J. (2004) Holidaytaking and the sense of well-being. *Annals of Tourism Research* 31(1), 103–121.

Gossling, S. and Schultz, U. (2005) Tourism related migration in Zanzibar, Tanzania. *Tourism Geographies* 7(1), 43–62.

Gustafson, P. (2000) Tourism and seasonal retirement migration. *Annals of Tourism Research* 29, 899–918.

Hall, C.M. and Muller, D. (2004) *Tourism, Mobility and Second Homes: Between Elite Landscape and Common Ground*. Channel View Publications, Clevedon, UK.

Jafari, J. (1987) Tourism models: the socio-cultural aspects. *Tourism Management* (June) 151–159.

Kang, S.K.-M. and Page, S. (2000) Tourism, migration and emigration: travel patterns of Korean-New Zealanders in the 1990s. *Tourism Geographies* 2(1), 50–65.

Kritz, M.M., Lin, L.L. and Zlotnik, H. (eds.) (1992) *International Migration Systems: A Global Approach*. Clarendon Press, Oxford.

Lee, J.A. (1976) *Lovestyles*. Dent, London.

Mannell, R. and Iso-Ahola, S. (1987) Psychological nature of leisure and tourism experience. *Annals of Tourism Research* 14, 314–331.

Maoz, D. (2008) The backpacking journey of Israeli women in mid-life. In: Hannam, K. and Ateljevic, I. (eds) *Backpacker Tourism: Concepts and Profiles*. Channel View Publications, Clevedon, UK, pp. 188–198.

Massey, D.S., Arango, J., Hugo, G., Kouaouci, A., Pellegrino, A. and Taylor, E.J. (1996) Theories of international migration: a review and appraisal. In: Cohen, R. (ed.) *Theories of Migration*. Elgar Publishing, Cheltenham, UK, pp. 431–466.

Niggel, C. and Benson, A.M. (2008) Exploring the motivations of backpackers: the case of South Africa. In: Hannam, K. and Ateljevic, I. (eds) *Backpacker Tourism: Concepts and Profiles*. Channel View Publications, Clevedon, UK, pp. 144–156.

Noy, C. (2004) This trip really changed me: backpackers' narratives of self-change. *Annals of Tourism Research* 31(1), 78–102.

Oigenblick, L. and Kirschenbaum, A. (2003) Tourism and immigration: comparing alternative approaches. *Tourism Management* 29(1), 1086–1100.

O'Reilly, C.C. (2006) From drifter to gap year tourist: mainstreaming backpacker travel. *Annals of Tourism Research* 33(4), 998–1017.

Palmer, C. (2005) An ethnography of Englishness: experiencing identity through tourism. *Annals of Tourism Research* 32(1), 7–27.

Pruitt, D. and LaFont, S. (1995) For love and money – romance tourism in Jamaica. *Annals of Tourism Research* 22(2), 422–440.

Rodriquez, V. (2001) Tourism as a recruiting post for retirement migration. *Tourism Geographies* 3(1), 52–63.

Rodriquez, V., Fernandea-Mayoralas, G. and Rojo, F. (1998) European retirees on the Costa del Sol: a cross national comparison. *International Journal of Population Geography* 4(1), 183–200.

Ryan, C. and Robertson, E. (1997) New Zealand student-tourists: risk behaviour and health. In: Clift, S. and Grabowski, P. (eds) *Tourism and Health: Risks, Research and Responses*. Pinter, London, pp. 119–138.

Salva-Tomas, P.A. (2002) Foreign immigration and tourism development in Spain's Balearic islands. In: Hall, C.M. and Williams, A.M. (eds) *Tourism and Migration: New Relationships Between Production and Consumption*. Kluwer Academic Publishers, Dordrecht, The Netherlands.

Sheller, M. and Urry, J. (2003) Mobile transformations of 'public' and 'private' life. *Theory, Culture and Society* 20(3), 107–125.

Singh, S. (2002) Love, anthropology and tourism. *Annals of Tourism Research* 29(1), 261–264.

Skeldon, R. (1997) *Migration and Development: A Global Perspective*. Longman, London.

Snepenger, D., Johnson, J.D. and Rasker, R. (1995) Travel-stimulated entrepreneurial migration. *Journal of Travel Research* 34(1), 40–44.

Taylor, J. (2001) Authenticity and sincerity in tourism. *Annals of Tourism Research* 28, 17–26.

Uriely, N., Yonay, Y. and Simchai, D. (2002) Backpacking experiences: a type and form analysis. *Annals of Tourism Research* 29, 519–537.

Urry, J. (2003) Social networks, travel and talk. *British Journal of Sociology* 54(2), 155–175.

Wickens, E. (2002) The sacred and the profane: a tourist typology. *Annals of Tourism Research* 29(3), 834–851.

Williams, A.M. and Hall, M.C. (2000) Tourism and migration: new relationships between production and consumption. *Tourism Geographies* 2(1), 5–27.

Williams, A.M., King, R., Warnes, A. and Patterson, G. (2000) Tourism and international retirement migration: new forms of an old relationship in Southern Europe. *Tourism Geographies* 2(1), 29–49.

Wilson, E. and Ateljevic, I. (2008) Challenging the 'tourist other' dualism: gender, backpackers and the embodiment of tourism research. In: Hannam, K. and Ateljevic, I. (eds) *Backpacker Tourism: Concepts and Profiles*. Channel View Publications, Clevedon, UK, pp. 95–112.

chapter 5

MODELS OF TOURIST BEHAVIOUR

Since the 1960s and 1970s, there have been attempts within the wider field of consumer behaviour to develop models that somehow encapsulate the different elements of behaviour and also show the relationships that exist, normally in some sort of chronological order, from the start to the finish of the behavioural process. Such early attempts at model creation are derived very much from psychology and driven very often by marketing. They are still immensely influential within the academic world but have been followed up with models that are deemed to be more tourist-specific – models that apply more especially to the tourism industry. These provide further focus but are nevertheless criticized for what they do *not* concentrate on – such as constraints on tourist behaviour.

It must also not be forgotten that there are models of tourist behaviour that come from outside the psychology specialism but nevertheless relate to tourist behaviour – such as can be found in the social science contributions of, say, sociology, anthropology and geography.

This chapter will consider each of the model types above and will pay particular attention to the potential application of the models to tourism and tourist sub-contexts, so that the relevance or otherwise of the models can be outlined and evaluated.

GRAND MODELS OR LARGE SYSTEM MODELS AND OTHER MODELS

American scholars were largely instrumental in developing the 'Grand Models' of consumer behaviour in the 1960s, 1970s and 1980s. The models often formed the organizing framework for their weighty, but normally very readable, consumer behaviour and/or marketing textbooks.

Some examples include the work of Nicosia (1966), Engel *et al.* (1968), Howard and Sheth (1969) and Lilien and Kotler (1983) – all of which generated multiple book editions.

Lilien and Kotler (1983) identify and suggest a taxonomy of models. They plot the stages of consumer behaviour that each model type highlights against the breadth of its coverage – the degree to which a model maps either the whole or a part of a decision-making process (from 'complete micro-detail' through to complete 'macro-detail').

Of course, the 'Grand Models' (or what Lilien and Kotler term 'Large System Models') mark out one extreme of the taxonomy – their purpose is to cover each of the consumer behaviour stages and also to include the most complete micro-detail. The 'Market Response Models' mark out the other extreme. They are not our concern here as they relate market changes (e.g. sales) to market activities (e.g. marketing) – without mention of any behavioural mechanisms – and rely completely on aggregate or market-level data. However, the large system models most certainly are our concern.

Any of the examples listed above can illustrate how the models work, though we choose Engel *et al.* (1968) – as reprinted in the 25th anniversary edition of the book in 1993.

The Engel *et al.* model is based on both rational decision making and also what Engel *et al.* (1993, p . 41; Fig. 5.1) term 'hedonic benefits' in which 'the consumption is viewed symbolically in terms of emotional responses, sensory pleasures, daydreams or aesthetic considerations'. The same model is claimed to apply to both limited problem solving (following a rule such as 'buy the cheapest product/brand') and extended problem solving – in which the decision process is detailed, rigorous and extended with much thought given to alternative brands. The model is divided into a number of stages and at its heart is the decision-process stage – similar to many large system consumer behaviour models. This comprises:

- need recognition;
- search for information – internal (memory) and external (marketer dominated);
- information processing (exposure, attention, comprehension, acceptance, retention);
- alternative evaluation (comparison of different products and brands) until the choice is narrowed to a preferred alternative;
- purchase; and
- outcomes (such as satisfaction and dissatisfaction).

As Engel *et al.* (1993, p. 48) clearly state their model 'specifies the building blocks (variables) and the ways in which they are inter-related'. But it is a conceptual model – like all the 'Grand Models'/'Large System Models' – a unifying aid to thought rather than an operational model. There are many assumptions that may not hold in the real world of consumers – such as an ability to recognize needs, draw from memory, seek and comprehend both marketing information and also information from the social environment, be aware of, and also evaluate, alternatives, act on feedback and so on.

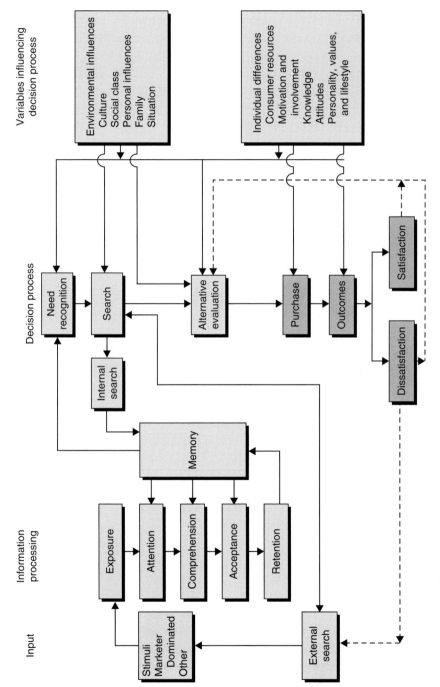

Fig. 5.1. Model of consumer behaviour showing purchase and its outcomes. (From Engel *et al.*, 1993, p. 53.)

Gilbert (1991, p. 93) considered that the grand models of consumer decision making 'share several commonalities':

- They all consider consumer behaviour as a decision process.
- They offer a comprehensive vision of the process with a focus on the individual – rather than the group.
- They consider behaviour to be rational and explicable – rather than random.
- The consumer actively searches and evaluates information that is both stored internally and is available from outside sources.
- As time goes on consumers narrow down information search and finally make a choice from alternatives.
- A feedback mechanism means that future decisions are affected by past experience.

Each of the shared commonalities is also a potential Achilles heel – for example, much decision making occurs in a group and a rational approach to decision making is not always central.

Other models that link to the narrower realm of information search (and beyond that to include perception formation and preference formation) will be considered in Chapter 8, 'Logical Decision or Lucky Dip?' (this volume). In terms of Lilien and Kotler (1983) such models occupy the middle ground both as regards their breadth of coverage and also the range of processes covered. For the most part, Chapter 8, 'Logical Decision or Lucky Dip?' (this volume), concentrates on models adapted by tourism academics and in it we give due note to the likes of the gather–analyse–decide models (Mansfield, 1992; Lye *et al.*, 2005); choice sets (Um and Crompton, 1990; Crompton, 1992); and the theory of planned behaviour (TPB) (Ajzen, 1991; Sparks, 2007).

TOURIST-SPECIFIC MODELS

The grand models are not tourist-specific and, moreover, are orientated more to products than to services. So, they do not encapsulate the well-established special characteristics of services such as intangibility, inseparability, heterogeneity and perishability detailed in Chapter 9, 'In-use Experience' (this volume) (Zeithaml *et al.*, 1985). Sirakaya and Woodside (2005) consider that the characteristics of tourism service offerings should not be neglected when building theories of decision making by travellers. They especially emphasize the intangibility service characteristic, the supposed high involvement of tourists and the tourists' need to find ways that can reduce high-perceived risk – for example, through more reliance on personal contacts for information (see Chapter 8, 'Logical Decision or Lucky Dip?', this volume). Other tourism-specific considerations might include the role of seasonality and demand fluctuations (and so over and under supply of capacity) and sub-sector interlinkage (Middleton and Clarke, 2001). Seaton and Bennett (1996) also argue that the tourism service offering partly comprises the dreams and fantasies of customers (certainly not comparable with many other services yet alone goods) and that much tourism relates to an extended service experience (not just extended problem solving) with no predictable critical evaluation point.

A credit list of tourist-specific consumer behaviour models would most probably need to mention the work in chronological order of Wahab *et al.* (1976), Schmoll (1977), Mayo and Jarvis (1981), Mathieson and Wall (1982), Moutinho (1987), Woodside and Lysonski (1989), Um and Crompton (1990), Moscardo *et al.* (1996) and Middleton and Clarke (2001). There are other valuable contributions to the body of knowledge that we could add – but we have to stop somewhere.

In general, Sirakaya and Woodside (2005) contend that such models do relate to the special nature of tourism purchase behaviour – they are more relevant in an evaluation of the tourist consumer than the more generic models. But we have not found a tourist-specific model that incorporates all such special characteristics. This is not the place for a comprehensive review of all the models – readers can follow up the references. But it is worth considering their limitations and asking whether any one model manages to combat some or most of the limitations. Hudson (1999), Hudson and Gilbert (2002) and Sirakaya and Woodside (2005) identify a role cast of limitations – supplemented below by further limitations from the authors of this book:

- bias towards a positivist stance that views decision making as a rational, formal, sequential, multistage process;
- non-empirical base in most cases – often linked to difficulties defining and/or operationalizing the terms – so, entirely hypothetical;
- lack predictive capability – cannot be used as a basis for forecasting tourist demand in a given tourist service or destination;
- emphasis on high-involvement decisions and extensive problem solving rather than moderate or low involvement and limited problem solving (as might occur in much tourist activity);
- emphasis on decisions that are made individually rather than jointly in groups – family or friendship or interest groups;
- emphasis on decisions that are single and independent rather than multiple and in a hierarchy or portfolio – that take other tourist and non-tourist decisions into account;
- elements missing and/or ill defined;
- linkage and, therefore, relationships between elements not clear;
- very complex relationships suggested among elements;
- lack of feedback loops – outcome of a decision can have effect on a subsequent decision, so without feedback model not dynamic;
- overgeneralized – for example, not relevant to particular tourist segments;
- orientated towards the USA and former Western Europe vis-à-vis, say, Asia, South America or the former Eastern Europe;
- lag behind technological change – the Internet, social networking and multifunction mobile phones;
- absence of time dimension – for example, no temporal order;
- limited mention of constraints.

On the surface this is a fiercely long range of shortcomings. If this is truly the state of the art as regards tourist-specific models of behaviour, after 30 years of endeavour, then the art is in some state! However, it is a composite list. And, even when a model seems to succumb to many of the limitations above there are normally some very positive redeeming features.

It is worth considering a case in point – such as the model of Mayo and Jarvis (1981; Fig. 5.2). The Mayo and Jarvis model was used, in the manner of the grand theorists, as the organizing framework for a very readable text – perhaps the first point of credit. Beyond that, Mayo and Jarvis do not blithely assume that all tourist decisions are extensive – decisions that take a long time to make have a high perceived need for information and a low perceived knowledge about alternatives. They suggest that some decisions may be routine or impulsive.

> The auto traveller needing overnight accommodations, for example, may almost automatically look for a Holiday Inn. In this case, the traveller makes a routine or habitual decision, so called because it is made so rapidly and with so little conscious thought that it appears to be based on habit. Similarly, the East Coast (USA) businesswoman who must travel to the West Coast might automatically and habitually choose to fly to her destination.
>
> (Mayo and Jarvis, 1981, p. 17)

In addition, they appropriately highlight the influence of social factors and psychological factors in decision making. There is an inner ring of defined, internal, psychological factors

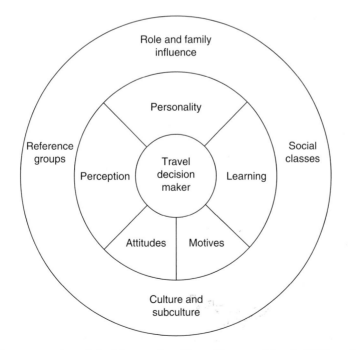

Fig. 5.2. Influences on travel decision maker. (From Mayo and Jarvis, 1981, p. 20.)

(perception, learning, personality, motives and attitudes) and there is an outer ring of defined, external, social factors (role and family influence, social class, culture and subculture and reference groups).

> Perception is the process by which an individual selects, organises, and interprets information to create a meaningful picture of the world. Learning refers to changes in an individual's behaviour based on his experiences. Personality refers to the patterns of behaviour displayed by an individual, and to the mental structures that relate experience and behaviour in an orderly way. Motives are thought as internal energising forces that direct a person's behaviour toward the achievement of personal goals. Attitudes consist of knowledge and positive or negative feelings about an object, an event, or another person.
>
> (Mayo and Jarvis, 1981, p. 19)

Such factors continue to strike a chord over 25 years since publication. On the other hand, while the model is very clear, there are shortcomings – like the lack of an empirical base, lack of predictive capability and so forth. This brings us back to our start point. Also, Mayo and Jarvis do not directly mention a number of key factors that would most likely influence the tourist – such as income or price or travel trade marketing. Indeed they state 'that there is ample reason to be disenchanted with purely economic explanations of travel behaviour. Income and price, though important, do not explain very much about the leisure and travel decisions' (Mayo and Jarvis, 1981, p. 234).

It is also worth considering the recent strides that have been made to deal with some of the identified shortcomings in these models. For example, although a consideration of constraints has not yet found a way into the most recent models, constraints on tourist behaviour are now well explored by Gilbert and Hudson (2000) and Hudson and Gilbert (2002; Fig. 5.3). They specifically relate their thoughts to constraints on skiing participation. For any reader who has harboured any doubts about such activity, their list of intra-personal, interpersonal and structural constraints – a division of constraints hypothesized by Crawford *et al.* (1991) – surely resonates very clearly. Some people are just scared of the ski lifts (an intra-personal constraint) – whether enclosed lifts or open lifts that are exposed to the elements and leave you dangling many metres above the ground. They may be concerned, too, that they will not be able to jump-off in time when they get to the ski station. Some people just cannot get their head around the whole gamut of equipment that seems to be required (a structural constraint), especially for downhill skiing rather than cross-country skiing; or are concerned that the lack of snow on the lower slopes, as induced by global warming or not, will inhibit their chances to get out on the snowfields. And some people may just think that they are not sufficiently glamorous to grace the ski scene (an interpersonal constraint), especially as falling over and flailing around without any balance can make even the most serene person look rather like a fool.

Gilbert and Hudson distinguish between the constraints facing non-participants and those facing existing participants and then consider the implications for marketers. They conclude

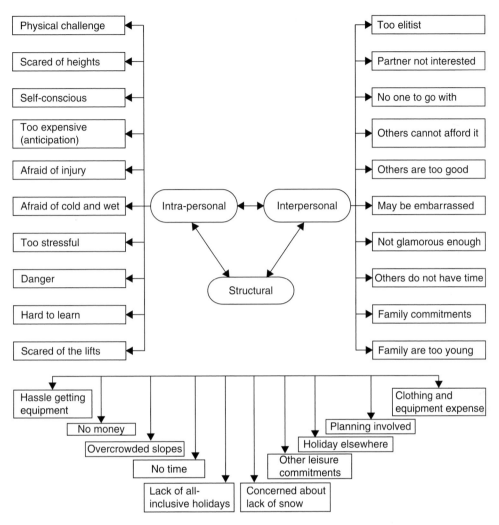

Fig. 5.3. Constraints on ski participation. (From Hudson and Gilbert, 2002.)

(2000, pp. 919–920) that 'non-skiers suffer intra-personal constraints on a significantly larger scale than do their counterparts'. Education is required – education through marketing:

> The question for the marketer is how to recapture the essence of skiing – the exhilaration, fascination, sense of independence and freedom, the beauty of the mountains, rush of adrenaline, the toned muscles and the incredible high that skiers feel at the end of a day's skiing.
>
> (Gilbert and Hudson, 2000, p. 920)

A similar set of constraints and resultant marketing implications can be produced for most other activities – and not just those requiring the accumulated skill level of skiing. It is indeed instructive to consider the intra-personal, interpersonal and structural constraints that can act as a break on the activity of otherwise outgoing and confident individual tourists – from swimming in the sea and lying on a beach through to canal boating, walking in the hills or enlisting on a cookery course or architecture course in an Italian city. What is of interest here though, apart from such considerations, is the role that a model such as Hudson and Gilbert (2002) can have in organizing and stimulating thought and suggesting practical action by tourism professionals.

SOCIAL SCIENCE CONTRIBUTIONS

There is an argument that suggests tourism academics have looked for too long at the general consumer behaviour/marketing theories – so that tourist models overdose on the ideas presented in the grand models. Moreover, as Przeclawski (1993, p. 17) suggests 'an investigator inclined to the materialist way of thinking should take into account that leaving aside the human spirit makes a true analysis of the market impossible'. We assume that the marketing pioneers who configured the grand models of consumer decision making, and many although not all of the tourism academics who adapted their models, would fit into what Przeclawski calls the 'materialist way of thinking'.

Arguably, social science contributions present a wider view of the tourist and the tourist experience than the tourist as a materialist consumer. Here, we turn primarily to some foundational articles from the pen of sociologists and anthropologists. For the most part such contributors do not produce visual models – but we start with one sociologist, Jafari (1987; Fig. 5.4), who does just that.

Jafari (1987, p. 151) uses a springboard metaphor – especially apt in a tourism context for those of us who have spent much holiday time diving off springboards and boats into a pool or sea – to describe how a tourist can leap temporarily into the tourist world and then fall back into ordinary life. The six main components or processes of the model include:

- Corporation – an obscure term until you think back to the Latin word (*corps*) for the English word 'body'. So, corporation is the 'corporated body of the ordinary life which breeds the need or desire to leave the springboard behind' (Jafari, 1987, p. 151).
- Emancipation – the act of departure.

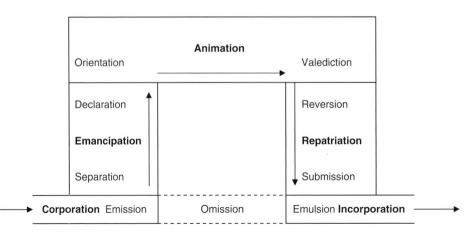

Fig. 5.4. The tourist springboard metaphor. (Adapted from Jafari, 1987, p. 156.)

- Animation – the tourist doing something in the non-ordinary world of tourism.
- Repatriation – the return from the temporary tourist position to the reality of ordinary life, the springboard platform.
- Omission – the ordinary current of life that continues when the tourist has left the springboard.
- Incorporation – getting back into the body of ordinary life and, indeed, overcoming the 'depression' caused by physical and mental exhaustion from a 'trip'.

Within each broad component, Jafari provides some further thought. For example, emancipation is split into spatial *separation* as the individual is drawn to the magnet, the destination; and also *declaration* as the individual moves beyond the sociocultural thresholds of home:

> Through a new identity and role, the individual is transformed into a tourist, familiar clothing and anxieties are shed, tourism becomes the script for the new character, and the magnet becomes the stage for the performance.
>
> (Jafari, 1987, p. 153).

The emphasis on the ordinary/profane (and workaday) and the non-ordinary/sacred (and touristic) is an echo of mainstream anthropological thought that Graburn (1989) attributes to Leach (1961). Graburn (1989) elegantly states that 'tourism…does not universally exist but is functionally and symbolically equivalent to other institutions that humans use to embellish and add meaning to their lives' (Graburn, 1989, p. 22). By which Graburn means aspects of life such as rituals and ceremonies, pilgrimage and religion – and we have commented elsewhere on how similar some terminology is in tourism and religion.

Sociologists and anthropologists also produce some strong non-visual conceptualizations that deserve to be brought together in this chapter – as a balance to the 'materialist way of thinking' in many models of tourist behaviour. It seems appropriate to expand at least one highly relevant conceptual debate – authenticity – to incorporate the human spirit. Other areas could also be chosen, but we lack space and authenticity sends out its tentacles far and wide – and links closely with the non-ordinary/sacred touristic time as outlined by Jafari and Graburn.

Authenticity and the tourist gaze

Authenticity, as debated in the tourist literature, largely originates in the work of MacCannell (1976). Essentially, in MacCannell's view, modern society is deemed to be inauthentic and alienating – and this spurs the tourist to seek the authentic. Taylor (2001, p. 10) elaborates:

> At the forefront of the account of the timeless and spiritually pure primitive, then, is a parallel story of alienation from nature, fragmentation, and loss.…Of course, authenticity is valuable only where there is perceived inauthenticity. Such is the plastic world of the consumer. Enamoured by the distance of authenticity, the modern consciousness is instilled with a simultaneous feeling of lack and desire erupting from a sense of loss.…Enter the business of tourism: a few hours of cushion-seated flying will bridge the span of 'modern nostalgia'; it will even take you back in time.
>
> (Taylor, 2001, p. 10)

MacCannell (1976) responds to the work of Boorstin (1964, p. 77), who saw (modern) tourist experience as trivial, superficial and frivolous – a quest for 'pseudo-events' rather than authentic experiences. But MacCannell (1976) also concludes that the search for authenticity fails and that the tourist is treated to a contrived and artificial 'staged authenticity' or even a deeper more insidious and dangerous 'false back' (MacCannell, 1976, p. 102). This is because the tourism industry – the supply side of the tourism equation – turns culture into a commodity that is packaged together and sold to the tourist with a loss of authenticity (so-called commodification). So, tourists are motivated towards authenticity but get short-changed by the conniving industry, the tourism establishment.

As an example of a conniving industry, Turnbull (2008) records in the *New York Times* that at the temple of Angkor Wat – the UNESCO World Heritage site in Cambodia – it is difficult for the tourist to imagine the customs and rituals of the Cambodian dynasty that flourished there during the 9th to 15th centuries. Few artefacts remain *in situ*. But an attempt to redress the problem in a new museum nearby – the Angkor National Museum – has been much criticized. It is Thai-owned (so causing political suspicion) and includes an adjoining retail mall (so causing aesthetic outrage). Moreover, its sense of history is authentic. The Cambodian National Museum (185 miles away; 1 mile = 1.609 km) and the Conservation d'Angkor agreed to hand over 1000 artefacts and 31 major pieces to the museum over a 30-year period – but subsequently reneged on the agreement and reduced the numbers. So, it seems that hundreds of Buddhas in the Angkor National Museum date back no further than the 20th century – hardly an authentic representation for the tourist:

> It remains to be seen whether the museum will embrace the growing scholarship and broad debates that currently characterise Angkorian studies, or be content to lure tourists to the knickknacks of the cultural mall.
>
> (Turnbull, 2008)

But Urry (2003, p. 11) mentions that there are 'multiple discourses and processes of the "authentic"'. For example, Selwyn (1996) refers to:

- cool (real, original or genuine) authenticity;
- hot (accepted but fake and enjoyed) authenticity.

Anyone who has stood with wry amusement in front of street-sellers who market their products as 'genuine fakes' will know exactly what Selwyn means.

Wang (1999) refers to:

- objective authenticity (a museum version – supposedly an undistorted standard);
- constructive authenticity (something that acquires social recognition);
- existential authenticity.

'Existential authenticity' is a term drawn from Cohen (1979) and details a condition 'in which people feel that they are much more authentic and more freely expressed than in everyday life, not because the toured objects are authentic, but rather because they are engaging in non-everyday activities' (Wang, 1999, p. 49).

Kim and Jamal (2007) recognize existential authenticity among repeat visitors to the Texas Renaissance Festival – a weekend festival that takes place through October and November in Plantersville, Houston, on a site that (supposedly) replicates selected features of a 16th-century European village – castles, knights, magicians and jousts! Kim and Jamal (2007, pp. 195–196) conclude that

> festival locations such as this are very important sites of self-making, meaning-making and belonging in the (post) modern world…active participation in bonding, friendship, identity-seeking and transcendence (self-transformation) become evident…the experience at such contrived, simulated carnivalesque settings is quite socially complex and cannot be generalized simply as post-modern, superficial (and) hedonistic.
>
> (Kim and Jamal, 2007, pp. 195–196)

There are advocates, too, of authenticity as a reality that is socially constructed – and so not static but changing through time. And back on the tail of MacCannell, Taylor (2001) questions what is wrong with 'false backs'. He records how in some instances local New Zealand Maori have moved their meeting place with international visitors from the museum, hotel and stage to the *marae*, the spiritual home of the community. There the Maori hope to 'redress the proliferation of negative images and stereotypes propagated by the industry and media at large' (Taylor, 2001, p. 22). Taylor includes a quote from *Te Maori News*:

> We didn't want to offer visitors just the memory of a culture, with haka, dance, and painted faces.…We also offer them an insight into a living culture of our people.
>
> (Taylor, 2001, p. 22)

Cole (2007) provides further support to such an intervention in a different culture and context – a study among villagers in Eastern Indonesia.

> Rather than unpacking authenticity into hot, cold, objective, constructive or existential, analysts need to be asking questions about how the notion is articulated and by whom. A better understanding is needed of how cultural tourism is used by marginalized groups to gain power and how they can use the identity and pride that commodifying their cultural identity appears to bring.
>
> (Cole, 2007, p. 956)

Linked to authenticity is not just the related concept of commodification but also the literature on the 'tourist gaze' (Urry, 1990). And the depth of work on the tourist gaze as an aspect of behaviour also deserves to be highlighted here, albeit briefly, to emphasize how social science fights for the inclusion of the human spirit into an evaluation of tourist consumption – mostly hidden in the standard models. The gaze 'organises and regulates the relationships between the various sensuous experiences while (the tourist is) away, identifying what is visually out of ordinary' (Urry, 2002). Among other things, it 'has the power to discipline and normalise the locals' behaviour…[and the locals] are influenced by this power and are objects of the gaze' (Maoz, 2006).

But herein lies the fight for the human spirit – almost a real fight – for Maoz (2006) has taken the concept of the tourist gaze further with her empirical examination of the *two-way* gaze between Israeli backpackers and Indian villagers. And Maoz finds that while the tourist gaze is dominant so that the locals have to adjust themselves, sell themselves and hide and protect themselves against the gaze – so as to resist and manage its power – the villagers also engage in their own 'local gaze'. The result is a 'mutual gaze'. Locals also exert power. And so, it might be argued, direct from such sociological and anthropological study, models need to be less centred on tourists only. As Maoz suggests (2006, p. 235) by being alert to the 'local gaze' we can maybe 'view a more complex, double-sided picture, where both the tourist and local gazes exist, affect and feed each other and the encounter they produce'.

In choosing authenticity as our key sociological debate we directly and indirectly enrich concepts contained in the grand models and the tourist models. For example, authenticity, in whatever form, is a major element of such components as 'felt need' and 'motivation' and 'desire' – all terms that are used extensively in our credit list of tourist models. The components of behaviour as identified in the tourist models hide the sort of fertile thinking engaged in by the social scientists (the sociologists and anthropologists). The social scientists deepen headline terms with more profound understandings. That is why we include a discussion of authenticity in this chapter.

Urry (2003) suggests that work related to the sociology of tourism is 'characterized by intellectual underdevelopment' (Urry, 2003, p. 9) and 'a kind of parasitism upon broader debates and controversies within sociology and cultural studies' (Urry, 2003, p. 18). That may be true in part – but there is a real contribution made by the social sciences that deserves a showing.

MODELS AND (NEAR) REALITY: SOME SCENARIOS

It is a very valuable exercise to plot the theory as represented by the tourist models against the reality of a particular sub-context – any sub-context because if a theory is supposed to inform then it should inform in a myriad of situations. So, take a scenario such as elder (55+) tourists – indeed, a more specific scenario such as elder tourists from China arriving in Europe 2010–2020. Then focus down more so that we look in particular at heritage tourists – and heritage tourists in a given historic European city. You can name the city – Bruges, Cordoba, Oxford, Berlin – and consider how the tourists' behaviour will match or fail to match a classic tourist behaviour model such as Mathieson and Wall (1982; Fig. 5.5).

The Mathieson and Wall model (incidentally produced by two geographers and so a contribution from another social science) is centred around a decision-making process that moves through a number of principal phases – travel desire, information search and image creation, assessment of alternatives, travel decision and finalization of arrangements, the travel experience and evaluation.

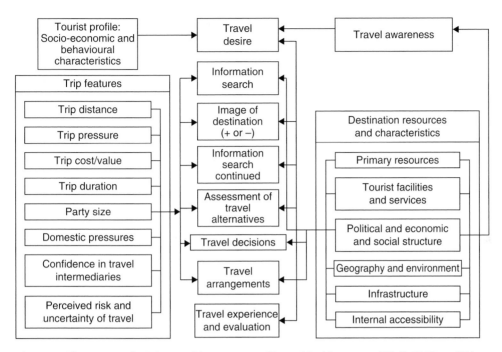

Fig. 5.5. The tourist decision-making process. (From Mathieson and Wall, 1982, p. 27.)

To satisfy our exercise, we need to fuse a likely but imagined reality with theory. First, consider the tourist profile – the socio-economic and behavioural characteristics (emotional, physical and spiritual *needs* and physical, cultural, personal and prestige and status *motivations*). We have mentioned the Chinese tourist on a number of occasions through this book, most notably in Chapter 2, 'Country-File: Tourist Nations' (this volume). As long as the international, external political and economic environment is not tilted from its axis – that is, even more than in the financial turmoil in 2008/09 – there is likely to be a growth in Chinese elder travellers arriving in Europe over the coming decade. The growth will not be as spectacular as some predicted in the early years of the 21st century – but there will be growth, because a large number of the current Chinese middle class will become elder tourists over the next 10 years. It is likely that in comparison to the early streams of elders – who started to travel as the list of Approved Destination Status (ADS) countries grew in the late 1990s and early 2000s – the new streams will be less bound by the collectivist traditions and frugality of the past and more willing to spend on the consumption of new experiences. Again, because of the greater variety of background compared to the earlier (and first) generation of 21st-century Chinese elder travellers, the new stream will be less homogeneous as a group – the middle-class 40–55-year-olds (the 55+ market in 2010–2020) are more educated, more open to the world and seek more new experiences than their earlier counterparts. They will fit more to the differentiated subgroups that are characterized in studies of the 'seniors market' in the West (Shoemaker, 1989; You and O'Leary, 1999) with differences based on economic resources, health status, marital status, comparative connection or disconnection to family and also motivation.

Shoemaker (1989) labelled the subgroups as 'family travellers', 'active resters' and the 'older set'. You and O'Leary (1999) identified passive visitors, enthusiastic go-getters and cultural hounds. These subgroups will not be replicated in the Chinese case. But it will be far less common to see comparatively uniform groups of Chinese elders travelling en bloc – almost as if in a large and conspicuous delegation. Instead groups will be smaller and more free-spirited. Dare one say that travel will no longer be the brief of those who have done well in China because of political party affiliation or connection?

The destination resources and characteristics listed by Mathieson and Wall (1982) already exist in European destinations. We can assume that with word of mouth complemented by word of mouse – and also a concurrent growth of other information sources from conventional guidebooks (translations of *Lonely Planet* and other such publications into Mandarin) through to film and television and the Internet – the new generation of Chinese elders will have a more rounded travel awareness regarding Europe and European cities than their current counterparts and will develop clearer destination images. Mathieson and Wall (1982, p. 31) remind us that 'tourists may be motivated to travel but, unless they are informed of what opportunities are available, they may be unaware of the means of meeting their requirements'. So with raised travel awareness, the elder travellers will make informed travel decisions based on an assessment of travel alternatives (one European country vis-à-vis another and one heritage city vis-à-vis another) and will settle on their required trip features.

Europe may even become less a place of fantasy and romance and more a place of real people and landscapes – and shopping. Or not, for what we are doing here is attempting to see if a model lends itself to be fleshed out. We are not offering a foolproof vision of the future. But if we take the first scenario, the word of mouth/mouse will serve to *enhance* a view of a fantasy and romantic Europe to the new elder tourist profile. Both the authentic, original city heritage and the reconstructed city heritage of Europe will bewitch in comparison to the 21st-century dazzle of glass and steel that has engendered the quick and rapid bulldozing of heritage in Chinese cities. And the elder tourists will pour through the doors of the best-preserved places of heritage while remembering their own heritage lost. Becker (2008) in a commentary on Beijing – the City of Heavenly Tranquillity – states that whereas in 1980 there were 6000 courtyard homes (*hutong*), there are just a few hundred now; and only one out of 44 princely palaces (*wangfu*) remains. He makes a telling comparison:

> Imagine the outcry if in less than a decade London underwent a similar transformation. If the West End, Notting Hill, Knightsbridge, Holland Park and the City of London were to be levelled and replaced by giant commercial and residential blocks. If every landmark…were to disappear at once.
>
> (Becker, 2008)

We think it is a strength when a model – like that of Mathieson and Wall (1982) – can be fused with such an imagined scenario even if it is open to much of the common criticism of tourist-specific models. And it clearly can be.

IN THE FUTURE...

Nearly twenty years ago, Gilbert (1991, p. 101) stated that

> [a]lthough...a great deal of written material has been produced to explain different aspects of the (consumer behaviour) process, much of it is general in nature or unsubstantiated empirically....While progress may be occurring on a partial, disaggregate level, the emergence of improved general theories is bound to follow.
>
> (Gilbert, 1991, p. 101)

This has not proven to be entirely the case. But there is some hope that the merging of theory from all quarters with empirical study of the sort detailed by the latest work on authenticity might lead to the creation of more hybrid and more complete models in the future – before another 20 years pass.

REFERENCES

Ajzen, I. (1991) The theory of planned behaviour. *Organizational Behaviour and Human Decision Processes* 50, 179–211.

Becker, J. (2008) *City of Heavenly Tranquillity: Beijing in the History of China*. Allen Lane, London.

Boorstin, D. (1964) *The Image: A Guide to Pseudo-events in America*. Harper and Row, New York.

Cohen, E. (1979) A phenomenology of tourist types. *Sociology* 13, 179–201.

Cole, S. (2007) Beyond authenticity and commodification. *Annals of Tourism Research* 34(4), 943–960.

Crawford, D., Jackson, E.L. and Godbey, G. (1991) A hierarchical model of leisure constraints. *Leisure Sciences* 13, 309–320.

Crompton, J.L. (1992) Structure of vacation destination choice sets. *Annals of Tourism Research* 19(3), 420–434.

Decrop, A. (1999) Consumer behaviour related to tourism. In: Pizam, A. and Mansfield, Y. (eds) *Consumer Behaviour in Travel and Tourism*. Haworth Press, London, pp. 103–133.

Engel, J.F., Kollat, D.J. and Blackwell, R.D. (1968) *Consumer Behaviour*. Holt, Rinehart and Winston, New York.

Engel, J.F., Blackwell, R.D. and Miniard, P.W. (1993) *Consumer Behaviour*. The Dryden Press, London.

Gilbert, D.C. (1991) Consumer behaviour in tourism. In: Cooper, C.P. (ed.) *Progress in Tourism, Recreation and Hospitality Management Vol. 3*. Belhaven Press, Lymington, UK, pp. 78–105.

Gilbert, D. and Hudson, S. (2000) Tourism demand constraints: a skiing participation. *Annals of Tourism Research* 27, 906–925.

Graburn, N.H.H. (1989) Tourism: the sacred journey. In: Smith, V.L. (ed.) *Hosts and Guests: The Anthropology of Tourism*. University of Pennsylvania Press, Philadelphia, Pennsylvania.

Howard, J.A. and Sheth, J.N. (1969) *The Theory of Buyer Behaviour*. Wiley, New York.

Hudson, S. (1999) Consumer behaviour related to tourism. In: Pizam, A. and Mansfield, Y. (eds) *Consumer Behaviour in Travel and Tourism*. Haworth Press, London, pp. 7–34.

Hudson, S. and Gilbert, D. (2002) Tourism constraints; the neglected dimension of consumer behaviour research. In: Woodside, A.G. (ed.) *Consumer Psychology of Tourism, Hospitality and Leisure*. CAB International, Wallingford, UK, pp. 137–150.

Jafari, J. (1987) Tourism models: the socio-cultural aspects. *Tourism Management* 8(2), 151–159.

Kim, H. and Jamal, T. (2007) Touristic quest for existential authenticity. *Annals of Tourism Research* 34(1), 181–201.

Leach, E. (1961) *Rethinking Anthropology*. Athlone Press, London.

Lilien, G.L. and Kotler, P. (1983) *Marketing Decision Making*. Harper and Row, New York.

Lye, A., Shao, W. and Rundle-Thiele, S. (2005) Decision waves: consumer decisions in today's complex world. *European Journal of Marketing* 39(1/2), 216–230.

MacCannell, D. (1976) *The Tourist: A New Theory of the Leisure Class*. Schocken, New York.

Mansfield, Y. (1992) From motivation to actual travel. *Annals of Tourism Research* 19(3), 399–419.

Maoz, D. (2006) The mutual gaze. *Annals of Tourism Research* 33(1), 221–239.

Mayo, E.J. and Jarvis, L.P. (1981) *The Psychology of Leisure Travel*. CBI Publishing, Boston, Massachusetts.

Middleton, V.T.C. and Clarke, J.R. (2001) *Marketing in Travel and Tourism*, 3rd edn. Butterworth-Heinemann, Oxford.

Moscardo, G., Morrison, A.M., Pearce, P.L., Lang, C.T. and O'Leary, J.T. (1996) Understanding vacation destination choice through travel motivation and activities. *Journal of Vacation Marketing* 2, 109–122.

Nicosia, F.M. (1966) *Consumer Decision Process: Marketing and Advertising Implications*. Prentice-Hall, Englewood Cliffs, New Jersey.

Przeclawski, K. (1993) Tourism as the subject of inter-disciplinary research. In: Pearce, D. and Butler, R. (eds) *Tourism Research: Critiques and Challenges*. Routledge, London, pp. 9–19.

Seaton, A.V. and Bennett, M.M. (1996) *Marketing Tourism Products*. International Thomson Business Press, London.

Selwyn, T. (1996) Introduction. In: Selwyn, T. (ed.) *The Tourist Image. Myths and Myth-making in Tourism*. Wiley, Chichester, UK, pp. 1–32.

Shoemaker, S. (1989) Segmentation of the senior-pleasure travel market. *Journal of Travel Research* (Winter) 14–21.

Sirakaya, E. and Woodside, A.G. (2005) Building and testing theories of decision making by travellers. *Tourism Management* 26, 815–832.

Sparks, B. (2007) Planning a wine tourism vacation? Factors that help to predict tourist behavioural intentions. *Tourism Management* 28, 1180–1192.

Taylor, J. (2001) Authenticity and sincerity in tourism. *Annals of Tourism Research* 28(1), 7–26.

Turnbull, R. (2008) Thai museum at Angkor draws tourists, and criticism. *New York Times*, 6 July 2008.

Um, S. and Crompton, J.L. (1990) Attitude determinants in tourism destination research. *Annals of Tourism Research* 17, 432–448.

Urry, J. (1990) *The Tourist Gaze*. Sage, London.

Urry, J. (2003) The sociology of tourism. In: Cooper, C. (ed.) *Classic Reviews in Tourism*. Channel View Publications, Clevedon, UK, pp. 9–21.

Wang, N. (1999) Rethinking authenticity in tourism experience. *Annals of Tourism Research* 26, 349–370.

You, X. and O'Leary, J.T. (1999) Destination behaviour of older travellers. *Tourism Recreation Research* 24(1), 23–33.

Zeithaml, V.A., Parasuraman, A. and Berry, L.L. (1985) Problems and strategies in services marketing. *Journal of Marketing* 49, 33–46.

chapter 6

ECONOMIC AND SOCIAL INFLUENCES

It is possible to consider a range of external influences that can affect tourist behaviour. During an academic conference in Australia one of the authors of this book was required to stay on a particularly tight budget and so spent 4 days in a static holiday caravan site practically opposite the main conference venue.

It was a surreal experience to retreat each evening from the lush surroundings, modern elegance and ample, well-balanced and healthy food of a five-star resort – good enough to act as a camp for the Australian Wallabies rugby union side during their immediate Rugby World Cup preparation – to the rather minimal bare setting and barbecue (BBQ) world of the caravans. Each caravan reeked throughout with the distinctive smell of a harsh detergent-cum-cockroach repellent and a caravan-site shop sold just the bare necessities of life. The holidaymakers were pleasant enough and in one sense there was more *holidaymaking* – making the holiday – in the caravan site than there was among the pampered tourists in the resort. Life revolved around a family trip to the beach (drive not walk), a simple pool surrounded by rusty railings, the ubiquitous BBQ, sit-down games of cards – and cans of beer both through the day and either side of sundown. The caravan site played host to the real working-class Australians – in a supposedly classless society – at play for the duration of the summer. It was poor tourism – that is tourism for the comparatively poor.

The experience illustrated more starkly than any conference paper that there are external influences – separate from internal psychological influences (learning, motivation and so forth) – that have an effect on the tourist. Especially to the fore were the influence of economic power in the form of disposable income – or more accurately the lack of economic power – and a couple of key social influences such as social class and the role of family (see Chapter 12, 'The Importance of Family', this volume).

In other situations, different social influences can shine through such as gender, ethnicity (including religion) and race – each of which can help generate cultural distance. Swain (1995, p. 248) has a succinct but elegant turn of phrase when she remarks that such influences 'intersect and affect each other'. But they are divided up below for ease of understanding.

ECONOMIC INFLUENCES

The science of economics has a marked effect on most tourist activity. Since our focus is the individual – the tourist – we should introduce some theory from microeconomics. Two key economic influences on the tourist are income and price. The way in which there are changes in demand depending on income is called 'income elasticity of demand' and is expressed in a simple formula:

$$\frac{\text{percentage of change in quantity demanded}}{\text{percentage of change in income}}$$

Some tourist products are deemed to be more income-elastic than others and so respond more strongly to a change in income. So, for example, a weekend break might be a second or third or fourth opportunity for a young, professional person to get away for a short holiday and if that person's income was to drop – for example, because of a change in job grading or a rise in taxation at source – then the person might decide not to take the weekend break. If the aggregate of all such decisions can be worked out, then it might be found that with a 10% drop in income there is a 20% drop in quantity demanded. The income elasticity is measured, therefore, as 20/10 = 2. The weekend break product is then known as an 'income-elastic' product – for elastic products are any products with an elasticity greater than 1 (such as in a scenario with a 10% change in demand and a 10% change in income). A visit to a close friend or relative (VFR), though, might be less subject to change as a result of the alteration in income (e.g. there might be a 5% drop in demand with a 10% drop in income 5/10 = 0.5). In such a case, VFR is considered to be income-inelastic – for the elasticity is less than 1.

A similar formula works, too, for price elasticity. This is the way in which demand changes depending on price – the so-called price elasticity of demand'. Again it is expressed in a simple formula:

$$\frac{\text{percentage of change in quantity demanded}}{\text{percentage of change in price}}$$

A price hike can send tourists tumbling out of the market, and bring them rushing back when the price falls – simple in principle, rather more complicated in practice as so many variables may intervene to interfere with any given demand pattern.

For example, in response to a sustainability agenda and an attempt to diversify a sun and sand tourism model, the Balearic Regional Parliament (the regional parliament that governs over the islands of Mallorca, Menorca and Ibiza in the Mediterranean) introduced in April 2000 a contested and emotive tax on tourist hotel accommodation (implemented May 2002, abolished October 2003 with a change in Government!). As described by Aguilo *et al.* (2005), the tax was set at a maximum of €2/day in a five-star hotel, €1/day in a three-star hotel and €0.25/day in rural tourism accommodation; was not levied on children; and was not applied in non-hotel accommodation. So, not an especially swingeing tax, you might think. But Palmer and Riera (2003) report a model of the demand for tourism – the price elasticity of demand – that showed a resultant fall of 125,000 international tourists. This seems to be complemented by the details that Aguilo *et al.* (2005) provide on the fall in numbers of tourists visiting the Balearics – 0.3% in 2000, 2.22% in 2001 and 7.9% in 2002.

However, in contrast to Palmer and Riera (2003), others such as Aguilo *et al.* (2005) link the fall in numbers to the stagnant German economy over the same period – and so, presumably, the effect of income elasticity rather than price elasticity caused by the introduction of the 'ecotax'. They conclude that 'the number of tourists lost due to the introduction of this tax was very likely minimal' (Aguilo *et al.*, 2005, p. 230).

Whatever is the reality in the Balearics (whether it is price or income elasticity that is paramount), one thing is certain. It is not correct to argue that tourism products or tourist segments as a *whole* are income-elastic or price-elastic. Some are price-elastic and income-elastic and some are price-inelastic and income-inelastic. Tribe (2005) contrasts the likely inelastic demand for business tourism with other forms of tourism – even VFR. Business, he argues, demands face-to-face, direct contact and is, therefore, not so responsive to price change as other forms of tourism. But as an aside, to add a further twist, we offer the thoughts of Larsen *et al.* (2007, p. 247), who argue that 'the stretching out of social networks makes (all forms of) tourism desirable and indeed necessary'. Face-to-face meetings glue social networks, not just business networks – phone calls, texting and e-mail do not suffice.

This is but a short dip into the murky world of tourist economics but its influence, its tentacles, should be clear enough. We could continue with many other examples of how tourists are forced to interact with economic reality as they build their fantasy world. Interest rates, exchange rates, the comparative cost of living and the availability of credit all have an effect on the tourist – as we see in daily newspapers and other media. On the demand side, it is up to the tourist to respond – for example, through social networking on the Internet that cuts the cost of accommodation and allows individuals to go local (as seen in Chapter 8, 'Logical Decision or Lucky Dip?', this volume). On the supply side, it is up to the producer to woo the visitor. New York, for example, is asking tourists to fall in love with it again through a reprise of its 1970s strap-line – '*I love New York*'. But in severe economic times it is emphasizing the comparatively local domestic market. As Elliott (2008) states in the *New York Times*:

> 'People drive less but they do not stop driving' said Thomas Ranese, chief marketing officer at the New York office of the Empire State Development Corporation … and more than 80 million people live within a three- to five-hour drive of New York State. New York State joins a lengthening list of destination advertisers, including Canada, Massachusetts and Virginia that are acknowledging a travel market where gas costs $3.50 a gallon or more.

Beyond the realm of price and income elasticity, there are non-tourism competitors for tourist money and time. A former marketing manager of Blenheim Palace, an historic house in England and a World Heritage site, always stressed that the main competitors to Blenheim Palace were the do it yourself (DIY) superstores. Potential tourists use their money in the superstores and use their time engaged in DIY. Tourism is by no means immune to the wider consumption system. Potential tourists can take action and substitute a tourist purchase for a non-tourist purchase – even though many see tourism as a comparatively inelastic necessity and even a *right* rather than an elastic luxury. In academic writing, Dolnicar *et al.* (2008, p. 44) also consider the truth that tourist expenditure does not exist in a vacuum. In their Australian study, they point out that past studies 'fail to take into account that tourism expenditures are affected by the plethora of expenditures that households make'. However, there is some good news. Dolnicar *et al.* (2008, p. 51) isolate a sizeable segment (comprising 16% of the Australian population) – mainly singles without children – who demonstrate 'a very distinct preference for diverting additional discretionary expenditure towards vacations'. Not for them are financial investments – and DIY. For them, tourist expenditure is the crucial *sine qua non* expense.

SOCIAL INFLUENCES

Social influences are truly many and varied and numerous frameworks exist to try and map out the range of elements that might fall within the remit of social influence. In the early 1980s, Mayo and Jarvis (1981) suggested an inner ring of defined, internal, psychological influences (personality, learning, motives, attitudes and perception) and an outer ring of defined, external, social influences (family; role; reference groups; culture and subculture; social class). With regard to the social influences, it is easy to envisage a young tourist, say, whose destination decision making is affected by external influences such as what is acceptable to his/her family (e.g. what destinations are deemed safe); his/her ongoing role in society (e.g. student or new worker); reference group (what student friends or workmates say); his/her culture and subculture (religious or other influence on way of life; sport or other recreation and leisure interests) and even actual or ascribed social class.

Mayo and Jarvis continue to strike a chord over 25 years since publication and, indeed, we take a closer look at their model in Chapter 5, 'Models of Tourist Behaviour' (this volume). The role of family has been detailed elsewhere in Chapter 12, 'The Importance of Family' (this volume) and the influence of role and reference groups is evident in several parts of this book (e.g. in the discussion on backpacker motivation). However, we identify here what we consider to be some remaining, key social influences on the tourist at the end of the first decade of the 21st century.

Religion

We apparently live in a world that is less bound by religion. Indeed, tourists are sometimes accused of breaking down religion and society in general – and Aziz (2001, p. 152) draws attention to the stereotype of Western tourists 'as shameless hedonists corrupting local morals through empty promises of economic benefit'. At a glib level, it is hard to counter such an argument but when you see a congregation gathering for evening prayer in one of the exquisite churches in Palma, Mallorca, or listen to the regular call for prayer that reverberates from the mosques in Turkey, you may wonder whether the supposed breakdown is absolutely correct.

Indeed, religion has a multi-pronged influence on the tourist. Religious belief can define the movement of tourists to some destinations that have a pilgrimage connection. Pilgrimage, of course, has a long and eventful history – and we should not forget the religious origin of the very phrase *holy day* – but pilgrimage is also as much a thing of the present as of the past. For example, Jerusalem, a sort of religious Disneyland but with real rather than cartoon characters, is a pilgrimage centre for the Jewish faith at the Western Wall ('Wailing Wall'); the Christian faith (and its various denominations) along the Via Dolorosa, The Church of the Holy Sepulchre, Gethsemane and so forth; and the Muslim faith at the Al Aqsa Mosque ('Dome of the Rock') from where the prophet Mohammed is believed to have ascended to heaven and encountered the divine (*israk* and *miraj*).

The Hajj to Mecca is gaining prominence in the general consciousness of pilgrimage and Aziz (2001, p. 151) provides details of its scope and organizational requirements. He claims that the Hajj is the 'largest voluntary and regular mass movement of population in the world'. About one million people make the pilgrimage during the designated 4-day period – and a further two million arrive on Umra, a visit to the holy sites, outside the period of Hajj. The experience of the Hajj to Mecca (a return to the centre of Islam, the birthplace of the prophet Mohammed) is one of Islam's five pillars of faith – alongside belief in Allah and the prophet Mohammed, daily prayer, fasting during the daylight hours of Ramadan and the giving of charity. As Aziz (2001, p. 157) states:

> Muslims from all social classes aspire to go on Hajj once in their lifetime, often spending their life savings to fulfil this religious requirement. For Muslims from lower socio-economic groups, it is usually the only chance to travel overseas, to meet Muslims from all over the world, and to be re-created in a spiritual and practical sense. Expenditure for such trips is considered to be for a divine purpose, enabling the pilgrim to be closer to God.

Aziz gives an insight to the rituals of the Hajj – for example, walking around the Kaa'ba, the site believed by Muslims to be the house of God built by the prophet Abraham, the father of all prophets, or a visit to the Mosque of the Prophet in Medina – and also suggests some similarities with mainstream tourism. At one level the pilgrims can be said to reach a liminal state – a state set apart from normal life – as the Kaa'ba is performed by men and women together rather than apart. At another level, tour operators and travel agents have developed niche, luxury packages for more wealthy pilgrims that 'contradict the principles of humility and equality' (Aziz, 2001, p. 157). Indeed, Kessler (1992, p. 150) highlights the work of Mary Byrne McDonnell – who investigated the changes in the Hajj from Malaysia – and records how it is now 'closely coordinated by a major Malaysian government agency (and is not) the same protracted, hazardous, and uncertain venture that it once was'. Trade and shopping are also said by some returning pilgrims (hajji) to verge on the tacky end of commercial – perhaps an inevitable consequence of such an event with so many people in one place. And television and radio shows in the Muslim world offer trips for Hajj and Umra as prizes. However, the Hajj is not an open event that tourists of any religion can observe or engage in. Apart from the efforts of individuals such as the Victorian explorer Richard Burton, who endured a mid-life circumcision to complete his disguise, the Hajj is restricted to non-Muslims.

Movements other than to Mecca are also important in Islam. Aziz details these as including ziyara (visits to local shrines) and rihla (travel in search of knowledge or trade). He also mentions how the Quran 'exhorts Muslims to travel in the land of God to experience His creation more widely, to acquire knowledge, and to meet people and spread the word of God among Muslims and non-Muslims' (Aziz, 2001, p. 152). The notion of hospitality for travellers has long been a fail-safe for backpackers, it must be said, in many parts of the Muslim world.

It is clear from the discussion of the Hajj – and what Kessler (1992, p. 148) calls the 'drama of movement, travel and transformation…(that) is at the very core of Islam itself' – that religion can impose a set of beliefs on an individual and encourage travel. However, such a spirit does not apply uniformly to all Muslims and Henderson (2003, p. 449) draws attention to the role of women in Islam observing that

> [g]ender differences in tourism involvement…(are) very striking in some patriarchal and ultra orthodox Islamic cultures that impose severe restrictions on women. Tourism movements and industry practice are determined by conditions in society and mirror unequal gender relations where these exist. Male pre-eminence is a characteristic of many Muslim countries where women are denied a place in public life.

The case outlined above is an extreme. There are examples of far less extreme situations in the Islamic world in which women have more equal position and power and so travel more freely – or in which women somehow subvert the established norms. Indeed, Kessler (1992, p. 152) also highlights the work of Nancy Tapper who investigated the world of ziyara among traditional, lower-class women in Turkey – a country founded since the 1920s on secular principles of government but nevertheless predominantly Muslim by religion. The ziyara are 'female outings…pleasant, even joyful occasions that express and in practice embody a gender equality…(for) through these opportunities for movement, women's inherent subordination to men in the Islamic tradition is modified and alleviated'.

But right or wrong – and let us argue wrong – the extreme case exists as well in which such outings would not be tolerated. Even a married non-Muslim expatriate is unable to travel through an international airport in Saudi Arabia without her husband as an escort.

The influence of religion on tourist behaviour can also arise from the connection a religious faith may have with a non-religious site. In an analysis of tourist motivation to visit heritage sites, Poria *et al.* (2006) study visitors standing in line waiting for entrance to the Anne Frank

House in Amsterdam (a memorial to the life of Anne Frank who hid in the house, with her Jewish family, during the Nazi occupation in World War II). They show that heritage tourists are a disparate group both as regards their personal heritage and their motivation for visiting but while some visitors certainly feel connected to the Anne Frank House by their own (Jewish) heritage others consider a visit as an opportunity to learn some history – presumably the intertwined history of Nazi occupation of The Netherlands and the Jewish (and non-Jewish) response to occupation. Visits are sometimes underscored by a sense of social obligation – and such a notion of obligation surely strikes a nerve of recognition with many readers. So the Anne Frank example illustrates several types of social influence on tourists – for those with a personal Jewish heritage (so a religious influence, a place of pilgrimage) and for those without a Jewish heritage (so an educational influence bound up with obligation). Some visitors, it must be said, consider the Anne Frank House as just 'an attraction' in which neither religion nor education nor obligation lies at the core of the visit.

Finally, an additional prong of religious influence on tourist behaviour is the perceived cultural distance that it creates between different cultures. The post-9/11 tension between Islamic nations and the West is one current example of cultural distance – one that may never be completely narrowed despite the best efforts of current and future generations. We return to cultural distance below.

Gender

The discussion on religion above has already opened up the influence of gender on tourists. In the real world supposedly separate influences intersect with one another. Kinnaird *et al.* (1994, p. 6) sum up the role of gender in tourism, and also hint at an intersection when they suggest that

> tourism involves processes which are constructed out of complex and varied social realities and relations that are often hierarchical and unequal. All parts of the process embody different social relations of which gender relations are one element.

The argument appears to be that since all tourists and all tourist suppliers are gendered and since the male gender is historically dominant over the female gender then social realities and relations in tourism have been historically hierarchical and unequal. As an illustration, Kinnaird *et al.* (1994) compare brochure representations in which men are associated with action, power and ownership and women are passive, available and owned. We are all most probably familiar with such representations – and not just in brochures. In this book we offer an additional perspective through an example of single, female tourists in Chapter 13, 'Of Fear, Flight and Feistiness' (this volume).

However, it is interesting to consider whether, at least in much of the West and North, some of the inequality argument has lost its venom. This is not to argue that parity between women and men is in any way universal. But who can question that the rise of women as a distinct tourist market with distinct non-subordinate tourist behaviours has gathered pace through the second half of the 20th century and beyond to the early 2010s? And who can question that tourist participation among women matches the enhanced participation of women in society (and the economy) in general?

There is research that indicates that gender is still important. For example, Collins and Tisdell (2002) in a study of life cycle travel patterns of outbound Australian travellers find that gender is a major influence on travel. Specifically, there are more women than men travelling for holiday purposes in all age groups up to 65 years of age; there are more women than men travelling to visit friends and family in all age groups up to 65 years of age; there are many fewer women than men travelling for business travel and to attend a conference or convention; and the peak of business travel is far earlier for women (25–34) than for men (45–54). Collins and Tisdell explain their findings in various ways – for example, women who travel with their partners on a business or conference trip may indicate the purpose of travel as 'holiday' and so boost the number of female travellers vis-à-vis men; and family and friends are supposed to offer security and assistance for 'women in the full-nest and single-parent group, if travelling with children' (Collins and Tisdell, 2002, p. 142).

As regards the future, Collins and Tisdell note the likely effect of the increasing participation of women in the workforce and the tendency for women to remain single and childless for a longer period of time – but also suggest that 'the changes are likely to be slow and may only bring minor variations in the observed pattern' (Collins and Tisdell, 2002, p. 142). On the other hand, in much of the West and North, women now participate in almost the full range of tourist activities and are indeed specifically targeted by marketers for some more exclusive women-only products. For example, there are women-only rooms in hotels and women-only floors in hotels and other accommodation types. In other sectors and sub-sectors of the tourism industry the same condition applies – there are genuine attempts to develop and promote women-centred tourist products that are not based on women as passive, available and owned subjects. In London, the mission of the Imperial War Museum (IWM), that 30 years ago had a very male dominant customer base is today orientated to a wider audience, including women, as can be seen in their flow of special exhibits from Forces Sweethearts in the 1990s (still playing to the subordination theme, we allow) through to the present. And then, too, there is the role of women in the decision-making process of families and other groups as documented in Chapter 12, 'The Importance of Family' (this volume).

We do not agree entirely with Marshment (1997, p. 18) who considers that 'the holiday market is not constructed along gender lines' – unlike the market for clothes, cosmetics, magazines and the like. Gender still plays a role – but it is a role that is likely to be less played out in the future. Moreover, as Swain states (1995, p. 253) it is as ever dangerous to write about 'the universal female experience as a converse to the universal male'. To do so is an old-style feminist approach that was probably necessary in its day to make a point – but does not provide a launch pad to present-day understanding. There are some women with a particular racial, ethnic and class background who are equal to men with similar race, ethnicity and class. But there are other women who are disadvantaged by any one of those influences – as well as their gender.

Ethnicity and race

There is a difference between race and ethnicity. While there are three races in the world – Negroid, Caucasian and Mongoloid – there are any number of ethnic divisions as determined by culture and subculture. So, a black Dutchwoman is distinct from a white Dutchwoman on grounds of race and can never be the same in purely physical terms – even though social constructions of what it means to be black or white might change through the course of her lifetime. However, the white and the black Dutchwoman *may* be ethnically similar not only in terms of country of origin or residence but also in terms of, say, language, religion, education, recreation interests and tourism. Yet in everyday life, race and ethnicity are sometimes incorrectly considered to be one and the same – and Hutchison (1988) points out that even seminal studies in leisure and recreation (tourism is not mentioned) have used race and ethnicity interchangeably. Caution should prevail so that we are aware of which writers recognize the difference.

Klemm and Kelsey (2004, p. 115), in a UK context, claim that 'the leisure activities and tourism preferences of non-white ethnic minorities in society are poorly understood and under-researched'. They contrast this with the comprehensive knowledge of the demography, income, health and education of UK ethnic minorities. This surprising dearth of knowledge has echoes in work on race and recreation, leisure and tourism, too. Klemm and Kelsey comment on the stereotypical view that ethnic minorities focus their tourist activity on VFR to the ethnic homeland. This can be related to the image of the ethnic minority as excluded economically, socially and politically – an image that is not always substantiated in the UK (their research context) despite media hype. Even more extreme is the assumption that the ethnic minorities are part of the tourist gaze – so the ethnic groups in the 'Little Italy' and 'Chinatown' and 'Arab Quarter' of various cities through the world are supposed to remain static and be the object of visitation rather than be visitors in their own right.

In a separate study, Klemm (2002) finds that South Asians in Bradford, England, have a frequency of holiday taking and holiday preferences not so different to that of the UK population as a whole. Specifically, a survey group shows some differences from the British mass market insomuch as they prefer city to country holidays, have less interest in beach holidays and prefer Muslim destinations (Egypt and Turkey) compared to Florida and California. But the differences are not large. So, Klemm (2002, p. 91) concludes that 'it is debatable whether this market forms a totally separate niche needing different holiday products'.

But in a USA context, Philipp (1994) suggests that there is some difference in the tourism preferences of American blacks and whites – that is, preference across race. In an interview survey of households in a medium-sized metropolitan area in south-east USA, Philipp researches differences across basic tourism dichotomies – dependence versus autonomy (independence); activity versus relaxation; order versus disorder; familiarity versus novelty. He finds a significant difference in five of the eight preference categories – specifically dependence, activity, disorder, familiarity and novelty. When socio-economic variables (education and household size) are controlled, he finds that 'all the significant differences ($p < 0.05$) continue to exist between the racial groups; suggesting that education and household size are not responsible for the reported differences' (Philipp, 1994, p. 483).

Philipp reviews the two major theoretical explanations that have dominated discussion regarding black/white differences – 'marginality' and 'ethnicity'.

> Marginality theory centres primarily on differences in income/class between blacks and whites (i.e. blacks are different from whites because of their 'marginal' economic position in society). While ethnicity theory refers to the 'cultural' characteristics of blacks (i.e. blacks have a distinctive and identifiable subculture apart from whites).
>
> (Philipp, 1994, p. 481)

Hutchison (1988, p. 15) expands on the ethnicity perspective. It involves a 'complex interplay of social values, social organization, and normative elements passed from one generation to the next through the socialisation processes of the family, local schools and the community'. And Floyd *et al.* (1994, pp. 158–159), in a US context, expand on marginality – 'under-representation of African Americans in certain leisure forms results primarily from limited economic resources, which in turn are a function of historical patterns of discrimination'. However, Philipp (1994) argues that theories based on the concepts of prejudice and discrimination offer more help in explaining his findings than either 'marginality' or 'ethnicity'. In a clear statement, Philipp writes:

> If the outside world has been associated with hostility and pain then it is not unreasonable to believe a group of individuals who have personally felt this hostility would travel in larger, more secure groups to known areas, patronize hotels and restaurants with familiar names, avoid streets they do not know, make few unplanned stops, and keep moving from one activity to another to avoid being in one place too long.
>
> (Philipp, 1994, pp. 485–486)

Floyd *et al.* (1994) in their contemporary study conclude, from a national random telephone survey in the USA, that there are complex interrelationships between class and gender and race such that while race is *not* so salient in differentiating middle-class leisure preferences among blacks and whites, it *is* salient in differentiating working-class white and black preference – especially among females. Philipp acknowledges that his study is preliminary or suggestive and indeed it is difficult to see how any one study could be conclusive. Philipp (1994) and Floyd *et al.* (1994) only refer to the USA – and even then in Philipp's case to one medium-sized metropolitan area in the 1990s – and so their work may lack any resonance in a consideration of a racial divide in, say, Brazil or France in the 2010s. Moreover, as Hutchison (1988, p. 21) points out 'both the marginality and ethnicity perspectives attribute a single, monolithic structure to the black population'. Such uniformity in the USA is hardly credible – as we discussed in other contexts elsewhere in this book.

CULTURAL DISTANCE

The effect of cultural distance as an influence on tourists is evident in annual straw polls that the authors conduct with students regarding their most recent international travel destinations. It is a simple ice-break exercise at the start of a taught course. Native English speakers show a notable propensity to travel to English-speaking destinations (Australia and New Zealand and the USA/Canada). The same linguistic divide can also be deduced from even the most cursory glance at the tour offerings of a British travel agent vis-à-vis a Spanish or German travel agent. South America as a destination is far more prominent in Spain – and the Spanish-speaking Caribbean is also more prominent than the English-speaking Caribbean. Of course, such observations are just as soon connected to the patterns of colonialism (McKercher and Decosta, 2007) – with the resultant linkage perpetuated in the form of VFR tourism or, where ties are less current, tourists searching for identity in distant family roots.

Language, of course, is a social influence, and each of the social influences can contribute to cultural distance. Ng *et al.* (2007) examine five different cultural distance measures and their impact on the destination selection of a sample drawn from an Australian consumer research panel (specifically from New South Wales). The destinations consist of 11 countries reflecting a range of cultural distance from Australia based on four parameters from Hofstede (2001) (individualism, power distance, masculinity and uncertainty avoidance). The study finds that the greater the perceived cultural similarity of a foreign destination to Australia, the more likely it is that Australians will visit the destination. Support for such a finding is linked to the greater perception of risk that comes from visiting less familiar, culturally distant destinations (Lepp and Gibson, 2003) that is supposed to lead to 'culture shock'.

But, of course, there is a counter to such an argument – very well expressed by Hottola (2004). She takes issue with the explanation of human intercultural adaptation suggested by Oberg (1960) – the U-curve of culture shock. According to this, the tourist is supposed to adapt to another culture through a five-stage process: euphoria (initial contact); disillusion-ment; hostility; adaptation; and assimilation. But, Hottola (2004, p. 449) considers that as applied to international tourism 'the U-curve is but one possible course of events, and cer-tainly not the most common one'. First, it is an idealized description of reality since many tourists do not adapt or do not want to step outside their 'environmental bubble' and adapt – and also adaptation is not a linear process. Second, a focus on shock should be replaced by a focus on learning. When tourists travel 'there often is neither shock nor depression, but they (tourists) usually get stressed and confused while learning new things or facing unexpected difficulties, even after repeated visits to the destination' (Hottola, 2004, p. 450). Third, Oberg (1960, p. 177) defined culture shock as a 'transitory concept precipitated by the anxiety that results from losing all one's familiar signs and symbols of social interaction'. But the tourist rarely succumbs to serious problems such as acute depression and an overwhelming sense of failure, anxiety and insomnia – the tourist interaction is transitory and as a result of globalization 'there is less and less uncontrolled exposure to cultural difference, especially when people travel within cultural regions or take part in the main stream of international tourism' (Hottola, 2004, p. 452).

Hottola based her study on interviews and participant observation of 'mostly young, well travelled and well educated' western backpackers in South Asia, a tourist segment that is different in some ways from the majority of international tourists. Her sample might be thought of as one attracted to cultural distance (McKercher and So-Ming, 2001; McKercher and Cros, 2003) – and to an extent aware in advance of some of the confusion and disorientation and tiredness that might confront them. But intuitively at least the logic of her work applies to a much wider tourist public who are not so fazed by difference because that is what they confront in their everyday lives.

CHANGE THROUGH TIME AND SPACE

Economic and social influences (and political and physical environmental influences) constantly affect the behaviour of tourists – even if they choose to live apart from the world of 24 h media. They vary from country to country and region to region within one country – and from time to time. While the Hajj has always been out of bounds for non-Muslims, there was a time when entry to the Al Aqsa Mosque in Jerusalem was not predicated on your religion. No more. There was a time when a single, male hitch-hiker in Western Europe did not run unacceptable dangers as he hitched a ride – and every major junction out of a town would host queues of male and (often) female hitch-hikers. No more. But there was also a time when black people in the Southern States of the USA or South Africa were restricted in where they sat in a bus or restaurant (or were even denied entry). No more, and just as well. And there was also a time when tourism was the preserve of the aristocracy. No more and (on balance!) just as well. Economic and social influences are ever fluid. They can be persistent, but they can also change very rapidly. Maybe it is not such a bad thing to carry your mobile with you, even when in escape mode – you may need mobile news to keep you travel savvy.

REFERENCES

Aguilo, E., Riera, A. and Rossello, J. (2004) The short-term price effect of a tourist tax through a dynamic demand model. The case of the Balearic Islands. *Tourism Management* 26, 359–365.

Aguilo, E., Alegre, J. and Sard, M. (2005) The persistence of the *sun* and *sand* tourism model. *Tourism Management* 26, 219–231.

Aziz, H. (2001) The journey: an overview of tourism and travel in the Arab/Islamic context. In: Harrison, D. (ed.) *Tourism and the Less Developed World: Issues and Case Studies.* CAB International, Wallingford, UK, pp. 151–160.

Collins, D. and Tisdell, C. (2002) Gender and differences in travel life cycles. *Journal of Travel Research* 41(2), 133–143.

Dolnicar, S., Crouch, G., Devinney, T., Huybers, T., Louviere, J.T. and Oppewal, H. (2008) Tourism and discretionary income allocation. Heterogeneity among households. *Tourism Management* 29, 44–52.

Elliott, S. (2008) Calling for tourists to come for New York City, but stay for the State. *New York Times*, 6 May 2008.

Floyd, M.F., McGuire, F.A., Shinew, K.J., and Noe, F.P. (1994) Race, class and leisure activity preferences: marginality and ethnicity revisited. *Journal of Leisure Research* 26 (2), 158–173.

Henderson, J.C. (2003) Managing tourism and Islam in Peninsular Malaysia. *Tourism Management* 24, 447–456.

Hofstede, G. (2001) *Culture's Consequences*. Sage, Thousand Oaks, California.

Hottola, P. (2004) Culture confusion: intercultural adaptation in tourism. *Annals of Tourism Research* 31(2), 447–466.

Hutchison, R. (1988) A critique of race, ethnicity, and social class in recent leisure–recreation research. *Journal of Leisure Research* 20 (1), 10–30.

Kessler, C.S. (1992) Pilgrims progress: the travellers of Islam. *Annals of Tourism Research* 19, 147–153.

Kinnaird, V., Kothari, U. and Hall, D. (1994) Tourism: gender perspectives. In: Kinnaird, V. and Hall, D. (eds) *Tourism a Gender Analysis*. Wiley, Chichester, UK, pp. 1–34.

Klemm, M.S. (2002) Tourism and ethnic minorities in Bradford: the invisible segment. *Journal of Travel Research* 41, 85–91.

Klemm, M.S. and Kelsey, S.J. (2004) Ethnic groups and the British travel industry: servicing a minority. *Service Industries Journal* 24 (4), 115–128.

Larsen, J., Urry, J. and Axhausen, K.W. (2007) Networks and tourism: mobile social life. *Annals of Tourism Research* 34(1), 244–262.

Lepp, A. and Gibson, H. (2003) Tourist roles, perceived risk and international tourism. *Annals of Tourism Research* 30(3), 606–624.

Mayo, E.J. and Jarvis, L.P. (1981) The Psychology of Leisure Travel. CBI Publishing Company Inc., Boston, Massachusetts.

McKercher, B. and Cros, H.D. (2003) Testing a cultural tourism typology. *International Journal of Tourism Research* 5(1), 45–58.

McKercher, B. and Decosta, P.L. (2007) The lingering effect of colonialism on tourist movements. *Tourism Economics* 13 (3), 453–474.

McKercher, B. and So-Ming, B.C. (2001) Cultural distance and participation in cultural tourism. *Pacific Tourism Review* 5, 23–32.

Ng, S.I., Lee, J.A. and Soutar, G.N. (2007) Tourists' intention to visit a country: the impact of cultural distance. *Tourism Management* 28, 1497–1506.

Oberg, K. (1960) Culture shock: adjustment to new cultural environment. *Practical Anthropology* (7), 177–182.

Palmer, T. and Riera, A. (2003) Tourism and environmental taxes. With special reference to the 'Balearic ecotax'. *Tourism Management* 24, 665–674.

Philipp, S.F. (1994) Race and tourism choice, a legacy of discrimination. *Annals of Tourism Research* 21 (3), 479–488.

Poria, Y., Reichal, A. and Biran, A. (2006) Heritage site management: motivations and expectations. *Annals of Tourism Research* 33(1), 162–178.

Swain, M.B. (1995) Gender in tourism. *Annals of Tourism Research* 22 (2), 247–266.

Tribe, J. (2005) *The Economics of Recreation, Leisure and Tourism*. Butterworth-Heinemann, Oxford.

chapter 7

THE DRIVING FORCE OF MOTIVATION

What motivates the tourist today? What motivates one tourist may not motivate another. Some tourists seek the most elemental of physical needs and some try to find their spiritual selves. Some, indeed, look for both at the same time and in the same place. Some know what motivates them and some either do not know or cannot explain what they know. Likewise, some businesses and organizations understand and articulate the motivation that drives their consumers to purchase their products and services – and classify consumers accordingly. Others, unlikely to survive for long in a market economy, neither understand nor articulate consumer motivations.

A review of tourism motivation theory shows that theorists and tourism researchers see motivations as fundamental reasons for behaviour (Snepenger *et al.*, 2006). Motivations are critical for understanding the vacation decision-making process and the foundation for assessing satisfaction from an experience, designing and planning tourism attractions and marketing tourism experiences. Motivation indeed seems like a driving force.

GENERAL CONSUMER MOTIVATION: SOME BACKGROUND

There is no shortage of writing on human motivations and it is certain that no single motivation theory can lead to full understanding. Motivation is the dynamic process in buyer behaviour, bridging the gap between the felt need and the decision to act or purchase (Middleton and Clarke, 2001). Wright (2006) sees motivation as the process that starts with some kind of need, the drive or action to satisfy the need and, finally, the fulfilment of the need. He refers back to the simple behavioural origins of motivation study and the supposed requirement for psychological equilibrium or 'homeostasis' brought about by the process of drive reduction.

Evans *et al.* (2006) also deal with drive and distinguish between physiological or biogenic drive and psychogenic drive (e.g. the drive to be appreciated or gain status) that originates more from the social environment. They make particular reference to Belk *et al.* (2003) who state that social desires are the driving force behind contemporary consumption, and also affect symbolic consumption (consumption related to who we are and the way we relate to ourselves and others in society) and experiential consumption (consumption related to the experience of ownership and consumption). Some argue, as we shall see more in Chapter 8, 'Logical Decision or Lucky Dip?' (this volume), that much tourist consumption is symbolic – for example, we choose destinations according to our own self-image (Beerli *et al.*, 2007). And much current tourist consumption is experience-based as we see repeatedly through this book.

Motivations are also considered in terms of a number of other categories – for example, positive motivations (the need to seek positive situations) and negative motivations (the need to escape from negative situations); internal motivations (the drive from within) and external motivations (the drive from external stimuli such as promotional marketing); cognitive motivations (linked to the need for meaning) and affective motivations (linked to the satisfaction of feelings and the achievement of emotional goals). Apparent differences, at opposite ends of each category, can lead to motivational conflict in which there is a need to choose between incompatible needs with different outcomes (e.g. 'instant gratification' and 'delayed gratification').

A general consideration of motivation, too, cannot pass without mention of Freudian theory, even though it is now discredited in some quarters, and the distinction between the following:

- conscious, rational motivations (the 'superego', the socially acceptable motivations that might be stated by a consumer);
- real, unconscious motivations (the 'id', subliminal motivations based on sex, aggression, violence or other past experiences);
- the subconscious mediator (the 'ego').

According to Freud, the unconscious mind can and does affect human motivation. Again, it does not take great imagination to think of an example related to tourists – consider how tourists on small group, soft adventure tours might overtly claim an interest in, say, culture and art and walking when they might be more motivated in the romantic and sexual opportunities that develop in such groups, with some inevitability, over an intensive 2- or 3-week adventure.

The hierarchy of needs developed by Maslow (1970) should also be mentioned, even though it may be more fashionable to skirt around his work – over-popularity with the general reader has made Maslow a victim of his own success. As Cooper *et al.* (2005) state, it is not clear why he selected five basic needs or ranked the needs in the way he did – and he did not carry out clinical observation or experiment to confirm or reject his model.

However, what Maslow calls higher-level 'aesthetic' and 'self-actualization' needs – that contrast with lower-level 'physiological' and 'safety' needs – closely accord with growing consumer individualism in the 21st century both in tourism and other consumer behaviour. Indeed, in much discussion there is an underlying assumption that motivation drives people (whether tourists or not) to develop their potential to the highest possible level, to make the best out of life. In reality, such a view may be too optimistic. It is judgemental to say so but it is difficult to appreciate the high-level motivation behind some of the more debauched tourist behaviour (or rather 'misbehaviour') so prevalent in some tourism destinations. But, as Ryan reckons (1998, p. 953), such a situation 'is perhaps beside the point and not a criticism of a theory, but an indictment of the nature of holidaymakers'.

SPECIFIC TOURIST MOTIVATIONS

Early thoughts

As regards more specific tourist motivation, Ryan (1991, pp. 25–29) identifies: escape, relaxation, play, social interaction, strengthening family bonds, prestige, sexual opportunity, educational opportunity, self-fulfilment, wish or dream fulfilment and (ultra prosaic as it might seem) shopping motivation. Bansal and Eiselt (2004) use the work of Crompton (1979), Lundberg (1971) and Shoemaker (1994) to assign tourist motivations to five classes: climate (or atmosphere or environment); relaxation; adventure; personal; and educational. Brown (1998), formerly long-time editor of the journal *Tourism Management*, considers that tourism is the most accessible, convenient (and legal) escape from the ordinary. This, she claims, is largely due to the new technologies of the 20th and 21st centuries with the associated advances in productivity – that have allowed tourism to develop so that it is within reach of the majority within industrialized Europe. She summarizes some of the work by Krippendorf (1987), Poon (1993), Ryan (1997) and Young (1973) regarding the question 'What reasons do tourists have for taking a holiday?' and she comes up with ten of her own very practical reasons:

- Have time with family and friends.
- Be with others and have fun.
- Rest and relax.
- Discover new places and things/experience a different culture.
- Experience nature.
- Broaden education.
- Get away from bad weather.
- Get good food.
- Get excitement and adventure.
- Visit places heard about/see famous attractions.

These are the sorts of reasons that would not be difficult to generate from the comfort of an armchair – or in an airport terminal frustrated by a delayed departure. At a more conceptual level, there are some obvious links between general consumer motivation and more specific

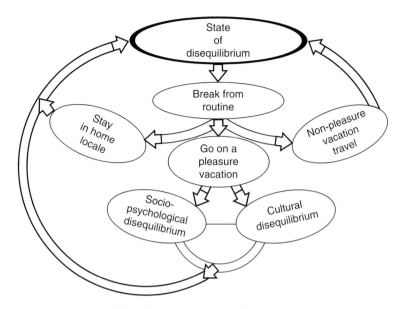

Fig. 7.1. Roles and relationships of tourist motives. (From Crompton, 1979, p. 414)

tourist motivation. For example, 'homeostasis' is dealt with by Crompton (1979), Crompton and McKay (1997) and Lee and Crompton (1992), and 'needs hierarchy' is dealt with by Chon (1989), Pearce (1982), Pearce and Lee (2005) and Ryan (1997).

Crompton (1979; Fig. 7.1) has a very clear exposition of homeostasis as applied to motivations for pleasure vacations – free of the clutter that sometimes gets in the way of clarity some 30 years later. His work was based on unstructured interviews with a small sample of adults from College Station (Texas) and Boston (Massachusetts) and he identifies and conceptualizes four main components in a model of respondents' motives:

- state of disequilibrium;
- break from routine;
- three behavioural alternatives (stay at home, go on a pleasure vacation, travel for other purposes such as VFR or a business trip);
- either socio-psychological (non destination-specific) or cultural (destination-specific) motives that satisfied the disequilibrium.

Meanwhile, with regard to a hierarchy of needs, Pearce (1988) developed his travel career ladder (TCL) based on the hierarchy (or ladder) idea and also on the idea that tourist motivations change with growing tourist experience. As Pearce and Lee (2005, p. 227) stated: 'From this (TCL) approach people may be said to have a travel career, that is a pattern of travel motives that change according to their lifespan and/or accumulated travel experiences.' TCL is dealt with further in Chapter 3, 'A Life in Travel' (this volume).

However, even though the work on motivation has moved apace in tourism studies, and even though some frameworks such as the TCL have entered (and remain) in the heads of a generation of students and practitioners, much work on tourist motivation tends to focus on the widely accepted framework of a motivational 'push' and a destination 'pull'. Dann (1977, 1981) and Iso-Ahola (1982) cover much early ground on tourist motivation studies – ground that has recurred time and time again. Dann (1981, p. 198) sees much 'definitional fuzziness surrounding tourist motivation (so that) sometimes it is difficult to discover whether or not researchers are studying the same phenomena'. Nevertheless two views shine through 'wittingly or otherwise' (Dann, 1981, pp. 189–190):

- travel as a response to what is lacking yet desired;
- travel as destination 'pull' in response to motivation 'push'.

Kozak (2002, p. 222), in a more recent review, also describes push factors as 'origin related' – the intangible, intrinsic desires of the individual traveller (the desire for escape, rest and relaxation, adventure, health or prestige) – while pull factors are mainly related to the attractiveness of, say, a given destination and its tangible characteristics. Uysal and Jurowski (1994) also categorize push factors as internal and pull factors as external. However, while the 'push' and 'pull' classification is simple, attractive and seemingly all encompassing, there is no need to consider push and pull as opposite ends of a dichotomy. Tourists may create their own balance between the escape from the ordinary and the mundane and the lure of the new and the different. Indeed, Iso-Ahola (1982, p. 259) proposes 'that both approach (seeking) *and* avoidance (escaping) components are present in leisure motivation in general…and tourism motivation in particular'. In other words, push and pull factors are not two separate decisions made at two separate points in time. An individual can engage both motives simultaneously. Moreover, each motive also has a personal (psychological) and interpersonal (social) component, so that four motivation dimensions emerge – personal escape, personal seeking, interpersonal escape and interpersonal seeking (Iso-Ahola 1982; Fig. 7.2). As Goossens (2000, p. 305) states, push and pull factors 'melt together in the brain of the consumer…and the individual is motivated, or not, to take advantage of the supply in the market'.

Later views

The power of the early tourism theorists can be seen in the way that even very recent tourism researchers still return to their work. For example, in an attempt to test theory, Snepenger *et al.* (2006, p.

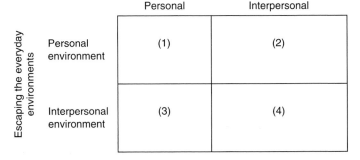

Fig. 7.2. A socio-psychological model of tourism motivation. (From Iso-Ahola, 1982, p. 259.)

142) provide practical item descriptors to characterize the four motivation dimensions of Iso-Ahola (1982). So, 'personal seeking' is itemized as 'to tell others about my experience' and 'to feel good about myself' and 'to experience new things by myself'. Snepenger *et al.* (2006) tentatively confirm the existence of Iso-Ahola's dimensions – albeit in a student population and not in all forms of tourism.

As another example, in what might seem a specialist study – but one that neatly illustrates potential complexity – Pomfret (2006) had much to say about push and pull motivation in relation to recreational mountaineers and adventure tourists. She developed a conceptual framework of influences on people's participation in mountaineering – and their experiences during involvement. These include, on the one hand, motivational push factors that encourage mountaineering participation. Here, Pomfret (2006) draws particularly on Ewert (1985) – and recognizes elements such as the need for challenge and risk, catharsis (relaxation and the slowing of the mind), recognition (prestige status), creativity (problem solving – finding routes and evaluating hazards), a sense of control and mastery of an activity and, of course, the natural mountain environment. The physical setting and favourable mountain weather conditions provide the motivational pull element. In a further layer of motivation, Pomfret (2006) goes beyond *mountaineering* push factors and also mentions generic, *tourist* push factors (such as escapism) and generic, tourist pull factors (such as commercial packages and related marketing stimuli and the provision of mountain huts, trekking routes, access and so forth). It is interesting, as an aside, to consider whether such a combination of generic and specific motives acts in other arenas of specialist tourist activity and not necessarily adventure tourism either – from art history through to zoology. Whether that is the case or not, Pomfret (2006; Fig. 7.3) provides additional complexity. Other elements are interlinked with motivation to influence tourist participation in mountaineering – such as the personality characteristics of mountaineers, their lifestyles and the emotional states (from terror to elation) that they experience and then seek to replicate in future experiences. Consideration of these lies beyond the scope of this chapter but is mentioned to show that there is a wide range of influences that act on tourists beyond straightforward motivational influences.

Further empirical examples of push and pull abound in the academic journals. They often focus on international tourists and destinations rather than domestic tourists – although one exception is that of Kim *et al.* (2003) who find simultaneous push and pull among a domestic sample of Korean park visitors in the setting of Korean national parks. Sparks (2007, p. 1188), too, in an Australian study, investigates the intentions of potential wine tourists to take a wine-based vacation. He finds three key wine tourism factors and observes that 'one of the factors, personal self-development, is related more to an internal or push motivator, whereas (the other two factors) destination experience and the core wine experience are pull factors'.

Uriely (2005) provides a thoughtful counterpoint to this section, hijacked as it is so far by notions of push and pull. He identifies conceptual developments in the study of the tourist experience and highlights the contrast between early conceptualizations and postmodern

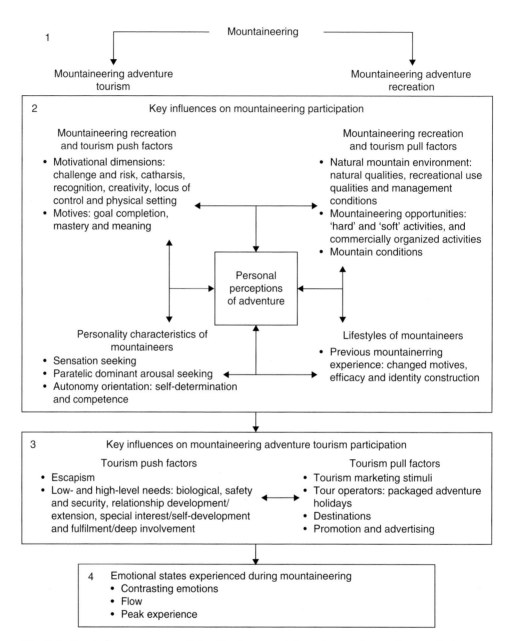

Fig. 7.3. Key influences on participation in mountaineering and experiences during involvement. (From Pomfret, 2006, p. 115.)

conceptualizations. Early thinkers emphasized the distinctiveness of tourism from everyday life, leisure as opposed to work, the authenticity of tourism experience vis-à-vis the inauthenticity of everyday life, the host versus the guest (Cohen, 1972; MacCannell, 1973; Smith, 1989). But as Lash and Urry (1994) also suggest, many tourist experiences – like enjoying aspects of other cultures – are accessible in the course of everyday life, so that people can become tourists (at least in their head if not according to a WTO definition of a tourist) most of the time. This is a theme that we also visited in Chapter 4, 'Life Change: Tourist Experience and Beyond' (this volume). So, from this perspective one can ask the questions 'What do tourists escape towards' and 'What is their motivation for such escape?'. As Munt states (1994, p. 10) 'tourism is everything and everything is tourism' – it is in the workplace in the form of leisure spaces and is also an essential part of many domestic or international business trips. Accordingly, there is a need for the 'de-exoticising' of tourism 'because tourism, visits and hospitality have moved to the centre stage of many people's more mobile lives' (Larsen *et al.*, 2007, p. 245). Stated more fully:

> [R]ecent work has begun to challenge the traditional distinctions between home and away, the ordinary and the extraordinary, work and leisure, everyday life and holidays, by arguing that in transnational times tourism moves into less obviously touristic places…tourism enters the lives of business people and global professionals, second homeowners and their friends and families, exchange students and gap-year workers abroad, migrants and (former) refugees, people with friends and families in distant places.

(Larsen et al., 2007, pp. 245–246)

Tourism is increasingly concerned with reproducing social networks, meeting face to face rather than just sightseeing, since 'one cannot hug one's mother or cuddle one's grandchild or kiss the bride over the telephone or through an e-mail or a videoconference' (Larsen *et al.*, 2007, p. 247). And even when tourists are 'away' they remain in contact with 'home' through mobiles and low-cost telephone lines, Internet cafés or portable computers so that they remain embedded in their social networks (White and White, 2007).

What often emerges across a variety of studies is that the situations are more diverse and in flux than early, widely established generic theory might suggest. In other words, the motivation listings, classifications (and typologies) and frameworks do not reflect the rich reality that emerges on the ground. As another example, Wickens (2002) in her study of British tourists in Chalkidiki, Greece (also mentioned in the context of Chapter 4, 'Life Change: Tourist Experience and Beyond', this volume), shows that 'individual mass tourists' commit themselves to organized package tourism and an 'institutionalized' role (Cohen, 1972). They are motivated by what Wickens calls after Giddens (1992, p. 64) one of several 'feeling states': escape from everyday life, the pursuit of pleasure and 'ontological security' (continuity, constancy, the force of habit). But, on the other hand, the individual mass tourist also takes the choice to step outside that role. So Wickens (2002) identifies five micro-types with specific interests and activities and views about the host community – and thus specific tourist motivations. Some of the tourists place an emphasis on the local culture while others search for sensual and hedonistic pleasures, wish for a romantic experience, seek sunshine and a hot climate, and enjoy the familiarity of a repeat destination.

Along a similar line, Uriely *et al.* (2002, p. 521) in their postmodern conceptualization – with evidence from a study of backpackers – question whether what they call *form* matches up with what they call *type*. 'Form' refers to institutional arrangements and practices by which tourists organize their journey:

- length of trip;
- flexibility of the itinerary;
- visited destinations and attractions;
- transportation and accommodation;
- contact with locals and so forth.

'Type' refers to less-tangible psychological attributes:

- fundamental values of tourists' own society;
- tourists' motivations for travel;
- meanings tourists assign to travel.

From in-depth interviews, they find that 'some (backpackers) visualized their trips as a period of recreation, while others sought new experiences to expand their knowledge and explore their own psyches' (Uriely *et al.*, 2002, p. 535). Form and type thus are not necessarily aligned. Moreover, 'a single backpacker (may) express various motivations and meanings' (Uriely *et al.*, 2002, p. 533) either during separate backpacker trips or even during the same trip (facilitated by the length of the trip and the variety of visited destinations and attractions). The single backpacker can cut across the range of tourist modes suggested by Cohen (1979), so that he/she is alternately motivated by mere pleasure or by the search for more profound experiences – for example, the 'quest for a centre' through immersion in local culture and lifestyle. Uriely *et al.* (2002) consider that such findings provide empirical support for the idea that motivations change through time – but they also veer towards Cohen's concept of a 'tourist biography' rather than Pearce's 'tourist career' since 'it should be stressed that the different experience types presented in this study do not represent lower or higher levels in a backpacker's career ladder' (Uriely *et al.*, 2002, p. 535).

MOTIVATION: FURTHER PRACTICAL RELEVANCE – TOURIST SEGMENTS, TOURISM STRATEGY

We started this chapter with reference to Snepenger *et al.* (2006) and their consideration of the conceptual and practical role of motivation in tourism. We have already provided many examples to illustrate the theory base. But it is worthwhile to emphasize the practical relevance of motivation study.

Pearce and Lee (2005, p. 226) recognize a number of difficulties in the study of motivation such as the wide range of human needs and wants, cross-cultural differences and methodological difficulties. They nevertheless suggest that 'travel motivation (is) a topic of central interest to tourism marketers and managers'. By knowing and exploring consumers' motivations for tourism, researchers are able to profile tourists into different segments and can examine similarities and differences among the segments. In academic work, many studies have produced typologies of tourists based on segments that are connected in some way to motivation. Decrop and Snelders (2005, p. 122) divide up typologies into two groups. The first group of typologies is based on segmentation criteria such as age, sex, education, family life cycle, income, expenditure, distance travelled, destination, frequency of travel and benefits sought. And it must be said that demographic variables and income, in particular, remain strong favourites of sales and marketing managers as well as academics for predicting motivation and wider tourist behaviour. The second group of typologies is based on socio-psychological variables – and these can certainly involve motivations. For example, consider the following:

- Gray (1970) identifies 'sunlust' and 'wanderlust' tourists.
- Cohen (1972) uses roles, motives and level of risk aversion/novelty seeking to identify four tourist types: drifter; explorer; individual mass tourist; and organized mass tourist.
- Cohen (1979) uses roles, motives and sought experiences and so identifies five tourist types: recreational; diversionary (seeking pleasure); experiential (seeking authentic experiences); experimental (seeking contact); and existential (seeking immersion in the culture and lifestyles).
- Smith (1989) identifies seven tourist types: explorer; elite; offbeat; unusual; incipient mass; mass; and charter.
- Plog (2002) identifies dependables (previously called psychocentrics by Plog) and venturers (previously called allocentrics) – with the conclusion based on a large, pragmatic tracking survey that different psychographic types generally pursue different types of activities. Venturers travel more than dependables and 'venturesomeness generally is more effective than income at pointing to the kinds of activities that people pursue when travelling' (Plog, 2002, p. 249).

The implication of motivation-based segments is that managers (and academics) may then develop and promote matching tourist products. This is because through empirical examination of motivations it should be possible to identify markets in which tourist motivations and destination characteristics or attributes and resources match (Bansal and Eiselt, 2004). For example, Sung (2004, p. 354) classified US adventure travellers into six clusters: (i) general enthusiasts; (ii) budget youngsters; (iii) soft moderates; (iv) upper high naturalists; (v) family vacationers; and (vi) active soloists; and suggested that '[t]argeting those who belong to the upper high naturalists group will be a good strategy for providers who offer a well organized itinerary in exotic destinations such as safaris in Kenya or arctic trips on tall sailboats'. Indeed, staying in a Kenyan context, Beh and Bruyere (2007, p. 1464) sought to understand the motivations of different types of visitors to three nature reserves in order to 'develop a tourism strategy aimed at enhancing tourist opportunities' – and through factor analysis reveal eight motivations (escape, culture, personal growth, mega fauna, adventure, learning, nature and general viewing) and three visitor segments (escapists, learners and spiritualists). The linkage between destination attributes and tourist motivations (what a destination offers and what a tourist gets from visiting a destination) and the development of a promotional strategy aimed at a tourist segment is a very practical reason for seeking to understand tourist motivation. Many tour operators would claim knowledge of this – most often without hard research evidence – and even though it is sometimes clear that the reality on the ground is a less than perfect match between client motivation and the chosen destination.

However, Bargeman *et al.* (2002, p. 321) contend that such typologies 'lack practical relevance for decision-making in tourism as the implied types are difficult to identify'. Moreover, the best-known typologies are sometimes ageing, imply universality and assume individual rather than group decision making. They also do not take account of the movement through the categories – either from one time to another or, indeed, on the same tourist visit – plainly not the case as shown in Wickens (2002). So, the search for general theoretical frameworks for understanding motivation should perhaps be superseded by a postmodern emphasis on the richness and diversity of life – a very practical point for a tourism manager to consider even if the manager has no knowledge of, or desire to know anything about, postmodernism! For example, if tourist motivations are indeed more diverse than the outward form would suggest – as in the case of Wickens (2002) and Uriely *et al.* (2002) – there is a need for some urgent practical planning and management of destinations to adapt to the new demands of the tourist.

As another illustration of practical relevance, De Guzman *et al.* (2006) review the range of ways in which analyses of motivations to visit festivals can help event managers. For example, planning and marketing event-programmes effectively, strengthening marketing and product development, monitoring satisfaction and so forth.

This is quite a range of advantages that individually or in tandem have a wider relevance in tourism – beyond event management. For example, at destination level, Tourism Australia (www.tourism.australia.com) has identified a global market segment of 'Experience Seekers' who share key characteristics and motivations which are, specifically, the following:

- They are experienced travellers for whom travel shares a big part of their life.
- They look for a challenge whether physically, emotionally or mentally.
- They desire a high level of engagement with the local people and culture.
- They wish to experience, not just witness, destinations.
- They like to avoid the tourist route preferring locations that are untouched.

Within each major market – such as Germany, the USA, the UK, Japan and so forth – Tourism Australia has analysed what travel products the 'Experience Seekers' consume so as to attain their higher-level travel needs. And so, in other words, Tourism Australia tracks the motivation process for its chosen global market segment – from the identification of some kind of need through to the drive or action to satisfy the need and, finally, the fulfilment of the need.

To illustrate, the endgame of a national tourism organization (NTO) tourism strategy may seem especially matter of fact. But many strategies have sought hard to understand the *meaning* of destinations to potential tourists. The meaning of destinations can be closely linked to motivation – and particularly perhaps in a postmodern tourism world in which social networks are replacing a sightseeing 'gaze'. As Larsen *et al.* (2007, pp. 251–252) state 'when tourists visit friends or kin they simultaneously travel to particular places that are experienced through the host's social networks and their accumulated knowledge of the local scene or of pertinent landscapes'. Tourist attempts to go local (as with the 'Experience Seekers') are tightly linked with a motivation to understand more about a place and what a place means. And friends or kin or contacts (even transitory ones from Internet travel-surfer networks) can offer a short cut to such understanding.

ECLECTIC THOUGHTS

A couple more thoughts can conclude this section. First, there are constraints placed on tourist motivations. Fleischer and Pizam (2002, p. 119) show in a study of Israeli seniors that following retirement the health constraint and the income constraint increase through time – just as the time constraint becomes 'obsolete'. The old adage that the mind is willing but the body is not applies in the reality of tourist experience. But other constraints also arise in other parts of the life cycle, too, as most tourists can confirm – and some constraints are not connected to the life cycle. We deal with the life cycle in Chapter 3, 'A Life in Travel' (this volume), and with constraints in Chapter 5, 'Models of Tourist Behaviour' (this volume).

Second, not every tourist is necessarily fired up by motivations. Bieger and Laesser (2002, p. 73) – in their study of domestic and international tourists from Switzerland – suggest that 'travelers from Switzerland form their motivation structure on the basis of a specific travel profile rather than making autonomous decisions and then structuring their trip. Generally they would like somebody or something to tell them what they want to do'. The key elements within the (anticipated) 'travel profile' include:

- destination;
- number of household members on a trip;
- total size of travel group (household + other);
- type of trip undertaken (city trip, cruise, etc.);
- duration of a trip.

The individual's needs or benefits sought are subsumed to the total structure of the travel group and the destination. This is a reverse of what marketers might suggest in the 'me-me' age. However, despite the surprise of Bieger and Laesser, it is not perhaps so unusual. How often have you thought to yourself that there is just too much planning involved in your next tourism adventure – and then willingly let your friend or partner take over?

Third, Ryan (1995, p. 42) – despite sometimes treating motivation and attitude together – suggests that the link between motivation and behaviour is not automatic. Moreover, the importance of the motivation is crucial, too – simply identifying a motivation is only a partial answer.

Fourth, there is the issue of true or false motives. Dann (1981) draws attention to a range of problems associated with motivation research. Tourists may not wish to reflect on real travel motives; tourists may be unable to reflect on real travel motives; tourists may not wish to express real travel motives; tourists may not be able to verbalize or otherwise express real travel motives. Dann asks:

> What actually constitutes motivation to travel? Is it the conclusion of the researcher or the explanation of the tourist?

(Dann, 1981, p. 209)

A variety of techniques are used to expose otherwise hidden motives. The positivist research philosophy and the use of quantitative techniques are evident in the many attempts to derive key motivation elements and then group them together through a technique such as principal components analysis (Kim *et al.*, 2006). In projective techniques, the respondents project themselves on to a third party. For example, a respondent might consider a question such as 'Why does the person in the photograph buy holiday X?'. In 'means–end chain analysis' a respondent progressively details product/service attributes and consequences/benefits and, finally, the motives and values that stem from purchase and ownership. However, it is the opinion of the authors that motivation study, dealing as it does with the unseen and the complicated working of the mind and emotion – in an evaluation of future consequences – lends itself more to the power of interpretivism and qualitative techniques as exemplified by participant observation and depth interviewing. Such an approach is more likely to tease out true tourist motivations. We return to this theme in the Epilogue.

IN EXTREMIS...

Sometimes it is useful to get away from academic thought patterns and/or the tourist analysis that comes out of businesses and organizations and see what particular, 'extreme-case' individuals say about their tourist motivations. Jan Morris (1989), for example, the doyenne of travel writers in the UK with then over 40 years experience of travelling and writing, suggested that she had a number of 'practical rules' for happy travelling, rules that closely resemble motivations. In the first instance, she suggests that you cannot see everything and do everything:

> Many frames of mind can sustain a journey – scholarly, sociological, gastronomic, carnal or just plain hedonistic: but try to employ too many of them at the same time, and travelling becomes messy and unsatisfying.

Morris (1989)

Morris also suggests the need for a travelling theme; to consciously expect journeys to be enjoyable and not expect to be 'robbed, raped or poisoned'; and to remember that most people are agreeable, whatever their nationality. Moreover, she most definitely does not try and put herself into other people's shoes because it is 'better to regard the world as kind of show, a tragic-comedy, kindly put on for my fascination'. Morris considered that her half-life of travel was an addiction – and a craft and not an art as there is 'nothing creative to it, nothing especially elevating, imaginative or even necessarily commendable'. Many would disagree, as the output of her travels in the form of journalistic articles and books was invariably creative, elevating, imaginative and commendable. But close to the 50th anniversary of her early travel dispatch, that recorded the first successful ascent of Mt Everest in 1953, Morris stated that she had finally lost the motivation to travel – the addiction had passed. She could see a lot more sense in staying at home in North Wales and argued that her garden provided sufficient stimulation. To an extent, this is an echo of Pliny the Younger, quoted in Brown (1998, p. 102):

> We travel long roads and cross the water to see what we disregard when it is under our eyes.

As another extreme case, Ffyona Campbell, considered to be the first woman to walk around the world, until she later admitted that she had missed out some parts after all, crossed America, Australia, Africa and Europe between the age of 18 and 27. When asked 'why?' by the journalist Alan Coren, she said that she considered it as a *rite de passage*. She wanted 'to confront fear head on, and beat it' and felt, after finishing, that 'I now feel that I have grown up'. Yet, she also recognized some domesticity in herself – and looking to the future she reckoned that she would 'find a home somewhere near water, near a river going into the sea if possible' (Coren, 1994). Such an account seems to fall neatly into the conceptualizations of the earliest tourism academics with their emphasis on escape, sense of liminality and return – although Campbell, in the same interview, stated that she had no home and no roots, a cause of envy in her when she compared herself with some peoples she had observed along the way (especially in Africa).

In the final analysis, motivation differs between individuals – and certainly among these extreme-case individuals – so that there is limited homogeneity. It also differs within diverse contexts, cultural or otherwise, and is also inherently dynamic and subject to flux based on ongoing experiences and reflection on past experiences. Moreover, it is worth remembering Crompton (1979, p. 411) who observed that while some motivations are 'uniquely satisfied by the pleasure vacation experience' other motivations 'can also be satisfied by alternative opportunities available from other sources'. Other things that go on in tourists' lives mediate tourist motivation and wider tourist behaviour.

REFERENCES

Baker, D. and Crompton, J. (2000) Quality, satisfaction and behavioural intentions. *Annals of Tourism Research* 27, 785–804.

Bansal, H. and Eiselt, H.A. (2004) Exploratory research of tourist motivations and planning. *Tourism Management* 25, 387–396.

Bargeman, B., Joh, C.-H. and Timmermans, H. (2002) Vacation behaviour using a sequence alignment method. *Annals of Tourism Research* 29(2), 320–337.

Beerli, A., Meneses, G.D. and Gil, S.M. (2007) Self-congruity and destination choice. *Tourism Management* 34(3), 571–585.

Beh, A. and Bruyere, B.L. (2007) Segmentation by visitor motivation in three Kenyan national reserves. *Tourism Management* 28, 1464–1471.

Belk, R.W., Ger, G. and Askegaard, S. (2003) The fire of desire: a multisided inquiry into consumer passion. *Journal of Consumer Research* 30(3), 326.

Bieger, T. and Laesser, C. (2002) Market segmentation by motivation: the case of Switzerland. *Journal of Travel Research* 41 (August), 68–76.

Brown, F. (1998) *Tourism Reassessed*. Butterworth-Heinemann, Oxford.

Cohen, E. (1972) Toward a sociology of international tourism. *Social Research* 39(1), 164–189.

Cohen, E. (1979) A phenomenology of tourist types. *Sociology* 13, 179–201.

Cooper, C., Fletcher, J., Fyall, A., Gilbert, D. and Wanhill, S. (2005) Tourism Principles and Practice, 3rd edn. Pearson Education Ltd, Harlow, UK.

Coren, G. (1994) The wandering star heads for home. *The Times* (London) 30 September 1994.

Crompton, J. (1979) Motivation for pleasure travel. *Annals of Tourism Research* 4, 408–424.

Crompton, J.L. and McKay, S.L. (1997) Motives of visitors attending festival events. *Annals of Tourism Research* 24(2), 425–439.

Dann, G.N.S. (1977) Anomie, ego enhancement and tourism. *Annals of Tourism Research* 4(4), 184–194.

Dann, G.M.S. (1981) Tourist motivation: an appraisal. *Annals of Tourism Research* VIII(2), 187–214.

Decrop, A. and Snelders, D. (2005) A grounded typology of vacation decision-making. *Tourism Management* 26, 121–132.

De Guzman, A.B., Leones, J.D., Tapia, K.K.L., Wong, W.G. and De Castro, B.V. (2006) Segmenting motivation. *Annals of Tourism Research* 33(3), 863–867.

Evans, M., Jamal, A. and Foxall, G. (2006) *Consumer Behaviour*. Wiley, Chichester, UK.

Ewert, A. (1985) Why people climb: the relationship of participant motives and experience level to mountaineering. *Journal of Leisure Research* 17(3), 241–250.

Fleischer, A. and Pizam, A. (2002) Tourism constraints among Israeli seniors. *Annals of Tourism Research* 29(1), 106–125.

Giddens, A. (1992) *The Consequences of Modernity*. Polity Press, Cambridge.

Goossens, C. (2000) Tourism information and pleasure motivation. *Annals of Tourism Research* 28(3), 221–232.

Gray, J.P. (1970) *International Travel – International Trade*. Lexington Heath: Lexington Books, Kentucky.

Iso-Ahola, S.E. (1982) Toward a social psychological theory of tourism motivation: a rejoinder. *Annals of Tourism Research* 9, 256–262.

Kim, H., Borges, M.C. and Chon, J. (2006) Impacts of environmental values on tourism motivation: the case of FICA, Brazil. *Tourism Management* 27, 957–967.

Kim, S.S., Lee, C.-K. and Klenovsky, D.B. (2003) The influence of push and pull factors at Korean national parks. *Tourism Management* 24, 169–180.

Kozak, M. (2002) Comparative analysis of tourist motivations by nationality and destinations. *Tourism Management* 22, 221–232.

Krippendorf, J. (1987) *The Holiday Makers: Understanding the Impact of Leisure and Travel*. Butterworth-Heinemann, Oxford.

Larsen, J., Urry, J. and Axhausen, K.W. (2007) Networks and tourism: mobile social life. *Annals of Tourism Research* 34(1), 244–262.

Lash, S. and Urry, J. (1994) *Economics of Signs and Space*. Sage, London.

Lee, T.H. and Crompton, J.L. (1992) Measuring novelty seeking in tourism. *Annals of Tourism Research* 19, 732–751.

Lundberg, D.E. (1971) Why tourists travel. *Cornell HRA Quarterly* February 75–81.

MacCannell, D. (1973) Staged authenticity: Arrangements of social space in tourist settings. *American Sociological Review* 79, 589–603.

Maslow, A.H. (1970) *Motivation and Personality*. 2nd edn. Harper Row, New York.

Middleton, V.T.C. and Clarke, J.R. (2001) *Marketing in Travel and Tourism*. 3rd edn. Butterworth-Heinemann, Oxford.

Morris, J. (1989) Trade secrets of the craft of travelling without tears. *The Times* (London) 14 October 1989.

Munt, I. (1994) The 'other' postmodern tourism: culture, travel and the new middle class. *Theory, Culture and Society* 11, 101–123.

Pearce, P. (1982) *The Social Psychology of Tourist Behaviour.* Butterworth-Heinemann, Oxford.

Pearce, P.L. (1988) *The Ulysses Factor: Evaluating Visitors in Tourist Settings.* Springer-Verlag, New York.

Pearce, P.L. and Lee, U.-I. (2005) Developing the travel career approach to tourist motivation. *Journal of Travel Research* 43 (February), 226–237.

Plog, S.C. (2002) The power of psychographics and the concept of venturesomeness. *Journal of Travel Research* 40, 244–251.

Poon, A. (1993) *Tourism, Technology and Competitive Strategies.* CAB International, Wallingford, UK.

Pomfret, G. (2006) Mountaineering adventure tourists: a conceptual framework for research. *Tourism Management* 27, 113–123.

Ryan, C. (1991) *Recreational Tourism: a Social Science Perspective.* Routledge, London.

Ryan, C. (1995) *Researching Tourist Satisfaction.* Routledge, London.

Ryan, C. (1997) *The Tourist Experience: a New Introduction.* Cassell, London.

Ryan, C. (1998) The travel career ladder: an appraisal. *Annals of Tourism Research* 25(1), 936–957.

Shoemaker, S. (1994) Segmenting the US travel market according to benefits realised. *Journal of Travel Research* 32, 8–21.

Smith, V. (1989) *Hosts and Guests: the Anthropology of Tourism* 2nd edn. Basil Blackwell, Oxford.

Snepenger, D., King, J., Marshall, E. and Uysal, M. (2006) Modeling Iso-Ahola's motivation theory in the tourism context. *Journal of Travel Research* 45, 140–149.

Sparks, B. (2007) Planning a wine tourism vacation? Factors that help to predict tourist behavioural intentions. *Tourism Management* 28, 1180–1192.

Sung, H.H. (2004) Classification of adventure travellers: behaviour, decision-making, and target markets. *Journal of Travel Research* 42 (May), 343–356.

Tourism Australia. (2008) Available at: www.tourism.australia.com (Accessed 19 November 2008).

Uriely, N. (2005) The tourist experience: conceptual developments. *Annals of Tourism Research* 32(1), 199–216.

Uriely, N., Yonay, Y. and Simchai, D. (2002) Backpacking experiences: a type and form analysis. *Annals of Tourism Research* 29, 519–537.

Uysal, M. and Jurowski, C. (1994) Testing the push and pull factors. *Annals of Tourism Research* 21(4), 844–846.

White, N.R. and White, P.B. (2007) Home and away: tourists in a connected world. *Annals of Tourism Research* 34(1), 88–104.

Wickens, E. (2002) The sacred and the profane: a tourist typology. *Annals of Tourism Research* 29(3), 834–851.

Wright, R. (2006) *Consumer Behaviour.* Thomson Learning, London.

Young, G. (1973) *Tourism: Blessing or Blight?* Penguin, London.

chapter 8

LOGICAL DECISION OR LUCKY DIP?

You want to go somewhere. Do you just do it? Or is there more to it than that? What stimulates you in the first instance? How and where do you search for information? Is it as straightforward as a rational thought process that drives the decision making or is there a separate emotional component? How do you organize information and assess alternatives? How do you come to your tourist decisions? When do you stop making decisions? Is your final decision – say, a destination choice – a logical decision or just a lucky dip?

All of these questions and many more are worthy of some thought by academics and practitioners alike. And, indeed, much thought has been applied – especially with regard to information search and (most often) destination decision making and destination image and destination choice.

INFORMATION SEARCH AND DECISION MAKING

Funnelling down

You do not have to search hard to find information and views on tourism. For example, we all know that the Internet is bursting with businesses and organizations – and fellow tourists – who are mad-keen to promote their products or get their views across. Bookshops give over much floor space to potential tourists seeking information and newspapers also fill their pages with articles that offer information – as well as straightforward commercial advertisements. The London-based *Guardian* newspaper has an extensive online archive of free-to-read travel articles – 8684 to be precise on the day we looked – arranged A–Z by type of trip. And such archives are replicated around the world. So, the problem is not so much a lack of information – in most instances – but how to deal with the information that exists and make a decision.

Many of the early models of consumer behaviour – the 'grand models' as they have come to be known – concern themselves deeply with information search, analysis and decision making.

Such models are dealt with more fully in Chapter 5, 'Models of Tourist Behaviour' (this volume). Specific tourist-based models build on the early generic models. Sirakaya and Woodside (2005) provide a succinct overview of what the models state:

> In general, this literature reports that tourists follow a funnel-like procedure of narrowing down choices among alternate destinations. Decision-making can be broken down in to a series of stages.…Evidently, this decision-making process is influenced by psychological or internal variables…and non-psychological or external variables.
>
> (Sirakaya and Woodside, 2005, pp. 815–816)

The psychological variables are listed as image, motivation, beliefs and intentions, and personality characteristics. The non-psychological variables are listed as time and the elements of the 'marketing mix' or, presumably, the extended marketing mix (product, price, promotion, place, physical evidence, process, people).

Sirakaya and Woodside (2005) go on to distinguish between two main types of decision-making models: 'behavioural' and 'choice set'. In the behavioural model, a decision maker moves from motivation to actual travel through a series of stages. Mansfield (1992) explains the process – although without empirical evidence – with reference to destinations:

- Collect formal, commercial information – and also informal, non-commercial information (the recommendations and impressions of other people).
- Search for additional information.
- Establish destination alternatives.
- Eliminate totally unacceptable destinations.
- Assess the remaining subset of destination alternatives.
- Make a final choice from among the alternatives.

Elsewhere this is characterized as a single-phase decision process and a gather–analyse–decide model (Lye et al., 2005).

Similar but different, the 'choice set' model, developed originally by Crompton (1992) and Um and Crompton (1990), contends that a decision maker generates a number of groups or 'sets' of (say) destinations to visit and then progressively narrows down the sets until a final choice is made. A tourist may start with a passive 'awareness set' of a range of countries in Africa but move on to actively search for information on (say) an activity such as a wildlife safari and so narrow down to the 'evoked set' of Tanzania, Kenya, Malawi, Namibia and South Africa. Then a positive attitude to Tanzania and Kenya (detailed by Um and Crompton (1992) as the difference between perceived inhibitors and facilitators) – together with constraints such as travel time and cost – further narrows down the 'evoked set' until Tanzania is chosen as the final destination. The model is an intuitively attractive one, simple and practical, and one that is said to be more open to empirical testing than the behavioural model. It is also said to play up the role of memory based on past experience and/or *passive* reaction to external information – such as marketing or word of mouth – rather than a determined search for information. Or at least until there are only a few alternative choices left. However, it is not without its critics. Jang *et al.* (2007), in a summary, suggest that it is monolithic in process, marginalizes time and situational factors, is more deterministic rather than probabilistic and lacks due consideration of the role of emotions. It is worth taking time out to work through such criticisms in relation to your own reality.

In an extension of theory considered so far and as an extension of the choice-sets idea, Lye *et al.* (2005) propose the adoption of 'decision-wave theory' to unravel the 'black box' of decision making. They link the idea of decision waves with image theory – as detailed by Beach and Mitchell (1998). Image theory suggests that a decision maker's values and principles ('value image') are connected to decision goals ('trajectory image') and plans for action ('strategic image'). So, a decision maker screens the multitude of alternatives that are incompatible with the three key images above. The choice set is then reduced until there is only one alternative remaining – or there is an empty choice set. The authors have not seen this model tested empirically in tourism. But it is tempting to conjure a scenario in which a tourist's value image (such as a sustainable approach to travel and plenty of host–guest interaction), trajectory image (such as the use of locally owned accommodation or adventure providers) and strategic image (such as an Internet search and assessment of suitable providers) are screened in a series of waves – until a choice set is reduced and a final decision is reached. As Lye *et al.* (2005; Fig. 8.1) state:

> Simply put, image theory utilises value, trajectory and strategic images in a multi-phase decision process, incorporating screening processes to eliminate the multitude of alternatives – and a choice phase to select between those alternatives surviving the screening process.

(Lye *et al.*, 2005, p. 222)

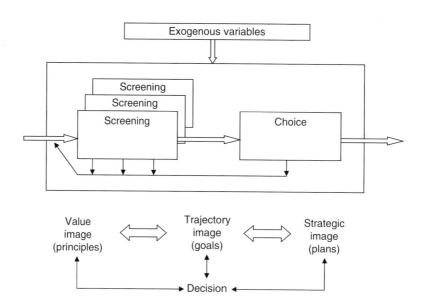

Fig. 8.1. Decision waves and consumer images and decision making. (Adapted from Lye *et al.*, 2005, p. 222.)

Theory of planned behaviour

There is another theory that is worth consideration in this chapter – for example, theory of planned behaviour (TPB) (Ajzen, 1991). The relevance to the question 'Logical decision or lucky dip?' should be obvious. A key deliberation in TPB is a consideration of the attributes that make up an experience – and these can sometimes be myriad. Consumers come to hold beliefs about what the attributes offer in terms of benefits – and then attach value to the benefits sought. That is, the consumer decides what an experience means to them. Such is the basis of expectancy value (Ajzen and Fishbein, 1980). One of the clearest explanations of TPB, a model that is used to predict intentions and actual behaviour, is given by Sparks (2007; Fig. 8.2).

> In brief the TPB proposes that three key constructs, in particular, will drive behaviour: attitude, subjective norms and perceived control. An attitude is the overall evaluation of the behaviour; a subjective norm is the influence of others about whether to engage in the behaviour; and control is the perceived ability to engage in the behaviour. The attitude construct in turn, comprises two elements: beliefs about the likely outcome of behaviour, and values attached to these outcomes.
>
> (Sparks, 2007, p. 1182)

In short, attributes that make up an experience exist. The tourist seeks information on them; develops an emotional attitude about them – and then fuses the attitude with a consideration of norms and perceived control. And so the tourist makes a decision. In a wine tourism context in Australia, Sparks uses a questionnaire survey with over 1250 usable responses from a

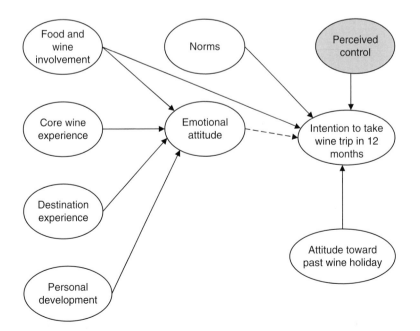

Fig. 8.2. Structural model of wine tourism intention. (Adapted from Sparks, 2007, p. 1184.)

CONTEMPORARY TOURIST BEHAVIOUR

company marketing list and identifies three key wine tourism factors based upon expectancy value: destination experience (e.g. beautiful surroundings), core wine experience (e.g. wine tasting) and personal development (e.g. opportunity to feel inspired). These are the important (composite) attributes of the potential wine tourism experience. But, as regards the TPB model, the *major* predictor of intention (at least in the case Sparks investigates) is the perceived control the respondent feels – for example, wine tourists seek to have more control over the time that the wine experience takes. There was no relationship found between emotional attitude and intention norms.

As another example, Lam and Hsu (2006) find in a study of potential Taiwanese travellers to Hong Kong, that it is subjective norm *and* perceived behavioural control that have direct impact on behavioural intention – not attitude. Past behaviour is also tested as a further variable because of the supposed strong connection between past behaviour and future behaviour (Sonmez and Graefe, 1998) – and it, too, has a direct impact on behavioural intention.

The TPB model is clearly useful (it has a long pedigree with reference to other social behaviours) and has some more mileage in tourism. For example, it has relevance in organizing and predicting tourist thoughts on intention and behaviour. Even as Lam and Hsu (2006) question the role of attitude, they also suggest that it is important for the Hong Kong Tourist Board to ensure that the attitude of travel agents in Taiwan is kept positive – as they are gatekeepers for the flow of tourists between the two areas.

Integration

Gursoy and McCleary (2004, p. 354) integrate what they see as three theoretical streams of consumer information-search literature:

- psychological/motivational approach;
- information processing approach that focuses on memory and information processing theory;
- economics approach that uses the cost–benefit framework.

Subsequently, they propose a model that integrates all the approaches. The model has many variables (and 21 untested propositions) but they are mediated by two main factors: 'familiarity' and 'expertise'. Gursoy and McCleary (2004, p. 359) state that '[b]asically, it (familiarity) represents tourists' subjective knowledge of the destination while their expertise represents the objective knowledge'. Familiarity relates to the early stage of learning while expertise relates to the later stage. Elsewhere, Kerstetter and Cho (2004) describe familiarity as an awareness or perception of a product or service or destination that does not require prior experience. It is easy to think of the familiarity that any intending tourists might generate through time with any destination – through reading guidebooks or other more general books, newspapers, magazines and web browsing; word of mouth with friends, relatives or other social networks; and general exposure to a variety of marketing media. Linking with Ajzen and Fishbein (1980) and Sparks (2007), it is possible to see how such familiarity can give the tourist a clear view on how intended behaviour relates to subjective norms. By contrast, expertise refers to a higher level of knowledge, or more advanced decision making (including travel-related decision making), so that tourists are able to produce and recall and evaluate incoming information better – and give a clear view on their perceived ability to engage in the intended behaviour. It must be said, though, that Kerstetter and Cho (2004) found that familiarity and expertise, so important to Gursoy and McCleary (2004; Fig. 8.3), were not necessarily separate within the overall concept.

Some other key considerations in the Gursoy and McCleary (2004) model include past experience with a variety of places and activities and the cost to the tourist of both an internal research strategy (drawing on individual memory) and an external research strategy (through the use of commercial and non-commercial information). Such costs relate to finance, time spent and cognitive effort balanced against expected outcome (Vogt and Fesenmaier, 1998). 'Involvement' in the whole process is also considered. This varies among individual tourists so that the highly involved decision maker will, for example, use more information sources; carefully examine the importance (and credibility) of information; want to know the strengths and weaknesses of possible alternatives in more detail; form attitudes that are more resistant

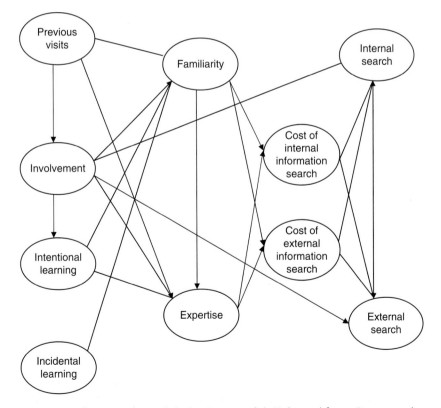

Fig. 8.3. Tourist information search behaviour model. (Adapted from Gursoy and McCleary, 2004, p. 365.)

to change; and learn in a style that is rather more intentional than incidental. So, the theory of information search and decision making really does embrace a gamut of elements and approaches.

Further empirical reality

Such theory may be news indeed for tourists as they go about their normal thing. And, of course, Gursoy and McCleary (2004, p. 354) are quick to point out that their proposed theoretical model has not been empirically tested so that they 'cannot confirm or disconfirm the existence of proposed relationships'. Jang *et al.* (2007), however, do manage to trace the choice-sets model for (engaged) couples as they go through their choice of honeymoon destination – and extend much work on choice sets with a focus on joint (rather than individual) decision making. Each partner in a couple reduces conflicts by adding some of the other partner's 'early consideration set' (similar to the 'awareness set' of Um and Crompton, 1990) into their own modified early consideration set. They build a 'late consideration set' (similar to the 'evoked set') with alternatives acceptable to both. When couples do not agree on their destination until the final stage, situation inhibitors (money, time) and couples' influence relative to one another determine the final destination. Out of 96 couples, 42 reached consensus before situational constraints were taken into account – and of the remaining 54 couples, 29 reached

consensus. As Jang *et al.* (2007; Fig. 8.4) point out there are limitations in their work – most obviously because respondents were engaged couples planning to go on their honeymoon within 3 months. And, as Jang *et al.* add with brevity and charm: 'These are typically happy couples, but other kinds of couples exist.' The theme

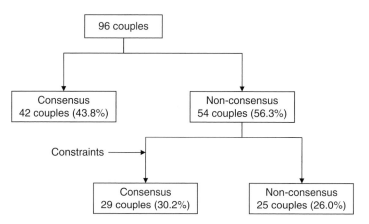

Fig. 8.4. Decision-making funnel for honeymoon couples. (Adapted from Jang *et al.*, 2007, p. 1305.)

of couple decision making for tourist products is further expanded in Chapter 12, 'The Importance of Family' (this volume).

In another empirical study, Bargeman and van der Poel (2006) point out that most theories assume individuals act rationally and evaluate options – and that most vacationers go through an 'Extended Problem Solving' (EPS) decision-making process (DMP) (rather than limited problem solving or routine problem solving). In their real-life study of Dutch households, however, they found a rather more diverse picture. Some vacationers did not go through an extended problem-solving route even though they were going on a foreign holiday. On the other hand, some vacationers who had gone on vacation in The Netherlands many times before (and so might be expected to make a quick decision) still went through an extended DMP:

> Sometimes they needed clarity and certainty, but often they were interested in the information per se. They seemed to search and process information as a leisure pursuit, a hobby, or an experiential form of entertainment and pleasure.
>
> (Bargeman and van der Poel, 2006, p. 717)

Decrop and Snelders (2004, p. 1011) also suggest that 'this DMP (decision-making process) is not related so much to solving a problem as it is to creating enjoyable feelings (such as fantasising whilst reading brochures), experiences (such as having fun with friends), and emotions (for example, while gazing at photographs of the Pyramids or other attractions)'. Working over a period of 1 year, in an inductive study with Belgian households (so not individuals), Decrop and Snelders provide some particularly interesting findings related to gathering information. The majority of the informants were low information searchers rather than high information searchers and gathering information was not the same as integrating or memorizing it. Some households created a physical archive of material in lieu of relying on memory. Also, while information was a good indicator of choice *preference*, it was a weak indicator of *actual choice* – so that one woman gathered information on Brittany but chose another destination 'about which she knew hardly anything' (Decrop and Snelders, 2004, p. 1020). Furthermore, information search was more an ongoing and incidental (rather than intentional) process. It occurred before, during and after the vacation – to prolong mood or fantasize about future projects – in a fashion that was 'à la carte, when the tourist really needed it' (Decrop and Snelders, 2004, p. 1020).

Van Raaij and Francken (1984) give one of the earliest and clearest views on the DMP in which a vacation sequence moves through five stages – generic decision, information acquisition, joint decision making, vacation activities, satisfaction and complaints – but for Decrop and Snelders the generic decision making was often late. This was due to 'situational variables' (e.g. the chance of an illness in the family); opportunity – the late availability of vacations in the now much more ubiquitous last minute.com society (although late generic decision making was not synonymous with impulse buying); and due to personality – 'the passive and day to day traits of some vacationers result in short term planning' (Decrop and Snelders, 2004, p. 1016).

In a wider consideration of the whole DMP, Decrop and Snelders (2005) conclude that

> there is not one but a plurality of vacation DMPs…there is a need to soften traditional tenets which characterise vacation decision-making as high involvement … extensive problem solving…and sequential…(and) one should pay more attention to adaptability and opportunism…(and) the daydreaming of hedonic vacationers.
>
> (Decrop and Snelders, 2005, p. 129)

And so to close on a wry note, much (although not all) of the information search and planning does not conform to standard theory – a condition that is most probably reflected in other tourist groupings, too.

IMAGE AND DESTINATION CHOICE

Some theory

We carry many images around with us in our heads – from memories, associations and what is in our mind's eye about a product or place. They can be retrieved at stages within the information search process if, indeed, there are stages. Customer decisions noticeably depend on image. So, it is worth considering image as a separate influence in information search. We illustrate this here mainly with reference to destination choice – often a key decision for the tourist. Images are an essential part of selecting (and differentiating) a destination (Baloglu and McCleary, 1999).

In an early attempt at a conceptualization of destination image, Gunn (1972) identifies 'organic images' that reflect deep memory, associations and imaginations formed from naive non-tourist information (family traditions, teachers, mass media such as television documentaries, books and so forth – that create 'familiarity'); 'induced images' (commercial efforts) and 'modified induced' images that result from personal experiences. In a further study, Echtner and Ritchie (1991, 1993) juxtapose three sets of opposing image continuums:

- 'functional' characteristics (tangible, directly observable like climate and prices) versus 'psychological' characteristics (intangible – atmosphere or romance of a place);
- 'common' characteristics versus 'unique' characteristics;
- 'holistic' characteristics (complete or overall) versus 'attribute-based' characteristics (individual elements).

Through a combination of open-ended and scaled questions they capture the components of destination image in an empirical study of Jamaica. Although Echtner and Ritchie state that the scores are most useful when used in relative terms (to compare Jamaica with another destination), they also interpret the scores in absolute terms. So, a number of factors are deemed to have high scores (over 5 on a 6-point scale – see Fig. 8.5):

Also, in another notable study, Gartner (1996) endorses three image components:

- 'cognitive' (thought produced – an internally accepted picture of destination attributes, the attractions or resources in a destination);
- 'affective' (emotion-produced – what is to be obtained from the destination);
- 'conative' (actions and behaviour that follow from cognitive and affective image).

Similarly, Keller (1998) categorizes image according to:

- 'descriptive attributes' – broadly similar to the cognitive component;
- 'benefits' – the personal value and meaning attached to an attribute – broadly similar to the affective component;
- 'attitudes' – the overall evaluation and basis for action and behaviour.

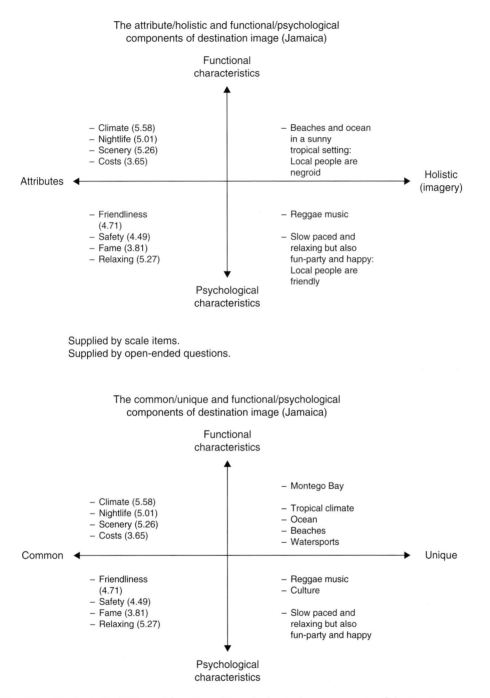

Fig. 8.5. Attribute/holistic and functional/psychological components of destination image. (Adapted from Echtner and Ritchie, 1993, p. 10.)

The jury is still out regarding which theory is closest to reality. But it is worth considering Hong *et al.* (2006) and their study of visitors to eight Korean national parks. Their model shows the close interrelationship that can exist between image and choice sets (two theory elements at the centre of this chapter). They also show the enhanced role for the affective component in image compared to the cognitive component. They argue that visitors categorize destinations into similar groups – with more similarity within than between the various groups – and then use affective image (more than the tangible attributes of cognitive image) to select. This is because there are just too many attributes to compare. If true, this runs counter to other work that puts less emphasis on the affective component in image creation. Just think of the positive, affective, intangible, image of cities such as Paris (romance), Rio de Janeiro (sensuality, carnival) or 1970s San Francisco (liberation) or any city with some particular, positive, personal connection and you can understand the power of affective image. Parisians may like to consider their city as the most romantic of all but there are many other cities with similar affective image and Hong *et al.* would argue that it is one of the key bases on which tourists organize their thoughts and so come to a destination choice.

Taken together, the strands of theory outlined so far provide a useful basis for thought and, more rather than less, underpin much practice. But they are a sliver of all the writing on the subject. Pike (2002) produces a review of 142 papers on destination image – the field is certainly extensive. In their review, Gallarza *et al.* (2002) detail image as:

- complex – there is more than one interpretation of what it means;
- multiple – the final composite image comes from multiple attributes;
- relativistic – image changes from person to person;
- dynamic – image is not static but changes according to time and space.

However, after considering over 30 definitions they offer a warning:

> The conceptual delimitation of destination's image is not unequivocal. Definitions are as many as the authors interested in conceptualising it.
>
> (Gallarza *et al.*, 2002, p. 68)

We believe, however, that Crompton (1979, p. 18) produces as succinct a definition of image as any other:

> An image may be defined as the sum of beliefs, ideas and impressions that a person has of a destination.
>
> (Crompton, 1979, p. 18)

Looked at from a slightly different angle, Beerli *et al.* (2007, p. 582), using the survey method on over 500 individuals living on Gran Canaria, Spain, find that destinations should try to develop an image close to that of the self-perception of the tourists – 'self-congruity' – a point also stressed by Sirgy and Su (2000) and Kastenholz (2004). Beerli *et al.* (2007, p. 582) consider that 'the greater the congruity between the destination's image and one's real and ideal self-concept, the greater the tendency for the tourist to visit the place'. There are shades here of Prebensen *et al.* (2007) as found in Chapter 2, 'Country-File: Tourist Nations' (this volume). Self-congruity decreases with previous experience of a destination but increases with tourists' involvement in the tourism process.

Finally in this theory section, Mossberg and Kleppe (2005) have recently portrayed the conceptual background differently by integrating thoughts on country image, product country image and destination image. Marketers have largely dealt with 'country image' (image associated with objects, events or persons from a country in politics and culture as well as international business) and 'product country image' (image associated with specific products) – while tourism researchers have largely dealt with 'destination image'. Mossberg and Kleppe suggest that the similarity between country image and product country image on the one hand and destination image on the other hand has not been explored, even though they often deal with nearly the same area of applied (international) marketing – export products to international consumer markets. Accordingly, they develop an integrated model that pulls together the two streams of research and thinking (Mossberg and Kleppe, 2005, p. 500; Fig. 8.6). They suggest that it can be illustrated in action with reference to Sweden in which the Space for Minds project (www. swetourism.se) attempts to integrate both products from Sweden and Sweden as a destination. So, instead of 'top down umbrella branding' the Space for Minds project has attempted to 'develop…a common platform that gives room for corporate, destination and product branding as part of the generic

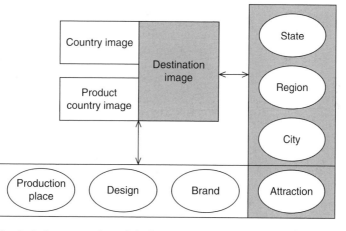

Fig. 8.6. Integrated model of country and destination image concepts and image objects. (From Mossberg and Kleppe, 2005, p. 500.)

country brand'. This integrates both products from Sweden (and specific attributes such as production place, design and brand) and Sweden as a tourist destination.

IMAGE SOURCES

National tourism organizations (NTOs)

It is interesting just how hard national tourism organizations (NTOs) work in order to create what they hope will be a common and striking image. Even though it may be an unfulfilled quest.

The role of governments in image formation, whether through NTOs or their forerunners, is not entirely new. Nor is their remit to use tourism for wider ends. Indeed, Ateljevic and Doorne (2002), in a comparative study of New Zealand in the 1900s and 1990s, place tourism imagery within an historical-political context and argue that the image presented by the early-20th-century New Zealand government was deliberate and most certainly influenced by ideology – specifically, symbols of progress and civilization (alongside an idealized and senti-mentalized image of 'Maori maidens'). Furthermore, imaging by the New Zealand Tourism Board (NZTB) in the 1990s is seen as 'in essence not so different from the agency's approach at the beginning of the century'. Ateljevic and Doorne (2002, pp. 661–662) identify:

- a scenic wonderland myth – images of the (civilized) spa;
- middle-class order;
- an 'exotic' Maori culture.

This image, of course, is nowhere near the organic image presented by the Maori gang films from the same period, that were widely distributed through cinemas in Western Europe, depicting life in the poorer suburbs of Auckland. Indeed as Ateljevic and Doorne state:

> [t]he reality of Maori as largely urbanised people suffering high levels of intergenerational unemployment, poverty, and incarceration rates are carefully avoided by the contemporary tourism discourse.
>
> (Ateljevic and Doorne, 2002, p. 662)

And who would blame the NZTB for such an approach? The alternative would hardly be a winning theme for the European, North American or South-east Asian market – perhaps keen on escape and escapism. Even so, convincing the disparate tourism sub-sectors and operators and other stakeholders of a common (positive) induced image can be an uncommonly difficult task. In New Zealand, the national press of the day (1998/99) carried some bitter exchanges between operators and (opposition) politicians as the NZTB built up to the launch of *Pure NZ* – by common consent one of the finer recent examples of NTO image creation. The opposition felt that the NZTB image strategy – then very much in the public forum – was a waste of money. They argued that money could either be diverted to other causes or not taken from the public purse at all – and also that the strategy was misguided in what it sought to represent (Knowles, 1999; Prebble, 1999).

Nor do the problems stop when and if the image sender has a unified image to present. After an image is agreed, there is the problem of getting the message out to potential international tour operators or tourists so that they pick up the (agreed) image in their intentional or unintentional search. This is not so straightforward. Indeed, Grosspietsch (2006) in a case study of Rwanda found that visitors and international tour operators had different images. The tour operators did not appreciate as much as the tourists either the diversity of the country's nature or the cultural attractiveness of the destination – the traditional lifestyles and the chance to interact with local, friendly people.

Brochures and guides

With regard to specific media as sources of image creation, it is possible to divide the stimuli up into deliberate, overt promotional efforts and rather more covert efforts. Other ways to divide up image creation are also possible such as non-media information sources – institutional brochures, commercial brochures, travel agents and Internet – and mass media information sources (Seabra *et al.*, 2007).

Most tourists from the pre-Internet age will be familiar with a brochure trawl as part of their information search. Indeed through time, brochures and guides have been used extensively to perform three main overt, interlinked promotional objectives – satisfy tourist need for information; create an image; and influence choice (Tian-Cole and Crompton, 2003). Molina and Esteban (2006) asked tourists in Madrid, Spain, to consider brochures on eight (other) Spanish cities. They concluded that destination image is predicted mainly by the visual format and the sense of wonder that is created in the brochure. But, in the modern age, the sense of wonder may be more obviously created by other media – and, indeed, the results of Molina and Esteban do nothing to stop recent questioning regarding the usefulness of commercial printed media. Moreover, Seabra *et al.* (2007) find that commercial brochures show a significant and negative relationship with the fulfilment of expectations – most likely related to an overly colourful image that does not match with reality.

The Internet

A more recent but burgeoning media addition to image creation comes from the Internet both as an overt and covert information source. Things continue to change fast. According to Elliott (2008) in the *New York Times*, there is a huge difference in the online marketing budget for the *I Love New York* campaign even between the consecutive years 2007 and 2008. Given that in 2008 Barack Obama created an image, through a savvy under-the-wire Internet operation, that was good enough to help elect him to the office of US President, such a growth trend might seem unlikely to abate. Indeed, it seems certain that the role of the brochure in image creation in the 19th and 20th centuries will be subsumed in the 21st century to the Internet.

However, a few words of warning are necessary. Frias *et al.* (2008) in a study among inbound tourists to Malaga airport, southern Spain, found that destination image is *worse* when tourists use the Internet rather than when they exclusively use the travel agency. This is because of information overload and disorientation – a situation that is compounded when the tourist does not have the ability to find, sift through and organize relevant information. Pan and Fesenmaier (2006), too, in a study of online information search among would-be USA-based tourists to San Diego, identify tourist knowledge and skills in relation to both travelling and also 'online space' – all the related sites that can be accessed – as key contributors to effective search. The requirement on the behalf of the provider, therefore, is to generate information that is 'relevant, precise, timely and up-to-date' (Frias *et al.*, 2008, p. 174) with first-rate web design that includes pictures rather than text. The tourist can more easily process pictures – newspaper editors found in a different age that pictures can tell a story quicker than pages of newsprint. As detailed by Luque-Martinez *et al.* (2007) in a sample of international (mainly European Union) holidaymakers, there are three main elements that determine tourist intention to use the Internet when searching for holiday information: usefulness – intuitive and user-friendly web sites; the total value of the acquired information; and satisfaction with the search activity.

However, and this is very relevant to image creation, Pan and Fesenmaier (2006) find that tourist Internet users are not subjugated to the marketers:

> [T]he marketer is the primary agent establishing the basic lens when representing a destination, its experiential aspects, as well as the process by which the tourist can gain access to information. Unlike other channels, however, the internet supports many different forms of communication thereby enabling users to assert their need for information that is framed within their personal context rather than that of the promoter. Indeed the incredible growth in online social networks tools and blogs is clearly in response to the perceived control by the producers.
>
> (Pan and Fesenmaier, 2006, p. 826)

The Internet also has a further influence that is relevant to image creation and wider information search. Social networking sites now exist (often dependent on donations) that can help a tourist find 'worldwide free accommodation with individual hosts who greet and meet each customer at the airport or rail station…and sometimes even provide free guided tours, leisure activities with their friends and tips on experiencing local life' (WTM, 2008a). So, the image of place is reflected through the lens of the locals:

> Travellers learn how locals live, discover a new country from an insider's perspective. Conversely, their hosts enjoy meeting visitors of different cultures and swap news and knowledge.
>
> (WTM, 2008b)

You might think that such a scenario is too good to be true – a wild extension of the free-and-easy offers and spontaneous hospitality that some individual tourists were lucky enough to stumble across in Europe, the USA and Asia in the 1960s and 1970s before the industry of tourism was fully developed. But it is not too good to be true if you are already a member of a non-profit organization such as couchsurfing.com – and most probably either single or under 25, or both – or a growing raft of other such fast-expanding social networking sites. The couch surfing project offers some statistics on just how far the movement has headed. As a suggestion of a trend the statistics from www.couchsurfing.com make interesting reading – 832,729 couch-surfers; 785,849 successful surf or host experiences; 933,259 friendships created; 1,539,987 positive experiences; 230 countries represented; 51,067 cities represented.

As with eBay and Amazon, the quality of interactions on such social networking sites can be made public through posting reviews – and so the online community is self-regulated. An individual fears that he/she will lose credibility and be banned from further participation by inappropriate behaviour as a tourist or host.

Television and film

Regarding covert efforts, there is some serious thought given by marketers to slip under the skin of hardened consumers. The use of television and cinema movies is the most obvious example. Television is examined less closely than movies in the academic literature. However, Kim *et al.* (2007) in a study of the effect of Korean television dramas on Japanese visitors, conclude that television dramas such as the highly successful 26-part Korean series Winter Sonata (that created a frenzy of excitement in Japan) can initiate considerable image change and enhancement – even among otherwise implacable nations.

Examples of image creation through movies (as opposed to television dramas) abound. However, while tourism marketers from tourist destinations are often in cahoots with television and film producers, the effect is not always controllable or predictable. For example, The Wizard of Oz was a forerunner for waves of movies that have set people talking and influenced destination image. But Hsu *et al.* (2004) find that the visitor image of Kansas, USA, from 12 major feeder states, is still closely affiliated with the movie – now nearly 100 years old. This seems to support the intuitive claim by Crompton (1979, p. 21) 'that images have considerable amount of stability over time, even in the face of dramatic changes in destination attributes'.

Mercille (2005), too, found that in Tibet the media image is incomplete. Survey informants based their image dominantly on the Hollywood movie Seven Years in Tibet (mentioned by 43% of survey informants); the guidebook the *Lonely Planet* (27%); and the magazine National Geographic (10%). Indeed, 'important absences in media productions, such as Sinification and Westernization, led to tourists being surprised by Tibet's relatively high level of modernization and Chinese presence upon arrival' (Mercille, 2005, p. 1051). Moreover, just to add some extra spice, the cultural and social background of tourists led them to interpret and decode messages differently – some accepted messages and some opposed and adapted them. So, even with the same information source, different effects can emerge.

Frost (2006) also throws a word of warning in relation to the (limited) effect of the Australian movie Ned Kelly that was projected to influence the promotion of North-east Victoria, Australia. It did not recreate a destination image, and it was not successful internationally – its limited contribution to the image of the area lay alongside other media. But at the time of writing, there is much fuss about the new epic Australia and with such an unambiguous title (and big movie stars), it is of much interest to destination marketers in Australia. Notwithstanding the case of Ned Kelly, if the reality is as good as the advance publicity, it should be a sure-fire image maker – maybe as much as the wave of 1970s movies such as Gallipoli and Picnic at Hanging Rock. You the reader will know. And testament to the power of television and film can be seen in the boost to visitor numbers that occur at the locations, or presumed locations, of television dramas and films across the world (see also Chapter 11, 'The Power of Brand and Celebrity', this volume).

Other devices

In a campaign with a model that has been worked through elsewhere, Mayor Bloomberg of New York City 'kicked off a tourist-welcoming campaign by encouraging confused new arrivals to "Just ask the locals" where to go and how to get around' (McGeehan, 2007). At the same time, the city also engaged in more conventional activities – like information handouts from greeters and airport taxi dispatchers.

It is the job of the marketer to produce innovative, covert images – and some thinking outside the box is increasingly required. One other recent attempt to catch the eye comes from the attempt by the Tourism Authority of Thailand and the Melbourne city tourism board to involve London taxi drivers in image creation. Black-cab drivers are offered free familiarization trips – and then engage their travelling passengers in conversation as 'ambassador drivers'. One such driver, quoted in the London-based *Times* newspaper stated:

> No one said I had to talk about it. They just know that if you send someone somewhere and they like it they are going to talk about it and if they are a cab driver they are going to talk to lots of people about it. I am certain that I have helped many of my customers to see Thailand in a different light, just as I am sure that I have persuaded many passengers to visit Melbourne, where I and my wife took a ten-day 'trip of a lifetime' courtesy of the city's tourist board.
>
> (Pavla, 2008, p. 3)

Another so far unintentional image creator, though not really exploited by the marketers, is the postcard – a true tourism icon. Yuksel and Akgul (2007) analyse the role of postcards as affective image makers. The figures are simple and powerful. They base their study on the international resort town of Kusadasi in Turkey, host to 500,000 visitors per year. A personal communication from the Post Office Director suggested that 300,000 postcards were posted during each season. This seems like a conservative estimate, but even if it is correct it does not take much imagination to realize the likely effect that such a number of postcards can have. At the very least it places Kusadasi in the 'awareness set' of potential tourists. Moreover, there would be high credence through later word-of-mouth endorsement from the postcard-sending friend or relative. As the authors suggest and then illustrate:

> [t]he postcard arriving by mail would evoke positive emotions; provoke curiosity in the recipient, and desire to know the other parts of the 'jigsaw puzzle'.
>
> (Yuksel and Akgul, 2007, p. 717)

Yuksel and Akgul go on to suggest a more intentional marketing effort that recognizes the postcard as an image maker. For example, the postcard producers might work alongside the destination authorities (and host community) so that postcards more closely reflect what the customer values or so that outdated or stereotypical views are banished. On the other hand, perhaps this is going too far – perhaps there is a need for some deliberate innocence so that the tourist does not feel manipulated at all points of the experience. It is worth reflecting how often tourists reject a free postcard – say with a picture of their hotel – for a commercial postcard that costs money but that somehow sums up their visit with their preferred destination image.

JUST SPIN THE GLOBE OR NOT...

This chapter has concentrated on a conceptual and empirical discussion of tourist information search and decision making and also the role of image in destination choice. The commentary on image as a source of information has focused on pre-visit image. After bombardment, or subtle intrusion, from so many information sources, tourists might want to put their head and heart in neutral and suppress their destination image. After all, image and reality can be two very different things and to an extent, certainly after deciding on a destination, it might be a good idea to wait for the reality to unroll. The post-visit image, however, is likely to be more realistic, complex and differentiated (Chon, 1991). Selby and Morgan (1996) distinguish between the pre-visit naivety of images and the post-visit re-evaluation – often resisted, as tourists do not like to be proved wrong. But, assuming that the tourist retains the motivation to travel, a *post-visit image* enters the mix for the next round of decision making and choice.

Sometimes, though, such decision making is not especially planned, particularly among individual tourists or tourists in small, non-tour groups. Kugel (2008), writing in the *New York Times*, records how one tourist, the operations manager of the Hale Centre Theatre in Salt Lake City, plans for his trips to New York. He 'waits for *The New Yorker* food issue to come out; rips out pages and makes a list of where to go and what to order the next time he is in town'.

Information from a large number of happenings can force a decision:

- a web browse the night before in a hostel or hotel;
- a chance conversation with other guests in a B&B;
- a chance conversation with some local people on the street;
- a fleeting glance at a guidebook;
- noticing places of interest from sets of direction signs;
- some other more overt marketing in a given location;
- flicking through a postcard stall;
- any combination of the above.

Increasingly, indeed, some tourists deliberately avoid pre-planning beyond the core framework of time and destination and main accommodation and transport. They will prefer to browse around, say, a city destination and just experience the daily life – without their head in a guidebook. They realize the frustration of 'discovering' a newly crowned 'local and authentic restaurant' in Rome or Bangkok only to find that everyone else has read the same guidebook and discovered it too. Such behaviour should probably be welcomed by tourist authorities because tourists then spread the effect of tourism beyond the must see and do places and so contribute to a more diversified economy, less overcrowding and, in all likelihood, less host–guest friction.

But such 'Lucky Dip' overthrows much of what we have written in this chapter. For the most part, we do still live in a logical world. We *could* choose a destination by spinning a globe or randomly selecting from an atlas. But for the most part that is not what we do.

REFERENCES

Ajzen, I. (1991) The theory of planned behaviour. *Organizational Behaviour and Human Decision Processes* 50, 179–211.

Ajzen, I. and Fishbein, M. (1980) *Understanding Attitudes and Predicting Social Behaviour*. Prentice-Hall, Englewood Cliffs, New Jersey.

Ateljevic, I. and Doorne, S. (2002) Representing New Zealand. *Annals of Tourism Research* 29(3), 648–667.

Baloglu, S. and McCleary, K. (1999) A model of destination image formation. *Annals of Tourism Research* 26, 868–897.

Bargemann, B. and van der Poel, H.T. (2006) The role of routines in the vacation decision-making process of Dutch vacationers. *Tourism Management* 27, 707–720.

Beach, L.R. and Mitchell, T.R. (1998) The basics of image theory. In: Beach, L.R. (ed) *Image Theory: Theoretical and Empirical Foundations*. Lawrence Erlbaum Associates, New Jersey.

Beerli, A., Meneses, G.D. and Gil, S.M. (2007) Self-congruity and destination choice. *Tourism Management* 34(3), 571–585.

Chon, K.S. (1991) Tourism destination image modification process. *Tourism Management* 12(1), 68–72.

Crompton, J. (1979) An assessment of the image of Mexico as a vacation destination and the influence of geographical location upon that image. *Journal of Travel Research* 17, 18–23.

Crompton, J.L. (1992) Structure of vacation destination choice sets. *Annals of Tourism Research* 19(3), 420–434.

Decrop, A. and Snelders, D. (2004) Planning the summer vacation. *Annals of Tourism Research* 31(4), 1008–1030.

Decrop, A. and Snelders, D. (2005) A grounded typology of vacation decision-making. *Tourism Management* 26, 121–132.

Echtner, C.M. and Ritchie, J.R.B. (1991) The meaning and measurement of destination image. *Journal of Tourism Studies* 2(2), 2–12.

Echtner, C.M. and Ritchie, J.R.B. (1993) The measurement of destination image: An empirical assessment. *Journal of Travel Research* 31(4), 3–13.

Elliott, S. (2008) Calling for tourists to come for New York City, but stay for the State. *New York Times*, 6 May 2008.

Frias, D.M., Rodriquez, M.A. and Castaneda, J.A. (2008) Internet vs. travel agencies on pre-visit destination image formation: an information processing view. *Tourism Management* 29, 165–179.

Frost, W. (2006) Bravehearted Ned Kelly: historic films, heritage tourism and destination image. *Tourism Management* 27, 247–254.

Gallarza, M.G., Saura, I.G. and Garcia, H.C. (2002) Destination image. *Annals of Tourism Research* 29(1), 56–78.

Gartner, W.C. (1996) *Tourism Development: Principles and Policies*. Van Nostrum, New York.

Grosspietsch, M. (2006) Perceived and projected images of Rwanda: visitor and international tour operator perspectives. *Tourism Management* (27), 226–234.

Gunn, C. (1972) *Vacationscape. Designing Tourist Regions*. Taylor & Francis, Washington, DC.

Gursoy, D. and McCleary, K.W. (2004) An integrative model of tourists' information search behaviour. *Annals of Tourism Research* 31(2), 353–373.

Hong, S.-H., Kim, J.-H., Jang, H. and Lee, S. (2006) The roles of categorization, affective image and constraints on destination choice: an application of the NMNL model. *Tourism Management* 27, 750–761.

Hsu, C.H.C., Wolfe, K. and Kang, S.K. (2004) Image assessment for a destination with limited comparative advantages. *Tourism Management* 25, 121–126.

Jang, H., Lee, S., Lee, S.-W. and Hong, S.-K. (2007) Expanding the individual choice-sets model to couples honeymoon destination selection process. *Tourism Management* 28, 1299–1314.

Kastenholz, E. (2004) Assessment and role of self-congruity. *Annals of Tourism Research* 31(3), 719–723.

Keller, K. (1998) *Strategic Brand Management: Building, Measuring and Managing Brand Equity*. Prentice-Hall, Englewood Cliffs New Jersey.

Kerstetter, D. and Cho, M.-H. (2004) Prior knowledge, credibility and information search. *Annals of Tourism Research* 31(4), 961–985.

Kim, S.S., Agrusa, J., Lee, H. and Chon, K. (2007) Effects of Korean television dramas on the flow of Japanese tourists. *Tourism Management* 28, 1340–1353.

Knowles, C. (1999) Tourism needs a helping hand. *New Zealand Herald*.

Kugel, S. (2008) Some tourists don't need advice. *New York Times*, 2 November 2008.

Lam, T. and Hsu, C.H.C. (2006) Predicting behavioural intention of choosing a travel destination. *Tourism Management* 27, 589–599.

Luque-Martinez, T., Castaneda-Garcia, J.A., Frias-Jamilena, D.M., Munoz-Leiva, F. and Rodriguez-Molina, M.A. (2007) Determinants of the use of the Internet as a tourist information source. *Service Industries Journal* 27(7), 881–891.

Lye, A., Shao, W., Rundle-Thiele, S. and Fausnaugh, C. (2005) Decision waves: consumer decisions in today's complex world. *European Journal of Marketing* 39(1/2), 216–230.

Mansfield, Y. (1992) From motivation to actual travel. *Annals of Tourism Research* 19(3), 399–419.

McGeehan, P. (2007) The mayor wants tourist to be welcomed. Hospitably. *New York Times*, 30 August 2007.

Mercille, J. (2005) Media effects on image: the case of Tibet. *Annals of Tourism Research* 32(4), 1039–1055.

Molina, A. and Esteban, A. (2006) Tourism brochures: usefulness and image. *Annals of Tourism Research* 33(4), 1036–1056.

Mossberg, L. and Kleppe, I.A. (2005) Country and destination image – different or similar image concepts? *Service Industries Journal* 25(4), 493–503.

Pan, B. and Fesenmaier, D.R. (2006) Online information search: vacation planning process. *Annals of Tourism Research* 33(3), 809–832.

Pavla, W. (2008) Spiel at the wheel? You must've had that adman in the front of the cab. *The Times*, 14 January 2008, p. 3

Pike, S. (2002) Destination image analysis – a review of 142 papers from 1973 to 2000. *Tourism Management* 23(5), 541–649.

Prebble, R. (1999) Tourism spending a waste. *The New Zealand Herald*.

Prebensen, N.K. (2007) Exploring tourists' images of a distant destination. *Tourism Management* 28, 747–756.

Seabra, C., Abrantes, J.L. and Lages, L.F. (2007) The impact of using non-media information sources on the future use of mass media information sources: the mediating role of expectations fulfilment. *Tourism Management* 28, 1541–1554.

Selby, M. and Morgan, N.J. (1996) Reconstruing place image. *Tourism Management* 17(4), 287–294.

Sirakaya, E. and Woodside, A.G. (2005) Building and testing theories of decision making by travellers. *Tourism Management* 26, 815–832.

Sirgy, M. and Su, H. (2000) Destination image, self-congruity and travel behaviour: toward an integrated model. *Journal of Travel Research* 38, 340–352.

Sonmez, S.F. and Graefe, A.R. (1998) Determining future travel behaviour from past travel experience and perceptions of risk and safety. *Journal of Travel Research* 37(4), 171–177.

Sparks, B. (2007) Planning a wine tourism vacation? Factors that help to predict tourist behavioural intentions. *Tourism Management* 28, 1180–1192.

Tian-Cole, S. and Crompton, J. (2003) A conceptualisation of the relationships between service quality and visitor satisfaction, and their links to destination selection. *Leisure Studies* 22, 65–80.

Um, S. and Crompton, J.L. (1990) Attitude determinants in tourism destination research. *Annals of Tourism Research* 17, 432–448.

Um, S. and Crompton, J.L. (1992) The roles of perceived inhibitors and facilitators in pleasure travel destination decisions. *Journal of Travel Research* 30(3), 18–25.

Van Raaij, W. and Francken, D. (1984) Vacation decisions, activities and satisfactions. *Annals of Tourism Research* 13, 1–9.

Vogt, C. and Fesenmaier, D. (1998) Expanding the functional information search model. *Annals of Tourism Research* 25, 551–578.

WTM (2008a) Free is new F-word *WTM (Press Release)*, London, 10 November 2008.

WTM (2008b) Travellers reject expert advice…and go local *WTM (Press Release)*, London, 10 November 2008. Available at: www.couchsurfing.com

Yuksel, A. and Akgul, O. (2007) Postcards as affective image-makers: an idle agent in destination marketing. *Tourism Management* 28, 714–725.

chapter 9

IN-USE EXPERIENCE

It is possible to view consumer behaviour as a set of interlocking elements. Some of these elements relate best to the pre-experience stage, such as motivation and information search and destination decision making; some relate best to the post-experience stage such as satisfaction and loyalty and life change; and some relate best to in-use experience – that is, behaviour that occurs when the tourist is actually engaged on the ground (or air or sea) doing tourist things.

What do we know about in-use experience? Often it is predictable. A tour leader frequently has limited autonomy over the choice of the next stopping place, eating place, attraction or means of transport – as even comparatively small decisions are made centrally and form part of the contract to the consumer. Individual tourists also make predictable in-use decisions. For example, Wansink and van Ittersum (2004, p. 328) detail the stopping decisions of tourists on their way by car to a given destination. They emerge with some understandable but non-startling findings: '[R]easons an average traveller stops are to buy gas, snacks, and to use the facilities (and) travellers often tend to wait until they have multiple needs before stopping.'

There have been various attempts made to provide a holistic framework for the different elements of the whole tourist experience. Chapter 5, 'Models of Tourist Behaviour' (this volume), deals with the so-called grand models of consumer behaviour and the spin-off tourist behaviour models that can certainly be thought of in terms of a whole (tourist) experience. The models mostly imply some temporal sequence of behaviour and the operation of a set of judgements that then modify future behaviour. However, in this chapter, we will concentrate more on the in-use experience – a part of the whole experience but the part that might be considered as its core. It is the part that involves the tourist act or action or *performance* (our preferred term) in which the tourist is an element in the overall production.

FRAMEWORKS

A focus on the in-use experience can lead to a discussion of in-use frameworks – such as 'visitor perception audits' and also 'service blueprints' or 'service maps' – all of which look at the totality of the in-use tourist experience with the tourism product. A visitor audit is a systematic perception and appraisal of a service from the point of view of a given visitor. The logic behind such an audit is provided by Middleton and Clarke (2001, p. 123) who state that

> [i]t is always highly instructive to analyse any service business operation in terms of the full sequence of contacts and processes between customer and business, from the time that they make initial enquiries (if any), until they have used the product and left the premises.

Johns and Clark (1994) provide a visitor perception audit for a visitor journey to a museum – although the framework could equally be applied to any tourism business or organization in any sector or sub-sector of the tourism industry. They outline five stages – adapted here to take into account technological change since 1994. The core of the in-use experience would extend from arrival to exit – after all, pre-visit relates more obviously to information search and follow-up relates more obviously to post-experience judgement making.

- Pre-visit: impressions obtained from web site including blogs, brochures, other marketing – and the site itself; adequate and accurate information on opening times, price structure and so forth;
- Arrival: road or rail access to the site and car parking; secondary transport to the entrance; signposting, maps and micro-location instructions; architecture such as covered walkways against rain, wind or sun;
- Entry: entry to the exhibits including restrictions – for example, dress code; queue lengths and queue times; payment methods, security, baggage deposit;
- Service experience: quality and availability of exhibits, guided tour, guide book or electronic interactive multimedia equipment; washroom facilities, rest areas; eating/drinking facilities and outlets and shops – the retail experience;
- Exit: exit from the exhibits; reclaim of baggage and deposit of hired items; marketing opportunities – discount or other promotion encouraging further visits by visitors, their friends or relatives; clear pedestrian, road or rail getaway;
- follow-up e-mail, text, postal or other contact with visitors; revisit suggestions; reinforcement opportunities – marketing to remind visitors about their (really good) experience; membership opportunities. (Adapted from Johns and Clark, 1994, pp. A18–A19.)

It is possible to extend and adapt the visitor audit framework. For example, each stage of the 'visitor journey' outlined by Johns and Clark could be viewed in tandem with the three major categories of 'service evidence' that Bitner (1993) considers to be experienced by each consumer – people, physical evidence and process. These are the three extra 'Ps' of the marketing mix (beyond product, price, place and promotion). For example, at the entry to an attraction the service personnel (people) are important in dealing with ticketing or answering any queries or just providing some entertainment to a line of tourists (as evident in many theme park entrances); physical evidence is important in conveying the values of the attraction – hence the often magnificent entrances of national museums; and the efficient and courteous approach inculcated by good attraction managers in their employees is an example of the importance of process.

Shostack (1985) developed service blueprinting or mapping as a tool for the diagnosis of service problems. Its relevance to a discussion on the tourist in-use experience should be evident from Fig. 9.1. It depicts a service blueprint for a stay in a hotel that considers the visible and invisible sides of production, the objective listing and diagrammatic ordering of the service elements. There are some clear potential service fail points (points in delivery of the service that are most likely to cause execution or delivery problems). The in-use experience will be enhanced when the visible and invisible sides of the service production are delivered without the occurrence of problems at any of the fail points – and when systems are in place to deal with complaints if problems do occur. This can rescue the situation and maintain (or enhance) consumer judgements on satisfaction, quality and value (for money and for time).

A service blueprint/map and so the process of service mapping or blueprinting takes a perspective beyond that of the tourist consumer – but the tourist performance can contribute negatively to the experience.

Bitner (1993, p. 362) states that

> [a] service map visually displays the service by simultaneously depicting the process of service delivery, the roles of customers and employees, and the visible elements of the service.

With some mental sidestepping, the visitor audit, service blueprint/map can be applied beyond one business to an amalgam of businesses – or even the wider tourism system (as envisaged by Leiper in 2004). It is only a matter of scale. So, the five components of a visitor audit can equally be applied to a whole destination (a town, city, region or country). There is a pre-visit phase, arrival, entry, service experience, exit and follow-up. The main difference is that the experience at a destination is less tightly manageable than in a single business or organization. There is much more scope for failure – for example, the tourist can be overcome by a negative experience on a taxi ride back to a hotel after a wonderful night out in a restaurant or a theatre.

THE TOURIST WITHIN TOURISM AS A SERVICE

What is revealed so far is just how much tourism as a product – and so the tourist in-use experience – is predicated by the characteristics of tourism as a service. Tourism management is clearly placed within the context of services management. In any study of consumer behaviour that is set within this context, it is important to revisit the key writings that have helped to distinguish the study of services management from that of other management in general and also to consider the more recent doubts that have crept into such a distinction. Specifically, the unique characteristics that have been assumed to exist under the services marketing paradigm are inseparability, heterogeneity, intangibility and perishability (Zeithaml *et al.*, 1985). The

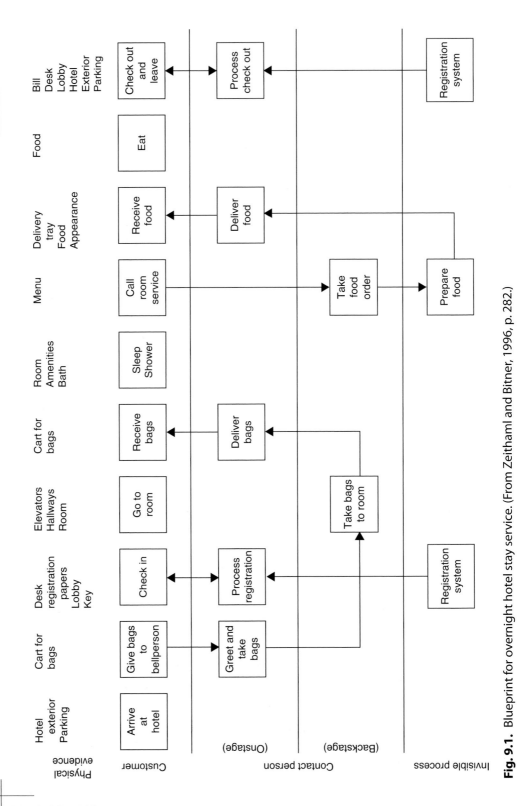

Fig. 9.1. Blueprint for overnight hotel stay service. (From Zeithaml and Bitner, 1996, p. 282.)

foundation of the services marketing paradigm vis-à-vis goods marketing revolves around the way in which these characteristics distinguish services from goods – and so how tourists as consumers are different from consumers of, say, cars or televisions.

We have already touched on *inseparability* – without giving it a name. Services are performances rather than objects and we have described the tourist as engaging in performance alongside the service provider. Inseparability is the term used to describe the simultaneous production and consumption of a service. The received argument is that goods are produced first, then sold and consumed, whereas most services are sold first and then produced and consumed simultaneously. The consumer and the producer participate in the production of the service and frequently, too, the production and consumption take place on the premises or in the equipment (owned or leased) of the producer. Additionally, consumers themselves may interact with *other* consumers in the production process. Booms and Bitner (1981) comment on such a distinct 'customer-interface'. There are exceptions to such a general view and Riddle (1986) identifies not only 'co-production' of services but also 'self-service' and 'isolated production'. There are many common examples of self-service in tourism (airport baggage recovery, say) and isolated production refers to a case in which part or nearly all of the service is performed outside the consumer's presence – as shown in the example of service mapping or blueprinting. However, there are examples in tourism that suggest management sometimes attempts to minimize the invisible element – for example, by creating open-view kitchens in restaurants. Each type of production has its merits in its place and can lead to greater satisfaction with the in-use experience – maybe not so much from self-service baggage collection but certainly from potential interaction with informed, empathetic tourist guides or like-minded fellow tourists, or a myriad of other interactions that inevitably spring from inseparability.

The *heterogeneity* characteristic of services, which is also referred to as *variability*, is largely connected with the vagaries of human interaction between and among service contact employees and consumers. No two customers and no two employees are alike and so no two service acts are alike. Middleton and Clarke (2001, p. 43), however, argue against such a position since 'in practice it (heterogeneity) is a somewhat academic concept and it is makes no sense to apply it to frequently used convenience service products such as those marketed by banks, transport operators, post offices, and other large-scale service operators, all of which are committed to the specification and quality control of service performance'.

On the other hand, many experiences, tourist experiences included, do exhibit rather more involvement than that found in banks – or surface transport operators and fast-food chains (both of which would be claimed as sub-sectors of the tourism industry). Deighton (1994, p. 24) memorably considered such involvement:

> It is a truism to say that all services are performed. To say that all services are performances, however, is to say something slightly different – and much more interesting. To go further and say that all performances are staged performances is very different and quite provocative.

Deighton (1994, pp. 124–126) makes a threefold division of performance.

- 'Non-performances' – occurrences that just happen without any intention to satisfy another party.
- 'Contractual performances' – actions that are done to fulfil an obligation, a debt or a contract to another party.
- 'Staged performances' – an extension of performances beyond the contractual level, put on with deliberate concern for the impression that they will make on the other party. The actor deliberately and intentionally contrives an effect.

Deighton (1994, pp. 127–129) also ascribes four motivations for performance.

- 'skill performances' – staged displays of competence in naturalistic settings for the benefit of passive observers;
- 'show performances' – deliverance of entertainment to passive observers in non-realistic settings;
- 'thrill performances' – active participation in naturalistic settings, in which the staging, although present, is not intrusive;
- 'festive performance' – active participation in a built context created by deliberate staging and costuming.

In order to succeed, a performance must *involve* an audience and capture its attention. This is the core of Deighton's argument and its link with the concept of heterogeneity. The performer needs to move the service encounter beyond perfunctory involvement and what Deighton calls 'divided attention' towards more 'focused attention' in which the consumer is more tightly involved with the performance, accepting and executing a more involving role. 'Engrossed attention' may even follow in which the consumer plays a role with an enthusiasm that begins to become its own reward. The consumer is empowered in this instance to co-produce the performance. It is difficult to conceive of equipment-based services or even highly scripted people-based services that create such a performance. That is because there is a need for producers – on both the provider and consumer side. Such involvement inevitably points toward the acceptance of the concept of heterogeneity. Deighton (1994, pp. 136–137) concludes:

> For contractual performance, the expectancy confirmation/disconfirmation paradigm guides service managers well. When the idea of satisfaction is applied to staged performance, however, (there are) some ways in which conventional views of quality and customer satisfaction are incomplete....It is usually unclear who should get the credit, the actor who performs or the object with which he or she performs or even the service institution within which the performance occurs...or the customer. Satisfaction is not simply a matter of ensuring that the event conforms to expectations...satisfaction with a performance is an interactive concept...failure to recruit the audience can damage an otherwise good performance. Satisfaction on one occasion is, therefore, no guarantee of satisfaction on a subsequent occasion.

Such a situation is truly heterogeneity writ large and it can be thought of as the core difficulty (and opportunity) that service managers face as they seek to manage employee and tourist behaviour during the consumer stage of in-use experience.

As regards *intangibility* Cowell (1984, p. 23) states:

> It is often not possible to taste, feel, see, hear or smell services before they are purchased. Opinions and attitudes may be sought beforehand, a repeat purchase may rely upon previous experience, the customer may be given something tangible to represent the service, but ultimately the purchase of a service is the purchase of something intangible.

On the other hand, Rathmell (1966) points out that a more relevant concept is that of a goods–service *continuum*, rather than a goods–service dichotomy – with pure goods at one end and pure services at the other. Shostack (1977) extends this into a tangible–intangible dominant continuum. Indeed, Enis and Roering (1981, p. 1) argue that consumers 'purchase neither tangible objects nor intangible features; rather they purchase a bundle of benefits – a product'. Such doubts can suggest that intangibility may not be as crucial a service element for consumer in-use experience as, say, inseparability or indeed heterogeneity. As a group of features, though, service characteristics do have a considerable influence on tourist in-use experience.

MICRO-EVENTS, MEMORABLE MOMENTS, MOMENTS OF TRUTH

Many of the ideas presented in this discussion of in-use experience come through in a study conducted by Bowen (2001, 2002) that seeks to discover the antecedents of tourist satisfaction and how satisfaction develops through time on a small group, long-haul, soft adventure and inclusive tour from the UK to South-east Asia (namely Malaysia and Singapore). Through a 2-week period of participant observation, Bowen was able to identify six antecedents. But more importantly for the discussion here, he observes that the in-use experience is composed of myriad sets of 'micro-events' – and sometimes especially noteworthy 'memorable events' or 'memorable moments' – that can last for a few minutes through to a much longer period of time. Below is one extract taken from a 35,000-word narrative and reproduced in Bowen (2002). The extract centres on in-use experience in the unpromising surrounds of Kota Bahru in the extreme north-east of Malaysia. Here, the tourists engaged themselves in an activity that owed much to their own ingenuity and effort – although it was partly based on ideas within the *Lonely Planet* guidebook and a tour leader's suggestions:

> The central idea was to get out of town to see the landing of a fish-catch by some local fisher-people. Accordingly, a deal was struck with a group of taxi drivers who duly, although not without some trouble, found the landing creek for the incoming fishing boats. Eventually, about twenty or so boats, slowly driven by elongated propellers, motored their way alongside the crumbling stakes and short quays that lined the creek. It was early afternoon, extremely hot and shade-less apart from inside an open-fronted drinks-place – set with bare trestle tables and selling only locally

produced soft drinks. The boats had nearly all moored, either to the stakes or to one another and the entire tour group, with the exception of Donald, were in the drinks-place. Here was a memorable moment…although with regard to expectation (an antecedent of satisfaction) it is worthwhile highlighting a conversation recorded in the field-notes.

Asif (the tour leader) asked:

'So what do you all want to do?'

No reply.

'So how long do you want to stay here?'

'All day'.

General laughter.

'That's just how I like to take things too'.

[T]he memorable moment was extended when Donald, who invariably ventured further a-field than any other Expedition Malaysia (EM) members, normally in great haste and earnestness, appeared on the opposite bank of the creek. He was in search of the ultimate photograph and appeared oblivious to the heat and the watching eyes.

Asif spoke generally to the group: 'I've asked before about what happened to all those crazy English people who came and planted rubber in Malaysia when no one wanted it – and then just caused an enormous boom – there's one of them over there! Just imagine Donald in a white pith helmet!' Asif suggested a rearrangement of the taxi groups…and six group members…continued on with the taxis a short distance across country roads to where there were reputed to be numerous good local traders selling batik, silver-ware workers and a renowned kite-maker called Ismail (a craft particular to the East Coast and especially Kota Bahru). Although contact with locals, even buyer–seller contact was not pronounced on the EM tour, this was an exception. Jane, Susi and Sinnead, stirred on by the stories told by Robbi, attempted some elementary haggling over prices in a number of batik places and Donald also attempted to do the same at Ismail the kite-makers place. This was perhaps inappropriate….Ismail's pride in his handicraft was such that he spent close on 30 minutes sewing-up two kites…in cardboard outer containers. The taxi drivers also entered into the spirit of the visit and bought miniature kites for themselves – Donald noticed this and believed that it rather suggested the special-ness of their trip. So, a part of the pleasure from the afternoon at the fishing creek (and at the sellers' places) was derived not only from the familiarity with the people within the group but also from the tentative, transient relationships with the local seller-people and taxi drivers.

(Bowen, 2002, pp. 4–5)

From such evidence, Bowen (2002; Figs. 9.2 and 9.3) derived a set of analytical diagrams that charted the development of satisfaction through time and so the development of the in-use experience. Each micro-event had a series of components: the satisfaction antecedent such as expectation or individual performance (as in the example); a specific context (North-east Malaysia, Kota Bahru, the drinks-place or Ismail's place); a general context (service industry characteristics); immediate or delayed judgement of satisfaction; action or inaction as a response to that judgement (whether extraordinary, like phoning through to the tour operator – or ordinary, like thanking the tour guide); and, finally, feedback. Sometimes the feedback was delayed and so the micro-event was unclosed and, sometimes, the feedback was immediate and

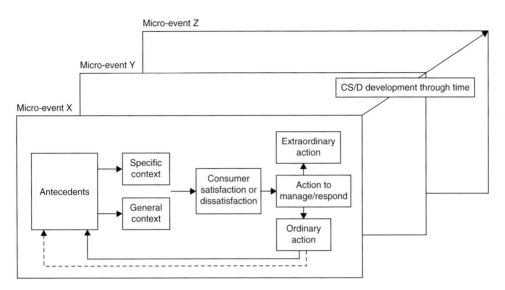

Fig. 9.2. Inter-event CS/D development through time. (From Bowen, 2002.)

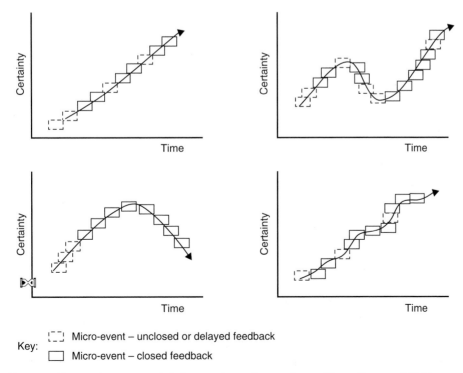

Key: ⌐ ¬ Micro-event – unclosed or delayed feedback
      ☐ Micro-event – closed feedback

Fig. 9.3. Time-certainty models for tourists – four variants. (From Bowen, 2002.)

so the micro-event was closed. Through time, though – and in this case through space as the tour moved through Malaysia and on to Singapore – there is a gathering certainty (based on the accumulated micro-events) regarding the overall satisfaction judgement of the in-use experience.

Now, of course, such a very specific study cannot be applied to all tourist experience although it is argued that there is some considerable wider resonance for the work and 'memorable moments' or 'moments of truth' are well recognized within discussions of in-use experience (Carlzon, 1989; Normann, 1991).

SYSTEMS AND MOBILITY IN SPACE AND TIME

Leiper (2004; Fig. 9.4) has a broader view of tourism than suggested by the frameworks outlined so far (visitor audits, service maps and blueprints). Tourism is considered as a system that can be viewed, as in all systems, at a variety of scales – a domestic system, an outbound system and an inbound system through to a potentially infinite number of subsystems. All of these are set within wider economic, sociocultural, political, legal and physical systems. Tourists move from traveller-generating regions to tourist destination regions through a transit route region that supports opposing flows of departing travellers and returning travellers. The tourist moves from point A to point B and back so that at its most basic the tourist in-use experience involves movement through geographic space over a given period of time.

Certainly at a macro level, this is what tourists actually do during the in-use experience. Much government and business resource is applied to measuring the macro-level flow of tourists through space over a given period of time so that we can state – within the limitations of statistical collection using structured questionnaire interviews – that in 2005 there were so many million visitors from Hong Kong to China compared to so many million visitors 5 years later in 2010. Or that so many thousand visitors looked around the Vatican City in January 2005 compared to so many thousand in July 2005. At a more micro level moving from point A to point B through a transit route can also be what tourists do – at least in part. For example,

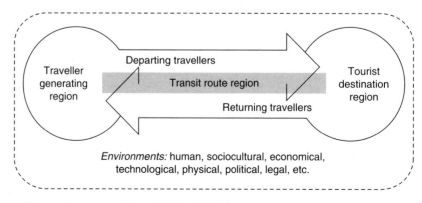

Fig. 9.4. The tourist system. (From Leiper, 2004.)

Hartmann (1988, p. 90) in a study of the 'recreational activities' and 'tourist habits' in Europe (specifically Munich) of young travellers from the USA and Canada found that the tourists 'only had very limited contact with outside persons'. Even the limited contact was 'brief (and) non-personal' – the tourists were viewed as 'strangers in town'. Moreover, Hartmann observes that they 'tended to return to familiar places in Munich in order to start their daily program from there' (Hartmann, 1988, pp. 99–100). In other words, they travelled in their 'environmental bubble' (Cohen, 1972, p. 166) from a micro-level-generating area (normally the Glockenspiel in the main city square) to various micro-level destinations (other local attractions) – along a recognizable transit route with very little host–guest contact!

Geographers in particular have been active in studying movement along tourist routes in a temporal and spatial context, often based on Hagerstrand (1973). So-called time-geography assumes that time and space are factors that directly influence the structure of life – including, therefore, tourist in-use experience – and Oppermann (1995) generates a model of travel itineraries.

Zillinger (2007) in a study of German car tourists in Sweden also analyses how tourists move through time and space. She investigated in what way the travel route depends on the previous number of visits and discovers that it does not do so directly, only indirectly through the location of the travel region. Thus, there is some contradiction here with the travellers in Munich, although the modes of travel are different. She also explores the existence of individual travel rhythms – the combination of mobility and staying put – and concludes, among other findings, that the longer the stay of car travellers in Sweden, the less they travel on average per day. So while space hardly affects the daily travel rhythm, time does. Tourists are mobile in order to be static. These are not startling findings – they are commonsense findings really and the familiar motive for many tourists who drive all day and all night to arrive at their destination. But they do add some reality to the basic model of Leiper (2004) and the perspective of in-use experience as involving movement from point A to point B and back through a transit zone.

Hartmann (1988) studies in-use experience through combined research methods that involve interviews and both non-participant and participant observation. The non-participant observation involves following a small group of the young travellers for 1 h and then allocating a time budget of activities such as walking, sitting, window-shopping and so forth. The participant observation involves the observer as an integral part of a small tourist group (two to five persons) – and very much helps to shed light on the purpose and meaning of activities (as detailed above). Zillinger (2007), by contrast, used travel diaries that respondents updated at least once a day. And as a very recent extension of such enquiry, Shoval and Isaacson (2007), with an eye on changing technologies, suggest that we could become more sophisticated in the way that we track tourists in the digital age and start to use Global Positioning System (GPS) or land-based tracking systems. Even at a comparatively micro level we could then see how tourists move in space and time – both in vehicles and on foot. Shoval and Isaacson show GPS in action on a tracked 4-h tour in Heidelberg, Germany, during which the tourist subject (actually one of the authors) covers nearly 20 km on foot, by car and bus. They suggest that GPS devices can be used to record the number and density of tourists visiting not just historic cities but also attractions, theme parks and the like – and so enrich conventional research methods such as questionnaires, interviews or diaries.

But what else will any innovatory methods find? For a start, we can assume a finding that crowds of people attract crowds of people (mostly guest–guest rather than host–guest) – and only a minority of individual GPS movements will be away from the herd. We all most probably have our own example of a favourite tourist town where the masses congregate around iconic sites – but where the more normal life continues apace just down an alleyway or across a block. And in the great outdoors, we all know similar destinations to the observed spatial behaviour in Yellowstone National Park, USA. Campers do not move more than a couple of hundred metres from their recreational vehicles/camper vans (RVs) – even though either true wilderness or partial wilderness beckons for the able-bodied person willing to stretch away from the crowds.

Movement through space among gregarious crowds, though, should not be mocked. Much tourism occurs in a public place and even when individuals choose to go alone and travel independently, they still need to find a way to interact within space – either to maintain their solitary state or to deliberately join with other like-minded people. For example, a study using video-based evidence of how visitors navigate, explore and experience museums (Vom Lehn, 2006) demonstrates, in the museum subsystem, our movement through museum space. Unless you are very lucky, or visit only obscure museums, you will find that human contact is inevitable – and a crucial part of in-use experience. Movements and actions of others – sometimes, indeed, micro-movements in which museum goers seek to hold on to a view area and/or make various subtle or not-so-subtle exclamations of interest or non-interest in a museum artefact/painting/display – influence how museum visitors negotiate their way through a museum. That is, how they use space and time.

> People's experience and understanding of exhibits arises in and through their bodily action.... They see and make sense of the artefacts through a range of activities, including walking and looking, glancing and inspecting, pointing and showing, talking and discussing and so forth. These activities are observable and reportable events that other visitors orient to and use as resources when exploring and examining exhibitions. By seeing others' engagement with exhibits people can...align and coordinate their actions with them....Their observation of others offers them information on an exhibit even before they have examined it. It may have an important influence on their decision to approach and examine the exhibit.
>
> (Vom Lehn, 2006, p. 1353)

FINALLY

Following the analysis of in-use experience – especially through applying the frameworks suggested by Johns and Clark (1994) and Zeithaml and Bitner (1996) – students often say that we have altered the way that they will think about their future tourist experiences. In other words, they will not be able to suspend reality in the way that most tourists often do and they will forever think about the 'visible' and the 'invisible', or the 'pre-visit' and 'arrival' in-use stages. We argue that it will make them better managers and better tourists – because they will appreciate the complex arrangements that are needed to satisfy the tourist face to face during production and consumption. Mention of satisfaction leads us neatly into the next chapter in which it is the key consideration.

REFERENCES

Bitner, M.J. (1993) Managing the evidence of service. In: Scheuing, E. and Christopher, W.F. (eds) *The Service Quality Handbook*. AMACOM, New York, pp. 358–370.

Booms, B.H. and Bitner, M.J. (1981) Marketing: strategies and organization structures for service firms. In: Donnelly, J.H. and George, W.R. (eds) *Marketing of Services*. American Marketing Association, Chicago, Illinois, pp. 47–51.

Bowen, D. (2001) Antecedents of consumer satisfaction and dissatisfaction on long-haul inclusive tours – a reality check on theoretical considerations. *Tourism Management* 22(1) February, 49–61.

Bowen, D. (2002) Research through participant observation in tourism: a creative solution to the measurement of consumer satisfaction and dissatisfaction among tourists. *Journal of Travel Research* 41(1) August, 4–14.

Carlzon, J. (1989) *Moments of Truth*. Harper & Row, New York.

Cohen, E. (1972) Toward a sociology of international tourism. *Social Research* 39, 164–182.

Cowell, D. (1984) *The Marketing of Services*. Butterworth-Heinemann, Oxford.

Deighton, J. (1994) Managing services when the service is a performance, Ch. 6. In: Rust Roland, T. and Oliver, R.L. (eds) *Service Quality – New Directions in Theory and Practice*. Sage Publications, London.

Enis, B.M. and Roering, K.J. (1981) Services marketing: different products similar strategy. In: Donnelly, J.H. and George, W.R. (eds) *Marketing of Services*. American Marketing Association, Chicago, Illinois, pp. 1–4.

Hagerstrand, T. (1973) The domain of human geography. In: Chorley, R.J. (ed.) *Directions in Geography*. Methuen, London, pp. 67–87.

Hartmann, R. (1988) Combining field methods in tourism research. *Annals of Tourism Research* 15, 88–105.

Johns, N. and Clark, S. (1994) Quality auditing at tourist attractions. *Insights*. ETB, A17–A22.

Leiper, N. (2004) *Tourism Management* 3rd edn. Pearson Education, NSW, Australia.

Middleton, V.T.C. and Clarke, J.R. (2001) *Marketing in Travel and Tourism*. 3rd edn. Butterworth-Heinemann, Oxford.

Normann, R. (1991) *Service Management, Strategy and Leadership in Service Business*. Wiley, Chichester, UK.

Oppermann, M. (1995) A model of travel itineraries. *Journal of Travel Research* 33, 57–61.

Rathmell, J.M. (1966) What is meant by services? *Journal of Marketing* 30(4), 32–36.

Riddle, D.L. (1986) *Service Led Growth*. Praeger Publishing, New York.

Shostack, G.L. (1977) Breaking free from product marketing. *Journal of Marketing* 41(2), 73–80.

Shostack, G.L. (1985) Planning the service encounter. In: Czepiel, J.A., Solomon, M.R. and Surprenant, C.F. (eds) *The Service Encounter*. Lexington Books, Massachusetts, pp. 22–25.

Shoval, N. and Isaacson, M. (2007) Tracking tourists in the digital age. *Annals of Tourism Research* 34(1), 141–159.

Vom Lehn, D. (2006) Embodying experience: a video-based examination of visitors' conduct and inter-action in museums. *European Journal of Marketing* 40(11/12), 1340–1359.

Wansink, B. and van Ittersum, K. (2004) Stopping decisions of travellers. *Tourism Management* 25, 319–330.

Zeithaml, V.A. and Bitner, M.J. (1996) *Services Marketing*. McGraw-Hill, London.

Zeithaml, V.A., Parasuraman, A. and Berry, L.L. (1985) Problems and strategies in services marketing. *Journal of Marketing* 49, 33–46.

Zillinger, M. (2007) Tourist routes: a time-geographical approach on German car-tourists in Sweden. *Tourism Geographies* 9(1), 64–83.

chapter 10

FULFILLING THE PROMISE: TOURIST SATISFACTION

What makes the tourist satisfied? What is the role of increased tourism supply and so further competition and choice? What is the effect of expectations – are tourists really able to carry their expectations with them through time and space? Do they really balance their expectations against what they actually do – their performance? How do their emotions affect their satisfaction – like the fear of the unknown and the surprise of new experiences? And does unfairness play its part? Is satisfaction enough? What happens when tourists get satisfaction? Do they know that they are satisfied and, if so, when do they know that they are satisfied? What happens after they are satisfied? Does satisfaction link with loyalty? What is the link between satisfaction, quality and value, too?

SATISFACTION AND TOURISM SUPPLY

Tourists are no longer shackled by a lack of choice and so need not return to where they have been dissatisfied – with regard to transport, accommodation, attractions, tour operators or travel agents, web sites or destination organizers or any other tourism provider. In many destinations, the rise in the supply of tourism businesses and organizations, along with the growth of the service economy in general, has created a far deeper and wider range of tourism facilities and products. This does not just apply to countries in the traditional heartland of both tourism supply and tourist generation in Western Europe and the USA/Canada. Over the last 20 years or so, the reintegration of East and West Europe and the opening up of South-east Asia and, latterly, China to mainstream market forces has created a new wave of supply in destinations that were otherwise supply-poor. Moreover, this has been allied to a growing understanding of management systems that highlight the need for tourist satisfaction. The opening words of the famous Rolling Stones lyric '(I can't get no) Satisfaction' should hardly apply to any tourist in any tourist setting. (For fans of the rock group, we refer to the face-value statement of the lyric and not its anti-commercialism message.) In a competitive world, there are unlikely to be repeat visits from tourists who are not satisfied. Logically and practically, tourists have the choice to go somewhere else and to spend their time and effort and money where they have a good chance of getting satisfaction.

This is not invariable, though. As startling as the growth in supply has become, and as quickly as this has been allied to improved systems, the tourism authorities in the likes of, say, China or Vietnam or Estonia or Poland would acknowledge that their tourism system is still immature. China, indeed, is focused on a 'state of perfection' in 2020 (Baumgarten, 2003) – see Chapter 2, 'Country-File: Tourist Nations' (this volume). In many sectors and sub-sectors of the industry in China, there is still a limited and controlled supply of tourism facilities and products. In such instances, a lack of choice and imperfect competition can militate against satisfaction for the international visitor – who may not feel obliged to undertake a repeat visit. Meanwhile, domestic tourists may find themselves making repeat visits to, say, established tourist resorts or facilities even when the tourist experience is less than satisfactory – rather like the tourists in the 1950s–1980s within the now more mature tourism system of the UK (Middleton and Lickorish, 2005).

ANTECEDENTS OF SATISFACTION

Expectation, performance and disconfirmation

Much as supply, competition and choice can influence tourist satisfaction, there are other more micro, behavioural forces, 'antecedents', that have come to be recognized as of key importance. They can shape satisfaction in cases of supply surfeit and supply dearth. In short and although different authors sometimes tweak the lists one way or another, these forces can be listed as: expectation; performance and disconfirmation (a measure of the difference between expectation and performance); attribution (blame); emotion; and equity (fairness).

Expectation, performance and disconfirmation are often subsumed into one measure known as 'expectancy disconfirmation'. The study of expectancy disconfirmation is bound up with the establishment of standards and involves elements of appraisal and comparison. A comparison of consumer expectations with outcomes goes back to Thibaut and Kelley (1959) and Kelley and Thibaut (1978) and their study of the social psychology of groups. Their articles were formative in later understandings (and misunderstandings) connected with expectations – and so are worthy of attention. In tourism they are particularly relevant, too, because so much tourism activity takes place in groups (family or friendship groups or business groups). Kelley and Thibaut, complemented by Helson (1964), explain the role of satisfaction through a framework that relates pre-consumption and post-consumption thought. They predict that satisfaction develops from the interaction among individuals and the discrepancy between outcomes and evaluation standards. Kelley and Thibaut (1978) summarize their framework in an overview:

> The outcomes for any participant in an ongoing interaction can be stated in terms of the rewards received and the costs incurred by the participant....By rewards we refer to whatever gives pleasure and gratification to the person. Costs refer to factors that inhibit or deter the performance of any behaviour.
>
> (Kelley and Thibaut, 1978, pp. 8–9)

As La Tour and Peat (1979, p. 434) comment, such a set of ideas explicitly recognizes that satisfaction is a relative phenomenon rather than an absolute phenomenon.

Miller (1977) actually defines four types of expectation comparison standards: 'ideal' (can be); 'lowest tolerable level' (must be); 'deserved' (should be); and 'expected' (will be). He suggests that the latter two are most realistic – 'ideal' and 'lowest tolerable level' standards are dismissed. And 'expected' standards are favoured vis-à-vis 'deserved' standards because the marketplace is supposed to respond to the realities of demand rather than considerations by consumers of elements such as socio-economic and political philosophy and the quality of life. Such an approach is comparable to discussion in the service quality literature and the division made by Parasuraman (1995) between 'desired' (normative) and 'adequate' (predictive) service expectations set within a zone of tolerance.

In a full and succinct account of the expectancy disconfirmation model, Oliver (1989) summarizes and extends earlier views (Oliver 1977, 1980):

> [C]onsumers are posited to hold pre-consumption normative standards or to form expectancies, observe product (attribute) performance, compare product with their norms and/or expectations, form disconfirmation perceptions, combine these perceptions with expectation levels, and form satisfaction judgments. Outcomes that are poorer than expected (a negative disconfirmation) are rated below a reference point, whereas those better than expected (a positive disconfirmation) are evaluated above a given point.
>
> (Oliver, 1989, p. 2)

This seems a very comprehensive and purposeful statement. However, one might question the seamless logicality that such a model suggests and query whether consumers – tourists – really behave in such a rational manner. True, a standard answer to a question such as 'what makes you satisfied as a tourist?' normally draws the immediate response 'expectations and meeting expectations, of course!' – a response that is a simplified version of Oliver's research – but the reality may be rather different.

In particular, the role of past experience is not stressed in its fullest sense. Past experience – not just immediate experience – is researched by Mazursky (1989; Fig. 10.1) in a specific tourism context (tourists visiting a stalactite cave). Mazursky suggests that while a consumer's predictions of performance may be superficial and vague the actual performance can cause

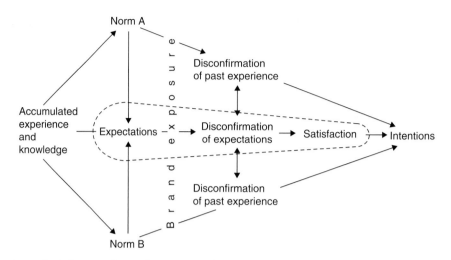

Fig. 10.1. Satisfaction, disconfirmation and past experience. (From Mazursky, 1989, p. 338.)

a retrieval of memories from past experiences and norms. These memories then function as comparative baselines. Effectively, therefore, expectations are overridden by the reality of the current experience that stirs up unanticipated memories. So, it seems that a wider set of product experiences is considered by consumers in the evaluation of satisfaction – experiences that go beyond the immediate product (focal brand), the product actually purchased and used.

Overall, there is a limited consideration of experience-based expectation in much traditional consumer satisfaction/dissatisfaction (CS/D) research – although Rodriquez del Bosque *et al.* (2006, p. 416) conclude, in an empirical study of the travel agency sector in northern Spain, that 'the users' past encounters with travel agencies can play a significant role in their expectation (from) a future encounter'. Other elements are important, too, such as perceived image that 'represents the true capabilities and skill of the travel agency in the eyes of the user' and communication through brochures and advertisements. But in line with Yuksel and Yuksel (2001), there is a suggestion that 'experience-based norms may be better than predictive expectations to explain the customer expectation process' (Rodriquez del Bosque *et al.*, 2006, p. 417).

On the other hand, Brehmer (1980) warns about the informational bias of experience and Hoch and Deighton (1989) cast some doubt on the efficacy of learning from experience. Experience, it is said, can provide an illusion of control, mistaken learning or no learning at all. However, this view does not truly square with much anecdotal evidence from practitioners and industry observers who frequently comment on the widened experience (and expectations) of tourists. In this respect, more tourists are now further up the tourist career ladder (TCL) (Pearce, 1982) and they get up the ladder faster through more frequent and greater variety of tourist experience than was formerly possible. Indeed, notwithstanding our discussion of a tourist career pattern (TCP) (Pearce and Lee, 2005) it may be as appropriate to speak about a tourist career *escalator* – with the associated explosion of experiences. This escalator allows tourist experience to be accumulated at greater speed, with fewer breaks in the ladder, and with less risk and effort. Straightforward analysis of the travel supplements of newspapers and magazines in many countries clearly shows the common journalistic assumption that the readers are travel-experienced. While this is not invariable, and a considerable percentage of people do not have an annual holiday, there are still many others who are accumulating considerable travel experience (at least in terms of the quantity of trips).

The work of Francken and van Raaij (1981) based on Olander (1977) is also worth consideration alongside the Oliver model (1989). They suggest that the standard against which satisfaction is judged – in general leisure-time activity – might be broader than an individual's expectation as derived from earlier experiences (what they call 'temporal expectation') and might encompass the individual's achievements in other spheres of life ('spatial expectation') and the perceived level of satisfaction others derived from the activity ('social expectation').

Performance

But the supremacy of the dominant disconfirmation paradigm does not pass without some criticism. Botterill (1987) appears to dismantle its foundations with a simple note based on both research findings and personal experience as a tourist. In a longitudinal study with a small number of international tourists, he finds that what he labels tourist 'anticipations' are often inadequate predictors of events in a vacation. Furthermore, it is the unpredictability of tourism events that lie at the heart of the tourism experience. Highly satisfied tourists do not have to make a perfect prediction of a vacation. Satisfaction, according to this view, is not achieved by narrowing the gap between expectation and performance so that consumer expectations are totally fulfilled. Rather satisfaction is related to the successful adaptation of the tourist to unpredictable events.

This suggestion favours the role of performance and indeed it has been suggested that each of the three components that make up expectancy disconfirmation may act independently as well as in tandem. Also, that one or other of the components may be suppressed or heightened in a particular tourism situation. For example, in their seminal study of river-rafting and extraordinary experience, Arnould and Price (1993) suggest that satisfaction may have little or nothing to do with expectations. In an attempt to recognize the various satisfaction components on a long-haul inclusive tour, Bowen (2002) finds that each of the elements is present but performance is dominant.

Performance, of course, is not confined just to the individual tourist. Other members of a tourist group or other tourists with no particular connection to an independent tourist also contribute to performance, as do any service personnel who the tourists come into contact with and people going about their day-to-day life in a host population. Even the most experienced tourists would not possibly be able to predict each and every element of performance that is likely to befall them, especially when travelling to a destination with which they are not familiar. Expectation is closely allied to prediction, so it is possible to quickly empathize with what Arnould and Price (1993) found on their river-rafting trip. Bowen (2002), too, was truly convinced some way into a period of participant observation on the long-haul inclusive tour (above) that performance was the key component – not only in the expectancy disconfirmation triangle but also in the whole satisfaction equation. Moreover, performance acts independently and the performance of the individual consumer is the key performance within the range of people performers and performances – more key than the tour leader. The tourist drives performance towards a satisfactory end. In the words of one manager, unusual in his take on the matter, 'the satisfaction comes from the performance … it can come from all sorts of activities too – from learning how to pack and fold a tent through to reaching the highest point on the Atlas Mountains'.

But most managers relegate the role of tourist performance in the creation of satisfaction. This can be explained by the default position of management – control. Consumers as performers are less amenable to control than the performance of, say, tour operator employees or more tangible attributes such as accommodation or transport. This is self-evident from the sort of elements that management attempts to measure on most consumer satisfaction questionnaires.

Bartikowski and Llosa (2004) in a review of how to weight and categorize service attributes in relation to their effect on satisfaction also remind us that not all attributes have the same performance impact. For example, some attributes have a strong weight whether the attribute performs well or badly – they give the example of the taste of food in a restaurant. Also, as another example, some attributes vary in weight depending on the performance – they give the example of how a clean restaurant can engender no (particular) satisfaction while a dirty restaurant strongly attracts negative feelings (and, presumably, thoughts). They call the first example the concept of 'invariant weights' and the second example the concept of 'variant weights':

> To sum up the concept of variant and invariant weights proposes four attribute categories: dissatisfiers influence CS strongly only in the case of low performance; satisfiers only in case of high performance; criticals impact CS in case of low as well as high performance; and the impact of neutrals on CS is relatively weak.
>
> (Bartikowski and Llosa, 2004, p. 69)

Fuller and Matzler (2008) follow a similar tack and distinguish between basic factors (dissatisfiers), excitement factors (satisfiers) and performance hybrids (that lead to satisfaction if performance is high and to dissatisfaction if performance is low). They call this the three-factor theory. The excitement factors add utility beyond that which is expected and so lead to 'customer delight' (Rust and Oliver, 2000), a term that can sometimes cause a groan as just another example of hyperbole and glib service industry speak, but which is nevertheless worth some thought. Fuller and Matzler (2008), in their empirical case in Alpine ski resorts, go on to show that different attributes can contribute to different satisfaction (or delight) among the five different lifestyle segments that they identify – non-family, family, sporty, demanding, settled.

ATTRIBUTION

Information, prior beliefs and motivation

Attribution theory deals with perceptions – in the same way as expectation, performance and disconfirmation also deal with perceptions. It is concerned with all aspects of perceived causal inference even when the inferences are suspect and not even logical or analytical. As with expectancy disconfirmation, attribution theory deals, too, with consequences as well as antecedents. Folkes (1984, p. 398) puts this interest succinctly:

> Given a certain attribution or explanation for product failure, what does the consumer do? Well one thing they may do is come to the conclusion that they are not satisfied. But the story has rather more twists in it than such a straightforward leap between cause and effect.
>
> (Folkes, 1984, p. 398)

A range of core concepts is central to attribution theory. Kelley and Michela (1980) consider that there are three antecedents for causal inferences – information, prior beliefs and motivations. With regard first to information, they refer to a variety of conceptions that differ in relation to what is specified as relevant information, the types of resulting attributions and the nature of the process linking information to attribution. For example, the notion of 'salience' suggests that an effect is attributed to the cause that is most salient in the perceptual (e.g. visual) field. This may have particular relevance in a high-contact consumer–employee industry such as tourism. Additionally, the notion of 'primacy' suggests that a person scans and interprets a sequence of information until an attribution is attained – and then disregards later information or assimilates it to the earlier impression. Again this may have a strong relevance to tourist situations in which there is a considerable amount of information available for assimilation. Weiner (1980) also introduces the notion that individuals have 'preferred informational cues' that are strongly weighted in their judgements. An example is a preference to rely on word-of-mouth information rather than web information – or vice versa.

Regarding prior beliefs, the argument runs that inferences do not rely solely on new information but are accompanied by prior beliefs. These beliefs interpret events.

Weiner (1980, p. 329) outlines this point with reference to memories that inform beliefs – also dealt with in the discussion of expectancy theory:

> To reach causal inferences, that is, to decide why one succeeds or fails, requires that various sources of information be utilised and combined. Some of this evidence will originate from the current situation, while other evidence is gleaned.
>
> (Weiner, 1980, p. 329)

Finally, Kelley and Michela (1980) succinctly class motivations as 'motivation for self-enhancement and self-protection' and 'motivation for the positive presentation of the self to others'. Intuitively, the potential for motivational bias, as one contributor to attribution, may be of special relevance in tourism. It is not difficult to conceive of tourists making rather un-objective attributions for their behaviour – to attribute good outcomes to self and bad outcomes to external or situational causes and to try and retain credibility. If you listen, you can hear it every day as tourists describe experiences. An explanation lies in the interrelated nature of consumption and production in tourism and the importance of (self) performance. The tourist may feel particularly disposed to present the tourism experience in a favourable manner. On the other hand, in defence of the consumer, Folkes (1988) argues, in a tourism situation (an airport), that it is the tourist alone who is truly aware of the effort that they may have devoted to the success of the product or service experience. Accordingly, the attribution of blame to others and some degree of self-aggrandizement may have a rational rather than a self-serving response.

Locus, stability and control

Altogether three underlying and independent dimensions or properties are identified to describe and explain causal inference. These are 'locus', 'stability' and 'controllability'. Attribution theorists derived these dimensions deductively but Weiner (1985) shows that there is a wide range of empirical studies in support. Heider (1958, p. 82) outlined a basic causal distinction fundamental to locus:

> In common sense psychology (as in scientific psychology) the result of an action is felt to depend on two sets of conditions, namely, factors within the person and factors within the environment.
>
> (Heider, 1958, p. 82)

This internal–external dimension, otherwise termed the locus dimension, has provided the focus of much research into the structure of causality. Locus is concerned with beliefs about the solution of problems – for example, the consumer or the firm, the tourist or the tourism business or organization. When a problem results from the actions of a consumer, it is suggested that the consumer should be responsible for the solution of the problem. This is internal locus. By contrast, if a problem results from the action of a firm, it is suggested that the firm is responsible for the solution. This is external locus.

Regarding stability, Weiner (1980) also comments on the degree to which a cause is considered by the consumers to be stable and permanent or unstable and temporary. Folkes et al. (1987) state that inferring a stable cause reduces the desire to repurchase a product compared with an unstable inference. They also suggest, after Weiner et al. (1982) and Brown and Weiner (1984), that stable causes increase anger more than temporary causes and that the degree of anger is related to the importance placed on the successful performance of the product.

Finally, the dimension of controllability refers to the degree to which consumers and firms are able to control outcomes. Weiner (1980) makes the distinction, stemming from Heider (1958), between control that is volitional/optional and control that is forced/constrained by a situation. Curren and Folkes (1987) report that when consumers recognize that control is volitional, they are more likely to complain in the event of product failure. Conversely, they are more likely to compliment a firm and recommend a product in the event of product success.

Weiner's seminal works from 1980 were specifically related to achievement-related contexts such as success and failure. As such, they have a clear relevance to satisfaction. Weiner classifies achievement factors within the frame of locus and stability. Ability is internal and stable; effort is internal and unstable; task difficulty is external and stable; and luck is external and unstable. It is shown that satisfaction scores are higher for ability and effort attributions than for attribution to task difficulty, others' efforts or luck. Furthermore, satisfaction more frequently describes internal locus attributions – a finding that matches with the heightened role of (self) performance in satisfaction.

Folkes *et al.* (1987) exemplifies the theory in an airport context. Such tourism exemplification is so rare from such a key writer in the attribution field that it is worth some attention. When fog or ice delayed a flight, the delay was not controlled by the airline. This contrasted with a delay caused by an airline's attempt to sell more tickets. The consumer response to each delay was different. When passengers perceived that delays or solutions to delays were controlled by an airline, they felt angry, did not want to fly on the airline again and wanted to complain about the delay. Different consumer responses also occurred when an airport delay was due to constant understaffing – a stable cause – or due to a shortage of staff that was perceived by consumers to be temporary in nature. According to Folkes *et al.* (1987) passengers would expect future delays and so be less willing to fly the same airline again if they perceived that the delay was due to a stable reason. By contrast, passengers who were subjected to delays caused by unstable causes were less certain of future delays and were more willing to fly the same airline again. Folkes *et al.* (1987; Fig. 10.2) also add that the importance of successful performance is a further influence on the desire to repurchase and the desire to complain through anger. So they go beyond a consideration of the antecedents of causal inference and also consider the consequences of causal inferences. Attribution theorists contend that the cause inferred for product (or service) failure influences how the consumer will respond. In the context of the airport example above the consumer response variously consists of a reticence to repurchase, a desire to complain and anger. It is one or two steps, rather than a giant leap, from this sort of consequence, as a result of attribution, to a judgement of satisfaction – or dissatisfaction and the first step on the road to litigation.

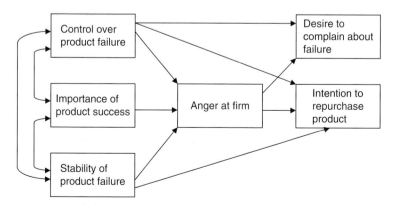

Fig. 10.2. Attribution model. (Adapted from Folkes *et al.*, 1987, p. 538.)

EMOTIONS

It has become customary for people to talk about emotions and for emotions to be more obviously expressed than in times past – even in societies that traditionally eschew such behaviour. So, it is not surprising that the role of emotions in consumer behaviour theory, and especially satisfaction, has come to play a larger role than was originally the case in the days when the (very) cognitive expectancy disconfirmation theories had their first airing. This is not to say that people immediately recognize the role of emotions in tourism, and specifically in satisfaction, when they are asked direct questions on the subject. But listen into tourist conversations and you start to realize that the tourist experience is replete with emotional reactions.

Of course, many books (sometimes contradictory) consume the study of emotion as an element of behaviour. Izard (1977) points out that emotion is not a simple phenomenon and that any definition must take into account the description that a person gives of an emotional experience, the observable expressive patterns of emotion (particularly those on the face) – and also electrophysiological occurrences that occur in the body systems. It would require a trained and specialist psychologist to truly identify the full range of such consumer emotions – and one can certainly doubt whether such could be achieved in the field. However, Izard (1977) reviews the supposed key questions relating to any study of emotion. She distinguishes between *emotion states* (particular emotion processes of limited duration) and *emotion traits* (the tendency for an individual to experience a particular emotion with frequency in day-to-day life). Additionally, she acknowledges the division of emotions into positive and negative classes – that are either more or less likely to have desirable consequences.

Other than the work of Izard, the psychological literature produced two early empirically based approaches to the description and categorization of emotion and the trick for a consumer behaviourist is to consider their different effects on consumption-related behaviour (tourist behaviour!) First, Plutchik (1980) viewed all emotions as stemming from eight basic emotional *categories* – fear, anger, joy, sadness, disgust, acceptance, expectancy and surprise. The approach does not attempt to determine the underlying cause of emotions – it concentrates on grouping according to similarity. Actually, the positive and negative classes of Izard (1977) were broadly comparable with Plutchik (1980) and included a positive category – interest and joy; a negative category – anger, disgust, contempt, distress, fear, shame and guilt; and a neutral category that in theory can amplify both positive and negative emotional experience – surprise. Second, Mehrabian and Russell (1974) distinguish emotional *dimensions* that all feelings have – pleasure, arousal and dominance (PAD; the level of felt control on a situation) – the so-called PAD paradigm. Each of the dimensions can range from high to low (e.g. high arousal) and each also has a positive and a negative element. This continues to be a popular conception. However, Watson and Spence (2007) outline a third approach, *cognitive appraisals*, which offer a more in-depth way of explaining the nuance of emotions on consumer behaviour. Specifically, cognitive appraisals go beyond dimensions and consider the interpretations that the con-

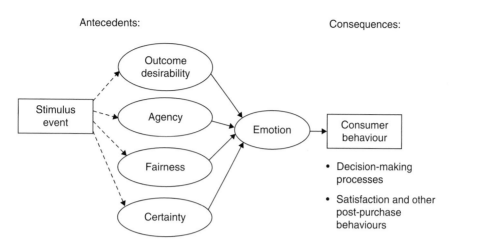

Fig. 10.3. Cognitive appraisal theory. (From Watson and Spence, 2007, p. 503.)

sumer makes of a situation. All consumers construct their own reality all the time. So, Watson and Spence, in a review of literature, show how researchers have demonstrated that different emotions with similar negative and positive valences and levels of arousal can lead to very different consumption-related behaviours.

There are some obvious similarities with the work of Folkes *et al.* (1987) – indeed Watson and Spence (2007; Fig. 10.3) used the work to illustrate the usefulness of the cognitive appraisal approach. Essentially, the consumer (tourist) interprets a stimulus event or situation and arrives at an emotional response by taking into account four elements. The resultant emotional response has an effect on consumer behaviour – including satisfaction and other post-purchase behaviour. The elements are:

- outcome desirability – the initial cognitive appraisal of whether the outcome of a situation is good or bad (positive or negative) with respect to personal well-being;
- agency – who or what had control over the event (oneself, someone else, circumstance);
- fairness – how morally appropriate an event is perceived;
- certainty – the likelihood of a particular event occurring in the future.

Elsewhere, in a crowded and clouded and closely related subject of study, Weiner (1985) makes a connection between studies on attribution and those on emotional response (what Weiner calls 'affective' response). A temporal sequence is proposed leading from thought/cognition (attribution) to affect (emotion) and on to action (behaviour) – a classic tripartite division within psychology. Weiner shows that attributions guide feelings, but that emotional reactions provide the motor and direction for behaviour. Oliver (1989, p. 12) develops these ideas and distinguishes between primary affects such as happiness and sadness that are largely automatic in nature (deriving from the evaluation '[i]s this good or bad for me?') and distinct emotions such as anger and guilt that require attributions.

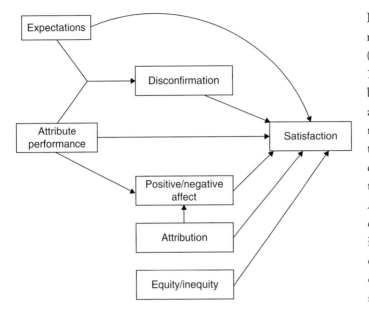

Fig. 10.4. Combined cognitive and affect-augmented CS/D model. (From Oliver, 1993, p. 419.)

In a synthesis of the full range of his ideas, Oliver (1993, pp. 419–420; Fig. 10.4) produced a combined cognitive and affect-augmented CS/D model. Disconfirmation is clearly not the dominant element in the satisfaction equation. Attribute performance can either have a direct influence on satisfaction or be mediated by affect or form part of the classic disconfirmation paradigm. Attribution can have a direct influence on satisfaction and can also be mediated by affect. Equity and inequity have a direct influence on satisfaction. The Oliver model was initially considered in the context of service (course instruction) – although not tourism. As such, it needs to be viewed with care – but its balanced and reasonable construction is an attractive framework for thought.

Mano and Oliver (1993) extend the theoretical and empirical evidence and conclude that

> the satisfaction response is not easily tied down. It does not respond as a pure affect nor does it exist in the absence of feeling. It is apparently a complex human response with both cognitive and affective components.
>
> (Mano and Oliver, 1993, p. 465)

What is clear from the above is that emotions have a key role in the formation of customer satisfaction judgements – and emotions in conjunction with cognitive assessments of a service encounter explain more variance in behaviour than either separately.

So far affect has been used as a synonym for emotion. But affect also includes mood. Gendolla (2000) identifies two assumptions in the literature on mood behaviour – first, it informs cognitive processes such as satisfaction (and other) judgements and, second, individuals seek to maintain a positive mood (pleasure) and repair negative mood (avoid pain). More recently, White (2006) states that little research has focused on the relationship between mood and satisfaction. But his exploratory work on the relationship between mood, emotions, service quality and loyalty is not related to tourism. So, until further research emerges we rely on intuitive considerations that mood is also an intermediary between a stimulus event or situation and a satisfaction judgement.

Tourism managers create products that respond to the overt demand for an emotional experience. At one end of the product spectrum, much of the soft adventure sub-sector of the industry is geared towards the creation of emotional highs – and even fear and anxiety, normally listed as negative emotions, may feature as a 'high' both during and after an experience. At the other side of the spectrum, in a sub-sector such as the hotel business market, there are emotions associated with luxury living – that seek to provide more than a home away from home. All tourist experience is influenced by emotions (and moods) and so understanding the reasons for different emotions and their effect on satisfaction and other judgements – as in cognitive appraisal (Watson and Spence, 2007) – is clearly useful.

Equity

Equity refers to the fairness element in satisfaction. Swan *et al.* (1985), Oliver and DeSarbo (1988), and Oliver and Swan (1989) state that in specific types of purchase transactions, consumers compare the inputs and outputs of salespersons and institutions with their own inputs and outputs. This is the basis of equity theory. In addition a consumer might also compare with another consumer (Fisk and Coney, 1982; Fisk and Young, 1985). The nature of tourism offers considerable scope for interpersonal comparisons – with inputs and outputs not only between a consumer, a salesperson and a firm at the time of a transaction but also a range of other representatives of the firm, customer service personnel, other tourists and the host population.

In Oliver (1993), equity has a direct influence on satisfaction, but the reality is not so clear cut. In Chapter 9, 'In-use Experience' (this volume), equity is seen to interact with all the other antecedent elements (see Figs 9.2 and 9.3) in a case study of satisfaction during a small group, soft adventure tour (Bowen, 2002). Individual tourists on the tour felt that they had been unfairly treated in a number of instances. For example:

- The price paid for the soft adventure tour – last minute discount reduced the price for some clients in the group by 10% and group members found out the variable amounts that each had paid for the same service.
- The inequitable seating arrangements – on the few occasions when public transport was not used and the group travelled in a private mini van. As ever the front seats had the best panorama but were occupied by a person who found it difficult to clamber to the back of the mini van.
- The sleeping arrangements – there was an even number of females in the group but an odd number of males and so with (shared) twin rooms there was a chance for males to organize a room rota so that they had a room to themselves on regular occasions. Some females thought that this was unfair.
- The (supposed) lack of attention that was paid by the tour leader to some members of the group vis-à-vis others.

As any tour leader will tell you, satisfaction can be affected by a sense of fairness or otherwise – among clients and between clients and the tour leader.

SATISFACTION AND OTHER JUDGEMENTS

So tourists juggle all the competing influences together – expectation, performance, disconfirmation, attribution, emotion and equity. Then what? Well, they come to a satisfaction judgement – not necessarily at the end of their experience, as is assumed in so many CSQs (customer service questionnaires), but most probably towards the end of the experience. Not a eureka moment either, but after a culmination of moments, some of which will be eureka moments and many of which will be quite mundane. If listened to, if asked face to face in conversation, they will suggest that they are satisfied (or not satisfied) with or without direct use of the s-word; and they will tick the requisite box on a self-completion questionnaire that says 'yes they are satisfied' (or 'no, they are not satisfied') or that summarizes their relevant level of satisfaction by asking them to offer a score out of 10. Bowen (2002) mapped this whole process. The competing influences interact at micro-moments, sometimes creating a mini-satisfaction judgement, and the mini-judgements add up incrementally until the tourist makes a final satisfaction judgement with a high level of certainty (see Chapter 9, 'In-Use Experience', this volume; Figs 9.2 and 9.3).

Quality, value and satisfaction

In much writing, quality and satisfaction are used interchangeably. However, this is a misinformed approach. Both in management and academic circles the separateness of quality and satisfaction needs to be more deliberate and certain. As Cronin and Taylor (1992, p. 57) state 'this distinction is important to both managers and researchers alike, because service providers need to know whether their objective should be to have consumers who are satisfied with their performance or to deliver the maximum level of perceived quality'. The key lies in analysing what tourists say about satisfaction and quality – and what they do not say. So, for example, while you can draw a judgement from a tourist on the quality of a hotel and restaurant that they have yet to visit, they will not be able to make a satisfaction judgement. Satisfaction is a judgement that necessitates experience of the product – unlike quality. Satisfaction, too, is really more of a consumer judgement than quality that is, by contrast, a management judgement on objective attributes such as room standard in a hotel, temperature control in an aircraft, service promptness in a restaurant and so forth. Satisfaction also has a key emotional component – while quality is a cognitive judgement only, confined to those attributes. In their study of satisfaction and recreational scuba diving, MacCarthy et al. (2006) provide some true insights from the deep. Apart from technical aspects of service quality ('What has been provided?') and functional aspects of service quality ('How has the service been provided?') – pithy summary questions suggested by Gronroos (1990) – MacCarthy et al. (2006) suggest that there are a myriad of experiential and subjective elements that determine diver satisfaction. Service quality is important but satisfaction is a separate and higher-order judgement compared to the technical and functional elements of service quality. So, 'experiential and subjective elements' go way beyond what the tourist judgement is as regards the hire equipment, the boat and fittings, the shop layout, the souvenirs and photos of previous dives, as regards the safety and operator experience. Experiential satisfaction is derived from water clarity; type, colour and variety of marine life and/or presence of rare species; mutual trust and support; staff rapport, camaraderie and conversational banter – and many other elements. Not enough elements for us to give up and assume that satisfaction is uncontrollable – but enough to suggest that the determination of satisfaction requires a broad rather than a narrow focus.

Value is another judgement and most now argue that it is as distinct from satisfaction as quality. Gallarza and Saura (2006, p. 438) in a review make an *initial* claim that while 'service quality and satisfaction have been dominating constructs since the very earliest studies of tourism marketing…in recent years it has been recognised that consumer behaviour is better understood when analysed through perceived value'. Gallarza and Saura explain the thought behind their claim but after an empirical study eventually conclude that the quality–value–satisfaction (and loyalty) chain holds more or less intact. That is, quality and value and satisfaction are all separate judgements but quality and value are antecedents to satisfaction.

Satisfaction and loyalty

But what happens next? What is the stage beyond satisfaction? Much of the work on loyalty in the service industry tries to outline connections between customer satisfaction and customer loyalty – and profitability. The common belief among academics is that satisfied consumers do not always become loyal ones. Indeed, Fuller and Matzler (2008, p. 116) in their review suggest that 'some empirical studies (find) that the loyalty curve is relatively flat within the zone of satisfaction (fulfilment of expectations)'. However, Javalgi and Moberg (1997) claim that developing satisfaction is crucial in building loyalty; Dube and Renaghan (1999) go so far as to conclude that customer satisfaction leads to customer loyalty; and Fuller and Matzler (2008, p. 16) go on to suggest that loyalty 'climbs rapidly as a result of delight or exceptionally high satisfaction' – although it seems that for 'variety seekers' even the super satisfaction of 'customer delight' might not lead to loyalty.

While the jury may still be out, the suggestion that a satisfied customer can become a loyal one remains as a key motivation behind business or organizational drive for customer satisfaction – because if satisfaction leads to loyalty then a series of benefits supposedly accrue. Indeed, Reichheld (2003) outlines seven financial benefits – continued profits, reduced marketing costs, increased per-customer revenue growth, decreased operating costs, increased referrals, increased price premiums, and provision of competitive advantage. Tepeci (1999) also indicates that costs of serving loyal customers are less because they require less assistance from the staff; and Kandampully and Suhartanto (2000) claim that loyal customers pay more than disloyal customers for the service they receive. On the other hand, Petrick (2004, p. 464) duly raises the possibility that 'repeat visitors spend less, are more price-sensitive, or are a less desirable market than first time visitors'. In an empirical study of cruise passengers, he shows some ambivalent findings. Loyal, attached cruise passengers are indeed more price-sensitive but provide more positive word-of-mouth publicity and show more intention to revisit – while less loyal customers and first timers spend more per passenger per day but are more likely to cause longer-term demand fluctuation. Alegre and Juaneda (2006) find a similar ambivalence in a study of British and German nationals staying in hotels and apartments in the Balearic Islands. Repeat visitors, with better knowledge of price and other destination elements, generally have a lower expenditure in comparison with spending by first timers – in both the country of origin and the destination itself. On the other hand, some exceptions exist – and these are thought to relate to either the search for higher quality or emotional attachment to place.

Jacoby and Chestnut (1978) subdivide loyalty into five types – such as 'brand purchase sequence' (undivided loyalty, divided loyalty, unstable loyalty, irregular sequences of loyalty), 'brand purchase proportion' (one brand, dual brand and triple brand loyalty) and 'brand purchase probability'. So, it immediately seems that loyalty is a relative rather than an absolute concept – loyalty does not require that a consumer purchase only one brand all the time (although that can be the case). Rather the consumer can break a sequence of purchase and can purchase one brand some part of the time and another brand another part of the time. This may not seem to be very loyal behaviour, but then product and service loyalty is not like loyalty to a partner – there is no common agreement, civil partnership or wedding.

Following on from Jacoby and Chestnut (1978), Backman and Crompton (1991) argue that loyalty refers to committed behaviour towards a particular service. They suggest a loyalty typology that evolves from a matrix of behaviour and attitudes. 'High loyalty' refers to a strong psychological attachment as well as high use intensity. 'Spurious loyalty' is high use intensity but a low psychological attachment. 'Latent loyalty' is low use intensity but a low psychological attachment. A simple behavioural approach, it is argued, does not distinguish between 'high loyalty' and 'spurious loyalty' – those who really are loyal and those who simply buy because of time convenience, monetary reward, lack of substitutes or lack of information on substitutes. But the introduction of 'attitudinal loyalty' does make such a distinction. And in order to be truly loyal a customer must both purchase (and so show behavioural loyalty) and have a positive attitude towards the purchase (attitudinal loyalty).

The concept of loyalty is not new in marketing – some trace its origin back to the 1920s. On the other hand, its application to tourism – and especially some fields such as destination loyalty – has not been extensively explored before or since (Oppermann, 2000). In his discussion, Oppermann identifies a number of issues and obstacles to the study of loyalty in tourism and, therefore, the meaning of the term 'loyal tourist'. These are worth consideration, especially with regard to destination loyalty – a particularly difficult case. First a destination is a composite product, a system. So how do we classify a tourist who is loyal to one part of the product but not another? Second, what length of time, between one purchase and another, identifies the loyal tourist – less than a year or more than a year or more than several years? What is the cut-off? Third, what about multi-purpose trips – trips that are for both business and leisure? Is a business tourist who returns to a destination on business and engages in tourist activity also a loyal leisure tourist? Fourth, what level of measurement should be taken – the micro (resort)-scale or the macro (regional)-scale? Fifth, is it at all feasible to measure attitudinal loyalty over a long period of time (as might be necessary) – or would it be better to just measure behaviour? Finally, do situational constraints – the influence of time, cost and opportunity – have a particularly strong influence?

SATISFACTION – NOT ENOUGH

There is a paradox in any academic- or industry-based discussion on satisfaction. Namely, the tourist wants more than 'satisfaction'. Satisfaction does not fulfil a dream or fantasy. Although satisfaction is one of the Holy Grails of consumer behaviour studies – notwithstanding some discussion of 'delight' (Rust and Oliver, 2000) and 'excitement factors' (Fuller and Matzler, 2008) – in ordinary parlance 'satisfaction' is not an especially high aspiration. This might go some way to explaining both high tourist 'satisfaction' scores and, sometimes, management complacency. The authors well remember an interview with a managing director of a tour operator group who was making a defence against a specific report of substandard tourist experience at a Spanish hotel:

> Well you say that people were complaining that the hotel looked out over a building site ... that the beds were uncomfortable (and not fire resistant) ... and that the kitchen and bathroom facilities were inadequate. But over the season the hotel achieved a satisfaction rating of 3.7 (out of 7). People were not dissatisfied or very satisfied – they were just average satisfied (!)

Despite the voluminous academic writings on the subject of satisfaction and the industry obsession with satisfaction scores, perhaps it is time to think more closely about what 'satisfaction' means in day-to-day conversation (something that is 'OK') – and figure out another more suitable term to capture what tourists truly seek.

REFERENCES

Alegre, J. and Juaneda, C. (2006) Destination loyalty: consumers economic behaviour. *Annals of Tourism Research* 33(3), 684–706.

Arnould, E.J. and Price, L. (1993) River magic: extraordinary experience and the extended service encounter. *Journal of Consumer Research* 20, 24–45.

Backman, S.J. and Crompton, J.L. (1991) Using loyalty matrix to differentiate between high, spurious, latent and loyal participants in two leisure services. *Journal of Park and Recreation Administration* 9(1), 1–17.

Bartikowski, B. and Llosa, S. (2004) Customer satisfaction measurement: comparing four methods of attribute categorisations. *Service Industries Journal* 24 (4), 67–82.

Baumgarten, J.-C. (2003) WTTC China policy recommendations. *WTTC* 13 October 2003.

Botterill, D.T. (1987) Dissatisfaction with a construction of satisfaction. *Annals of Tourism Research* 14, 139–140.

Bowen, D. (2002) Research through participant observation in tourism: a creative solution to the measurement of consumer satisfaction and dissatisfaction among tourists. *Journal of Travel Research* 41(1), August 4–14.

Brehmer, B. (1980) In one word: not from experience. *Acta Psychologica* 45, 223–241.

Brown, J. and Weiner, B. (1984) Affective consequences of ability versus effort ascriptions. *Journal of Education Psychology* 76 (1), 148–158.

Cronin, J.J. and Taylor, S.A. (1992) Measuring service quality: a re-examination and extension. *Journal of Marketing* 56(3), 55–68.

Curren, M.T. and Folkes, V.S. (1987) Attributional influences on consumers' desires to communicate about products. *Psychology and Marketing* 4 (Spring), 31–45.

Dube, L. and Renaghan, L.M. (1999) Building customer loyalty. *The Cornell Hotel and Restaurant Administration Quarterly* 40, 14–27.

Fisk, R.P. and Coney, K.A. (1982) Post-choice evaluation: an equity theory analysis of consumer satisfaction/dissatisfaction with service choices. In: Hunt H.K. (ed.) *Conceptual and Empirical Contributions to Consumer Satisfaction and Complaining Behaviour*. Indiana University, Indiana, pp. 9–16.

Fisk, R.P. and Young, C.E. (1985) Disconfirmation of equity expectations: effects of consumer satisfaction with services. *Advances in Consumer Research* 12, 340–345.

Folkes, V.S. (1984) Consumer reactions to product failure: an attributional approach. *Journal of Consumer Research* 10, 398–409.

Folkes, V.S. (1988) Recent attribution research in consumer behavior: a review and new directions. *Journal of Consumer Research* 14, 548–563.

Folkes, V.S., Koletsky, S. and Graham, J.L. (1987) A field study of causal influences and consumer reaction: the view from the airport. *Journal of Consumer Research* 13, 534–539.

Francken, D.A. and van Raaij, F.A. (1981) Satisfaction with leisure time activities. *Journal of Leisure Research* 13, 337–352.

Fuller, J. and Matzler, K. (2008) Customer delight and market segmentation: an application of the three-factor theory of customer satisfaction on lifestyle groups. *Tourism Management* 29, 116–126.

Gallarza, M.G. an d Saura, I.G. (2006) Value dimensions, perceived value, satisfaction and loyalty: an investigation of university students' travel behaviour. *Tourism Management* 27(3), 437–452.

Gendolla, G. (2000) On the impact of mood on behaviour: an integrative theory and review. *Review of General Psychology* 4(4), 378–408.

Gronroos, C. (1990) *Service Management and Marketing: Managing the Moments of Truth in Service Competition*. Lexington Books, Lexington, Massachusetts.

Heider, F. (1958) *The Psychology of Interpersonal Relations*. Wiley, New York.

Helson, H. (1964) *Adaptation-level Theory*. Harper and Row, London.

Hoch, S.J. and Deighton, J. (1989) Managing what consumers learn from experience. *Journal of Marketing* 53, 1–20.

Izard, C.E. (1977) *Human Emotions*. Plenum Press, New York.

Jacoby, J. and Chestnut, R. (1978) *Brand Loyalty Measurement and Management*. Wiley, New York.

Javalgi, R.G. and Moberg, C.R. (1997) Service loyalty: implications for service providers. *The Journal of Services Marketing* 11(3), 165–179.

Kandampully, J. and Suhartanto, D. (2000) Customer loyalty in the hotel industry: the role of customer satisfaction and image. *Journal of Contemporary Hospitality Management* 12(6), 346–351.

Kelley, H.H. and Michela, J.L. (1980) Attribution theory and research. *Annual Review of Psychology* 30, 457–501.

Kelley, H.H. and Thibaut, J.W. (1978) *Interpersonal Relations*. Wiley, New York.

La Tour, S.A. and Peat, N.C. (1979) Conceptual and methodological issues in consumer satisfaction research. *Advances in Consumer Research* 6, 431–437.

MacCarthy, M., O'Neill, M. and Williams, P. (2006) Customer satisfaction and scuba diving: some insights from the deep. *Service Industries Journal* 26 (5), 537–555.

Mano, H. and Oliver, R.L. (1993) Assessing the dimensionality and structure of the consumption experience: evaluation, feeling, and satisfaction. *Journal of Consumer Research* 20, 451–466.

Mazursky, D. (1989) Past experience and future tourism decisions. *Annals of Tourism Research* 16, 333–344.

Mehrabian, A. and Russell, J.A. (1974) *An Approach to Environmental Psychology*. MIT Press, Cambridge, Massachusetts.

Middleton, V.T.C. and Lickorish, L.J. (2005) *British Tourism: The Remarkable Story of Growth*. Butterworth-Heinemann, Oxford.

Miller, J.A. (1977) Studying satisfaction, modifying models, eliciting expectations, posing problems, and making meaningful measurements. In: Hunt, H.K. (ed.) *Conceptualisation and Measurement of Consumer Satisfaction and Dissatisfaction*. Market Science Institute, Cambridge, Massachusetts.

Olander, F. (1977) *Consumer Satisfaction: A Sceptics View*. Institut Markedsokonomi, Aarhus, Denmark.

Oliver, R. (1993) Cognitive, affective, and attribute bases of the satisfaction response. *Journal of Consumer Research* 20, 418–430.

Oliver, R.L. (1977) Effect of expectation and disconfirmation on post-exposure product evaluations: an alternative interpretation. *Journal of Applied Psychology* 62 (4), 480–486.

Oliver, R.L. (1980) A cognitive model of the antecedents and consequences of satisfaction decisions. *Journal of Marketing Research* XVII, 460–469.

Oliver, R.L. (1989) Processing of the satisfaction response in consumption: a suggested framework and research propositions. *CS/D&CB* 2, 1–16.

Oliver, R.L. and DeSarbo, W.S. (1988) Response determinants in satisfaction judgements. *Journal of Consumer Research* 14, 495–507.

Oliver, R.L. and Swan, J.E. (1989) Consumer perceptions of interpersonal equity and satisfaction in transactions: a field survey approach. *Journal of Marketing* 53, 21–35.

Oppermann, M. (2000) Tourism destination loyalty. *Journal of Travel Research* 39 (1), 78–84.

Parasuraman, A. (1995) Measuring and monitoring service quality. In: Glynn, W.J. and Barnes, J.G. (eds) *Understanding Services Management*. Wiley, Chichester, UK, pp. 143–177.

Pearce, P. (1982) *The Social Psychology of Tourist Behaviour*. Butterworth-Heinemann, Oxford.

Pearce, P.L. and Lee, U.-I. (2005) Developing the travel career approach to tourist motivation. *Journal of Travel Research* 43 (February), 226–237.

Petrick, J.F. (2004) Are loyal visitors desired visitors? *Tourism Management* 25, 463–470.

Plutchik, R. (1980) *Emotion: A Psychoevolutionary Synthesis*. Harper Row, New York.

Reichheld, F.F. (2003) *Loyalty Rules: How Today's Leaders Build Lasting Relationships*. Harvard Business School Press, Cambridge, Massachusetts.

Rodriquez del Bosque, I.A., San Martin, H. and Collado, J. (2006) The role of expectations in the consumer satisfaction formation process: empirical evidence in the travel agency sector. *Tourism Management* 27, 410–419.

Rust, R.T. and Oliver, R.L. (2000) Should we delight the customer? *Journal of the Academy of Marketing Science* 28(1), 86–94.

Swan, J., Sawyer, J.C., Van Matre, J.G. and McGee, G.W. (1985), Deepening the understanding of hospital patient satisfaction: fulfilment and equity effects. *Journal of Health Care Marketing* 5(3), 7–15.

Tepeci, M. (1999) Increasing brand loyalty in the hospitality industry. *Journal of Contemporary Hospitality Management* 11(5), 223–230.

Thibaut, J.W. and Kelley, H.H. (1959) *The Social Psychology of Groups*. Wiley, New York.

Watson, L. and Spence, M.T. (2007) Causes and consequences of emotions on consumer behaviour: a review and integrative cognitive appraisal theory. *European Journal of Marketing* 41(5/6), 487–511.

Weiner, B. (1980) *Human Motivation*. Holt, Rinehart and Winston, New York.

Weiner, B. (1985) An attributional theory of achievement motivation and emotion. *Psychological Review* 92 (4), 548–573.

Weiner, B., Graham, S. and Chandler, C. (1982) Pity, anger and guilt: an attributional analysis. *Personality and Social Psychology Bulletin* 8, 226–232.

White, C.J. (2006) Towards an understanding of the relationship between moods, emotions, service quality and customer loyalty intentions. *Service Industries Journal* 26(8).

Yuksel, A. and Yuksel, F. (2001) Comparative performance analysis: tourists' perception of Turkey relative to other tourist destinations. *Journal of Vacation Marketing* 7(4), 333–355.

1. Travel career

The ladder has been equated to the development of a person's tourist career. This ladder in the Swiss Alps has plenty of rungs – apt for the experienced vacationer. But in reality, is the travel career as rigid in form?

2. Red Capitalism Café

The *Red Capitalism Café* in Yangshuo near Guilin, China, can be thought of as a symbol of an emerging tourist nation – even one as diverse as China. It offers a nod to a communist past even though the emphasis in Yangshuo is much more on the capitalist future.

3. Tourist system

We are used to the idea of travelling from A to B on the railway system. Leiper (2004) applies the system idea to tourists and tourism. Tourists move from 'traveller-generating regions' to 'tourist destination regions' – through a 'transit route region' that supports opposing flows of departing travellers and returning travellers.

4. Reflections of reality

Tourist behaviour models reflect key variables – but tourist behaviour is complex and the variables do not run straight. The merging of theory from all quarters might lead to the creation of more hybrid and more complete models in the future.

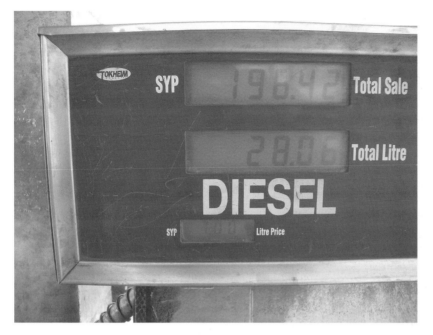

5. Gas stop

A short stop in the world of economics makes it clear just how strong the influence of a rise and fall in price is on tourists.

6. Home away from home

Even when tourists are 'away' they remain in contact with home through mobiles and low-cost telephones, Internet cafes or portable computers. Tourists can immediately chart what they have done – and send a photo image – so that they stay connected to their friends, contacts and family.

7. Authentic experience

The tourism industry turns culture into a commodity that is packaged and sold to the tourists. This floating market in Thailand is a favourite for tourists on the lookout for a trip within reach of Bangkok. But MacCannell (1976) argues that the search for authenticity fails and that the tourist is treated to a contrived and artificial 'staged authenticity'. However, the floating market still feels authentic enough to most tourists.

8. Organic image

'Organic images' (Gunn, 1972) reflect deep memory, associations and imaginations formed from naive non-tourist information. The year-round rain in the UK – and other particular weather types elsewhere in the world – can form a powerful and sometimes negative organic image.

9. Social network lens

With the growth of social networks – that link otherwise unknown hosts and guests – the image of a place is reflected through the lens of the locals. The tourist can get to see the non-tourist product – the backstreet restaurant, the up-and-coming music venues – and get an insider perspective.

10. Poster power

Sometimes decision making is not especially planned, particularly among individual tourists or tourists in small, non-tour groups. A quick glance at a poster, or some other chance occurrence, forces a decision.

11. Tale of the unexpected

'Anticipations' (Botterill, 1987) are often an inadequate predictor of events in a vacation. Unpredictability lies at the heart of the tourist experience – like watching this group of Australian children as they learn how to be lifeguards.

12. Tourist loyalty: a conundrum

There are issues and obstacles to the study of the loyal tourist. You may not walk through these arches in a favourite city more than once or twice a decade – when you return for a short weekend. But you may seek out other historic cities when you have a chance to travel for leisure or business. So are you loyal to your favourite city? And/ or are you loyal in a general sense to historic city tourism?

13. Family decisions

Style of parenting affects the sort of influence children are likely to have in any family vacation decision process – like whether to stay in this Australian guest house with a swing and trampoline or move on to another guesthouse! Early socialization in the family can influence later tourist decision making as an adult.

14. Fear is the key

Different tourists have different fears and perceptions of risk. A slow-moving pleasure ride with views of London is something to be avoided for those with a fear of heights.

15. Footprint in the sand

The ultimate question for tourists is whether the best contribution they can make to sustainable development is to stay at home – a step beyond leaving nothing but footprints. The most socially and environmentally aware tourist may inadvertently act as an 'early warning system' for an alert tour operator – on the look out for the next development opportunity.

REFERENCES

Botterill, D.T. (1987) Dissatisfaction with a construction of satisfaction. *Annals of Tourism Research* 14, 139–140.
Gunn, C. (1972) *Vacationscape. Designing Tourist Regions.* Taylor & Francis, Washington, DC.
Leiper, N. (2004) *Tourism Management* 3rd edn. Pearson Education, NSW, Australia.
MacCannell, D. (1976) *The Tourist: A New Theory of the Leisure Class.* Schocken, New York.

chapter 11

THE POWER OF BRAND AND CELEBRITY

The authors of this book live and work in Oxford, England, and it is with Oxford as an example that we begin this chapter. Oxford as a destination for tourists offers attractions (colleges, river, botanic gardens, museums, etc.), activities (punting on the river, walking tours and sightseeing buses, ice skating, cycling, rickshaws, theatre, etc.), accommodation (hotels, guesthouses, self-catering, backpackers, etc.), services (tourist information, currency exchange, bicycle hire, etc.) and hospitality (restaurants, pubs, bars and cafes, clubs, etc.).

Yet this listing of what is actually there in Oxford does not quite capture the essence of the city for tourists. For Oxford is the city of Roger Bannister and the 4 min mile, the university of scholars such as Francis Bacon and the scientists Hooke and Boyle, the educator of world leaders such as Bill Clinton and Margaret Thatcher, the literary city of Lewis Carroll and his Alice, of Tolkien and his hobbits, of Colin Dexter and his Inspector Morse (guidebook available on Morse's Oxford), of Philip Pullman and his heroine Lara (guidebook also available) and many other guises. It is a rich concoction of what is actually there and what tourists perceive to be there – a melting pot of a place's history, its people and their creativity – part fact, part legend, part fiction, part tourist dream and fantasy. Therefore, different tourists will have different images of Oxford – their Oxford – and to rely on the one-size-fits-all 'City of Dreaming Spires' even for first-time visitors is an oversimplification.

Images are the building blocks of brands and brands are specifically engineered and managed to influence our purchase decisions and buyer behaviour. Oxford, we would argue, is a destination brand. It may require more cooperation and negotiation between interested parties than in the case of a commercial sector brand, but it conjures up a distinctive image with meaning for the consumer beyond the mere physicality of its presence. Brands exist in every sub-sector of the tourism industry, although indeed they may only make up a handful in terms of the numbers of suppliers available.

We are going to delve into some of the theory of branding as applied to tourism to see what we can understand about our tourist behaviour. Then by taking the idea of branding across to humans – the 'human brands' – we will examine what we can learn about the influence of modern-day celebrity on our holiday-taking habits. We also offer an offshoot of celebrity in the form of the film tourist or the 'set-jetter'.

THE POWER OF THE BRAND

What do we mean by a brand? We hope even from the introduction that we have established that any brand is much more than just a product with a logo attached. A true brand exists as a collection of enduring intangible values in the mind of the consumer (Southgate, 1994). It has been imaginatively expressed by a branding practitioner as 'the intangible values created by a badge of reassurance' (Feldwick, 1996, p. 86). A strong brand has a history and a personality, and it has meaning for the consumer that is triggered by the use of the logo, slogan or some other brand property (e.g. the distinctive orange colour of the Easy group so that you can swiftly identify its aircraft or hire cars).

There are a number of reasons (Clarke, 2000) as to why strong branding might be particularly useful in tourism:

- Tourism is generally, though not exclusively, a complex, high-involvement product, so that strong brands can help simplify the individual consumer's purchase decision. It narrows the choice set and uses the brand property as a trigger to access information about the company and product previously absorbed by the buyer – thus shortening the usual extensive information search associated with a complex product. In short, a strong brand can provide a time-saving device during decision making.
- Strong brands can assist in countering the effects of intangibility, from the basic prompt of a tangible logo at the point of sale, through post-purchase anxiety, to the creation of a set of values in the potential holidaymaker's mind. Buyer familiarity with the brand's physical attributes and symbolic meaning offsets intangibility, particularly if reinforced by positive previous experience of the brand.
- In a sector vulnerable to variability of tourist experience due to its reliance on the quantity and quality of human contact, strong brands convey consistency across multiple outlets and across time – reassuring potential holidaymakers that standards encountered will meet their expectations (and that the company takes implicit responsibility embedded in the brand to rectify any possible shortfall).
- Strong brands are valuable as a risk-reducing mechanism. In particular, from the consumer's perspective, misspent time through a poor holiday decision cannot be replaced; the 2-day or 2-week leave period is forfeited. So, alongside the performance risk (failure in the product itself), social risk (as a group experience reliant on the behaviour of others), psychological risk (to an individual's self-concept or self-identity) and economic risk

(which, as with other products, can be redressed to some extent), branding can reduce the temporal risk associated with the purchase of a perishable product. It can help ensure that the consumer's limited resource of time is used in the best possible way.

- Strong brands facilitate precise segmentation. Given the inseparable nature of tourism and the resultant desirability of segment compatibility both spatially and temporally, branding contributes to the task of enhancing tourist satisfaction. A strong youth tour operator brand like Club 18–30 in the UK attracts only those in the right demographic and lifestyle group, simultaneously repelling those falling outside the profile (over thirties; married couples, young families and so forth), thereby enhancing the brand's image – a virtuous circle.

- Strong brands provide a focus for the integration of producer effort, helping different employees to work towards the same outcomes. With a high-contact service such as tourism, motivation and teamwork have a high priority both for the single company and for the destination brand.

- Strong brands provide their owners with a powerful strategic weapon for expansion into other sectors, either within tourism or externally in other sectors. The Virgin Group uses the values of the Virgin brand to enter new sectors and compete with existing suppliers. In stretching its brand in this way, the Virgin Group never allows their brand to be associated only with one product category.

The global advertising agency Saatchi & Saatchi and CEO Kevin Roberts refer to extremely strong brands as *lovemarks*, or super-evolved brands that they claim engage consumers through deep emotional connections. Such brands, according to Saatchi & Saatchi, are infused with a sense of mystery, sensuality and intimacy (Roberts, 2004). This idea of moving beyond brands to the 'lovemark' is not without its detractors; it must be remembered that the commercial world of communication is cut-throat and that Saatchi & Saatchi seek to differentiate themselves on their creative thinking. However, far from attaining 'lovemark' status, not all brands in travel and tourism have yet evolved to become strong brands. For example, there are large tour operator brands that have excellent awareness among their potential consumers, but whose names trigger virtually no meaning, values or brand personality in consumer minds. At the end of the 1990s, the Marketing Director of the giant tour operator, Airtours, declared that

> we commissioned research and found that while consumer recognition of our name was generally high, the brand had no meaning…in other words, our performance on brand emotion was miserable.

> (Rogers, 1998, p. 17)

As authors, we would argue that there are still examples of travel and tourism brands today that find themselves in a similar position, namely with high awareness of their brand names but little in terms of a distinctive personality and meaning for the consumers that they are trying to attract.

Tourism brands as functional, emotional and expressive devices

Tourism brands deliver a carefully crafted set of benefits to the consumer or holidaymaker. Some of these benefits are functional or performance benefits. For example, all part and parcel of a cruise brand is the convenience of online booking, the notion of value for money as against the price paid, the reliability of departure and arrival times, the atmosphere created by the decor and lighting, the quality of the food and drink, the attractiveness of the on-shore excursions, the comfort and layout of the cabins, and the quantity and quality of on-board facilities and entertainment. Other benefits are of the emotional kind – how does the brand make you feel as a consumer? Relaxed? Pampered? Energized? Emotionally close to your partner or family? Important? Successful? The third type of benefit are expressive, symbolic or representational (De Chernatony and McDonald, 1992, 2003), where consumers use brands as symbolic devices or as non-verbal communication tools. A consumer uses a brand high in selected representional benefits to help ease social interaction, to convey something about themselves to other people, or to glean information about the people or social environment surrounding them. People use representational brands to appeal to their aspirational reference groups, reinforce a given lifestyle and enhance their self-image. A glimpse of a Rolex watch, the choice of a designer dress, shoes or handbag – these brands flash unmistakable signals to others about the personality and supposed 'tribe' of the brand user. These expressive brands have high social visibility, for the products are used in public (we do not see the same person under the shower, brushing their teeth and so forth). This combination of representation with strong visibility is a natural one; such a brand cannot perform if there is no desired audience to witness its consumption and absorb its messages. The types of benefits – functional, emotional and expressive – are illustrated in Fig. 11.1.

We can transport this visibility feature across from physical goods to tourism and leisure, and apply the same principle because it is still all about visible consumption (Clarke, 2000). The tourism brands you choose relay information about your identity to others. Which bars, restaurants and nightspots send out the right messages to people? After all, others see you as you enjoy your food or drink or music. When on holiday, how often do you accept or reject a particular place based on a quick sighting of the people you see inside? A restaurant with the wrong (dissociative) or right (associative) sort of person – be they tourists or local residents – already seated? What do other people believe they know about you from your choice of beach resort or cruise ship or hotel brand? Where is the aspirational or in-crowd holidaying this year? The World Tourism Organization (WTO) refers to the future of the tourism destination as a *fashion accessory* (World Tourism Organization, 1997, p. 28), stating that it is probable that

> the next century [21st century] will mark the emergence of tourism destinations as a fashion accessory. The choice of holiday destination will help define the identity of the traveller and, in an increasingly homogenous world, set him apart from the hordes of other tourists.
>
> (Luhrman, 1998, p. 13).

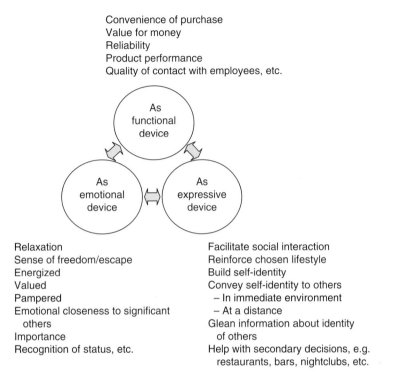

Convenience of purchase
Value for money
Reliability
Product performance
Quality of contact with employees, etc.

As functional device

As emotional device

As expressive device

Relaxation
Sense of freedom/escape
Energized
Valued
Pampered
Emotional closeness to significant
   others
Importance
Recognition of status, etc.

Facilitate social interaction
Reinforce chosen lifestyle
Build self-identity
Convey self-identity to others
   – In immediate environment
   – At a distance
Glean information about identity
   of others
Help with secondary decisions, e.g.
   restaurants, bars, nightclubs, etc.

Fig. 11.1. How consumers use tourism brands.

In other words, your choice of destination makes a statement about your identity to other people, just as your choice of shoes, jewellery or handbags announces you (whether you like it or not, or are the least part concerned) to a room of people. Interestingly, fashion accessories by their very nature are subject to frequent change, and so the analogy imparts a certain ephemeral quality to destination preference.

Of course, as well as signalling things about yourself to those in the immediate vicinity who witness your use of a particular tourism brand, you can send messages to others at a distance too. For example, you can extend the visibility of your holiday destination choice through the logo-emblazoned merchandise that you buy, the postcards with the implicit 'wish-you-were-here' messages that you send to those back home, the photographs and digital film clips that you take for later display, and the handicrafts, typical souvenirs and presents that you accumulate – with each one selected for its association with the destination. All such tourist behaviours publicize to a wider audience your use of a particular holiday destination or tourism brand (Clarke, 2000).

Nation brands and tourist behaviour

There is some fascinating and ongoing work called the Anholt Nation Brands Index that seeks to analyse the ranking of the world's country brands. It measures the power and appeal of a nation's brand image across six dimensions – exports, people, governance, culture and heritage, immigration and investment, and tourism (Anholt Nation Brands Index, 2005). Four times a year, the Index polls the opinions of 25,000 people from round the world on their perceptions of over 35 different countries. It is a research service that destination management organizations such as national tourist organizations buy into for more detailed reports, so that they can pinpoint changes in existing or emerging tourist markets and adjust their marketing activities accordingly. The web site (www.nationbrandindex.com) gives access to an interesting picture of how the residents of different countries round the world perceive the tourism appeal of their own and other countries. The self-confidence of a country's own citizens is indicated in the way they perceive their own nation brand.

Using the data from the tourism 'hexagon' point only (Anholt Nation Brands Index, first quarter 2007 survey, personal communication), Italy emerges as the world's leading tourism country brand. In terms of actual international arrivals, it is fifth in the world rankings as at 2006 (WTO, 2007). Of course, the Anholt Nation Brands Index is not looking at behaviour but at perceptions of the brand and, as such, is indicative of future potential and aspirations. For example, one of the questions contributing to the overall tourism ranking asks respondents to rate countries for 'most likely to visit if money was no object'. In contrast, the WTO figures map actual behaviour, here in terms of visits or international arrivals. The latest performance of Italy as the top choice for tourism in the Anholt Nation Brands Index is not unexpected. In 2005, for example, Italy was the premier tourism brand for American, Australian, Brazilian, British, French, German and Japanese citizens (Anholt Nation Brands Index, 2005).

Following Italy in the Anholt Nation Brands Index ranking is France in second place, then Spain, Egypt, Australia, UK, Canada, Switzerland, New Zealand and then Japan ranked tenth (Anholt Nation Brands Index, first quarter 2007 survey, personal communication). Of these nine (for we have already considered Italy), only France, Spain and the UK are in the top ten in terms of international tourist arrivals, with France at one, Spain at two and the UK at sixth (WTO, 2007). Earlier findings show Egypt to be a particularly strong tourism brand for Chinese citizens (Anholt Nation Brands Index, 2005). With the predicted growth in outbound Chinese tourism and other things being equal, we might expect Egypt to move up the WTO rankings for international tourist arrivals in the future, with its success rooted in this expression of brand attractiveness.

THE POWER OF THE CELEBRITY

The holiday and the celebrity are a natural combination in our contemporary consumer society. Alongside the USA, it might be argued that the UK presents an extreme case of celebrity culture. Certainly, the travel guide series *Lonely Planet* refers to the UK as *fame-obsessed* when summarizing the characteristics of the British for the benefit of incoming tourists. Other countries may not exhibit this celebrity fascination to the same degree. And not all tourists are influenced by it.[1] The linkage between holiday and celebrity is neatly captured by the UK broadsheet newspaper, *The Observer*, perhaps a touch tongue-in-cheek:

> No one goes on holiday as often, or as visibly, as celebrities. Flamboyant, regular holidaying is a contractual obligation for them. Dangling off yachts, frolicking along white sands, thrifting in little Ibizan marketplaces – it's an integral part of A-list life.
>
> (*The Observer*, 2005)

If our destination choices are a type of 'fashion accessory' (as claimed by the WTO) that say something about us to others – a form of visible consumption – then a case can be made for aligning our holiday choices with selected stars to boost our message and our image.

Celebrities are famous people, or, in the case of some through a more caustic reflection of our society, just famous for being famous. As a society, we avidly soak up celebrity holiday destinations from newspapers, lifestyle magazines, web sites and other media. Thus, an individual's match of ski resort to that of the younger British royals is unlikely to pass unnoticed by their peers (see Fig. 11.2). And in case you believe yourself immune to such celebrity influence in your holiday decisions, a recent study by the Internet travel community site, TripAdvisor, found that 68% of respondents had been to a holiday hotspot known to have celebrity tourists (TripAdvisor, 2006). According to Tourism Australia (2006), the national tourism organization for that country, after the celebrities Nicole Kidman and Keith Urban honeymooned in Bora Bora, the number of visitors to the destination increased markedly. Celebrity power over holiday decisions is interconnected with the tangle of lifestyle choices, reference groups and social aspirations.

A closer scrutiny of Fig. 11.2 shows two main types of celebrity influence, namely the informal type of 'news' telling us the destinations that celebrities visit on holiday – a sort of word of mouth that helps to sell the magazine or paper – and the formal type of promotion when celebrities are deliberately integrated with the marketing campaign of companies or destination management organizations. Those readers with keen eyesight will spot the additional example in the bottom left-hand corner where celebrity influence is engaged to halt the flow of tourists to a destination, rather than to endorse it.

There are many examples of the ways in which tourism companies and destination management organizations use celebrity in their marketing practice. Travel company Thomas Cook (2006) linked celebrity names to destinations in an e-marketing sales promotion in 2006, appealing to recipients to *follow the stars*. The promotion trumpeted that Majorca was the favourite hideaway of Catherine Zeta Jones and Claudia Schiffer, and that Jude Law and Elle Macpherson go to the Spanish island of Ibiza. The Bourne Leisure Group launched a brand in 2005 offering short-break packages

---

[1] Of course, the extent of celebrity influence in travel and tourism decisions can be debated. For example, a short piece by the British paper, *The Telegraph*, cites an online travel company's survey result that only 1% of people claim to have been influenced by a celebrity visitor (*The Telegraph*, 2006). Yet research by nVision on the cult of celebrity declared 'avowed susceptibility to celebrity endorsement is something of a stigma and so the proportion of consumers who admit to it is low' (nVision, 2007, p. 4). Overall we as authors find the phenomenon worth exploring, if perhaps with a touch of devil's advocate.

Fig. 11.2. Celebrity influence – our colourful media.

that combined talks and performances by celebrities with accommodation in country house hotels, thus building celebrity appearance into the actual product for sale. Expedia has released a travel experience theme of Indiana Jones packages that allows adventure-seeking tourists to experience the same sights and places as Indiana Jones in the films. Local celebrities were used by the Puerto Rico Tourism Company in a campaign to boost domestic tourism. The US$1 million campaign 'Ven Celebra tu Isla' (come, celebrate your island) used three celebrities in a series of television, cinema, print and radio advertisements (Guadalupe-Fajardo, 2002). The Dubai Department of Tourism and Commerce Marketing used public relations techniques in treating football star Cristiano Ronaldo to a desert safari and city tour during his stay in 2007 (Iglu Tropical, 2007). In 2004, UK tour operator First Choice sponsored the third series of 'I'm a Celebrity....Get me out of here', a reality television show of a mixed group of celebrities (and therefore someone for everyone in the audience to identify with – supposedly) competing in the Australian jungle. The success of that particular celebrity-based campaign (mirrored elsewhere in many other countries) – rumoured to have cost around £1.25 million and reaching some 11 million television viewers – was recognized in the UK Institute of Practitioners in Advertising (IPA) Effectiveness Awards. This use of celebrity in marketing is not atypical to tourism; it has been suggested that in the UK, one in five of all communication campaigns use celebrities (Erdogan *et al.*, 2001).

How are celebrities chosen for tourism campaigns?
The industry perspective

The use of celebrity endorsement in marketing practice has been much researched, though never – as far as we can ascertain – from a purely travel and tourism perspective. None the less, quite a lot is known about how the advertising industry around the world chooses the best celebrity for a given brand. Figure 11.3 shows the factors commonly agreed as being used by agencies when selecting a celebrity. We will briefly pick up on three different ways that the advertising industry summarizes such information for practical use.

First, the Director General of the Institute of Practitioners in Advertising in the UK explains these ideas through the 'Four Fs'. He talks about the following:

- Fit – how good is the match between a particular celebrity and the product or brand?
- Fame – how well known is a particular celebrity?
- Facets – which of the six areas (customer, sponsorship, employee, owner, placement and testimonial) can a particular celebrity get involved with?
- Finance – how much can the company or brand afford? (Pringle and Binet, 2005).

Second, the FRED acronym as used by the advertising agency Young & Rubicam, an older example based on global research comprising around 30,000 interviews and some 6000 brands. For Young & Rubicam, FRED stands for:

- familiarity – of a particular celebrity for the target audience or group of people;
- relevance – the match between a particular celebrity's image, reputation, values and appearance and the product or brand involved;
- esteem – the personal credibility of a particular celebrity and whether he/she is held in high regard by the target audience;
- differentiation – the distinctiveness of the celebrity against other high-profile people (Miciak and Shanklin, 1994).

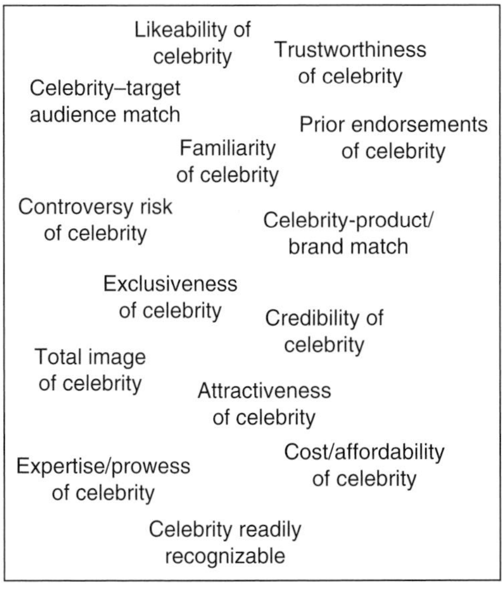

Fig. 11.3. Factors considered by the advertising industry when choosing a celebrity.

Third, the advertising industry may look to the Performer Q score to identify the best celebrity for a particular campaign. Developed in 1963 by an American company, Marketing Evaluations Inc. (www.qscores.com/performer.asp), the Performer Q score measures the familiarity and appeal of a celebrity as calculated from consumer-panel data that assess around 1700 celebrities in different categories (e.g. chefs, models, sports personalities, actors/actresses, reality show participants, etc.). The consumer panel comprises around 1800 consumers – including children and teenagers as well as adults. To arrive at the Performer Q score, a sort of 'recognition' measurement, the percentage of the consumer panel rating the celebrity as 'one of my favourites' is divided by the percentage of the consumer panel who are familiar with the celebrity. Thus, from sample data, if 27% of the consumer panel rate celebrity Brad Pitt as 'one of my favourites', and 91% of the consumer panel claim to be familiar with him, then Brad Pitt is assigned a Performer Q score of 30. An interested company can purchase a detailed breakdown of celebrities so they can best match a particular celebrity to a given target audience and product or brand. A 21st-century alternative to the Performer Q score is the Davie-Brown Index (DBI, www.dbireport.com/home.aspx). This score system of approximately 1500 celebrities was developed by an American company, David Brown Entertainment, and uses Internet-based research to access a consumer panel of 1.5 million. Consumers rate celebrities on eight key attributes – awareness, appeal, aspiration, endorsement, influence, notice, trendsetter and trust. The resulting score is designed to show a celebrity's ability to influence brand affinity and consumer buyer behaviour.

These three examples – the 'Four Fs', FRED, and the recognition scores – demonstrate the advertising industry's effort and investment in selecting celebrities best able to influence our purchase decisions. And that includes our holiday choices. The competitive nature of the industry and the pressure to justify the marketing spend on a tourism campaign prohibits the gratuitous use of just any celebrity. A well-selected celebrity can cut across a number of international markets, and most destinations will target a portfolio of different nationalities in their tourism marketing activities. The examples given here offer some insight into the practitioner's perspective on the problem.

How are celebrities chosen for these tourism campaigns?
The academic perspective

Academics have also examined the problem of how to select celebrities for marketing campaigns more effectively. To balance the three examples from industry, we now outline the three best known models from academia – the 'source credibility model', the 'source attractiveness model' and the 'meaning transfer model'. We top off these models with the briefest consideration of attachment theory. The first two models are referred to as the source models as they share the idea that the characteristics of the celebrity may have a beneficial effect on how the message is received (Erdogan, 1999). It is these two models that we look at first. Parallels can be spotted between these source models and the approaches adopted by practitioners as outlined previously.

The source credibility model, with its roots in the 1950s, proposes that the effectiveness of an advertising message depends on the source or celebrity's perceived credibility with the consumer. The concept of credibility combines the celebrity's particular expertise, knowledge, qualifications and skills (e.g. athletic prowess, fashion savvy, artistic ability and so forth) with the celebrity's trustworthiness or honesty, integrity and believability (Erdogan, 1999; Charbonneau and Garland, 2005) – or at least the consumers' perception of this.

In contrast, the source attractiveness model of McGuire (1985) argues that the effectiveness of an advertising message is reliant on a perceived similarity between the source (or the celebrity) and the receiver (or the tourist), the source likeability in terms of physical appearance and behaviour, and the source familiarity through repeated exposure in the media (Charbonneau and Garland, 2005). In other words, the source attractiveness model rests on the trio of similarity, likeability and familiarity. The core idea is that the celebrities who are known to, liked by and/or are similar to the consumer or tourist are attractive, and therefore persuasive (McCracken, 1989). The tourist accepts the information in the campaign because of a desire to identify with the attractive celebrity presenting it.

The meanings transfer model as formulated by McCracken (1989) lays out a very different explanation for the success of celebrity endorsement. The source models, in McCracken's view, are hindered in their usefulness through failure to recognize that even the most stereotyped celebrity encompasses a rich yet subtle and often contrasting bundle of meanings that simple dimensions and measurement just cannot tap into. Borrowing from the general meanings transfer process, McCracken argues that celebrities are experts in the art of construction of self. That is, they absorb selected meanings from the objects, culture, people, roles and situations that surround them better than the average consumer. Perhaps we could think of them as a 'super-self', as individuals electric with accumulated meaning. For example, Audrey Hepburn delivers iconic elegance, delivering this more powerfully than any elegant but anonymous model. She does so because she has absorbed this meaning through her film roles, photographs, public activities and style status. In McCracken's words, she *owns* her meaning of a particular nuance of elegance. The ordinary consumer or tourist is also looking to construct a sense of self from purchases made, objects owned, and, indeed, holidays taken – but we have to work harder at it. We lack the expertise of the celebrities in doing this, and so rummage around our material world in search of useful meanings with which to adjust our identities in the way we wish. A celebrity-endorsed product, whether physical object, boutique hotel or island destination, offers the consumer a short cut in this process, for a well-chosen celebrity transfers elements from their super-charged bundle of meaning to the product itself – and this transferred meaning can subsequently be reclaimed by the consumer to attach to their own construction of self. As a hypothetical example, Audrey Hepburn would have delivered elegance to any island destination she visited, and facets of that elegance would transfer to the tourist holidaying there, providing they were receptive to absorbing it. Thus, celebrities ease the flow of meaning through our contemporary society. Prised open by McCracken, celebrity power is exerted because

> working together, individualism and alienation have conspired to give individuals new freedom to define matters of gender, class, age, personality, and lifestyle. The freedom to choose is now also an obligation to decide, and this makes us especially eager consumers of the symbolic meanings contained in celebrities and the goods [and services, including tourism] they endorse.
>
> (McCracken, 1989, p. 318. Authors' brackets)

The phenomenon of celebrities and tourist behaviour can also be explored through 'attachment theory', explained under these circumstances as 'intimacy at a distance' (Thomson, 2006). Attachment theory argues that autonomy, relatedness and competence are three fundamental human needs, and that if a celebrity or human brand – even at their relational distance – can respond to these needs, then a strong attachment may develop because of the emotional security delivered to the individual person. The first of these three needs, autonomy, is defined as an individual's need to feel that their activities are self-selected, self-governed and self-endorsed (Thomson, 2006), in other words, that a person feels free from pressure to express themselves and to behave as they wish, with neither constraint nor coercion. Relatedness is defined as an individual's need to feel a sense of closeness or connectedness with others (Thomson, 2006). Finally, competence is defined as an individual's life-long tendency to search for feelings of effectiveness, achievement and challenge in the activities that they undertake. Such mastery enables an individual to see themselves as both skilled and inquisitive in life. The upshot is that you are likely to form a stronger attachment to a celebrity (or human brand) that is responsive to these innate needs. The untested assumption would be that the stronger the attachment, the greater a particular celebrity's influence on your holiday-taking behaviour.

An offshoot: the influence of the film industry on tourist behaviour

An offshoot of this discussion relates to the influence of film celebrities on tourist behaviour. Celebrities are often locked into the world of film and television so that any discussion of the influence of celebrity on our holiday-taking habits invariably draws in the influence of the film industry as well (we first turned to the role of television and film in our consideration of image creation in Chapter 8, 'Logical Decision or Lucky Dip?', this volume). In the main, our examples in this chapter take a Western and often Hollywood perspective. However, 'set-jetting' is not a solely Western phenomenon. Bollywood films are believed to be driving Indians to holiday in foreign destinations. According to Fawkes (2006), New Zealand as a tourism destination became popular with Indian set-jetters following the Bollywood film hit, Kaho na Pyaar hai (Tell me this is love). Some national tourist organizations and regional bodies actively encourage film tourism or screen tourism by producing maps and brochures to highlight the different film locations that a tourist could visit. Others – including cities and larger attractions – might have dedicated film tourism officers whose job it is to boost the number of television series, films and documentaries that are shot in their particular destination, a form of what marketers call 'product placement'. As many tourists like to visit the locations (or purported locations) where their favourite films were shot, bragging rights with regard to set locations can be fierce. Witness the battle in 2007 between the different towns of Springfield in the USA to win the accolade of being *the* Springfield for the first feature length film of the cartoon celebrities, The Simpsons.

Thomson Holidays, the UK outbound tour operator, labels the British set-jetters as 'cinema sightseers', with up to 20% visiting destinations that featured as settings for favourite films at the cinema (Thomson Holidays, 2004). Likewise, VisitBritain claims that a similar 20% of incoming tourists to Britain are inspired to visit by either cinema or television images (Majendie, 2007). The blockbuster films, such as The Beach, Amelie, Lord of the Rings or Captain Correlli's Mandolin (among others), have all become successful, if sometimes controversial, 'virtual holiday brochures' for Phi Phi Le Island in Thailand, Montmartre in Paris, New Zealand and the Greek island of Cephalonia, respectively. According to Thomson Holidays, top film scene locations for the British include the cafe in When Harry met Sally, Fifth Avenue, New York in Breakfast at Tiffany's, and Laughing Waters Beach, West Indies, famed as the spot where Ursula Andress comes out of the sea in the James Bond film Dr No (Thomson Holidays, 2004).

Academics have been documenting examples of film and television tourism on tourist numbers for over a decade (e.g. Riley and Van Doren, 1992; Tooke and Baker, 1996; Evans, 1997; Hudson and Ritchie, 2006). So when Alnwick Castle in Northumberland, England, nearly trebles its visitor numbers in 2006, and Christ Church Cathedral in Oxford boosts its revenue by 50% (Majendie, 2007), the influence of the Harry Potter films on tourist statistics is not unexpected. Set-jetting is an established tourist phenomenon.

OF TOURISTS, BRANDS AND CELEBRITIES

In this chapter, we have looked at the influence of brands on your holiday decisions, and whether or not celebrities can sway your tourism choices. The evidence is not incontrovertible – as we acknowledged at the outset – and you may remain unmoved by the suggestion that you personally fall under the spell of either brands or the human brand of the celebrity. But we hope that we have convinced you of its relevance in deciphering the behaviour of some tourists today – even if that tourist is not you. We have introduced more contemporary concepts, such as Saatchi's Lovemark, the Anholt Nation Brands Index and set-jetting associated with film tourism.

Our next chapter is equally colourful, but whereas in this chapter our celebrities belong to more distant reference groups, in the next chapter we look at a much more intimate reference group in our tourist decision making – the family.

REFERENCES

Anholt Nation Brands Index (2005) *How the World Sees the World, 3rd Quarter*. The Anholt Nation Brands Index, UK. Available at: www.nationbrandindex.com

Charbonneau, J. and Garland, R. (2005) Talent, looks or brains? New Zealand advertising practitioners' views of celebrity and athletic endorsers. *Marketing Bulletin* 16, 1–10.

Clarke, J. (2000) Tourism brands: an exploratory study of the brands box model. *Journal of Vacation Marketing* 6(4), 329–345.

De Chernatony, L. and McDonald, M. (1992) *Creating Powerful Brands*. Butterworth-Heinemann, London.

De Chernatony, L. and McDonald, M. (2003) *Creating Powerful Brands*, 3rd edn. Butterworth-Heinemann, London.

Erdogan, B.Z. (1999) Celebrity endorsement: a literature review. *Journal of Marketing Management* 15(4), 291–314.

Erdogan, B.Z., Baker, M.J. and Tagg, S. (2001) Selecting celebrity endorsers: the practitioner's perspective. *Journal of Advertising Research* 41(3), 39–48.

Evans, M. (1997) Plugging into TV tourism. *Insights*, March, D35–D38.

Fawkes, P. (2006) Bollywood driven tourism. Available at: www.psfk.com/2006/07/bollywood_drive.html

Feldwick, P. (1996) What is your brand equity anyway, and how do you measure it? *Journal of the Market Research Society* 38(2), 85–104.

Guadalupe-Fajardo, E. (2002) Local celebrities promote tourism. *Caribbean Business* 30(12), 18.

Hudson, S. and Ritchie, J.R.B. (2006) Film tourism and destination marketing: the case of Captain Corelli's Mandolin. *Journal of Vacation Marketing* 12(3), 256–268.

Iglu Tropical (2007) Tropical holiday news. Ronaldo does Dubai. Available at: www.iglutropical.com/news/article.cfm?artID = 18045613

Luhrman, D. (1998) World tourism. Crystal ball gazing. *Tourism, the Journal of the Tourism Society*, 96, 13.

Majendie, P. (2007) Harry Potter casts spell on location vacations. Available at: www.uk.reuters.com/article/filmNews/idUKL1435592420070615?src=070307_1419

McCracken, G. (1989) Who is the celebrity endorser? Cultural foundations of the endorsement process. *Journal of Consumer Research* 16(3), 310–321.

McGuire, W.J. (1985) Attitudes and attitude change. In: Gardner, L. and Elliot, A. (eds) *Handbook of Social Psychology Volume Two*. Random House, New York, pp. 233–346.

Miciak, A.R. and Shanklin, W.L. (1994) Choosing celebrity endorsers. *Marketing Management* 3(3), 50–59.

nVision (2007) *The Cult of Celebrity. A Review of the Impact of Celebrities on Wider Consumer Behaviour.* nVision, London.

Pringle, H. and Binet, L. (2005) Practice paper. How marketers can use celebrities to sell more effectively. *Journal of Consumer Behaviour* 4(3), 201–214.

Riley, R.W. and Van Doren, C.S. (1992) Movies as tourism promotion. *Tourism Management* 13(3), 267–274.

Roberts, K. (2004) Indoor fireworks. Kevin Roberts' speech at the launch of Lovemarks: The future beyond brands. Available at: www.lovemarks.com/media/speechprint.php?id = 19

Rogers, D. (1998) Travel: sun, sea and brands. *Marketing*, 26 March, 17.

Southgate, P. (1994) *Total Branding by Design: How to Make your Brand's Packaging More Effective.* Kogan Page, London.

The Observer (2005) Follow that star. *The Observer*, 30 January.

The Telegraph (2006) Tired of celebrities. *The Telegraph*, 22 July.

Thomas Cook (2006) Award winning offers to your favourite movie locations. E-marketing sales promotion sent 19 May 2006.

Thomson, M. (2006) Human brands: investigating antecedents to consumers' strong attachments to celebrities. *Journal of Marketing* 70 (July), 104–119.

Thomson Holidays (2004) Sun, sand, sea and cinema. Why Hollywood stars are the new travel agents. Available at: www.lexispr.com/thomson

Tooke, N. and Baker, M. (1996) Seeing is believing: the effect of film on visitor numbers to screened locations. *Tourism Management* 17(2), 87–94.

Tourism Australia (2006) Changing world – changing consumers. Operator opportunities. Available at: www.tourism.australia.com/content/Research/Factsheets/Consumer_Trends_Industry_Handout_Sep_2006.pdf

TripAdvisor (2006) Press release. Travelers reveal likes and dislikes in travel for 2007 in annual TripAdvisor survey. Available at: www.tripadvisor.com/PressCenter-i93-cl-Press_Releases.html

World Tourism Organization (1997) *Tourism 2020 Vision: Executive Summary*. World Tourism Organization, Madrid.

World Tourism Organization (2007) *Tourism Highlights 2007 edition*, United Nations World Tourism Organization, Madrid. Available at: www.unwto.org/facts/menu.html

chapter 12

THE IMPORTANCE OF FAMILY

The family is an important force in tourist consumer behaviour. You only have to think about the number of holidays that are taken together as a family over an individual's lifespan, or the influence that family considerations have on other vacation decisions or even the cumulative effects of family holiday choices on a country's tourism seasonality patterns to see the truth in the statement.

Family tourism can comprise multigenerational trips, where grandparents, parents and children all enjoy the same holiday together. Look at the emphasis given to the family holiday programme as the backbone of the business for many large tour operators, resorts and destination attractions or at the expertise of the family brands such as DisneyLand or LegoLand. The tourism industry has long saluted the family market.

Tourism is not unique in terms of family power in buying decisions. Many marketers for other products and services are moving towards treating the family as what they term a 'single consumption unit', and in doing so, removing the traditional emphasis on the individual. You can see this with particular car brands that have shifted campaign attention from a sole focus on the male head of household to also feature the perspectives of children, or the way in which advertisements for detergent brands in the UK have evolved from the wife next to her washing machine to the outdoor activities of adolescents. As thoughtfully expressed by two Scandinavian academics:

> [M]ost of the current literature in marketing sees consumption as an activity that is mostly motivated by individual and hedonistic concerns. New perspectives on consumer behaviour suggest that other motives, such as care or love for others and meaning creation in everyday life, are very important [motives] in family consumption.
>
> (Kleppe and Gronhaug, 2003, p. 314)

We have already looked at one key family concept in Chapter 3, 'A Life in Travel' (this volume), namely the family life cycle. In this chapter, we continue to build our understanding of

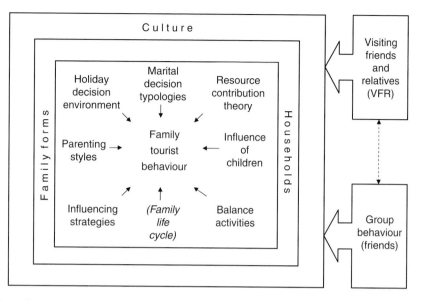

Fig. 12.1. Concepts and ideas used to explain family tourist behaviour.

families and their vacation decisions by exploring some of the other frameworks and concepts associated with family consumption behaviour. These ideas are drawn from generic consumer behaviour, leisure studies, tourist behaviour and from industry bodies with responsibility for 'Visiting Friends and Relatives' (VFR) – a regular hotchpotch of sources but all offering valuable insights. Recognizing the 'Friends' component of VFR, we have extended the chapter into the issues surrounding friendship and travel in groups. After all, statistics in Western countries show that an increasing number of people today are not living in family groups but in single households, and even individuals from family households are known to take non-family holidays with friends. Figure 12.1 is a simple diagram that shows the concepts and ideas that will be introduced to try and make sense of the ways in which families partake in tourism.

In society today, families take different forms. In a humorous take on the family, American poet Ogden Nash describes it as 'a unit composed of a man, a woman, children, an occasional animal, and the common cold' (Jarski, 2004, p. 70), a quirky acknowledgement of the overarching interdependence and sometimes irascible closeness of family members. Please note that the inclusion of the family pet is not entirely to be laughed at, as a family holiday will often involve taking the dog. There are plenty of guides and advisory web sites for choosing pet-friendly holidays.

However, in an official vein, family forms might be usefully classified as:

- nuclear family (composed of parents and offspring) and the extended family (including other relatives);
- family of orientation (the family that a person is born into) and the family of procreation (the family that a person creates with their chosen partner);
- blended or step family (following separation or divorce) and the intact family (that has not experienced such division).

These family forms only take partial account of the single-parent family, cohabiting couples or the complicating factor of child adoption. Is it necessarily accurate to portray the family in today's Western societies as a married couple plus two children? The evidence would suggest that it is not, and, for example, tour operator brochures targeting the family allow a flexible interpretation by potential consumers through favouring photographs of one or other parent carrying out holiday activities with children.

Some definitions of family are close to those of a household, with its task sharing and residential criteria – the idea of living together under one roof. In practice, where marketers consider the family as a 'single consumption unit', it is likely to take the form of a household with family members residing at one address and sharing purchase decisions. However, the family is more accurately defined in terms of kinship and kinship networks – fathers, mothers, offspring, siblings, grandparents, in-laws, aunts, uncles, cousins and any corresponding second, removed and step-counterparts. In most cultures, this implies a spread of relatives across a number of household units and indeed geographic location. It is this spatial dispersion of family members, itself aided by the fluid migration policies of governments and ease of access to efficient transport systems, that partly stimulates the substantial global V(F)R market. For example, the World Travel Market (2007) highlighted 'diaspora tourism' as including heritage tourists who travel back to their origin country to discover their ancestry and culture, and festival tourists who travel back to their origin country for key events and festivals such as Easter, weddings or christenings.

An important point to note, and one that holds true throughout the chapter, is that whatever form the family takes – nuclear, procreation, intact, etc. – the actual translation into family behaviour will be shaped under the influence of culture. For example, a family in Malaysia with its emphasis on collectivism, cooperation and valuing of the group above the individual (Ndubisi and Koo, 2005) is quite distinctive in its characteristics from the individualistic family, say, of the USA. This cocoon of culture wrapped around the family will affect family behaviour in holiday decisions – we fully recognize this, but knowing that we have examined the theory of culture and subculture in Chapter 2, 'Country-File: Tourist Nations' (this volume), we choose here to delve in and explore the family itself.

FAMILY DECISION MAKING

There are a number of theories that help to explain different aspects of families and tourist consumption. We include some better-known concepts that are well established in the tourist behaviour literature, for example, marital decision typologies, but also ideas from other literature sources that have yet to be tested through tourism research but make a useful contribution to understanding family behaviour in a tourism context. It is, after all, quite a complex phenomenon that merits attention from different perspectives.

Marital decision typologies or how couples decide

One of the most explored concepts relating to families in the tourism literature is the idea of marital decision typologies. These typologies set out to categorize the possible options for decision making between husbands and wives, for even a team of two has to have some way of organizing the task. Building on previous work (Herbst, 1954; Davis, 1970) and using research across different product categories including vacations, Davis and Rigaux (1974) identified four types of decision making among husbands and wives, namely:

- Husband-dominant – the husband takes the primary role in decision making.
- Wife-dominant – the wife takes the primary role in decision making.
- Autonomic – the decision is taken by an individual partner independently, sometimes described as solitary or unilateral.
- Syncretic – the decision is made jointly or equally between husband and wife.

Remember this is early research published in the 1970s (Davis and Rigaux, 1974), yet the results identified the vacation decision as syncretic or joint in style – arguably a modern response for some 40 years ago.

This marital decision typology has been pursued within tourism research across different countries. In the USA, early work by Jenkins (1978) examined the 'total' vacation decision plus nine sub-decisions incorporated in the overall decision to travel (e.g. information collection, whether to take children, destination choice, length of stay, mode of transportation, etc.). In measuring the perceptions of both husbands and wives, he found joint decision making to be a very important influence in each of the ten decision areas, and to be the modal type of decision making for five sub-decisions – whether to take children, transportation mode, activities, accommodation selection and destination choice. Jenkin's choice to examine vacation decision making by sub-decisions rather than by the classic decision-making stages was informed by his focus group work, which suggested that couples preferred to think of the task in this manner. In the current century, Litvin *et al.* (2004) revisited Jenkin's idea of breaking down the vacation decision process by sub-decision for marital decision typologies, only this time using data from America (specifically Kansas) and from Singapore. They drew comparisons for seven sub-decisions that they could match with Jenkin's work – information collection, length of stay, vacation budget, destination choice, accommodation, activities and overall vacation decision – and asked for both husband and wife opinions on the matter. The American data showed a dominance of joint decision making in five of the seven areas – the overall vacation decision, length of stay, budget, destination choice and activities. The Singaporean data showed a dominance of joint decision making in six of the seven areas – all but information collection. They concluded that over a generation a significant trend towards joint husband–wife decision making for vacations had emerged.

Although Jenkin's (1978) work is the most often cited, other published research conducted in the late 1970s in Canada (Filiatrault and Ritchie, 1980) suggested rather more joint decision making for vacation decision making than did Jenkin's findings. Filiatrault and Ritchie (1980) assessed 17 vacation sub-decisions from the perspective of both husband and wife.

They found that husbands and wives agreed that ten of the 17 sub-decisions were taken jointly between them. A later Canadian study (Zalatan, 1998) also adopted a vacation sub-decision approach, this time dividing the tasks to be done into four categories – initial trip tasks (e.g. vacation dates, collecting information), financing tasks (e.g. arranging financing, purchasing tickets), pre-departure tasks (e.g. accommodation arrangements, preparing luggage) and destination tasks (to be carried out once at the destination, for example, restaurant choice, sightseeing choices). However, unlike the Filiatrault and Ritchie (1980) study and the Litvin *et al.* study (2004), Zalatan only collected the opinions of the wives. He found that wives were least involved in financial decisions concerning the vacation and most involved in sub-decisions made at the destination.

Switching countries again, a recent study carried out in Taiwan by Wang *et al.* (2004) found that husband and wife joint decisions dominated ten of the 13 sub-decisions made for a group package tour. However, the wife dominated decisions regarding the accommodation, shopping and selection of travel agent. She also appeared to be more active in the information search. Published the same year, an Irish study (Mottiar and Quinn, 2004) concluded that holiday decision making was largely a joint decision between couples that when broken down into stages showed a female dominant role in the early stages of the process – for example, initiating the discussion or searching for information. Using a Malaysian sample, Ndubisi and Koo (2005) linked marital decision typologies and family characteristics to vacation decision making. They found that 'strong cohesive' families (described as showing strong interdependence between members, harmony, altruism and consideration for others) and 'modern' families (described as exhibiting equal division of power between marital partners, short power distance between parents and children, and joint decision making) do indeed make more joint decisions when choosing a holiday than traditional or weakly cohesive families.

After examining the evidence above drawn from the 1970s onwards and from around the world, what can we conclude? If a broad consensus for marital decision roles in tourism can be reached, then a trend of increasing wife influence and a corresponding syncretic decision style musters support (Dimanche and Havitz, 1994; Belch and Willis, 2002; Mottiar and Quinn, 2004; Bronner and de Hoog, 2008). It is the view best recognized in the generic marketing textbooks, where vacations are described as the *most democratic* of a family's purchase decisions (Blackwell *et al.*, 2001, p. 368). Part of the explanation for this may lie with the rise of a companionship ideology or a fostering of togetherness, as the chosen model for modern committed sexual relationships. But perhaps this marital decision typology research into vacation decision making is most useful because it has been firmly structured around the sub-decisions that need to be made. Therefore, its value lies not so much with any congruence in results across the different nationalities, but in the application of a sub-decision structure to a given vacation purchase situation. Individual tourism businesses would be best advised to examine the patterns exhibited by the segments of consumers most important to them. This would entail specific and tailored research to reap the reward of focused understanding of the ways in which husbands and wives tackle the decision-making process.

Introducing the resource contribution theory

One of the most interesting theories that helps to flesh out the marital decision typology is the comparative resource contribution theory of Blood and Wolfe (1960) – a memorable duo if there is a trace of the Goth in you. This theory suggests that comparative resources will determine the balance of power between husband and wife – the resources that each brings to the family purchasing decision. Solomon (2006, p. 433) refers to these resources as *spousal resources*. Such resources include income, education, competence, personal attractiveness and the performance of each in the various roles of homemaker, companion and sexual partner. Some of these resources will fluctuate with time. For example, a wife leaving employment to bring up children may find that her influence in decisions wanes with her loss of financial input. Research using a hospitality scenario found that earning wives had greater influence over a restaurant decision than non-earning wives (Lee and Beatty, 2002). It might be surmised that increasing wife influence and syncretic decision making for vacations correspond to the rise in dual-income families and to the career progression of women in many countries.

The holiday decision environment

The models that seek to explain tourist decision making (as portrayed in Chapter 5, 'Models of Tourist Behaviour', this volume) can seem overly clean and exact, as though precision is an underlying feature of vacation decisions. Some of the generic research in family decision making really highlights the messiness, confusion and perhaps even exhaustion that may surround family vacation decisions in the real world. Vacation decisions are seldom made under perfect conditions. Busy, multitasking parents may feel stressed, fatigued or downright exhausted from the combination of work and the demands of daily family maintenance tasks – perhaps the very stimuli that turn their thoughts to a holiday 'break'. However, there are almost certainly other important decisions to be taken by the family around the same time, for example, moving house, planning an extension to the garage, changing schools for children, what to do for an elderly grandparent, updating the home entertainment system or family car, and so on.

These key decisions all compete for precious decision time, effort and skill – the family holiday is just part of what is termed the 'decision load'. Under such circumstances, perhaps the decision arrived at fits the concept of 'satisficing' – that is, the holiday choice is not perfect but it will do what is required, for example, allow parents to recharge, give the family quality time together or escape from the everyday setting to somewhere special. In other words, the final holiday decision is adequate rather than perfect.

Family parenting styles

Parents adopt particular parenting styles with their children, so that the family has specific characteristics in the way that it communicates and operates as a unit. These styles or types affect offspring involvement and influence in family purchase decisions. Some children play a greater role in decision making than others when the family is making a purchase.

To step back a stage, such parenting styles also play a vital role in consumer socialization, a concept defined by Ward (1980, p. 382) as the 'processes by which young people acquire skills, knowledge, and attitudes relevant to their functioning as consumers in the marketplace'. For tourist consumer behaviour, this translates as how children develop their vacation decision-making abilities – the family unit is a powerful and early learning environment whose influence carries over into adulthood.

In one classification of parenting styles, there are two dimensions that make up the structure (McLeod and Chaffee, 1972; Moore and Moschis, 1981). These two dimensions are labelled as:

- socio-orientation;
- concept-orientation.

A socio-orientation aims to achieve parental deference in the child and to create harmonious relationships within the household. It relies on monitoring and controlling child behaviour with an eye to ensuring social conformity. Children learn to avoid controversy and the risk of offence to others; social acceptance and obedience are paramount. Parents choosing this approach try to control what their children learn as consumers and do not discuss purchase activities with them.

Conversely, a concept-orientation hinges on children forming and expressing their own opinions. Children are exposed to controversy and any resulting personal friction, and are supported by parents in developing consumer competence through open discussion on purchase decisions and by making their own purchase decisions. Some of these purchase decisions may be poor, but parents allow them to happen, as it is all part of the learning process. Perhaps unsurprisingly then, research conducted in Malta by Caruana and Vassallo (2003) found that the children of concept-oriented parents have an influence on purchase decisions, while those of socio-oriented parents do not.

These two dimensions can be developed up into a matrix of family types, depending on whether the family scores high or low on each (Moschis, 1985; Carlson et al., 1992; Rose et al., 1998; Caruana and Vassallo, 2003). The four types are:

- The laissez-faire family that scores low on both socio-orientation and concept-orientation. In this family, there is little communication between parents and children.
- The protective family that scores high on socio-orientation and low on concept-orientation. In this family, parents emphasize child obedience and family harmony.
- The pluralistic family that scores low on socio-orientation and high on concept-orientation. In this family, parents emphasize open discussion and the development of autonomous viewpoints with little parental interference.
- The consensual family that scores high on both socio-orientation and concept-orientation. In this family, parents encourage independent thinking while maintaining overall control.

There are other classifications discussed in the literature. One such work discusses an alternative classification (Carlson *et al.*, 1992) summarized here as:

- authoritarian parents: restrictive, maintain high levels of control over children, favour parental supremacy over children;
- neglecting parents: detached, little parental control, warmth or emotional involvement;
- authoritative parents: balance rights and responsibilities of parents and children, encourage self-expression in children, enrich learning environment with educational opportunities allowing freedom and autonomy within family rules; and
- permissive parents: more lenient than restrictive, remove constraints, may be detached or anxiously involved with children, allow children adult rights without the responsibilities.

The two classifications are in many ways similar. Taking either, you can see that the style of parenting an individual experiences as a child will influence how they develop as consumers of tourism as well as the sort of influence as children they are likely to have in any family vacation decision process.

Influencing strategies in the family decision process

An alternative subheading to this section could have been 'How to get your own way' in the family vacation decision process. After all, we have acknowledged the marital roles, the decision load, the imperfect environment, the 'satisficing' outcome and the variations in family type – so, amidst this group turmoil, how do you ensure that your voice is heard? Individual preferences are unlikely to dovetail, so how might any resulting conflict be resolved?

Early work by family decision process expert Davis (1976) argued for two broad representations of an ideal family decision process. The first is consensual, and the group problem solves and searches for alternatives until a solution is agreed that meets all members' minimum requirements. The second is accommodative, acknowledging that individual preferences are irreconcilable. Compromise becomes necessary and the influencing strategies of individual members swing into action.

Table 12.1 highlights the most common influencing strategies in family purchasing decisions. To date, there has been little research dedicated to applying these ideas directly to the family vacation decision. One such vacation decision study in The Netherlands (Bronner and de Hoog, 2008) found that a disagreement resolution strategy of the 'golden mean' (explained as give-and-take-and-reach-a-compromise) dominated family behaviour. Another vacation decision study that just touched on influencing strategies (Filiatrault and Ritchie, 1980) found that children did use a coalition strategy with one or other parent in order to gain influence. However, a third study (Kang and Hsu, 2005) found little use of any coalition strategy in destination selection. A study of Cornish (UK) holidays examined activity decisions taken during the holiday through use of space-time diaries (Thornton *et al.*, 1997) and found that negotiation between parents and children for these on-site secondary decisions was typical behaviour.

Anecdotally, you have probably witnessed at least a few of these influencing strategies in action – both for initial holiday decisions taken as a family and for subsequent decisions made at the

Table 12.1. Common influencing strategies used by individuals – child or adult – in family decision making. (Adapted from Davis, 1976; Spiro, 1983; Palan and Wilkes, 1997; Lee and Collins, 2000 and Shoham and Dalakas, 2006.)

Influencing strategy	Definition and features
Expert	Superior knowledge of the product category in question, or at least individual makes this case
Negotiation	Use of logical and practical arguments
Emotional	A display of feeling that may be non-verbal. For example, anger, crying, pouting, silent withdrawal, sweet talk, guilt trip or humour
Legitimate	Based on shared role expectations. For example, how the husband or wife or child should act in a given case
Bargaining	A trade-off based around negotiation which may or may not include financial offers or 'deals'. It implies a willing agreement with respective parties in a win–win situation
Persuasion (Coercion)	A way of forcing another member into agreement; unlike bargaining, the feature of willingness is absent, especially in its extreme form of coercion. Can include pleas of feminine intuition, begging, whining, manipulation, nagging and the media love child, 'pester power'
Coalition	The formation of alliances with other members of the family to outmanoeuvre an opponent. Families are generally cohesive groups, so this can be an effective tactic to bring an individual round to the majority view

destination (activities, sights, restaurant choice and so forth). You might even recognize your own influencing techniques, even if you would not choose to admit them publicly.

The influence of children

Research across different types of products (household goods, cars, computers, holidays and so on) suggests that the involvement of children in family decision making is greatest at the stage of problem recognition or at the start of the process (Swinyard and Sim, 1987; Shoham and Dalakas, 2005). Tourist-specific research from Taiwan investigating child influence in family decisions for group package tours concurred with this (Wang *et al.*, 2004), so one might surmise that children across an assortment of cultures have most influence in family holiday decisions at the point of problem identification – before the process truly commences.

There are some interesting findings from a study of child influence in vacation decisions across four European countries, namely the UK, Italy, Belgium and France (Seaton and Tagg, 1995). For one thing, the study sought the opinion of children as well as parents, and in doing so accessed well over 400 families across the social spectrum in each country. However, it only asked for the opinions of older children or adolescents, as participants were all between the ages of 13 and 18 – therefore, we do not know how the findings might differ for younger age groups. There was general agreement between the children of all four nationalities that the vacation decision was principally a joint decision of the parents, but parental consultation with the children was not less than 60% in any of the four countries. However, there were some marked differences in child influence. For example, Italian and French children were consulted more about family vacation decision choices than were their Belgium or UK counterparts. Concerning the magnitude of their involvement, almost half of the Italian children felt they had a 'big part' in the selection. Conversely, half of the UK children claimed only a 'small part' or 'no part' in the family vacation decision. Over 10 years on, a replication of the study would be useful to see if the findings still hold or whether there have been shifts in the pattern of behaviour.

A LEISURE STUDIES PERSPECTIVE ON THE FAMILY

The classic concept of leisure is one of respite from a strenuous work life (Larson and Gillman, 1997). It implies both free time and freely chosen activity in which to indulge. As described by Shaw and Dawson (2001), leisure involves freedom of choice by the individual, intrinsic motivation and enjoyment of experience. Leisure taken together as a family has traditionally been recognized as a powerful force in developing family cohesiveness and solidarity, improving family communication and encouraging positive interaction between family members. However, there is also recognition of the burden of work for women in organizing leisure activities for partners and children (Shaw, 1997). The responsibility often falls to the wife, and the energy, emotion and effort expended in ensuring the family spends quality time together can be interpreted as another form of unpaid work. The result? What is leisure for some becomes work for another. Family leisure participation can be a duty and a responsibility rather than an individual's freely chosen activity.

An interesting contribution is the idea of core and balancing leisure activities in family life. To operate effectively as a family, individual members need stability and change, structure and variety, and familiarity and novelty (Zabriskie and McCormick, 2003). Family leisure can provide this through a mix of core and balance activities. Core leisure activities tend to be home-based, regularly undertaken, easily accessible, and predictable. Examples include television watching or playing a family game. Balance activities tend to be away from home, less frequent and more unusual – that is, something of a challenge. Relevant examples include different forms of tourism from the short break to the longer vacation. To elaborate:

> [C]ore family leisure patterns address a family's need for familiarity and stability by regularly providing predictable family leisure experiences that foster personal relatedness and feelings of family closeness or cohesion. On the other hand, balance family leisure patterns address a family's need for novelty and change by providing new experiences that require families to negotiate and adapt to new input, to be challenged, and to develop as a working unit in a leisure context.
>
> (Zabriskie and McCormick, 2003, p. 169)

The argument is that if a family has a poor mix of core and balance activities, they are unlikely to function well as a family unit and show signs of frustration, boredom, irritability and communication breakdown. We can see that a short family city break taken in another country might require effort in a foreign or second language, map-reading across different city areas, frequent searching for, and processing of, new information (car hire, transport options, prices, restaurant options, navigation of attraction layouts) and trouble-shooting when things go wrong (malfunctioning bathroom suites, errors on bills, cultural misunderstandings) – a myriad of incidents that make the short city break a balance activity to test and develop the family spirit and redress a pattern of family leisure activity that is out of kilter.

A final word on families

It is possible to leave this chapter with an uplifting and positive view on family decision making for holidays. There is little research that considers the potential downside of family holidays, but we feel we should mention its existence. Not all families experience successful family holidays. Each year, the UK relationship support organization, Relate, experiences an increase in telephone calls during the month of September from couples dealing with post-holiday issues. Research by the tour operator, Just You (which specializes in holidays for single tourists), found that nearly 60% of their sample admitted to arguing with a partner while on holiday (Just You, 2006). Family holidays might not in themselves cause relationship problems, but as couples take time out of their usual routines, holidays do emphasize any existing difficulties (Just You, 2006). A wider study of this aspect of family holiday consumption would be a useful addition for a better understanding of family and vacation decisions.

VISITING FRIENDS AND RELATIVES

Previously in this chapter, we have examined how families make vacation decisions as a unit. In a switch of focus, we now explore the phenomenon of individual people who choose, either voluntarily or under a sense of duty, to visit another family member who lives a distance away. The travel industry refers to this type of tourism as 'Visiting Friends and Relatives', and uses the abbreviation 'VFR'. We have therefore included 'Friends' in this section in order to follow accepted terminology.

At the root of VFR is the geographic spread of perhaps the nuclear and certainly of the extended family both within a country and abroad. For any given country, the historical and current patterns of immigration and emigration are reflected in the volume and type of international VFR tourism (Lehto et al., 2001). For example, there are currently nearly 580,000 Indian-born UK residents and around 550,000 'A12' nationals (nationals of countries which have joined the European Union since May 2004) living in the UK today. Conversely, there are approximately 5.6 million British people permanently living abroad (see Chapter 4, 'Life Change: Tourist Experience and Beyond', this volume, for further discussion) who register as tourists whenever they visit Britain (VisitBritain, 2008). The same research also highlighted the number (approximately 49,000) of overseas residents studying at UK universities during 2007 – family and friends are likely to visit while they are studying. All these movements help to fuel the VFR market and this is just an illustration of current flows. There are also those UK-born nationals whose ancestry is non-British and those nationals of other countries whose ancestry is British to consider – the reflection of past immigration and emigration patterns.

Destinations are now alert to the potential size of today's VFR market. For example, in South Africa, research highlights over half of all domestic tourism in the country as VFR travel (Human Sciences Research Council of South Africa, 2003). In Canberra, Australia, around 38% of domestic tourism constitutes VFR travel (Australian Capital Tourism, 2005). In the UK, VFR tourism in 2007 made up 30% of inbound tourism by volume and 23% by value, being described as 'one of the main locomotives of growth for the UK's inbound visitor economy during the past decade and a half' (VisitBritain, 2008). There is something solid and reassuring about the VFR market. This family or friendship connection multiplied across the population offers a certain stability that makes the segment very attractive to destination management organizations. For in VFR tourism, the emotional tug of family and friendship is an additional destination pull that operates beyond the normal pull factors. Moreover, as pointed out by Visit-Britain (2008), whenever a friend or relative comes to visit, the likelihood for the host family to take meals out, visit attractions and participate in tourist-type activities increases – the 'missing piece of the jigsaw' (VisitBritain, 2008) that is often overlooked.

As a result, many destinations devise specific campaigns to appeal to the VFR market. For example, in 2005, Tourism Northern Territories, Australia, launched a 6-week campaign involving the resident population of Darwin to bring more domestic VFR to the 'Top End' of Australia between December and February, a season of storms, Asian-style markets, barramundi fishing, crocodile spotting and wet season waterfalls (Tourism NT, 2005). A direct mail package to residents included an 'invitation' postcard for sending to relatives elsewhere in Australia, and was supported by newspaper, radio and television advertising, plus incentive voucher booklets. For the Anchorage Convention and Visitors Bureau in Alaska, the incentive voucher booklet took the guise of a 'VFR Passport' for Alaskan residents (Anchorage Convention and Visitors Bureau, 2004); in Durham City, an historic cathedral city in the UK, a 'Free VFR Kit' for Durham residents (Durham Convention and Visitors Bureau, 2006). As part of the tourism recovery programme following the foot-and-mouth epidemic and 11 September 2001, VisitScotland offered a telephone VFR 'hotline' for Scots to ring in and nominate friends and relatives living outside Scotland to receive an information pack on holidaying in Scotland – the campaign used postcards to urge Scots to tell their loved ones 'wish you were here' (Visit-Scotland, 2002). As seen in these examples, there is plenty of scope to engage residents as ambassadors for a destination seeking to develop the VFR market – after all, they will be the ones acting as 'hosts' when their friends and family arrive and will take the lead in deciding the group's activities. It makes sense for marketers of destinations to recognize the importance of the VFR host and to target them accordingly.

Morrison *et al.* (2000) sum up the range of marketing tools that could be included in a VFR campaign to attract such tourists. In among the list are genealogy events and the provision of local genealogy resources, the establishment of reunions and homecomings to appeal to former residents and the creation of gifts such as calendars that appeal to VFR tourists – all sound yet imaginative ideas. With VFR, one of the hardest things for destination marketers is to generate a sense of immediacy, the necessary trigger that means the decision to visit is taken *now* rather than drifting off on a cloud of possibility into the indeterminate future. Where the relationship in VFR is close, the emotional tie can be the focus of the campaign; where the relationship is more distant, then the VFR connection better serves as a 'stepping stone' to explore the country (VisitBritain, 2004).

The VFR tourist can be visiting friends (VF), visiting relatives (VR), domestic or international – as we have seen in the examples. For international tourists, VFR opens up the opportunity of getting beneath the surface of a destination through the depth of social contact afforded by a friend or relative living in the area. It is interesting to note that international VFR tourists to Britain are receptive to being treated as a 'non-tourists' (VisitBritain, 2004), perhaps because they perceive tourists – which of course they are – as only catching superficial glimpses of the 'real' Britain. The VFR component can either:

- form the core motive – for example, visiting the brother who emigrated is the central purpose of the trip; or
- be one component of a parcel of experiences to be enjoyed, perhaps as a by-product of being in the area (Moscardo *et al.*, 2000) – the 'stepping stone' analogy of VisitBritain.

It is, however, a mistake to think that VFR tourists do not make use of commercial accommodation because they are staying with their relatives. This is a tourism myth. Research in America (Lehto *et al.*, 2001) concluded that international VFRs make substantial use of commercial accommodation and spend significantly on food, transportation, gifts, souvenirs and entertainment during such trips. Findings from the UK point to potential VFRs holding anxieties such as being trapped at the hosts' home, lack of personal privacy and freedom, conforming to restrictive behaviour patterns, being a burden to the host either financially or socially, or getting caught up in family politics (VisitBritain, 2004). For these and similar worries, commercial accommodation offers a solution.

Work by VisitBritain examining inbound VFR tourists (VisitBritain, 2008) highlighted the following five characteristics – here serving as an illustration of some of the points already made within the chapter:

- International VFR tourists can be of merit in a crisis; in 2001 (a year when British tourism was beset by crises), the volume of inbound tourism to the UK fell by around 10%. However, the inbound VFR increased by 1%.
- International VFR tourists exhibit an encouraging spread in terms of seasonality; about 47% of these VFR trips in 2007 occurred outside of the busy April to September period.

- International VFR tourists exhibit an encouraging spread in terms of regional coverage; about 60% of VFR spending by inbound visitors in 2007 occurred outside London (compared to 40% for holiday trips).
- International VFR tourists engage in a wide range of tourism activities; for example, during 2006, these inbound visitors made 1.8 million visits to museums and galleries, 2.6 million visits to castles, churches or historic houses and over 800,000 visits to theatres, operas or ballets.
- International VFR tourists do stay in 'free' accommodation with their friends and relatives, yet many also use commercial accommodation; for example, during 2006, inbound VFR tourists whose main journey purpose was to visit friends or relatives spent eight million nights in paid forms of accommodation.

GROUP BEHAVIOUR OF FRIENDS

We finish the chapter by considering the behaviour of groups that are not families but friends. We feel this is necessary as:

- Many of the concepts that help explain family group behaviour also help explain the behaviour of non-family groups in tourism.
- In the real world, tourism decision making is not discrete. A person involved in a family vacation decision may also be part of a decision-making unit (DMU) for a skiing trip with a group of friends.
- Children will eventually break away from the family unit and start to take holidays with friends – another form of consumer socialization and the learning and practising of vacation purchase skills.
- VRF tourism recognizes the influence of friends as much as relatives in holiday decisions, and treats the two under the same nomenclature.

How might the decision process and the behaviour of groups of friends involved in holiday decisions compare to that of families? Of course, unlike the relatively stable nuclear family, a group of friends for a holiday decision purpose is likely to be fluid across time and type of holiday; an individual might ski with three friends one year, a different group of ten the next and plan a series of short breaks with other friends sometimes blending into 'friends of friends'. To date, there is little research in this area of friendship group decision making, but early findings from Decrop (2005, 2006) suggest the following:

- Personal and situational factors such as budgets, interests and time schedules may vary greatly across the group of friends, making the finding of an agreeable solution taxing.
- Individuals in the group are likely to have commitments to other vacation DMUs, such as couples or families and these will invariably take priority over the friendship group.
- Communication between the individuals will be less extensive than for the family unit, which gathers together on a more regular basis.

- Most decisions involve all individuals in the group, and not subgroups; the decision making is largely syncretic or joint in style.
- A leader may emerge to push along the process. Other friends will abdicate their wishes in order to allow the emerged leader to finish the details of the plan. These actions are less likely to cause anger or frustration than in family decision making.
- The end decision may be weaker because individuals favour group consensus and group conformity ahead of their own critical deliberations (termed 'groupthink'). The group is more concerned with agreement and reaffirming affective ties than with maximizing the quality of the final decision. In other words, group cohesiveness takes priority above the details of the actual vacation planned, and a satisficing decision becomes very acceptable. It is the adequate decision again.

THE LAST WORD

Throughout this chapter we hope that you have deepened your understanding of family behaviour in the context of tourism and even caught glimpses of your own or other families in action. We have acknowledged the pervading influence of culture, and addressed the different family forms and approaches to definitions. By bringing together a range of concepts, we have attempted to shed light on the way that families behave during the decision process – and the process emerges as a messier procedure than suggested by the clean-cut lines of the tourist consumer behaviour models.

Our following chapter (or slide in the show) looks at series of themes of a quite different nature and we have titled it 'Of Fear, Flight and Feistiness'. But – in looking for a common thread – you will see that we have picked upon the VFR tourist of this chapter to illuminate some very different evidence of tourist behaviour.

REFERENCES

Anchorage Conventions and Visitors Bureau (2004) News release. Discounts for visiting friends and relatives. Available at: www.anchorage.net/995.cfm

Australian Capital Tourism (2005) Visiting friends and relatives market to the ACT. Available at: www. tourism.act.gov.au/CA256E140014A4CF/Lookup/Research_Market_Segments_FILES/$file/MS_Visiting_Friends_Relatives_Dec_05.pdf

Belch, M.A. and Willis, L.A. (2002) Family decision at the turn of the century: has the changing structure of households impacted the family decision making process? *Journal of Consumer Behaviour* 2(2), 111–124.

Blackwell, R.D., Miniard, P.W. and Engel, J.F. (2001) *Consumer Behaviour*, 9th edn. Harcourt College Publishers, London.

Blood, R.O. and Wolfe, D.M. (1960) *Husbands, Wives: the Dynamics of Married Living*. Free Press, Glencoe, Illinois.

Bronner, F. and de Hoog, R. (2008) Agreement and disagreement in family vacation decision making. *Tourism Management* 29(5), 967–979.

Carlson, L., Grossbart, S. and Stuenkel, J.K. (1992) The role of parental socialisation types on differential family communication patterns regarding consumption. *Journal of Consumer Psychology* 1(1), 31–52.

Caruana, A. and Vassallo, R. (2003) Children's perception of their influence over purchases: the role of parental communication patterns. *Journal of Consumer Marketing* 20(1), 55–66.

Davis, H.L. (1970) Dimensions of marital roles in consumer decision making. *Journal of Marketing Research* 7(May), 168–177.

Davis, H.L. (1976) Decision making within the household. *Journal of Consumer Research* 2(4), 241–260.

Davis, H.L. and Rigaux, B.P. (1974) Perception of marital roles in decision processes. *Journal of Consumer Research* 1(1), 51–62.

Decrop, A. (2005) Group processes in vacation decision-making. *Journal of Travel and Tourism Marketing* 18(3), 23–36.

Decrop, A. (2006) *Vacation Decision Making*. CAB International, Wallingford, UK.

Dimanche, F. and Havitz, M.E. (1994) Consumer behaviour and tourism: review and extension of four study areas. *Journal of Travel and Tourism Marketing* 3(3), 37–57.

Durham Convention and Visitors Bureau (2006) Visiting friends and relatives. Out of town guests? Want to tell them where to go? Available at: www.durham-nc.com/visitors/vfr.php

Filiatrault, P. and Ritchie, J.R.B. (1980) Joint purchasing decisions: a comparison of influence structure in family and couple decision-making units. *Journal of Consumer Research* 7, 131–140.

Herbst, P.G. (1954) Conceptual framework for studying the family. In: Oeser, O.A. and Hammond, S.B. (eds) *Social Structure and Personality in a City*. Macmillan, New York.

Human Sciences Research Council of South Africa (2003) Media releases 2003. Most popular form of tourism: visiting friends and relatives 10 September 2003. Available at: www.hsrc.ac.za/media/2003/9/20030910.html

Jarski, R. (2004) *The Funniest Thing You Never Said. The Ultimate Collection of Humorous Quotations*. Ebury Press, London.

Jenkins, R.L. (1978) Family vacation decision making. *Journal of Travel Research* 16(4), 2–7.

Just You (2006) Media release. Harmonious holidays or travel tantrums? New research reveals a nation of quarrelsome Brits abroad. 30 July 2006.

Kang, S.K. and Hsu, C.H.C. (2005) Dyadic consensus on family vacation destination selection. *Tourism Management* 26(4), 571–582.

Kleppe, I.A. and Gronhaug, K. (2003) No consumer is an island – the relevance of family dynamics for consumer welfare. *Advances in Consumer Research* 30(1), 314–321.

Larson, R.W. and Gillman, S.A. (1997) Divergent experiences of family leisure: fathers, mothers, and young adolescents. *Journal of Leisure Research* 29(1), 78–98.

Lee, C.K.C. and Beatty, S.E. (2002) Family structure and influence in family decision making. *Journal of Consumer Marketing* 19(1), 24–41.

Lee, C.K.C. and Collins, B.A. (2000) Family decision making and coalition patterns. *European Journal of Marketing* 34(9/10), 1181–1198.

Lehto, X.Y., Morrison, A. and O'Leary, J.T. (2001) Does the Visiting Friends and Relatives' typology make a difference? A study of the international VFR market to the United States. *Journal of Travel Research* 40, 201–212.

Litvin, S.W., Xu, G. and Kang, S.K. (2004) Spousal vacation-buying decision making revisited across time and place. *Journal of Travel Research* 43(2), 193–198.

McLeod, J.M. and Chaffee, S.H. (1972) The construction of social reality. In: Tiedeschi, J.T. (ed.) *The Social Influence Process*. Aldine-Atherton, Chicago, Illinois, pp. 43–56.

Moore, R. and Moschis, G. (1981) The role of family communication in consumer socialisation of children and adolescents. *Journal of Communication* 31, 42–51.

Morrison, A., Woods, B., Pearce, P., Moscardo, G. and Sung, H.H. (2000) Marketing to the visiting friends and relatives segment: an international analysis. *Journal of Vacation Marketing* 6(2), 102–118.

Moscardo, G., Pearce, P., Morrison, A., Green, D. and O'Leary, J.T.O. (2000) Developing a typology for understanding visiting friends and relatives markets. *Journal of Travel Research* 38, 251–259.

Moschis, G.P. (1985) The role of family communication in consumer socialisation of children and adolescents. *Journal of Consumer Research* 11(4), 898–913.

Mottiar, Z. and Quinn, D. (2004) Couple dynamics in household tourism decision making: women as the gatekeepers? *Journal of Vacation Marketing* 10(2), 149–160.

Ndubisi, N.O. and Koo, J. (2005) Family structure and joint purchase decisions: two products analysis. *Management Research News* 29(1/2), 53–64.

Palan, K.M. and Wilkes, R.E. (1997) Adolescent–parent interaction in family decision making. *Journal of Consumer Research* 24(2), 159–169.

Rose, G.M., Bush, V.D. and Kahle, L.R. (1998) The influence of family communication patterns on parental reactions towards advertising: a cross-national examination. *Journal of Advertising* 27(4), 71–85.

Seaton, A.V. and Tagg, S. (1995) The family vacation in Europe: paedonomic aspects of choices and satisfactions. *Journal of Travel and Tourism Marketing* 4(1), 1–21.

Shaw, S.M. (1997) Controversies and contradictions in family leisure: an analysis of conflicting paradigms. *Journal of Leisure Research* 29(1), 98–112.

Shaw, S.M. and Dawson, D. (2001) Purposive leisure: examining parental discourses on family activities. *Leisure Sciences* 23(4), 217–231.

Shoham, A. and Dalakas, V. (2005) He said, she said … they said: parents' and children's assessment of children's influence on family consumption decisions. *Journal of Consumer Marketing* 22(3), 152–160.

Shoham, A. and Dalakas, V. (2006) How our adolescent children influence us as parents to yield to their purchase requests. *Journal of Consumer Marketing* 23(6), 344–350.

Solomon, M.R. (2006) *Consumer Behavior: Buying, Having, Being*. Pearson Prentice-Hall, New Jersey.

Spiro, R.L. (1983) Persuasion in family decision-making. *Journal of Consumer Research* 9(4), 393–402.

Swinyard, W.R. and Sim, C.P. (1987) Perception of children's influence on family decision processes. *Journal of Consumer Marketing* 4(1), 25–38.

Thornton, P.R., Shaw, G. and Williams, A.M. (1997) Tourist group holiday decision making and behaviour: the influence of children. *Tourism Management* 18(5), 287–297.

Tourism NT (2005) Visiting friends and relatives campaign launched. Ministerial media release – 28 October 2005. Available at: www.tourismnt.com.au/nt/nttc/news/media_releases/mr/2005/mr_Oct28_VFR.htm

VisitBritain (2004) VisitBritain's strategy and insight division visiting friends and relatives (VFR) – Summary. Available at: www3.visitbritain.com/corporate/links/visitbritain/tips.htm

VisitBritain (2008) Issue of the month – the value of inbound visits to friends and relatives. *Foresight* Issue 57 July 2008. VisitBritain Strategy and Communications Division, London.

VisitScotland (2002) News Release. Scots urged to say 'wish you were here'. Available at: www.scotland.gov.uk/News/Releases/2002/02/1052

Wang, K.-C., Hsieh, A.-T., Yeh, Y.-C. and Tsai, C.-W. (2004) Who is the decision maker: the parents or the child in group package tours? *Tourism Management* 25(2), 183–194.

Ward, S. (1980) Consumer socialization. In: Kassarjian, H. and Robertson, T. (eds) *Perspectives in Consumer Behaviour*, 3rd edn. Scott Foresman, Glenville, Illinois, pp. 380–396.

World Travel Market (2007) There's no place like home. Available at: www.wtmlondon.com/page.cfm/ link=50

Zabriskie, R.B. and McCormick, B.P. (2003) Parent and child perspectives of family leisure involvement and satisfaction with family life. *Journal of Leisure Research* 35(2), 163–189.

Zalatan, A. (1998) Wives' involvement in tourism decision processes. *Annals of Tourism Research* 25(4), 890–903.

chapter 13

OF FEAR, FLIGHT AND FEISTINESS

Unfortunately, today the perception of risk that an individual will be a victim of terrorism, an international conflict, or a health hazard is higher than ever before. There is a growing perception of the world as a more risky place to live and travel.

(Reisinger and Mavondo, 2005, p. 212)

We continue our slide show of tourist behaviour with a rather more unexpected topic (or amalgamation of sub-topics) than in the previous chapter. We have used the word 'fear' to sum up this aspect of tourist behaviour which in recent years has been researched through the lens of different types of man-made and natural crises, health risks and crime. We have used the word 'flight' to highlight both the avoidance response and in a more literal sense to pin down fear of flying as a sub-topic. And we have used the word 'feistiness' to capture something of the resilience of tourists and the behavioural adaptations that you the tourist might make.

While we examine fear both in the context of the decision-making process and the in-use experience, we attend in the main to the more extreme end of the spectrum of fears, anxieties and perceptions of risk felt by tourists and their corresponding behaviour. Therefore, what might be considered the everyday risks inherent in tourist decision-making processes as understood by consumer behaviourists – such as social risk, financial risk or time risk – are of less concern to us here. It is appropriate to paraphrase Harold Macmillan,[1] British Prime Minister at the end of the 1950s, that what blows the tourist off-course is 'events dear boy, events'.

---

[1] A saying attributed to Harold Macmillan when asked by a journalist what was most likely to blow a government off course.

Tourist feelings of vulnerability are not new. Indeed, as modes of travel have progressed from foot to horse, boat, carriage, train, coach, car and aeroplane, so too have the names given to the associated form of attack (Foreman and Iljon, 1994). Thus, we have progressed through footpads, pirates, highwaymen, steamers, carjackers and hijackers (Foreman and Iljon, 1994). Much research indicates that tourists, most being risk-averse creatures, are particularly susceptible to threats relating to crime, political instability and violence, personal health and natural disasters (Bianchi, 2007). In his book on crisis management for destinations, Beirman (2003) categorizes his case studies as terrorism and political violence, natural disasters, health concerns and epidemics and diseases, crime,

Fig. 13.1. Tourists, crises and media coverage.

war, and combinations of crises. Even today, as this chapter is written, acts of terrorism in Mumbai are conveyed around the world by the media and government travel advisories warn of the dangers of travel to this city.

There is an argument that tourists are the targets of terrorist attacks because they represent Western capitalism and values and that attacks on tourists symbolize attacks on their respective governments (Reisinger and Mavondo, 2005). Tourists embody a mobile form of conspicuous consumption. Some writers contend that the emergence of violence against tourists is a distinctly contemporary phenomenon which has grown in tandem with the internationalization of tourism and the spread of the global communications media (see Bianchi, 2007, p. 67). The interface between tourists and different types of natural and man-made crises or events makes newsworthy and saleable media coverage (see Fig. 13.1 for examples).

FEAR AND PERCEIVED RISK

In this section, we briefly define fear and perceived risk as concepts for better understanding tourist behaviour.

Fear is a term used to denote an emotion caused by imminent danger, apprehension or dread and is connected to our desire to avoid risk (Wilson and Little, 2008, p. 169). We anticipate that something unpleasant is going to happen. The response of fear sounds straightforward, but as explained by Wilson and Little (2008) fear is

> complexly tied to social expectations and messages, our individual expectations and histories, our gender, our class and/or our capacity or belief in our capacity to be able to manage fearful or dangerous situations.

(Wilson and Little, 2008, p. 169)

In the past, this emotion of pain or uneasiness triggered by the sense of impending danger was used only to refer to the most violent extremes. Today, fear is a somewhat general term for varying strengths of this emotion (Oxford English Dictionary, 2008) and we could think of terms such as nervous, apprehensive, stressed, vulnerable, uncomfortable, disturbed, scared or panicked in a similar light. Some tourism research refers to anxiety rather than fear (see, e.g., Reisinger and Mavondo, 2005) but, outside of the medical research work, it has much the same meaning.

Risk can be defined as exposure to the chance of injury, a hazard or perilous chance or as the potential to lose something of value (Reisinger and Mavondo, 2005; Oxford English Dictionary, 2008). At the extreme end lies *dread risk*, the low-probability high-damage event with many deaths such as a large-scale terrorist attack or the 2004 tsunami (Gigerenzer, 2006). Real or actual risk is probably less important to tourist behaviour than perceived risk. Perceived risk refers to a person's perceptions of the hazard or potential loss. It has been calculated that the actual risk of death is about the same for 12 miles (1 mile = 1.609 km) of car driving as it is for a non-stop flight from Boston to Los Angeles; therefore, by the time you have driven safely to the airport, the greatest actual risk of death has past (Gigerenzer, 2006). Yet people are more fearful of flying – where the perceived risk lies and there is lack of personal control – than of the journey by car. This example may be culturally specific, but it is none the less memorable.

This concept of perceived risk was introduced by Bauer in 1960 (Dolnicar, 2005). Perceived risk in tourism can be split into the positive and the negative. The positive equates to the sensation-seeking behaviours where the perceived risk is actively sought – such as in adventure tourism with its inherent thrills. In this chapter, however, we are interested in the negative connotations – the arousal of fear – and the responses in tourist behaviour that it provokes. To follow on from our previous example of car versus airplane, after the terrorist attacks of 11 September 2001, millions of Americans avoided air travel, preferring the car instead for an aftermath of around 12 months (Gigerenzer, 2006) – an avoidance behaviour stimulated by fear and perceived risk. None the less, this switch in transport mode was estimated by Gigerenzer (2006) to have caused approximately 1500 additional fatal road crashes.

Perceived risk research in tourism has been ongoing since the 1980s (Dolnicar, 2005). For example, Roehl and Fesenmaier (1992) identified three groups of tourists based on their risk perceptions; the functional risk group (who weigh up mechanical, equipment and organizational risks), the place risk group (who perceive tourism and travelling as risky) and the risk-neutral group. Distinctly different patterns of perceived risks emerge for different destination contexts and for different segments of tourists (Dolnicar, 2008) and there are marked differences in perceptions of risk between domestic (low-risk) and overseas travel (higher-risk). In summarizing the literature, Reisinger and Mavondo (2005) indicated that factors such as the balance between familiarity and novelty desired in a holiday, personality type and nationality or culture could influence tourist risk perceptions.

It is worthwhile to study a particular tourist segment and its perceptions of risk and corresponding response behaviours. Here, we pick up on the international tourist as international tourism is typically perceived of as carrying greater risk than domestic tourism and on the single-female tourist as these tourists typically perceive greater risks to their physical safety while on holiday (Stone and Nichol, 1999). Combining these two bases, solo female international tourists make an informative example for study.

SOLO FEMALE INTERNATIONAL TOURISTS

Some fascinating research set in the context of the *geography of women's fear* examined the fears of solo female international tourists (Wilson and Little, 2008). The literature review is summed up as showing that women's use of tourist space is governed by a patriarchal system of fear, social control and judgement about what is 'appropriate' female travel behaviour. The research used depth interviews with around 80 women from different nationalities, although Australian informants predominated. Some of the fears discussed related to the decision-making process and others to the destination experience itself. Thus, the study addressed fears prior to undertaking the tourism experience and fears encountered during the tourism experience. The researchers also stressed that the solo female international tourists 'resisted' the geography of fear that they encountered – underscoring our point about tourist resilience.

Four main themes of fear emerged for these solo female international tourists (Wilson and Little, 2008). First, there are fears revolving around the influence and concerns of the perceptions and opinions of others. Feelings of doubt, fear and a sense of restriction were instilled in the female tourist prior to departure through often well-intentioned expressions of concern from friends, colleagues, family and partners. Typical comments included praise of bravery, the social inappropriateness of such travel and the vulnerability of women travelling alone. These comments reinforced feelings of fear prior to travel. Second, there are fears based on a personal sense of vulnerability in unknown places; the female tourist's own perception that travel is more difficult for women and that they are more vulnerable to attack and sexual harassment. Third, there are fears resulting in a sense of restricted access both spatially and temporally. These female tourists felt that certain destinations were off-limits for Western female tourists travelling alone – examples cited included the Middle East, Morocco or South America. Thus, fear led to a restriction in destination choice during the decision-making process. It was also evident in movement around social spaces within the destination. Alleyways, remote villages and off-the-beaten-track places were avoided; solo female international tourists stayed – in the words of one informant – where they *were meant to be*. Temporally, strong feelings of vulnerability were felt at night. Wilson and Little (2008, p. 179) reiterated that the combination of 'patriarchal societies, unknown places and evening activities all served to instil a level of fear in solo women travellers' experiences'. Fourth, there are fears stemming from feelings of conspicuousness and being prone to the male gaze while travelling, although this final fear was not always a problem and often accepted as part of being a tourist in a different country and culture.

Solo female international tourists adopted coping strategies, in particular *accommodating techniques* (Wilson and Little, 2008), which we equate to offering some form of tourist resilience. Examples included modifying their dress, fitting to local female norms of behaviour, remaining constantly vigilant or mindful of what was happening around them and extracting themselves from places where they felt fearful. However, a by-product of this behavioural adaptation meant that solo female international tourists can become 'weary of having to constantly gauge the tourist landscape' (Wilson and Little, 2008, p. 181). This particular type of 'weariness' is unlikely to be felt by other groups of tourists.

THE STRESS OF GETTING THERE

Much leisure tourism is about relaxation and freedom from stress, but ironically the act of travel itself often exposes individuals to stress. For instance, culture shock has been identified by the International Society of Travel Medicine as a psychocultural issue within the overall study of travel medicine (Kozarsky, 2006). Severe forms of culture shock involve nausea, disorientation and hostile reactions to the destination and unknown people (Smith, 2008a). Re-entry shock (Foreman and Iljon, 1994) on returning home also involves feelings of disorientation and disturbance. Together, culture shock and travel stress are two major psychological barriers to international travel (Smith, 2008a).

Let us explore the notion of travel stress a little deeper. Intense emotional reactions can be triggered by apparently mundane events, for instance parking the car at the terminal or port (Bor, 2007). Travel, and particularly travel by air, can induce depression, anxiety, panic attacks and even psychosis in vulnerable people who have left their familiar and secure everyday environment. Bor (2007) contends that as the human species has not evolved to fly naturally, we are best adapted to terrestrial travel modes and that we come up against *evolutionary barriers* when we attempt activities we are not designed to do (jet lag, motion sickness, heightened stress and so forth). As described by Bor (2007):

> [E]ven the most seasoned travellers appear to carry an 'emotional charge' when they fly, catch a train or join a cruise. This may be due to a range of factors including fear of separation from loved ones, anxieties and fears associated with safety, disorientation, worry about disrupted routines, fear of dependency on others who are in control, and even seemingly less significant issues such as whether the 'right' food will be available or fear of being separated from one's luggage.
>
> (Bor, 2007, p. 208)

Travel by sea in the form of cruise ships is part journey and part destination. We mention it here because it carries its own health risks as well as the general stresses indicated above. Indeed, the World Health Organization (2008) identified over 100 disease outbreaks associated with ships since 1970; diseases associated with disembarking and embarking passengers and diseases associated with contaminated food and water on board a ship, with the norovirus the most common pathogen implicated in outbreaks of gastrointestinal illness.

So as we can see, alongside generalized fears are unique anxieties associated with certain forms of transport. We have highlighted aviation. It is to fear of flying that we now turn our attention.

Fear of flying

Although the figures are in need of updating, fear of flying in its differing levels of intensity is believed to affect between 10% and 40% of the general population of developed countries (Van Gerwen *et al.*, 2004; Nousi *et al.*, 2008). Numbers have probably increased as a consequence of recent terrorist attacks (e.g. 11 September 2001) and health scares (e.g. SARS) (Van Gerwen *et al.*, 2004).

Fear of flying is defined by the American Psychiatric Association as a specific phobia characterized by a marked, persistent, excessive fear that is precipitated by the experience or immediate prospect of air travel (Bor, 2007). It matters because, aside from the unpleasant physical and psychological aspects, fear of flying can impact badly on marital and family relationships and hinder career prospects.

It is generally agreed that fear of flying is a complex phenomenon comprising a combination of underlying fears such as fear of crashing, heights, confinement and instability (Bor, 2007). An important trigger for many phobic passengers can be the perceived loss or lack of control (Borrill and Foreman, 1996; Bor, 2007); 'loss' in the sense that they 'lose it' themselves and 'lack' in the sense that they have to hand across control over their lives to others (pilot, aircrew, ground staff involved in aircraft safety maintenance). Thus, as expressed by Foreman and Iljon (1994), underlying fears can either be external (e.g. threat of terrorist attack, crashing, aircraft malfunction and so forth) or internal (e.g. fear of having a panic attack, heart attack, fainting, embarrassing themselves with unseemly behaviour and so forth). Fear of flying can also be divided into anticipatory anxiety preflight and in-flight anxiety during the flight with a possible third category of generalized flight anxiety too (Nousi *et al.*, 2008).

Of course classic behavioural responses to fear of flying include avoidance behaviours such as refusal to fly. Some passengers adopt their own self-help strategies such as searching out statistical information regarding flight safety, practising relaxation techniques, using in-flight films as a distraction, seeking medical reassurance preflight (Foreman and Borrill, 1994) and more dubious strategies for those suffering from flight phobia such as taking alcohol or relaxation drugs. But in the true spirit of feistiness and resistance, the traveller can also embark on professional treatments to overcome fear of flying.

In the decades prior to the 1960s, treatment for fear of flying was typically long-term explorative psychodynamic therapy with a focus on unconscious causes. Fear of flying in this era was regarded as a symptom of deeper problems such as hostility towards a parent figure or a fear of attachment (Bor, 2007). Today, Cognitive Behavioural Therapy (CBT) is a recognized treatment with claims for effectiveness (Foreman and Iljon, 1994; Van Gerwen *et al.*, 2004; Bor, 2007). The use of CBT rests on the belief that an individual's behaviour is dependent not just on their reaction to a stimulus but on their thoughts and emotions about it. So it is not the events themselves but an individual's interpretation of these events that causes anxiety and fear. If any of the three – think, feel and do – is modified, then changes can be expected in the other two components. This is what CBT aims to do by training the individual to think about the events in a different way (Foreman and Borrill, 1994). As part of the programme of treatment, CBT uses confrontation of the fear of flying through graded exposure to flying and gradual desensitization to break the established avoidance behaviour patterns.

It is not just those who have never flown who might exhibit fear of flying. It is important to realize that it can develop in tourists with a long track record of problem-free flying too. Figure 13.2 shows how flight phobia develops (Bor, 2007) and you can see how a bad experience (such as a near-miss take-off or landing), life changes (such as a birth of a child or bereavement) and underlying depression can feed into this vicious circle (Bor, 2007).

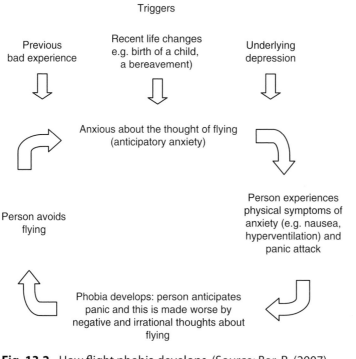

Fig. 13.2. How flight phobia develops. (Source: Bor, R. (2007) Psychological factors in airline passenger and crew behaviour: a clinical overview. *Travel Medicine and Infections Disease* 5(4), 207–216, p. 211 (with permission).)

Defence lawyers in legal cases for those accused of 'air rage' have sometimes argued fear of flying as a contributory factor (Bor, 2007). However, the vast majority of fearful flyers do not exhibit this extreme form of behaviour (Bor, 2007; World Health Organization, 2008). Before we leave the tourist on the journey element of the trip, we detour to briefly look at anti-social passenger behaviour and more extreme disruptive passenger behaviour or its moniker 'air rage'.

Pax[2] behaving badly

You have almost certainly observed some if not all of the behaviours noted by Bor (2007) while flying yourself – we hope in other passengers but maybe in yourself? Have you observed passengers who become unreasonably demanding? Who regress in their behaviour to a child-like state? Who tell utter strangers the intimate details of their lives? Who appear to have little regard for the needs of other passengers? Or who become clingy, boisterous or withdrawn?

You may have observed more extreme behaviour entering the realms of air rage. Abuse of alcohol? Smoking on board the aircraft? Sexual harassment of another passenger or crew? Verbal abuse or physical assault? Flagrant disobeying of crew instructions? Earlier work by Bor (2003) demonstrated that air rage is not as widespread in the UK as the frequency of media portrayals ('Jet diverted after families fight at 35,000 feet' and so on) might lead you to believe. A serious disruptive passenger incident occurs in roughly one of every 30,000 flights or for every two million airline passengers carried (Bor, 2003). The bulk of pax behaving badly can best be described as low-level anti-social behaviour – irritating, annoying, but not illegal or endangering the safety of others.

The behaviour of passengers is influenced by a number of factors: culture, age, gender, personality are all included (Bor, 2007). We have chosen to highlight three factors that we found particularly interesting from Bor's list.

First, the physical and mental condition of the traveller, including alcohol intake, prescribed medication, recreational drugs and sleep disruption all have the potential to influence behaviour (Bor, 2007). In particular, excessive alcohol intake relates to incidents of air rage (World Health Organization, 2008). The physical effects of air travel have psychological repercussions for tourists in the form of irritability, sleep deprivation, boredom and restlessness. These are particularly true for passengers on transmeridian long-haul flights (Bor, 2007).

Second, the purpose of the trip provides a unique social context which guides behaviour, emotional state and reactions to the flight experience. Bor (2007) cites a rowdy group of sportsmen, a stag or hen group, a lone business traveller wanting to work and a couple on their way to a funeral. These very different travellers are mixed together on the same flight (the characteristic of inseparability) – tensions can be rife.

Third, the precise environmental conditions on board the aircraft that are encountered by passengers affect behaviour. Examples include the space available, seat comfort, ventilation and air temperature. Deviations from normal conditions can give rise to irritability, hypoxia, claustrophobia and stress. Cramped conditions can even lead to

> acts of violence as passengers seek to establish dominance over an armrest or an empty seat.
> Emotional reactions are observed to intensify when personal space is invaded by strangers.
>
> (Bor, 2007, p. 209)

---

[2] Pax is airline terminology for passengers.

Today, disruptive passenger behaviour may be on the decline. Greater passenger compliance with crew instructions in the aftermath of 11 September 2001 and greater confidence of airline companies in enforcing zero-tolerance policies without damage to their brand images may have contributed to this decrease in passengers behaving badly (Bor, 2003).

THE STRESS OF BEING THERE

Having survived the stress of getting there – the journey – we now examine the stress of being there – the destination. There are many types of crises, fears and anxieties that influence tourist numbers, tourist behaviour and the destination image. We decided to focus here on less-frequented topics in tourism research and have selected health risks and crime as associated with the destination.

Destinations and health risks

There are, of course, physical health risks associated with flying (e.g. deep vein thrombosis, decompression sickness for incautious divers who fly too soon after their last dive or gas expansion in the body following certain types of surgery – World Health Organization, 2008), but in this section we have chosen to focus on the health risks associated with you the tourist and the destination that you visit.

Media coverage has lately spread awareness of three major global health fears for the average traveller, namely avian influenza (H5N1), Severe Acute Respiratory Syndrome (SARS) and the ongoing World Health Organization influenza pandemic alert (Smith and Leggat, 2008). The media headlines of infectious disease threats – in particular, avian influenza, SARS and a global influenza pandemic – deflect tourist attention away from demonstrated and defined infectious disease risks (Gushulak et al., 2007) such as dengue fever or chikungunya fever. For example, a recent epidemic of chikungunya fever in Réunion (a French island close to Mauritius and popular with tourists for its dramatic volcanic landscapes) affected over one-quarter of the island's small population of 777,000 (Gushulak et al., 2007). All in all, the International Society of Travel Medicine (ISTM) reported well over 40 different diseases of concern to tourists and travellers. Among the categories (Kozarsky, 2006) are diseases associated with vectors (such as dengue fever or malaria), diseases associated with person-to-person contact (such as tuberculosis or influenza), diseases associated with intake of food and water (such as cholera or travellers' diarrhoea), diseases connected with bites and stings (such as rabies or envenomation from jellyfish, snakes or spiders), diseases associated with water or environmental contact (such as schistosomiasis or legionella) and medical conditions associated with environmental factors (such as sunburn, heat exhaustion, hypothermia, altitude sickness or respiratory distress caused by air pollution). Far from the headline making health fears, travellers' diarrhoea appears to be the most commonly occurring infectious health risk (Pai and Lai, 2008; Steffen et al., 2008).

Tourist behaviour with regard to health risks is important not only for the well-being of the individual, but also for wider society. The home population is vulnerable to the tourist importing infectious diseases; that is, to the tourist bringing back an infectious disease from the destination visited (Dawson, 2007). During the 2003 episode of SARS, the five cases imported to Canada resulted in 251 other cases and serious impact on travel to Toronto (Gushulak *et al.*, 2007). Conversely, the destination population is vulnerable to the tourist exporting infectious diseases; that is, to the tourist introducing an infectious disease from the origin country (Dawson, 2007). GeoSentinel, a network of travel and tropical medicine clinics around the world established by the ISTM and the Centers for Disease Control, tracks geographic and temporal trends in infectious diseases among travellers as part of its work. A small illustrative example from GeoSentinel research focusing on travellers to China in the lead up to the Beijing Olympics showed that respiratory illness and injuries were common among tourists seen at clinics during their travel and that acute diarrhoea and dog bites were common among tourists seen at clinics after their travel (Davis *et al.*, 2008). Part of the body of knowledge of travel medicine as a field is therefore to better understand the *knowledge, attitudes and practices* of tourists in relation to travel health (Lopez-Velez and Bayas, 2007) – in short, their behaviour. To date, there are few studies in travel medicine that examine the effectiveness of pre-trip advice and consultation in terms of tourist behaviour and risk taking (MacPherson *et al.*, 2007a).

The World Health Organization (2008) stressed that the characteristics of the destination itself, the duration and season of travel, purpose of travel, standards of accommodation and food hygiene, the underlying health of the traveller and the behaviour of the traveller were all important factors in determining the actual health risks of the trip. The underlying health of the tourist is an interesting point, for, with the decreasing cost of air travel, more and more vulnerable groups are flying for vacations in more distant places – the elderly, the very young and those with pre-existing chronic illnesses (Gushulak *et al.*, 2007). The ISTM recognizes distinct travel activities or itineraries that demand specific attention; included in the list are cruise ship tourism, diving, extended stay travel, extreme or remote wilderness travel, last minute trips, mass gatherings (such as might be experienced during religious festivals) and high-altitude tourism (Kozarsky, 2006). We can separate out the behaviour of tourists into pre-trip behaviour (such as information gathering and seeking credible medical advice), in-trip behaviour (such as taking medication according to instruction, covering up at dusk in malarial areas, washing hands frequently and taking precautions with food and water) and post-trip behaviour (such as continuation of medication if required and having a prompt medical check up if untoward symptoms present or persist).

An analysis of the behaviour (aka knowledge, attitudes and practice) of Spanish travellers to high-risk destinations (in health terms) in the tropics found that over one-quarter had sought no information at all about health risks prior to departure (Lopez-Velez and Bayas, 2007). Trips were planned around 40 days in advance, with health advice – where used at all – only sought an average of 19.5 days in advance of the trip. The worst-informed travellers tended to be older than 50 years and had visited the destination several times previously on business trips. The best-informed tended to be travellers younger than 40 years visiting the destination for the first time with an organized tourist package. In addition, approximately 40% of Spanish travellers to high-risk destinations failed to correctly assess the risk for various infectious diseases. For example, almost one-quarter visiting malarial endemic destinations did not perceive malaria as a risk disease (Lopez-Velez and Bayas, 2007). As a single illustration of Spanish tourists, we have to be guarded about generalization to tourists from other countries – but there appears to be scope for improvement in tourist information seeking and behaviour with regard to travel health.

The Spanish study mentioned the concentration of VFR travel during the Christmas holidays. Indeed, VFR tourists have been highlighted by the ISTM as a *special population* for travel medicine and behaviour (Kozarsky, 2006).

VFR tourists with a twist

The twist of the sub-heading refers to the main focus in this section being the international VFR tourist who is travelling from a developed country to a developing country. The World Health Organization (2008) labels VFR tourists generally as immigrants from a developing country to an industrialized country who subsequently return to their home countries for the purpose of visiting friends and relatives. We can appreciate the relevance of this movement from a travel medicine perspective. In fact, from a tourist management perspective and as explained in Chapter 12 (this volume), VFR tourists have many guises and the domestic VFR tourist and the short-haul international VFR tourist between developed countries are more important in terms of volume and frequency of trips. However, for this section, we adopt the nuance of the international VFR tourist travelling from a developed to a developing country.

Typically, such VFR tourists perceived less personal risk from travel-related diseases than other tourists, probably due to the VFR tourists' cultural and geographic familiarity with the destination country and its endemic diseases (Angell and Cetron, 2005). As a result, they are less inclined than other tourists to seek travel-related medical care pre-trip, less likely to be vaccinated and are less likely to adhere to recommended medications or precautions too (Angell and Cetron, 2005; World Health Organization, 2008). In the UK, one-third of outbound international VFR tourists are believed to have inadequate medical insurance (Foreign and Commonwealth Office, 2003).

Yet these VFR tourists are often at greater risk for many travel-related illnesses, including diseases routinely vaccinated against in childhood which they may well have missed if foreign-born (Angell and Cetron, 2005) or have lost natural immunity against if second generation immigrants (Gushulak *et al.*, 2007). Also, they are more likely than other tourists to undertake last minute trips (World Health Organization, 2008), thus minimizing preparation time for health advice.

Actual risk is also greater due to the in-trip characteristics of international VFR tourism to developing countries. For example, such VFR tourists are more likely to visit rural destinations, have close contact with local populations, have longer lengths of stay and make repeat visits. Sleeping accommodation with relatives may not include the precautions of window screens or bed nets in malarial areas, and with food and drink prepared by the host, they are more at risk of untreated water and uncooked foods. In short,

> by approximating the living conditions of the local community, these behaviors increase VFR travelers' risk for disease exposure to a level similar to that of the local population in the developing country.
>
> (Angell and Cetron, 2005, p. 68).

With such preconceptions of health risk and in-trip behaviour, the results are not surprising. For example, the GeoSentinel surveillance data show that eight times more VFR travellers present with malaria upon their return than other tourists. In fact, VFR travellers are believed to account for more than half the imported malaria cases in Europe and North America (World Health Organization, 2008).

Destinations and crime

Just as for health risks, there are crime risks associated with the journey or travel component of tourism too. Train travel in Italy has its dangers with gangs gassing tourists on overnight sleeper trains in order to steal their belongings, for example (Ryan, 1993). Much more recently, acts of piracy off the coast of Somalia have escalated to over 120 reported attacks in the first 11 months of 2008 alone (International Maritime Organization, 2008) and although the majority of these attacks were not against cruise ships (but against cargo ships and tankers), an American cruise ship with around 1000 people on board was attacked in December 2008 (Associated Press, 2008). However, in this section, we focus on the crime risks associated with you the tourist and the destination that you visit.

To structure the section, we use Fig. 13.3 as guidance. It is a simplified diagram that simply seeks to link the different components of this section together. Thus, it shows the impact of fear of crime on the destination image and its role in the tourist's decision-making process. It also shows the tourist as

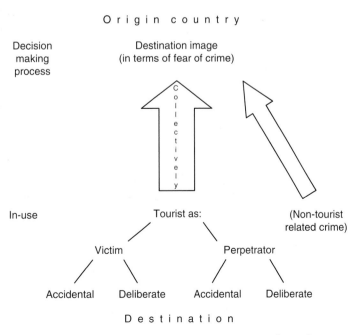

Fig. 13.3. Simplified diagram to structure tourist fear of crime.

both victim and as perpetrator at the destination itself; in other words, in-use behaviour. At the extreme end, research into Canadian travellers showed that the chance of being murdered was over three times greater for travellers than for non-travellers (MacPherson *et al.*, 2007a). Gruesomely, some serial killers target tourists (Gibson, 2006). But we are also concerned here with crimes such as muggings, assaults, rape and theft from person or property. A selection of evidence points to violence against tourists resulting in declining visitor numbers for destinations (Pizam, 1999).

Despite our iteration above of the likelihood of a violent demise, this section is not devised to add to any fear you might have of crime, but to better understand its effects on tourist behaviour. It is important to bear in mind that holidays only last for short durations (so all other things being equal you are more likely to encounter crime at home) and that fear and anxiety about crime will also vary by individual, depending on proneness in personality to anxiety and worry, social and physical vulnerability, and any previous experience of crime (Brunt *et al.*, 2000).

The tourist as victim can be divided into the accidental victim and the deliberate victim. The tourist as an accidental victim refers to the tourist being in the wrong place at the wrong time. They have not been singled out because of their status as a tourist. There may be differences in crimes rates (and types of crimes) between the origin country and the destination; if the tourist moves from a comparatively safe country to one with a higher crime rate, he/she is more likely to become an accidental victim. Related to this is the fact that tourists – through the 'tourist culture' – are more likely to be relaxed, to experience a 'loosening of a sense of responsibility' (Ryan, 1993, p. 178), to be free from home constraints and to be in an unfamiliar environment or culture where they cannot easily spot any warnings of trouble that a local person might perceive. By being a tourist, you are more likely to be out and about and less inclined to be inside your accommodation than local people (Brunt *et al.*, 2000). Furthermore, mature destinations or resorts can have innate characteristics that make them attractive for criminal activity (Ryan, 1993). For example, these places are typified by temporary mass movements of strangers who stay for short periods of time making detection a harder task. Thus, comparative crime rates, the tourist culture and the inherent characteristics of tourist honeypots all contribute to the tourist as accidental victim of crime.

The tourist can also be deliberately targeted as the victim of crime; in other words, selected out because of their tourist status (Ryan, 1993; Brunt *et al.*, 2000). Tourists can be particularly vulnerable as victims to crime for they are conspicuous. In poorer destinations, tourists stand out as particularly affluent and carry valuable items (wallets, cameras, mobile phones, credit cards and so forth). Their tourist culture (relaxed, off guard, unwary, careless, etc.) enhances their vulnerability. If they are targeted as a crime victim, they are less likely to press charges because of the requirement to return as witness – the cost, the distance, the effort of arranging time out from work, the distress of returning to a destination that failed to deliver a memorable holiday for positive reasons, are all disincentives (Ryan, 1993).

Knowledge of this tourist characteristic plays into the hands of criminals, for they are more likely to escape justice.

Tourists are not always the victims of crime. More recently, they have been examined in their role as the perpetrators of crime or offenders (Brunt *et al.*, 2000). Again, tourists can either be accidental perpetrators or deliberate perpetrators of crime. On the one hand, tourists can be less inhibited in their behaviour than while at home (the tourist culture again). In certain segments this can give rise to alcohol abuse, binge drinking and alcohol-related crimes such as assault. For example, there is plenty of media coverage of *boozy Britons* in various Mediterranean resorts and the associated crimes (not to mention accidents and injuries) (Smith, 2008b) and of British football hooligans. Other tourists may be deliberate and considered when engaging in criminal activity. For example, importing illegal goods or seeking out child prostitutes (Brunt *et al.*, 2000). However, a study of the pattern of arrests of Canadian international travellers indicated that drug-related offences were an important reason for this tourist segment (MacPherson *et al.*, 2007b). This finding corresponded to the combination of America as the most visited country by Canadians and America's stringently enforced drug policies. For some tourists, it may not be a matter of deliberately committing a crime but a misunderstanding of the laws and regulations between different countries (for prostitution, indecent behaviour, drugs, importing illegal goods and so on) that labels them as criminal. Tourists are more likely to be familiar with the laws of their home country than with the laws of the receiving country and thereby make an error. Thus, tourists as offenders can be deliberate or accidental.

Finally, as shown in Fig. 13.3, crime against non-tourists or local residents also contributes to the destination image in respect of fear of crime. Cities infamous for crime against residents had hammered out for themselves images of violence that made the potential tourist fearful without attacks specifically against tourists gaining publicity (Pizam, 1999). New York, Washington, DC, and New Orleans are cited by Pizam (1999) as such cities in the 1990s. Today, one could perhaps think of Johannesburg, Rio de Janeiro or Naples. During the decision-making process, tourists appear to use the 'fear of crime' aspect of destination image to screen out certain countries or areas perceived as unsafe from the choice set (Brunt *et al.*, 2000). However, tourists appear less likely to actively choose a destination because of its image as a safe destination (Brunt *et al.*, 2000). Evidence for this filter effect is limited and further research in this area of decision making would be useful.

ALLAYING THE FEAR...

If perusing through the fears and behaviours of solo female tourists and contemplating the fear of flying, disruptive passengers, health risks and crime have left you with the side effects of heightened anxiety, we apologize and would like to leave you with the thought that the tourist is a feisty and resilient beast. Tourist numbers following a crisis invariably improve with time and much energy is exerted by tourism authorities to aid this recovery.

With time, scenes and locations of great disaster or personal tragedy can give rise to thana-tourism or dark tourism where tourists are attracted precisely because of the terrible events that occurred in the past.

Our next chapter is almost diametrically opposed to this one on fear, flight and feistiness. It is about the pleasures and processes of giving and receiving gifts that are tourism experiences – in other words, the tourist behaviour associated with the purchasing of tourism for consumption by other people whom we seek to please.

REFERENCES

Angell, S.Y. and Cetron, M.S. (2005) Health disparities among travellers visiting friends and relatives abroad. *Annals of Internal Medicine* 142(1) 67–72.

Associated Press (2008) U.S. cruise ship escapes fire from pirates in Gulf of Aden. *New York Times* 3 December 2008. Available at: www.nytimes.com/2008/12/03/world/africa/03pirates.html?_r=1

Beirman, D. (2003) *Restoring Tourism Destinations in Crisis. A Strategic Marketing Approach.* CAB International, Wallingford, UK.

Bianchi, R. (2007) Tourism and the globalisation of fear: analysing the politics of risks and (in)security in global travel. *Tourism and Hospitality Research*, 7(1) 64–74.

Bor, R. (2003) Trends in disruptive passenger behaviour on board UK registered aircraft: 1999–2003. *Travel Medicine and Infectious Disease* 1(3) 153–157.

Bor, R. (2007) Psychological factors in airline passenger and crew behaviour: a clinical review. *Travel Medicine and Infectious Disease* 5(4) 207–216.

Borrill, J. and Foreman, E.I. (1996) Understanding cognitive change: a qualitative study of the impact of cognitive-behavioural therapy on fear of flying. *Clinical Psychology and Psychotherapy* 3(1) 62–74.

Brunt, P., Mawby, R., and Hambly, Z. (2000) Tourist victimisation and the fear of crime on holiday. *Tourism Management* 21(4) 417–424.

Davis, X.M., MacDonald, S., Borwein, S., Freedman, D.O., Kozarsky, P.E., von Sonnenburg, F., Keystone, J.S., Lim, P.L. and Marano, N. (2008) Short report: health risks in travelers to China: the GeoSentinel experience and implications for the 2008 Beijing Olympics. *American Journal of Tropical Medicine and Hygiene* 79(1) 4–8.

Dawson, A. (2007) What are the moral obligations of the traveller in relation to vaccination? *Travel Medicine and Infectious Disease*, 5(2) 90–96.

Dolnicar, S. (2005) Understanding barriers to leisure travel: tourist fears as a marketing basis. *Journal of Vacation Marketing*, 11(3) 197–208.

Foreign & Commonwealth Office (2003) *Campaign and partners. Visiting Friends and Relatives (VFR).* Available at: www.fco.gov.uk/servlet

Foreman, E.I. and Borrill, J. (1994) Long-term follow-up of cognitive behavioural treatment for three cases of fear of flying. *Journal of Travel Medicine* 1(1) 30–35.

Foreman, E.I. and Iljon, Z. (1994) Highwaymen to hijackers: a survey of travel fears. *Travel Medicine International*, 12(4) 145–152.

Gibson, D.C. (2006) The relationship between serial murder and the American tourism industry. *Journal of Travel & Tourism Marketing* 20(1) 45–60.

Gigerenzer, G. (2006) Out of the frying pan into the fire: behavioural reactions to terrorist attacks. *Risk Analysis* 26(2) 347–351.

Gushulak, B., Funk, M. and Steffen, R. (2007) Global changes related to travelers' health. *Journal of Travel Medicine* 14(4) 205–208.

International Maritime Association (2008) *November 2008: IMO chief makes direct appeal to Security Council for Somalia piracy action*. Available at: www.imo.org/Facilitation/mainframe.asp?topic_id=1178

Kozarsky, P. (2006) The body of knowledge for the practice of travel medicine. *Journal of Travel Medicine* 13(5) 251–254.

Lopez-Velez, R. and Bayas, J.-M. (2007) Spanish travellers to high risk areas in the tropics: airport survey of travel health knowledge, attitudes, and practices in vaccination and malaria prevention. *Journal of Travel Medicine* 14(5) 297–305.

MacPherson, D.W., Gushulak, B.D. and Sandhu, J. (2007a) Death and international travel – the Canadian experience: 1996 to 2004. *Journal of Travel Medicine* 14(2) 77–84.

MacPherson, D.W., Gushulak, B.D. and Sandhu, J. (2007b) Arrest and detention in international travellers. *Travel Medicine and Infectious Disease* 5(4) 217–222.

Nousi, A., van Gerwen, L. and Spinhoven, P. (2008) The flight anxiety situations questionnaire and the flight anxiety modality questionnaire: norms for people with fear of flying. *Travel Medicine and Infectious Disease* 6(1) 305–310.

Oxford English Dictionary online (2008) Available at: www.dictionary.oed.com/cgi/entry

Pai, H.-H. and Lai, J.-L. (2008) Health problems among international travellers: from a subtropical region to tropical and non-tropical regions. *Travel Medicine and Infectious Disease* 6(4) 201–204.

Pizam, A. (1999) A comprehensive approach to classifying acts of crime and violence at tourism destinations. *Journal of Travel Research* 38(1) 5–12.

Reisinger, Y. and Mavondo, F. (2005) Travel anxiety and intentions to travel internationally: implications of travel risk perception. *Journal of Travel Research*, 43(3) 212–225.

Roehl, W.S. and Fesenmaier, D.R. (1992) Risk perceptions and pleasure travel: an exploratory analysis. *Journal of Travel Research* 30(4), 17–26.

Ryan, C. (1993) Crime, violence, terrorism and tourism. An accidental or intrinsic relationship? *Tourism Management* 14(3) 173–183.

Smith, D.C. (2008a) Pulling the plug on culture shock: a seven step plan for managing travel anxiety. *Journal of Global Business Issues* 2(1) 41–46.

Smith, D.R. and Leggat, P.A. (2008) Editorial. Impact factors and the Journal of Travel Medicine. *Journal of Travel Medicine* 15(6) 389–390.

Smith, H. (2008b) Curse of the boozy Britons returns to Greek resorts. Foreign Office is launching an anti-rape campaign as resorts are invaded by young holidaymakers. *The Observer* Sunday, 27 July. Available at: www.guardian.co.uk/world/2008/jul/27/Greece.drugsandalcohol/print

Steffen, R., Amitirigala, I. and Mutsch, M. (2008) Editorial. Health risks among travellers – need for regular updates. *Journal of Travel Medicine* 15(3) 145–146.

Stone, J.G. and Nichol, S. (1999) Older, single female holiday makers in the United Kingdom – who needs them? *Journal of Vacation Marketing* 5(1) 7–17.

Van Gerwen, L., Diekstra, R.F.W., Arondeus, J.M. and Wolfger, R. (2004) Fear of flying treatment programs for passengers: an international update. *Travel Medicine and Infectious Disease* 2(1) 27–35.

Wilson, E. and Little, D.E. (2008) The solo female travel experience: exploring the 'Geography of Women's Fear'. *Current Issues in Tourism* 11(2), 167–185.

World Health Organization (2008) *International Travel and Health 2008 Edition*. World Health Organization, Geneva.

chapter 14

GIVING TOURISM: THE INTANGIBLE GIFT

It was a Saturday morning in September. Through the post arrived an A4 leaflet with a photograph of a ribbon tied in a bow on the front. It was from the National Trust, a UK heritage conservation charity with over 300 houses and 200 gardens to visit. As the leaflet illustrated, the National Trust had clearly started thinking about seasonal presents. The accompanying letter informed the reader thus:

> [F]inding the perfect gift to buy someone is always tricky. What books do they read, what music do they like, what perfume do they wear? Which is why we'd like to tell you about National Trust gift membership. It's the perfect idea for a present as it really does have something for everyone to enjoy, even better, it can be enjoyed throughout the whole year.
>
> (National Trust, 2008)

The timing of the mail shot was perfect – not because either of the authors had got round to thinking about what to buy our respective family and friends for Christmas and the New Year, but because we were about to start writing this chapter.

During your lifetime, it is likely that some of the tourism that you undertake will come to you by way of a gift. You will not have purchased it yourself, but will have been given it by family, friends or perhaps work colleagues. Indeed, you may already have shunned the physical object – the books, the music and the perfume – and either been a donor or a recipient of an intangible experience. It may have been something simple such as a weekend away or a spa day, or something more exotic such as 'walking with wolves' or a day of sphereing.[1]

---

[1] Sphereing essentially involves rolling down a mountainside in a human-sized hamster ball and speeds can reach 30 mph. As a sport, it is probably not for the faint-hearted. It is also possible to go 'aqua sphereing'.

If you have not either given or received an experience as a present, try asking friends and family – we think you will know someone who has.

These experiences – whether tourism- or leisure-based – are popular 21st-century gifts. The 'experience sector' may be worth around £200 million a year in the UK (Gohlar, 2007). On the other side of the Atlantic, Unity Marketing's Gift Tracker survey in America describes the experience as a *hot gift category* for the future (Anonymous, 2005). We think its popularity as a gift will grow.

Of course, there are other forms of gift-giving behaviour that touch on travel and tourism. For instance, there is corporate gifting and charitable giving and something termed as 'self-gifting' (gifts to oneself), not to mention the gifts (such as local handicrafts) that tourists purchase for others while on holiday. But in this chapter, we are looking at the gift of a tourism or leisure experience between two or more individual people who are using such gifts within their relationship.

There are plenty of options for weekend or short-break packages as gifts, but the majority of experience gifts offered by the experience sector are not tourism products. Many are really about leisure and hospitality and may be carried out in the recipient's immediate area with only localized travel. In practice, however, many of these leisure-type experiences have a more substantial travel element or an overnight stay subsequently built in by the donor. For example, in taking a white-water rafting experience, the recipient may need to travel to a different and more mountainous part of the country and use accommodation overnight. In doing so, they become tourists. Once this potential of extending the leisure experience is recognized, the experience gift could become a useful marketing tool for boosting domestic tourism. For example, in November 2007, VisitBritain launched a new initiative with Red Letter Days, the market leader in the experience sector in the UK, to do just this.

This chapter examines the phenomenon of experience gift-giving behaviour in more depth. We use the term 'experience' as this is how the industry often refers to it, but, of course, we are really interested in travel and tourism when overlaid with the status of a gift. In the simple terms of the decision-making unit (DMU), the buyer is not the same person as the end user, as access to the experience has changed ownership between purchase and consumption. We look at some of the reasons why experience gifts have emerged as a popular choice of gift. We outline the key concepts and components to understanding gift-giving behaviour as portrayed in the gift-giving literature of the social scientists. We consider the structure of the experience gift industry and a typology of experience gifts – the purchased, the modified and the created. And, of course, we highlight the behavioural characteristics observed in experience gift giving that are of particular importance to this intangible present. Throughout, we use recent primary research into experience gift giving conducted by one of the authors (Clarke, 2006, 2007, 2008a,b, 2009).

WHY HAVE EXPERIENCE GIFTS BECOME POPULAR?

There are a number of reasons for the rise of the experience gift (Clarke, 2006). Fundamentally, Western societies are affluent societies with individual people in many segments well able to buy a physical item on impulse as and when they want it. There is no necessity for them to wait to be given a digital camera for a birthday or festival day as they can buy it now with cash or credit card. This makes it harder for the potential donor of a gift to know exactly what the intended recipient already has or might have by the date of gift exchange. Donors might like to buy them a camera, but do recipients have one already or will they purchase one in the intervening months? Of course, a donor could tell the recipient that he/she is going to buy him/her a camera for his/her birthday, but if he/she does this, the element of surprise – an important element in gift giving – is gone. The recipient knows what to expect. On top of this are the unchartered dangers of buying the wrong brand (size, colour, speci- fication) of camera. Recipients can be very exacting. Jewellery, clothes, artwork and items for the home are all subject to very individual tastes – even bath oils and shower gels can be the wrong brand. Can a donor get it right and still give a gift that is a surprise? It has been suggested that about £1.2 billion is spent each year on unwanted presents in the UK alone (BBC, 2005).

In addition, there appears to be a backlash in certain groups against the accumulation of yet more physical things (Clarke, 2006). Recipients talk of presents of physical goods becoming *dust collectors*, *liabilities* and *white elephants* (Clarke, 2006, p. 539). They describe how they try to ban friends from giving presents that require dusting, moving and maintenance and consume precious space in the home. They talk of trying to downsize their lifestyles, de-cluttering their everyday environment and habitually shedding physical things. They take things to car boot sales, recycling centres and charity shops, or post them on eBay to sell. These people are often aged 40 plus who have achieved a certain level of material comfort. To such people, a physical gift can become another *meaningless item* (Clarke, 2006, p. 539), whereas an experience allows only an accumulation of memories. Intangibility is the very advantage that experiences hold in the gift attractiveness stakes.

CORE CONCEPTS FOR ANY GIFT GIVING

Before we continue examining experiences as gifts, it is worthwhile laying the groundwork about what we know about gift-giving behaviour in general. A gift – any gift – has been described as a 'ritual offering that is a sign of involvement in and connectedness to another' (Cheal, 1987, p. 153). People give to celebrate important life events, nurture personal relation- ships, foster economic exchange and socialize their children into desirable behaviour patterns (Belk, 1979). The practice of giving gifts has been studied by social scientists for decades (e.g. Mauss, 1954) and gift giving is widely recognized as 'a pervasive form of consumer behaviour' in contemporary society (Banks, 1979, p. 324).

There are core concepts that are relevant to any type of gift giving, whether physical good or experience. It is the interaction between the donor, the recipient, the occasion and the gift that creates the uniqueness of a specific gift exchange. Driving the whole system is the social obligation to give, receive and reciprocate (Mauss, 1954). Not all gift-giving occasions involve the mutual exchange of gifts. Therefore, in any relationship between two people, there is a staggering of reciprocity so that 'balanced reciprocity' (defined as equilibrium between donor and receiver) is unlikely at a stated point in time (Sahlins, 1972). Instead, donor and recipient roles are continually reversed in order to sustain the relationship through time.

The donor

Donors – whether singular or plural – have different motivations when they choose gifts. Sherry (1983) describes altruistic motives as focusing on anticipated recipient pleasure. The donor's perception of the recipient is reflected in gift selection (Wolfinbarger, 1990), as one might expect, but so too is the donor's own ideal self-concept, sometimes to the point of over-riding the recipient's characteristics (Belk, 1979; Sherry and McGrath, 1989). In these situations, the gift says more about the donor than it does about the recipient. There is a darker side that potentially lurks within some donors who focus on self-satisfaction, for a donor may be motivated by displays of power or status – labelled as agonistic motives by Sherry (1983). For example, it may be that the gift of a digital camera is really about displaying the donor's superior wealth in choosing the latest luxury model.

Donors have different quantities of assets – or productive resources – when choosing gifts. These productive resources that are invested in gift decisions are money, time and personal effort, thought or labour. A Belgian study suggested that higher-income groups tend to substitute a shortage of time with more financial outlay so that the emphasis for the gift is on the price paid (Mortelmans and Damen, 2001). Once invested, these productive resources transcend into the concept of 'donor sacrifice' or what the donor has given up or invested in order to provide the gift.

The recipient

The recipient may be surprised by a gift, but likewise, they may be involved in the gift selection itself. The classic is the issuing of a 'wish-list' of presents, with the ubiquitous wedding list as a notable example. Recipients may also participate in a less obvious way by dropping hints or casual window shopping with donors, an indirect tactic that Durgee and Sego (2001) refer to as 'sleuthing out'. According to Wooten (2000), recipient affluence raises the level of anxiety for a donor who is unsure what to buy the person who has everything.

And the link between …

The link between the donor and the recipient (or between a number of donors and recipients in various configurations) is the relationship. A gift has to be appropriate to the type of relationship (Cheal, 1996; Ruth *et al.*, 1999) – for example, godmother and godchild, two close friends, husband and wife, a group of work colleagues, father and child, parent and school-teacher and so on – and to its longevity, geographical distance and emotional intensity. It follows that expressive gifts tend to mark the emotionally close relationship and utilitarian gifts the more distant relationship (Sherry, 1983).

The occasion

Different societies create different occasions for the exchange of gifts. An initial list in the UK would include birthdays and coming of age, Christmas and other religious events, Valentine's Day, weddings and wedding anniversaries, job retirement, graduation, thank yous, baby christenings, hospital visits and so on. Rather than creating a definitive list, occasions can be usefully categorized. Some occasions are calendrical events, such as birthdays and religious events and others are more fluid and emergent – or non-calendrical – such as periods of illness, reconciliations or job promotions (Ruth *et al.*, 1999). What is important is that the selected gift is well matched to the occasion. The relationship may be the same, but you would not take the wedding gift to the stag night and the stag night gift to the wedding. Specific occasions demand different rituals and ceremony for gift exchange. Gift wrapping is a common element for many occasions, with the choice of wrapping helping to differentiate the occasion as well as disguising the gift (Hendry, 1993).

The gift itself

The chosen gift is highly symbolic, emotional and laden with meaning which the donor hopes will be communicated to the recipient without recourse to language (Belk, 1996a). In fact, the gift may be valued more by the recipient for its symbolism than for any material benefit (Wolfinbarger, 1990). We know something about the attributes of the perfect gift in Western societies – for example, the gift should demonstrate donor sacrifice, be uniquely matched to the recipient and (ideally) surprise the recipient (Belk, 1996b; Durgee and Sego, 2001). These three themes are developed later in the chapter in respect to experience gifts.

THE SUPPLY SIDE: THE EXPERIENCE GIFT INDUSTRY

We have already touched on the industry structure for experience gifts, but it is important to realize that any travel or tourism product can become a gift if that is the intention of the purchaser. This means that all businesses and organizations that sell tourism products to consumers have the potential to be involved in the gift-giving market. An outline of the industry structure would consist of:

- experience companies that are generalists;
- experience companies that are specialists;
- tourism, hospitality and leisure companies and organizations;
- facilitators.

The experience companies that are generalists are third party organizers which package up activity and other components such as insurance and then sell to the consumer. They often have a strong online presence, although they may distribute the experiences through high-street shops too. In the UK, examples would include Red Letter Days, Virgin Experience Days and Experience World. Typically such companies offer hundreds of different experiences to the consumer and also operate flexible gift voucher schemes. Table 14.1 illustrates an A to Z of examples drawn from the web sites of experience companies, and, although we admit defeat in our search for 'X', there was plenty of choice for the other letters, passing from the sedate to the active to the way-out. If Harry Potter's game of quidditch ever becomes a possibility, we are sure it will be offered! For the time being, however, the table gives you an idea of the range of pre-prepared packages currently being marketed as gifts.

The experience companies that are specialists are third party organizers that specialize in a particular area of expertise. In the UK, examples would include Balloons over Britain specializing in hot air balloon trips, or Everyman Driving Experiences specializing in different types of driving experiences, such as the Lamborghini Gallardo Thrill, Formula 1 driving and the Hummer and Corvette experience.

Then there are the vast number of tourism, hospitality and leisure companies and organizations. Some of these organizations have recognized the potential of their leisure and tourism products as gifts and are actively marketing them as such. For example – as you saw in the introduction to the chapter – the National Trust recognizes that its annual

Table 14.1. An A to Z of examples of gifts offered by experience companies in the UK.

Aqua sphereing	Necker Island holiday
Big cat encounter	Overnight wine-tasting experience
Celebrity gardening experience	Polo day
Deluxe short-break explorer	Quad biking
Eagle handling day	Rock 'n' Roll legends tour
Ferrari versus Lamborghini experience	Stand up comedy weekend
Glenmorangie whisky break	Teepee retreat
Husky dog sledding	Ulusaba private game reserve holiday
Italian cookery and master class	Virtual soldier
JCB racing	Wakeboarding
Kasbah Tamadot break	X
Llama trek	Yamaha off-road biking
Multi-activity weekend	Zero gravity flight

membership scheme has gift-giving potential and runs campaigns to promote it as such. However, most tourism and leisure organizations will not be actively pursuing the gift-giving market, even if they are aware that a few or more of their products are bought and consumed as gifts. For example, a tour operator may be aware that a small percentage of its short-break packages are purchased each year as gifts for other people – a Valentine's Day gift or a 30th birthday celebration – but they are not investing marketing resources to attract this segment.

Finally, there are the facilitators. These are the companies and organizations that may not come to the consumer's attention but are supporting the experience gift market in its widest sense. For example, the company SK Chase provides a gift certificate and software system that enables small hotels to sell hotel breaks online as gifts. Such companies help a myriad of smaller tourism and leisure companies to engage more formally with the gift-buying public.

PURCHASED, MODIFIED AND CREATED EXPERIENCE GIFTS

A typology of experience gifts derived from the consumers' perspective shows how consumers behave in this market (Clarke, 2008a, 2009). According to this typology, there are three types of experience gifts, namely the purchased gift, the modified gift and the created gift. Correspondingly, donors can be typecast as buyers, as adaptors and either as competitors or as complementary buyers (Clarke, 2009). Although the typology relates to the industry structure, it remains a consumers' take on the types of experience gifts that are available to them.

The purchased gift is the experience bought from an experience company (generalist or specialist) or from a tourism, hospitality or leisure provider and subsequently conferred gift status by the donor without any significant modifications taking place (Clarke, 2009). To all intents and purposes, the gift remains the original product as sold by the company. Some of these purchased gifts may be bought as impulse purchases, particularly if they are visible to the potential buyer. Perhaps the buyer sees the experience being used by others, such as helicopter rides at a festival, or perhaps the experience has been packaged up with some tangible items in a box for a merchandising display in a retail outlet. Other purchased gifts show more evidence of planning. Buyers often use the Internet to identify options and to compare features between competing offers.

The modified gift is the experience bought from an experience company or from a tourism, hospitality or leisure provider and conferred gift status after significant modifications have been made (Clarke, 2009). These modifications include the addition of meals, transport, or accommodation, or other experiences added by the donor. This may be done to personalize the gift to ensure the best fit with the recipient, to enhance appreciation of the effort invested by the donor or to ensure that the donor and recipient spend quality time together (a further investment of donor resources in the relationship). From the point of view of the tourism industry, this extension of the experience is an exciting way forward for domestic tourism (as noted in the introduction).

The created gift is the experience invented by the donor from a mix of possible commercial and non-commercial elements into a hand-crafted experience (Clarke, 2009). As the gift is the design and creation of the donor, there is plenty of scope for imagination and flair. Such gifts tend to involve considerable planning by the donor, secretively if the gift is planned as a surprise, and the emphasis within the gift's meaning lies with the personal effort, thought and time invested by the donor, rather than with its monetary value. This is very much the individualized gift, carefully engineered to the recipient's idiosyncrasies. In this situation, the actions of the donor might be seen as competitive to the experience companies (for the donor is replacing their pre-prepared products with their own) and as complementary to the tourism, hospitality and leisure companies (from whom the donor might purchase the ingredients for their own gift). For example, a created experience gift to London could include travel, accommodation, a trip on the London Eye, a visit to the aquarium, meals and a night out at a jazz club – all individual elements sold by the supplier to the donor who creates their own 'London experience' out of the mix. As an example at the other end of the financial spectrum, a created experience gift could include travel to an historic property, entrance fees and a surprise picnic in the grounds of the estate. Along with the surprise element, much of the emphasis here lies with the shared leisure time of donor and recipient – the pleasure of being together.

THE BEHAVIOURAL CHARACTERISTICS OF EXPERIENCE DONORS AND RECIPIENTS

In considering contemporary tourist behaviour, what really interests us is to examine how the donors and recipients of experience gifts actually behave. How do they make decisions regarding gift choice? How does the exchange process unfold? How is gift consumption managed? And how do they behave in the aftermath? Figure 14.1 outlines the key stages of the process from initial problem recognition through to the notions of role reversal and reciprocity. As a linear process, this representation is open to critique (see Chapter 5, 'Models of Tourist Behaviour', this volume), but it offers a simple sequential framework to which the concepts and behaviours discussed can be attached, at least for initial perusal. We will refer to this figure as we explore some of the ideas that help to explain the behaviour of people who give and receive gifts that are experiences.

The process in Fig. 14.1 starts with problem recognition, when a donor recognizes that a gift is needed. Into this problem recognition feeds the characteristics of the occasion, the recipient, the donor (including donor resources) and the relationship, as discussed earlier in the chapter. The information search and evaluation of alternatives may well involve online searching to identify experiences and to compare different options. The decision will result in an experience that may be categorized as either a purchased, modified or created experience gift.

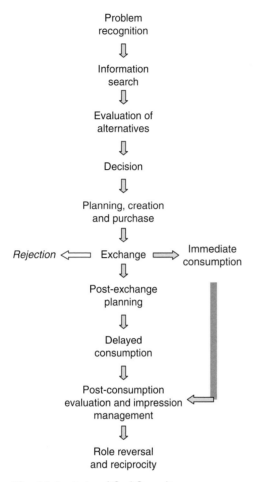

Problem
recognition
⇩
Information
search
⇩
Evaluation of
alternatives
⇩
Decision
⇩
Planning, creation
and purchase
⇩
Rejection ⟸ Exchange ⟹ Immediate
consumption
⇩
Post-exchange
planning
⇩
Delayed
consumption
⇩
Post-consumption
evaluation and impression ⟸
management
⇩
Role reversal
and reciprocity

Fig. 14.1. A simplified flow diagram to help explain experience gift-giving behaviour.

Further donor resources will be invested as the experience is then acquired, planned and created, as appropriate. Where a group of donors is involved, it may elect a 'project manager' to delegate the tasks (Clarke, 2006).

The exchange of the experience between donor and recipient might be considered the central point of the process. The social and physical setting and the observance of ritual suited to the occasion (including gift wrapping) are all elements of gift exchange. Recipients may need to think about 'impression management' upon gift revelation so that they relay the message they would like back to the donor, even if the gift is not liked in itself.

Some experience gifts will be designed for immediate consumption, and others will be designed for delayed consumption. During the time lag between exchange and usage, post-exchange planning, in the form of final travel details, meals en route and so forth, may be necessary. Both donor and recipient may be engaged in this post-exchange activity. Obviously, the recipient will be participating in the consumption of the experience (unless the experience was rejected as a gift), and there are good reasons why a donor might also elect to join in. Post-consumption evaluation of the experience will take place, with the recipient aware of impression management after the experience as the donor seeks feedback as to how much they enjoyed themselves. The final stage in the process as indicated on the flow diagram is that of role reversal and reciprocity, alluding back to the staggered nature of reciprocity and the social obligation to repay. It is unlikely that the next gift within the donor–recipient relationship will be a second experience. However, the original recipient who has a satisfactory experience is likely to absorb the idea of an experience as a good gift for future use in other relationships. The experience gift becomes part of their gift-giving repertoire. In addition, the impact of the experience gift, successful or unsuccessful, may have repercussions for the ongoing relationship between donor and recipient in terms of strengthening or weakening the bonds.

Having moved sequentially through the different stages of Fig. 14.1, we now examine more of the behavioural characteristics of the donors and recipients of experience gifts.

Building in surprise

We know from the literature that one of the attributes that can make a gift in Western society successful is its ability to surprise the recipient. It is the gift that was not expected, the one that was not on the list. Of course, we are referring to the positive surprise; a negative surprise, common sense tells us, would be most unpleasant (although possible if planned by a donor with extreme agonistic motivation). To keep the recipient from guessing, a donor might recruit an 'accomplice', someone close to the recipient who can block out dates in a diary and help organize things behind the recipient's back (Clarke, 2006). This accomplice can help with evaluating the alternatives too, advising on what experience would be best suited in the light of any quirky recipient likes, dislikes or health issues. These donors adopt a decision style of 'plotting' (Clarke, 2008b) so that the details are planned without the recipient's knowledge. The opposing decision style is 'discussing', where the recipient is informed and involved; however, unlike plotting and use of an accomplice, this does not build and maintain surprise for the recipient. According to one recipient, an experience gift is successful as a surprise only if it is a 'workable surprise' (Clarke, 2007) – the practical details have to fit with the recipient's lifestyle – and this requires empathy and careful planning on the part of the donor.

As the experience is intangible, there is a dilemma for the donor as to how to actually give the gift to the recipient at the time of exchange. An envelope is a popular wrapping choice, but has instant connotations of money or vouchers. However, presenting the gift as a written promise in a box immediately transforms the experience into the guise of a physical object. The box is skilfully used to mislead the recipient into thinking about what object might be hidden inside. Boxes used by experience companies are often big (to symbolize the magnitude of the gift) or ornate (to symbolize the luxuriousness of the gift). Such boxes can also be used for post-exchange display on a cabinet or mantelpiece, a piece of physical evidence that might alleviate any post-exchange anxiety or stoke up excited anticipation. An alternative to a box is to use a physical surrogate as a wrapping strategy (Clarke, 2008a). For example, a box of wrapped up golf balls to symbolize a golfing holiday, or a teddy bear in flying jacket and goggles to symbolize a weekend away flying historic aircraft. Such use of physical surrogates is also a popular wrapping choice for exchange; after all, it makes the experience tangible in a way that gives plenty of scope for donor creativity.

As noted, experience gifts can either be designed for immediate or delayed consumption following exchange. Donors giving an experience for immediate consumption sometimes build in a 'follow me' tactic (Clarke, 2007) to maintain surprise. Instead of revealing the gift to the recipient, the donor demands that the recipient joins them for a period of time, and the experience, location and other participants (if any) are gradually revealed in piecemeal fashion. For example, unexpected guests turning up at the recipient's house can commence the gift of a day trip on a river launch (but she does not know this yet). Then a previously hidden hamper can be loaded (with guests) into a car – so that the recipient only guesses at what is occurring until the donor finally drives into the boatyard. Her only instruction (delivered in a box at the point of exchange) was to be ready at 9 a.m.!

Donors giving experiences for delayed consumption sometimes build in a 'decoy' tactic (Clarke, 2007) to pump up the continued suspense as to what the gift actually is. The donor might pass over a list of things that the recipient must have ready and packed for the trip in 2 weeks' time. These listed items include plenty of items to fire up the recipient's imagination, as well as those actually required. For example, a trip to a music festival might include a passport, black tie and buoyancy aid, as well as the camping gear and waterproofs genuinely needed. For one research informant (Clarke, 2007, 2008a, 2009) the decoy strategy was so successful that she believed she might be going bog snorkelling in Wales, and the canoeing trip remained a surprise until the donor chose to reveal it.

In addition, during consumption or usage, we must remember that, like all tourism products, the experience gift has an inbuilt characteristic of variability. Its performance is reliant on the interplay between human beings – the recipient, possibly donor, co-consumers, supplier employees and other third parties. Thus, during consumption, there is always the possibility of the unexpected event in the sense that it is not planned as part of the gift, for example, a canal-based cruise where other river users at a lock joined in to sing 'Happy Birthday', or simply bumping into old school friends during an experience gift to London (Clarke, 2007). Such incidents can provide additional surprises for the recipient, although if they are not positive ones, they need to be managed by the donor to reduce the impact. A service marketer would label these surprises as 'critical incidents' (Zeithaml and Bitner, 1996), because of the influence on recipient satisfaction.

Of course, in the early 21st century, it might be easy to surprise a recipient with an experience gift, because experience gifts are largely off the potential recipient's radar. In the grand gifting scheme, they are not commonplace. This situation might change as the possibility of experience gifts is absorbed into the gifting repertoire of individuals, aided and abetted by role reversal and the need to reciprocate – a sort of virtuous circle for the general expansion of experience gift-giving practice.

A new emphasis for donor sacrifice

Although experience gifts can be expensive and absorb plenty of the donor's financial resources, it seems that the real emphasis for these gifts lies with donor effort and donor time. We have already alluded to this when we examined purchased, modified and created experience gifts. We also know from the literature that successful gifts need to demonstrate donor sacrifice and be uniquely matched to the recipient.

Donors can invest a great deal of personal labour, time, thought and effort into designing, plotting and planning a created or modified experience gift. Even the purchased experience gift – though less adept – can demonstrate time spent in searching and evaluating the alternatives, particularly if donors move on to plan the practical details. With the created gift, the what, when, where, how and with whom all need to be mapped out by the donor, typically before gift exchange. Post-exchange, the donor might still be investing time and effort in the planning of final arrangements. This demonstrable effort may be more pleasing to the recipient than the actual price tag associated with the experience.

Even more powerful is the investment of donor time during consumption, whether for an immediate or delayed experience. In Western society, we appear increasingly starved of quality time to spend with the people closest to us. Family and friends can often be squeezed out of our hectic 24/7 schedules. Time has become a most precious resource. We might think of ourselves as cash-rich but time-poor; we grow less accustomed to 'taking time', 'finding time' or to others 'giving us' time. For us, 'time flies' (Clarke, 2007). So where the donor chooses to invest discretionary leisure time (rationed) ahead of money (easier to expand), the gift is particularly satisfying for the recipient, for time is the resource that we hanker after and is therefore more expressive of the true value placed on our relationships.

Experience gift consumption shows four possibilities with regard to patterns of participation (Clarke, 2007, 2008a,b). The first two involve the donor and are of most concern to us here. The first is the most powerful and involves the donor as an additional participant. In this situation, the donor undertakes the experience alongside the recipient, be it making clay pots or white-water rafting. Donors join in. The time is shared together, whether for a day, a weekend or a longer holiday. The second involves the donor as a spectator. Here, the donor watches the recipient undertake the experience, but travels with them for the journey and joins in meals and other add-on activities. The donor as a spectator tends to occur for one of two reasons – when the experience is too expensive for the donor to pay for another and when the experience is too dangerous or extreme for the donor to enjoy, perhaps on grounds of health. The remaining possibilities for patterns of consumption do not involve the donor in experience consumption. The recipient might share the experience with other chosen friends or significant others (perhaps because the donor lives too far away to join in), or the recipient might attend on their own, relying on co-consumers whom they had not previously met for ensuring satisfaction. As you might imagine, this final option is the most risky in terms of recipient satisfaction with the gift.

The imagination, creativity and thought that a donor may invest in a created experience gift also enable the gift to be uniquely matched to the recipient. This care and attention is also embedded in the gift to be decoded by the recipient as symbolizing the relationship. An interesting example (Clarke, 2009) highlighted a London experience trip which included an 'open cheque' at Harvey Nichols, the upmarket department store. On the surface, this appears to be a straightforward investment of money in the gift. However, 'Harvey Nics' was blended into this couple's favourite television programme and they had a private on-running joke about it. The fact that the husband wove Harvey Nichols into the experience was a reference to the humour in their relationship and his appreciation of it. The nuance behind the gift was very individual to the recipient. So the created experience gift (and to an extent the modified experience gift) is very versatile when personal thought and imagination are emphasized as components of donor sacrifice. The created experience gift has the capacity to be unique to the recipient.

The possibility of recipient sacrifice

We have emphasized donor sacrifice, both in terms of the actual resources invested and in terms of the balance of resources most appreciated by the recipient (personal effort, time shared and so forth). The nature of an experience means that the recipient has to spend time actually consuming the gift. However, it is possible for recipients to find themselves obliged to use other resources – such as money, personal effort or time spent planning – in order to undertake the experience. So, in giving the gift, the donor is demanding recipient sacrifice beyond the actual time spent enjoying the experience (Clarke, 2007). Recipients can find themselves responsible for scheduling diaries, cancelling other commitments, finding friends to go with, and for travel and other not-so-incidental costs. One recipient talked about the 'hassle' of a surprise experience gift (Clarke, 2007). This recipient sacrifice can be particularly evident in the case of purchased experience gifts that are not well thought through by the donor, as much of the planning is offloaded on to the recipient. But it can also occur with modified and created experiences where the donor has not paid adequate attention to the balance between donor and recipient resources; where too much is expected of the recipient, the experience is less likely to be a successful gift. It can also result in gift rejection.

MYSELF: THE CONFIDENT EXPERIENCE GIFT DONOR

In this chapter, we have explored the phenomenon of the behaviour of donors and recipients of experience gifts. In doing so, we have highlighted key gift-giving concepts, outlined the structure of the industry and examined a typology of experience gifts (purchased, modified and created). We then moved on to look in more detail at the behaviour of donors and recipients with the aid of a simple process diagram; we incorporated the concept of surprise, donor and recipient sacrifice, and engineering the gift uniquely for the recipient – three ideas linked to successful gifts. We also referred to third parties in the process, such as accomplices and co-consumers.

Having read the chapter, you may feel inspired to experiment yourself with experience gifts, if you have not already done so. There are, after all, plenty of tips about how to go about it with confidence. On a serious note, an experience gift is all about doing and being, rather than having, and there is evidence that experiences in general are more conducive to happiness than material possession (Van Boven and Gilovich, 2003) because experiences are more open to positive interpretation and are more central to a person's identity. The following are the words of one donor informant in the experience gift-giving research carried out in the last few years:

> I've got a better sense of what they like to do than what they like to have. You consume experiences in a way that you don't consume [objects]. You don't accumulate experiences – I mean, you accumulate in another way, of happy memories, which is very nice – but they don't gather dust, they don't become white elephants and a liability.

(Female, 46–55)

This quotation brings us neatly round to our starting point – the appeal of the intangible experience as a gift over the physical good.

REFERENCES

Anonymous (2005) New survey finds gift giving on the rise. *Souvenirs, Gifts and Novelties* 44(8), 92–111.

Banks, S. (1979) Gift-giving: a review and interactive paradigm. *Advances in Consumer Research* 6(1), 319–324.

BBC (2005) Unwanted presents cost UK £1.2bn. Available at: http://news.bbc.co.uk/cbbcnews/hi/newsid_4450000/newsid_4459400/4459446.stm

Belk, R.W. (1979) Gift-giving behaviour. In: Sheth, J. (ed.) *Research in Marketing*. JAI Press, Greenwich, Connecticut, pp. 95–126.

Belk, R.W. (1996a) The meaning of gifts and greetings. *Advances in Consumer Research* 23(1), 13.

Belk, R.W. (1996b) The perfect gift. In: Otnes, C.C. and Beltramini, R.F. (eds) *Gift Giving. A Research Anthology*. Bowling Green State University Popular Press, Bowling Green, Ohio, pp. 59–84.

Cheal, D. (1987) Showing them you love them: gift giving and the dialectic of intimacy. *Sociological Review* 35(1), 150–169.

Cheal, D. (1996) Gifts in contemporary North America. In: Otnes, C.C. and Beltramini, R.F. (eds) *Gift Giving. A Research Anthology*. Bowling Green State University Popular Press, Bowling Green, Ohio, pp. 85–98.

Clarke, J. (2006) Different to 'dust collectors'? The giving and receiving of experience gifts. *Journal of Consumer Behaviour* 5(6), 533–549.

Clarke, J. (2007) The four S's of experience gift giving behaviour. *International Journal of Hospitality Management* 26(1), 98–116.

Clarke, J. (2008a) Experiences as gifts: from process to model. *European Journal of Marketing* 42(3/4) 365–389.

Clarke, J. (2008b) Gifts of tourism: insights to consumer behaviour. *Annals of Tourism Research* 35(2) 529–550.

Clarke, J. (2009) Purchased, modified created: consumer voices in experience gifts. *Service Industries Journal* (in press).

Durgee, J.F. and Sego, T. (2001) Gift-giving as a metaphor for understanding new products that delight. *Advances in Consumer Research* 28(1), 64–69.

Gohlar, R. (2007) Red letter days picks agency for Christmas push. *Marketing Week*, 7 September.

Hendry, J. (1993) *Wrapping Culture. Politeness, Presentation and Power in Japan and Other Societies*. Clarendon Press, Oxford.

Mauss, M. (1954) *The Gift. Forms and Function of Exchange in Archaic Societies*. Cohen & West, London.

Mortelmans, D. and Damen, S. (2001) Attitudes on commercialisation and anti-commercial reactions on gift-giving occasions in Belgium. *Journal of Consumer Behaviour* 1(2), 156–173.

National Trust (2008) *A Gift Your Friends Can Enjoy Time and Time Again Throughout the Year*. The National Trust mail shot promotion piece for the Membership Department, Autumn, Warrington, UK.

Ruth, J.A., Otnes, C.C. and Brunel, F.F. (1999) Gift receipt and the reformulation of interpersonal relationships. *Journal of Consumer Research* 25(4), 385–402.

Sahlins, M. (1972) *Stone Age Economics*. Aldine, Chicago, Illinois.

Sherry, J.F. (1983) Gift giving in anthropological perspective. *Journal of Consumer Research* 10(2), 157–168.

Sherry, J.F. and McGrath, M.A. (1989) Unpacking the holiday presence: a comparative ethnography of the gift store. In: Hirschman, E. (ed.) *Interpretive Consumer Research*. Association for Consumer Research, Provo, Utah, pp. 112–129.

Van Boven, L. and Gilovich, T. (2003) To do or to have? That is the question. *Journal of Personality and Social Psychology* 85(6), 1193–1202.

Wolfinbarger, M.F. (1990) Motivation and symbolism in gift-giving behaviour. *Advances in Consumer Research* 17(1), 699–706.

Wooten, D.B. (2000) Qualitative steps towards an expanded model of anxiety on gift-giving. *Journal of Consumer Research* 27(1), 84–95.

Zeithaml, V.A. and Bitner, M.J. (1996) *Services Marketing*. McGraw-Hill, New York.

chapter 15

LIMITS TO TRAVEL? THE ENVIRONMENTAL TOURIST

Back in the early 1990s, a director of what was then the biggest tour operator group in the UK was invited to speak on ecotourism at a Royal Geographical Society gathering. He described his situation as being 'rather like a cattle baron addressing a congress of vegetarians' (Brackenbury, 1992, p. 10).

Beneath the amusement was a serious point. Mass or large-scale tourism was popularly perceived of as 'bad', while so-called alternative or small-scale tourism was popularly perceived of as 'good' (Clarke, 1997). Thus, if you as a tourist took a package holiday to a Mediterranean resort by charter plane, you were something of a villain, whereas if you as a tourist took an ecotourism trip with a specialist operator to a nature-based destination, you were rather more virtuous. Even in the 1990s, this perception of tourism was simplistic (see, for example, early criticism by Wheeller (1991) of the 'us' good and 'them' bad dichotomy). Yet the sheer volume of international tourism and its negative characteristics – the consumption of fossil fuels through air transport, or use of fresh water at resorts in developing countries or the undesirable social impacts on host communities – makes you the tourist thoroughly implicated in the problem of achieving sustainability whether you choose or not.

Think briefly about just one issue, that of carbon dioxide emissions. In 2005, tourism (both domestic and international) accounted for approximately 5% of global emissions of carbon dioxide – with transport contributing roughly three-quarters of the tourism contribution and energy consumption in tourism establishments (like heating, lighting and air conditioning in hotels) contributing the remaining quarter (WTO, 2007a).

The ultimate question for tourists is whether the best contribution they can make to sustainable development is to stay at home. In other words, not to participate in tourism at all. After all, there are vested interests in the tourism industry among most of the bodies and associations that comment on it. They are not likely, therefore, to advocate less or zero tourism as the best way forward.

The tourism industry is grappling with the practicalities of action to tackle climate change. For example, in the UK, there is a coalition of tourism industry companies working on a blueprint project 'Tourism 2023'. The coalition recognizes the options for possible future government intervention such as flight restrictions (*Travel Trade Gazette*, 2008) – just how far down the scale of constraints they as a coalition will contemplate will be seen when they report in 2009.

We draw your attention to the WTO (2007a) definition of sustainable development as

> [T]he continuous effort to balance and integrate the three pillars of social well-being, economic prosperity and environmental protection for the benefit of present and future generations.
>
> (WTO, 2007a, pp. 4–5)

You will clearly see the lineage of this definition when we discuss sustainable development in the section that follows.

In this chapter, we consider the interface between sustainable development or sustainability and your behaviour as a tourist. We look briefly at the bigger picture driving sustainable development before examining something about the detail of tourist behaviour. We consider the different positional viewpoints such as techno-centrism and eco-centrism, which are useful for understanding the opinions and actions of ourselves and others in the sustainability debate. At the macro level, we look at how and why tourist flows and patterns might alter in response to climate change, using an example of both winter and summer tourist flows. We move on to explore the soft management tool of tourist codes of conduct. We then use the notion of confusion to examine tourist behaviour and introduce the concept of 'greenwash' and its impacts on you the tourist. We talk about the gap between consumer attitudes to the environment and realized behaviour, and whether motivation in the context of environmental behaviour really matters. Taking a 'fast' example and a 'slow' example, we focus on aviation and tourist behaviour and the emergence of 'slow tourism'.

A SNAPSHOT OF THE BIGGER PICTURE

Achieving sustainability is a complex problem. We may have agreed a national consensus (e.g. the Stern Review (2006) for the UK government) and an international consensus on the recognition of climate change (e.g. the Intergovernmental Panel on Climate Change, 2007a,b). The latter indicates further global warming of between 1.8 °C and 4 °C by the end of the 21st century, but the corresponding coordinated and global preventative action required is a challenging problem. There are many strands to the problem. A leading environmentalist, Jonathon Porritt (2005), describes two interlocking data sets, the first ecological and the second social.

On the ecological side (Porritt, 2005), we can think about the depletion of natural resources and fossil fuels; global warming, carbon emissions and the production of ozone-depleting substances; extreme climatic events such as tsunamis, droughts, hurricanes; security of food production; deforestation; damage and depletion of coral reefs and wetlands; desertification, soil erosion and the salinization of agricultural land; and loss of biodiversity. We are sure you can add to this ecological roll-call. On the social side (Porritt, 2005), there are issues of population growth; disparities across the globe in terms of people's access to resources as basic as clean water, food, fibre and fuel; equity in the provision of health care and immunization; and the alleviation of poverty in developing countries.

These two data sets – ecological and social – interlock because of the complexities of the relationships between the different strands. You have only to think of the media attention given to biofuels – on the one hand, as part-solution in the search for alternative energy to fossil fuels and, on the other hand, as a competitor for the arable land also needed for global food production.

Tourism has been described by the WTO as both 'victim' and 'vector' in sustainability. That is, tourism is both affected by the manifestations of climate change such as rising sea levels, desertification and the melting of snow and glaciers which damage the tourism economy, and itself contributes to the global environmental crisis – as illustrated by our example of global carbon dioxide emissions. According to the WTO, 'we [tourism] are part of the problem and will be part of the solution' (WTO, 2007b). In the past, tourism has been criticized for being too parochial and narrow in its focus on sustainable tourism, rather than considering its role and participation in worldwide sustainable development. In other words,

> for tourism to really contribute towards security and sustainable development, it needs to be placed within the bigger picture of human mobility, lifestyle, consumption and production.
>
> (Hall, 2005)

Outside of tourism, a recent call for papers for a special issue on sustainable consumption in the *International Journal of Consumer Studies* highlighted such issues as consumer rights and responsibilities in a finite and fragile world, consumption reduction, sustainable lifestyles and households, alternative consumption practices and communities, and localization versus globalization trends in consumption and production.

Today, climate change and what to do about it is a pressing 21st-century problem. However, its current elevation in international political circles should not obscure the fact that the issues were highlighted and action urged in the second half of the 20th century. For example, Rachel Carson's book *The Silent Spring* published in 1962 documented the negative effects of pesticides on the environment. Its success on the public stage meant that the book was credited with helping to launch the environmental movement. Internationally, the World Conservation Strategy (IUCN, 1980) was one of the first notable contributions. Indeed, you may have heard the oft-paraphrased ethical vision of the World Conservation Strategy: 'we have not inherited the earth from our parents, we have borrowed it from our children' (IUCN, 1980). Seven years later, the World Commission on Environment and Development's influential report, 'Our Common Future', commonly referred to as the Brundtland Report, heralded sustainable development as a process of change that promoted both inter- and intra-generational equity and one that grounded the economy firmly in its ecological roots. The Brundtland Report described sustainable development as

> a process of change in which the exploitation of resources, the direction of investments, the orientation of technological development, and institutional change are all in harmony and enhance both current and future potential to meet human needs and aspirations.
>
> (World Commission on Environment and Development, 1987, p. 46)

In short, and with echoes of the ethical vision of the World Conservation Strategy, sustainable development is 'development that meets the needs of the present without compromising the ability of future generations to meet their own needs' (World Commission on Environment and Development, 1987, p. 43). However, even in the 21st century, sustainable development can still be labelled as 'a relatively young and unfinished concept' (Porritt, 2005, p. 3).

The World Conservation Strategy and the Brundtland Report pre-date the 1990s and the landmark event of the so-called Rio Earth Summit or – using its formal title – the United Nations Conference on Environment and Development held in 1992. The Rio Earth Summit established the Agenda 21 principles to aid the implementation of sustainable concepts and was the forerunner to the agreement on the Climate Change Convention and the negotiations leading to the Kyoto Protocol which came into force in 2005.

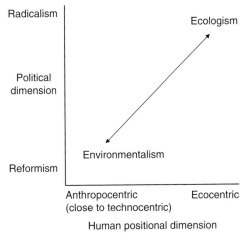

(Adapted from Kilbourne, 1995)

Fig. 15.1. Ideas that help to explain views towards sustainability.

Techno-centrism versus eco-centrism

By now, you will have certainly recognized the range and variety of opinions on sustainability that exist among organizations and individuals alike. Here, we present concepts that help to sort and better understand any given stance that you might come across. Figure 15.1 displays these ideas visually. Adapted from Kilbourne (1995) who built on the work of others, an individual's or organization's attitude and approach to sustainability is dependent upon their placement on the political dimension and on the human positional dimension.

In essence, the political dimension stretches from reformism (or the altering of tourist behaviour, regulation and so forth without challenging the existing social paradigm and power structures) to radicalism (rejection of the existing social paradigm to be replaced by new social and political systems). The former might be illustrated by notions such as increasing the public's environmental intelligence quotient (IQ) (Kangun and Polonsky, 1995), altering tourist purchase behaviour for environmental benefit or legislation to push tourism businesses into environmentally friendly practice. Conversely, the transformation of society to markedly alternative lifestyles or the overthrow of capitalism would illustrate the latter. For example, the stance taken by Porritt (2005) is distinctly one of working within capitalism as a system to reform it and he speaks of

> embracing capitalism as the only overarching system capable of achieving any kind of reconciliation between ecological sustainability, on the one hand, and the pursuit of prosperity and personal well-being, on the other.

(Porritt, 2005, p. 7).

The human positional dimension captures the individual or organization's perspective on the relationship between mankind and the natural environment. It ranges from anthropocentric (human dominance in the relationship) to eco-centric (humans absorbed into the ecological system where non-human elements have equal rights). Techno-centrism, or the belief that advances in science will discover solutions to environmental issues, is closely aligned to the anthropocentric viewpoint. Clearly, tourism businesses concerned about the environment are generally reformist and anthropocentric, often with a good dose of techno-centrism. They are likely to believe that technology will find a way forward – through new forms of renewable energy, new ways of storing energy or new energy-efficient vehicles that will replace the car as we know it – a position labelled by Kilbourne (1995) as environmentalism. Those at the other end of the spectrum (ecologism) will hold firm to the view that the only form of green tourism is no tourism, that all potential tourists should stay at home.

SUSTAINABLE TOURISM DEFINED

The WTO (2007a) emphasized that sustainable tourism principles, guidelines and management practices are relevant to all forms of tourism in all types of destination, including mass tourism and niche tourism products. Thus, sustainable tourism should

- make optimal use of environmental resources, maintain essential ecological processes, and help to conserve natural heritage and biodiversity;
- respect the sociocultural authenticity of host communities, conserve cultural heritage and values and contribute to inter-cultural understanding;
- provide socio-economic benefits to all stakeholders and are fairly distributed, including stable employment and income-earning opportunities and social services to host communities, contributing to poverty alleviation (WTO, 2007a).

This definition by the WTO is aligned with the three-pillar (environmental, social, economic) approach to sustainable development. You can see the three pillars of sustainability echoed in the bullet points above and in the definition of sustainable tourism that we highlighted in the introduction to the chapter.

TOURIST FLOWS

At the macro level, we might expect a shift in tourist flows or patterns in response to climate change. After all, the growth of mass tourism in the northern hemisphere during the last century was largely about a temporary migration to places with sunnier climates or predictable winter snowfall to pursue winter sport activities. This is the oft-cited North–South flow of tourists within Europe. Changes in climate will reorientate tourist flows both in winter and in summer. Table 15.1 looks at examples of projected region or country-specific impacts of climate change which might be expected to affect tourist flows. The table is illustrative only, but helps establish something of a global context for our snapshots of winter tourist flows and summer tourist flows that follow.

Winter tourist flows: example of the European Alps

According to a recent report by the Organization for Economic Cooperation and Development (OECD) (Agrawala, 2007), the Alps are very sensitive to climate change and recent warming has been approximately three times the global average. At present, around 90% of the Alpine ski areas in Austria, France, Germany, Italy and Switzerland may be considered as naturally snow-reliable. However, if temperatures were to rise up to 1 °C, then naturally snow-reliable areas would drop to 75%. A rise up to 2 °C would mean that only 60% were naturally snow-reliable – and a rise up to 4 °C would render only 30% naturally snow-reliable (Agrawala, 2007). Receding snowlines will mean that ski resorts at lower altitudes, such as those in the low-lying ski areas of Bavaria, Germany, will be highly affected or pushed out of the ski market (Burki et al., 2003; Agrawala, 2007). The process of tourists moving up to higher altitudes will further concentrate skiing activity and place further pressure on the sensitive environment of high mountains (Burki et al., 2003; Agrawala, 2007). In addition, the ski season will shorten as the first snows are predicted to fall later (Benfield UCL Hazard Research Centre, 2007). Thus, in the future, there will be fewer skier days available. Climate change will result in unreliability of snowfalls, rising snowlines and shorter ski seasons – the effects of these on tourist numbers will be compounded by an increased risk of avalanches, and major landslides, rock falls and mudflows associated with the melting of the permafrost (Benfield UCL Hazard Research Centre, 2007).

Currently, the use of artificial snowmaking machines and other adaptation strategies (a techno-centric response) often has accompanying environmental issues such as high energy consumption. As of 2003, there were over 300 projects in the Alps to open up the high mountain regions to winter sports activities (Burki et al., 2003). However, many skiers

Table 15.1. Examples of climate change impacts on tourism destinations.

Europe (region)[a]	Climate change expected to magnify regional differences in natural resources and assets
	Increased risk of inland flash floods, more frequent coastal flooding, increased erosion due to storminess and sea-level rise
	Mountainous areas will face glacier retreat, reduced snow cover and winter tourism and extensive species loss
	Southern Europe, higher temperatures and drought, reduced water availability, hydropower potential, summer tourism and crop productivity
	Climate change projected to increase health risks due to heat waves and frequency of wildfires
France (Provence and Côte d'Azur)[b]	Higher maximum temperatures and heat waves
	Increased wildfire risk; water shortages; flash floods
	Beach erosion and damage to wetlands
Southern Spain (Costas and Balearics)[b]	Higher maximum temperatures and heat waves
	Water shortages; increased wildfire risk
	Potential for malaria and other vector-borne diseases
	Beach erosion
	Increased aridity and desertification
North America (region)[a]	Warming in western mountains projected to cause decreased snowpack, more winter flooding and reduced summer flows, exacerbating competition for over-allocated water resources
	Cities that currently experience heat waves are expected to have heat waves more frequently and of longer duration and greater intensity with potential for adverse health
	Coastal communities and habitats will be increasingly stressed by climate change impacts interacting with development and pollution
USA (Florida)[b]	More powerful hurricanes; wildfires
	Coastal inundation and flooding due to storm surges
	Erosion and loss of beaches
	Damage and loss of coral reefs and other coastal ecosystems

(Continued)

Table 15.1. Continued.

	Emergence of vector-borne diseases such as malaria and dengue fever
India and Indian Ocean (Goa, Kerala, Maldives, Seychelles)[b]	Potential for more powerful cyclones in Goa and Kerala
	Erosion and loss of beaches
	Inundation and flooding of coastal zones and further inland
	Damage and loss of coral reefs in Seychelles and Maldives
	Potential evacuation of some islands in Maldives due to saltwater penetration of aquifers

[a] Intergovernmental Panel on Climate Change (2007b) *Climate Change 2007: Synthesis Report. Summary for Policymakers.* IPCC, Geneva, pp. 11–12.
[b] Benfield UCL Hazard Research Centre (2007) *Holiday 2030.* Benfield UCL Hazard Research Centre, London, pp. 37–38.

will choose or be obliged to switch to a ski resort that is more snow-reliable or to ski less often (Burki *et al.*, 2003). A paper by the International Institute for Peace through Tourism (IIPT, 2007) recounted that British tourists travelled more to the Rocky Mountains and less to the Alps during the 2006–2007 winter season due to the disparities in snow conditions. This serves as an illustration of possible shift in winter sports tourist flows by continent (as opposed to altitude within the Alps) as skiers search for reliable snow conditions and a longer ski season.

Summer tourist flows: example of Europe

European summer holiday destinations in the North–South flow are chosen mainly for the high temperatures and sunshine hours. For instance, British tourists are attracted by climates with average daytime temperatures of about 29 °C (Benfield UCL Hazard Research Centre, 2007). Human comfort is harder to maintain once temperatures move above around 31 °C, especially if humidity is high. By 2030, the level of physical comfort for many tourists visiting Southern Europe will be a problem. Health-related issues will also influence this North–South flow. For example, a near threefold increase in cases of malignant skin cancer for the UK is predicted by 2035, primarily due to UK tourist exposure to increased ultraviolet radiation in ever-hotter Mediterranean resorts. The Benfield UCL report also highlights expected increases in cases of eye cataracts, salmonella food poisoning, heat stress for those with respiratory problems, West Nile fever, dengue fever and malaria (Benfield UCL Hazard Research Centre, 2007) – all rooted in climate change impacts. These health risks (see Chapter 13, 'Of Fear, Flight and Feistiness', this volume, for further discussion) can be expected to contribute to a reorientation of traditional summer tourist flows within Europe.

The report outlines three possible summer tourist flow trends as a result of climate change in Europe, alongside the most obvious one of more tourists from Northern Europe opting to be domestic tourists and holidaying in their country of residence:

- The first trend is a switch in the timing of Mediterranean holidays to the winter or shoulder months of autumn and spring.
- The second trend is the shunning of large Mediterranean cities to avoid both the 'heat island' effect whereby such cities are frequently 1–2 °C hotter than the surrounding countryside and the poor air quality.
- The third trend is greater flows of summer tourists to mountains and other more temperate destinations on the international tourism scene (Benfield UCL Hazard Research Centre, 2007).

Other impacts and influences on tourist flows

Aside from winter sports and beach holidays, other particular forms or types of tourism will also be influenced by climate change. Take nature-based tourism. For example, many of the species in Canadian nature-based tourism (caribou, polar bears, otters, whales) will experience rapid changes in their habitat due to climate change thus raising the risk of extinction (Icarus Foundation, 2008). It is these top-of-the-food-chain iconic species that inspire nature-loving tourists – in short, no bears, no nature-based tourists. Such tourist flows would dwindle. Similarly, the bleaching and destruction of coral reefs will result in a decline in dive tourists and the associated macro-level flow of tourists between origin countries and coral reef destinations.

The impacts of national and international government's adaptation and mitigation policies in response to climate change will also be important influences on tourist flows and patterns. For example, government policies and regulations on energy consumption, carbon taxes and budgeting, and other mechanisms designed to internalize the hitherto external costs of consumption behaviours associated with climate change, will result in higher costs or even restrictions for the tourist (Icarus Foundation, 2008). Such government actions can also alter tourist flows and patterns, perhaps by lowering overall demand, altering transport modes or causing a reorientation away from long-haul international tourism to a stronger domestic tourism focus. For instance, the UK government's independent watchdog on sustainable development recommends just this – a stronger focus on the encouragement of domestic tourism (Sustainable Development Commission, 2006). Within a country, domestic tourist flows and patterns will change as hitherto outbound tourists choose to adopt domestic holiday alternatives or are squeezed out of the international market by higher prices – or even by travel allowances or consumption caps of some form.

BEHAVING BETTER: CODES OF CONDUCT FOR TOURISTS

Patterns and flows of tourists as they travel en masse can seem remote at times to the individual tourist. However, one of the things that you will most certainly have noticed is the effort

Responsible Travel.com Ltd
Tips for Responsible Travel
www.responsibletravel.com/copy/copy101891.htm

The Travel Foundation's Insider Guide
on Sustainable Tourism
www.thetravelfoundation.org.uk

Green Globe 'Responsible Travel Tips'
www.ec3global.com/products-programs/
green-globe/for-consumers/responsible...

The Himalayan Tourist Code
www.unep.org/bpsp/Tourism/Codes%20of20Conduct.pdf

International Association of Antarctica Tour Operators
Guidelines: Visitors
www.iaato.org/visitors.hmtl

WWF International Arctic Programme
Code of Conduct for Arctic Tourists
http://assets.panda.org/downloads/
codeofconductforarctictourists(eng).pdf

The International Ecotourism Society
Your travel choice makes a difference
www.ecotourism.org/webmodules/webarticlesnet/templates/
eco_template_travel...

WWF's Code of Conduct for Mediterranean Tourists
www.monachus-guardian.org/library/medpro01.pdf

Tourism Concern
How to avoid the guilt trips
www.tourismconcern.org.uk/index.php
?page=avoid-guilt-trips

Fig. 15.2. Codes of conduct for you the tourist.

made by many hotels, tour operators and destinations to encourage your own behaviour during your stay to be more sympathetic to the environment and local community. Commonly called 'codes of conduct' for visitors, these ideas are guidelines or tips on how to behave in a better fashion. For example, at your hotel you may have been urged to replace your towels on the rails to be reused by yourself, a message reinforced by an accompanying explanation on freshwater consumption and accumulated detergent pollution when towels are washed every day.

Even back in the early 1990s, there were over 100 guidelines and codes of conduct identified and monitored by the World Travel and Tourism Environment Research Centre (WTTERC, 1993). With the rise of the Internet, there has been a proliferation in such guidelines. Figure 15.2 shows some examples of codes of conduct drawn from round the world and all of them designed to improve the environmental behaviour of tourists. Where produced by larger businesses, these codes of conduct and their ilk are often embedded into wider environmental management systems and notions of Corporate Social Responsibility (CSR). These codes of conduct for tourists can be thought of as soft management tools used to try and influence tourist behaviour for the better.

To take one example from a single organization in the commercial sector, the UK tour operator brand, First Choice, use their web site to suggest practical ways that holidaymakers can support the environment. Seven bullet points summarize the advice:

- Packaging waste should be discarded before leaving home.
- Buy locally made souvenirs and use local services wherever possible.
- Avoid damaging flowers, plants and coral and buying products from endangered plants or animals.
- Use water sparingly – showers rather than baths – and let hotel staff know if you would like to reuse your towels and linen.
- Save energy by turning off air conditioning, lights and televisions when not in use.
- Learn about appropriate forms of behaviour, dress codes and how much to tip.
- Ask whether you can take photographs of local people or their homes and do not have photographs taken of yourself with animals from the wild (First Choice, 2008).

To contrast, take one example from an umbrella organization, the International Ecotourism Society. The International Ecotourism Society advises tourists to avoid negative impacts on local cultures, economies and the environment through:

- speaking the language: learning and using a few words of the local language;
- asking at the hotel: about environmental policies and practice, staff working conditions and any community projects supported by the hotel;
- dressing: according with local conventions, e.g. for modest dress;
- behaving respectfully: towards local residents' privacy and asking permission before entering sacred places, homes or private land;
- respecting the natural environment: by following designated trails, not touching or harassing animals and supporting conservation by paying entrance fees to parks and protected sites;
- refusing to buy animal products made from protected or endangered species;
- paying the fair price: not engaging in overly aggressive bargaining for souvenirs or short-changing on tips for services;
- buying local: choosing locally owned accommodation, using local buses, car rental agencies, local restaurants, local markets, and visiting local events and festivals;
- hiring local guides: asking guides if they are licensed and live locally and whether they are recommended by tour operators (International Ecotourism Society, 2008).

As a corollary to these codes of conduct, it is worth considering the apparent conflict between the pleasure principle that drives much leisure tourism and the visible, utility cost-cutting measures that tourists are aware of when they stay in hotels (e.g. being urged to reuse towels, not shower too long, switch off lights and air conditioning and so on). Traditionally holidays are about using as much water as you want, having fresh towels every day and appreciating standards similar to, or higher than, at home. Reduced consumption smacks of reduced comfort and is not – for the average tourist – an appealing message as a basis for a tourism purchase (Clarke and Hawkins, 2008).

YOU THE CONFUSED TOURIST

Many tourists are confused when it comes to sustainability.

Tourists are confused because they often do not know what the terms 'responsible', 'sustainable', 'ethical', 'green', 'eco' mean in respect of tourism and sustainable development – such terms (though often used) have limited resonance for the consumer (Clarke and Hawkins, 2008). Such confusion is not unique to tourism – the Sustainable Development Commission (SDC), the UK government's independent watchdog on sustainable development, found that few people could explain what sustainable development actually meant (SDC, 2006).

Tourists are confused by the profusion of ecolabels or tourism certification schemes that they encounter. You may yourself be aware of some of these certification schemes in different countries. You might think of Green Globe (global), Green Key (France and Denmark), Legambiente Tourismo (Italy), Green Tourism Business Scheme (UK) or Ibex (Switzerland). You might be aware of a few of the myriad more local schemes. Probably you are not a typical tourist when it comes to recognizing and understanding ecolabels. But still, do you know what each ecolabel actually represents? For instance, do you know whether it is based on self-certification or independent verification? For the majority of tourists, confusion reigns. What do the logos – the green leaves, acorns, animals and so on – that they see in accommodation reception areas and attraction ticket booths really mean? Moreover, how far can they trust their credibility? According to Futerra (2008), across all product categories, around 90% of UK consumers mistrust the green information that they receive from businesses and government.

Tourists are confused about the process of making the best choice, as they do not know how to assess the different options even if they can find out the necessary information. According to the SDC:

> [T]he truth is that the complexity of information required to make a judgement on product sustainability can leave even the most dedicated green consumer confused and disempowered.
>
> (SDC, 2006, p. 15)

How do you make the trade-offs? Even for a frequently consumed product such as an egg, the options are confusing if you start to really think about it. Is it better to buy free-range eggs that are locally produced or buy organic eggs produced elsewhere with higher associated food miles?

For a holiday purchase, the tourist has to consider the destination, the transport to, from and within the destination, accommodation, attractions and activities, restaurants, excursions, perhaps the inclusive tour package and the individual businesses that provide all of these services (and others such as travel agencies, travel insurance, foreign exchange providers, guiding services and so forth) and their respective corporate social responsibility programmes and equivalents. There might be trade-offs to be made between the different issues surrounding the environmental consequences, the social consequences and the economic consequences, as well as between the merits of the different businesses or options. Is it better to fly to a long-haul ecotourism destination where you have close economic contact with the local community, or is it better to take the train and stay in locally owned accommodation within your own country? Should you take a short-haul flight to an urban destination with a high carrying capacity and excellent public transport for a short break and shopping spree, or drive the car for 4h to a National Park and spend the weekend cycling and camping and spending very little money? The holiday choice is so much more complex than the egg choice. Even with the inclination, ability and access to all the necessary information (a somewhat doubtful proposition), and assuming a rational thought process (also a doubtful proposition), the decision process would be trying. You might need a second holiday or short break just to recover from the decision process of the first![1]

[1] Although you need to take into account that it is better to increase the length of your stay for your first trip to make your recovery rather than to increase the number of short breaks that you take by aircraft (Responsibletravel.com, 2008; WTO, 2007a). We said it was confusing.

In other product categories, a strategy of 'choice editing' by governments, regulators, retailers or businesses has proved useful in shifting the field of choice for mainstream consumers – by eliminating unnecessarily damaging products and getting the better sustainable products into the retail outlets (SDC, 2006). Choice editing has been defined by the SDC as the pre-selection of the particular range of products and services available to consumers, in this case taking into account sustainability criteria. So, rather than having to choose between 27 alternatives which may or may not be sound sustainable choices, the consumer is presented with, say, five pre-selected products all of which meet a minimum sustainability threshold. Such a strategy reduces the potential of misinformation, information overload and consumer confusion as how to make a satisfactory product purchase on environmental grounds. According to the SDC, choice editing for sustainability is seen as increasingly desirable by consumers as they look to others (government, regulators, businesses, retailers) to organize the choices that they face in a given product category.

In its generic form, choice editing is not a new idea. An independent travel agent selecting which inclusive tour brands to display in the brochure racks is indeed a retailer practising the general art of choice editing. It is the use of sustainability criteria that gives choice editing a twist. In this context, choice editing has reduced consumer confusion for product categories like white goods such as fridge freezers and washing machines, but does it have a role for travel and tourism products? In the future, could certain tourism product categories (e.g. inclusive tour packages) be choice edited so that only those meeting certain sustainability criteria are available as options for the tourist to buy?

Linked to choice editing is the policy of creating 'product roadmaps' for high impact products (SDC, 2006), such as cars or airplanes, that cannot easily be transformed to environmentally benign products in a short timespan. With product roadmaps, governments set out a long-term series of environmental performance objectives for a given product category, usually with a supportive and timetabled programme of interventions (such as fiscal incentives and staged rises in minimum product standards) – a mixture of carrot and stick. Thus, investment in product design and research and an outcome of better-performing environmental products are coaxed, provoked and demanded from an industry over a decade or more. Product roadmaps allow choice editing to be brought into play at a suitable point in the process of product improvement in environmental performance.

Greenwash: aiding and abetting tourist confusion

According to Futerra, a communications agency specializing in sustainability, 'greenwash' is an environmental claim made by a business or organization which is either unsubstantiated (a fib) or irrelevant (a distraction) (Futerra, 2008). The existence of greenwash is of greatest concern because of the way it undermines consumer confidence and trust in environmental performance – it exacerbates consumer confusion as to whom and what to trust. Furthermore, it is those businesses that are genuine in their environmental information and intention that feel the consumer backlash. Because of this, many governments regulate against greenwash as part of their advertising standards procedures.

Unsurprisingly, communication campaigns that make use of the environmental credentials of an organization are on the increase. In the UK, nearly £17 million was spent between September 2006 and August 2007 on advertising that included the words 'CO$_2$', 'carbon', 'environmental', 'emissions' or 'recycle'. This represents a dramatic 38-fold increase in spend from 2003 (Futerra, 2008). Mentions of greenwash on blogging sites show an explosion in number. And in 2007, environmental claims complaints to the UK Advertising Standards Authority increased fivefold from the figures in 2006 (Futerra, 2008), reflecting corresponding consumer concern with greenwash as environmental advertising proliferates.

Holiday and travel companies were not listed for environmental claims complaints to the UK Advertising Standards Authority in 2006, but by 2007, holiday and travel companies made up 9.5% of the number of environmental claims complaints made by consumers in the UK (Futerra, 2008). As far back as the 1990s, Wheeller (1991) and other academics warned tourism companies against falsely hopping on the back of the green environmental bandwagon.

MIND THE GAP!

It seems a logical progression from tourist confusion to the significant gap between what holidaymakers say they will do and what they actually do with regard to sustainable tourism. When it comes to sustainability, there is a difference between how tourists claim they would behave and their demonstrated behaviour (Clarke, 2002). Referring to all consumers as opposed to just tourists, the World Wildlife Fund (WWF, 2008) calls this gap the 'attitude–behaviour' gap. The attitude–behaviour gap is described as the disparity between the importance that an individual ascribes to environmental issues when interviewed and their real behaviour patterns. The Sustainable Development Commission (2006) refers to the gap as the 'value–action' gap. The value–action gap is described as the discrepancy between an individual's attitude (quite often pro-environmental) and their everyday behaviour. The gap, whatever its title, is a well-recognized phenomenon.

To take the argument back to tourists, a survey for Tearfund carried out in 1999 using a representative sample of over 2000 UK adults asked specific questions about the willingness of the tourist (both package and independent) to pay extra money for holidays which offered the ethical characteristics that they wanted. A total of 59% of respondents replied that, yes, they would be willing to pay more for their holidays if the money went to guarantee good wages and working conditions for workers at the destination, preserved the environment and reversed some of the negative environmental impacts or went directly to a local charity (Goodwin and Francis, 2003). However, Goodwin and Francis (2003) noted that the views expressed were aspirational and indicated how respondents would like to behave, rather than their actual tourist behaviour. Classically, many types of leisure tourism and much of its 'mass volume' products (as opposed to niche specialist or upmarket ecotourism offers) are sensitive to price, and so an increase in price typically leads to a decrease in demand. People say they are willing to pay more for environmental credentials and therefore seem an attractive segment proposition to tourism businesses that enhance their sustainability – but companies would be well advised to mind the gap.

The uneasy truth is that many tourists do not act on their convictions when it comes to purchasing ethical or sustainable tourism products, for such products only make up a very small percentage of total sales. Research by the Thomson Future Holiday Forum (2004) suggested that less than 1% of people buy sustainable holidays. The Cooperative Bank (2007) calculated that about £103 million was spent by UK tourists on holidays from responsible tour operators during 2006. However, this is less than 0.001% of the approximate £23 billion (ABTA, 2008) spent on holidays with the Association of British Travel Agents (ABTA) members in 2006. Tourists who choose genuine ethical or sustainable holidays are a small minority of all holiday takers. This is not to state that tourists are disingenuous when they state environmental concerns. Confusion may well play a role in the gap between words and deeds.

DOES YOUR MOTIVATION MATTER?

If you, the tourist, purchase a more sustainable holiday option for reasons other than a desire to minimize your carbon footprint and protect the environment, does it matter? Even when tourists do make sustainable choices (e.g. to take public transport in and around the destination rather than the car), the behaviour is not necessarily motivated by the desire to do environmental good. For example, leaving the car behind for a weekend short break may be motivated by the wish to escape traffic congestion and the associated unpredictable travel times, rather than by the active wish to reduce carbon emissions.

Many would argue that the motivation does not matter and that it is the action – in particular, the accumulated action across a society – that does. This is the general and popular assertion that people do not have to do the right thing for the right reasons. However, a provocative report by the WWF (2008) argued otherwise. If you buy a hybrid car because of the money saved on petrol and road tax or because of the car's social status with neighbours and the way that it improves your self-image, then you may very well divert that saved income into less-sustainable purchases because you were not motivated in the first place by environmental concerns. The problem with encouraging people to change their buying habits in favour of sustainability using appeals to self-interest or personal benefit is that it may only reinforce negative patterns of behaviour. For a specific individual, if pro-environmental behaviour equates to saving money (on energy costs in the home, on car fuel and so forth – and as typically used in environmental campaigns in the UK), then that individual is unlikely to pay more to travel by train rather than take a low-cost flight to a holiday resort in the Mediterranean. If their pro-environmental behaviour indeed equates with reducing their environmental footprint, then that individual is likely to pay for the more expensive train and to reject the low-cost flight. Thus, for pro-environmental behaviour to spill over into other lifestyle and product choices, the motivation and the values that underpin that initial purchase are important. For this WWF report, motivation matters.

The report highlights self-determination theory (WWF, 2008). Self-determination theory purports that when an activity or behaviour is pursued to uphold a set of intrinsic values (e.g. personal development, emotional intimacy or community involvement), this results in more energetic and persistent engagement than when the activity or behaviour is pursued to uphold a set of extrinsic values (e.g. acquisition of material goods, physical attractiveness, financial success, social recognition or status). There is evidence that suggests that an intrinsic value orientation exhibits both higher levels of well-being (or happiness) and stronger engagement with pro-environmental behaviour. Conversely, an extrinsic value orientation exhibits lower subjective well-being and less interest in protecting the environment. Therefore, the best strategy for increasing good environmental behaviour in a society is to use methods that increase the likelihood of individuals embedding intrinsic values into their self-identity.

The same report (WWF, 2008) is also argumentative about the merits of relying on many small easy-to-make behavioural changes (small, painless steps) in the expectation that this will eventually result in individuals engaging in the more fundamental harder-to-make behavioural changes (big, painful steps). Such strategies that rely on this 'foot-in-the-door' approach (WWF, 2008) can result in either people who passively rest on their laurels or people who actively undertake the small steps (switching televisions off rather than leaving them on standby) to ease their conscience in avoiding the big steps (such as giving up frequent flying). Memorably phrased in an opinion piece in *The Guardian* newspaper:

> [A]pparently, the more people bang on about how ecologically aware they are, the more likely they are to nip off on a plane for skiing holiday or some other indulgence…sanctimoniousness is little more than a leper-bell for hypocrisy.

> (Lezard, 2008)

A research report by TGI (2008) showed that 2% of the population of France, America and the UK could be labelled as 'eco-adopters'. These eco-adopters display an environmentally conscious mindset and a willingness to put these beliefs into action. They are, for example, interested in green media issues, buy eco-friendly household goods, belong to environmental organizations and donate to wildlife charities. Yet the report noted as follows:

> [W]e should not assume that their 'green' conscious dictates every part of an Eco-Adopter's lifestyle, particularly when it comes to personal travel … the most environmentally-aware 2% of the population in each of these three countries have personal carbon footprints that are larger than average.

> (TGI, 2008, p. 16)

For instance, over half of the eco-adopters in the UK flew in the past year, as did a quarter in France. In fact, French eco-adopters are 63% more likely than average to have taken three or four flights in the previous year. In America, eco-adopters are consistently more likely to fly domestically and internationally than the average person and are 122% more likely to be members of a frequent-flyer scheme (TGI, 2008). As a sting in the tail, according to Futerra (2005), confronting someone about the difference between their attitudes and their actual actions on climate change is unlikely to produce the desired effect.

Connected to motivation is the notion of equity in participation and fairness with regard to environmental changes in consumer behaviour across individuals in society. To illustrate, why should one person forgo flying when another will not? The SDC felt that equity had come through so strongly in their research among UK consumers that it took centre stage as the title to the report, 'I will if you will'. Unpacked, the idea means that progress in better environmental behaviour needs to be collective – individuals are willing to change their behaviour to tackle climate change but only if they see others doing so too. When equity is apparent – when everybody is acting – then an individual feels their own behavioural changes are worthwhile (SDC, 2006).

ARE YOU A FAST AND FREQUENT FLIER?

Aviation as a transport option between origin and destination is but one component of tourism, but an important one. First, it is because of the number of tourists – particularly international – who choose to fly rather than use other means of transport. Of course, countries that are islands are typically more dependent on air transport than land-locked countries and others sharing borders. For example, in 2006, three-quarters of the UK's 32.7 million inbound visitors came by airplane to visit the UK and those travelling by air accounted for 87% of all inbound visitor spending – almost £14 billion (VisitBritain, 2007). Second, it is because of the environmental impacts attributed to aviation and the accompanying media coverage. It is a much talked about story.

The three main contributors from aviation to climate change are carbon dioxide (CO_2) emissions, oxides of nitrogen (NO_x) emissions, and contrails and cirrus clouds that under certain atmospheric conditions are triggered by the freezing of the water vapour from the engine's exhaust (SBAC, 2008). The fact that this occurs at high altitudes is a specific problem as the effect of these greenhouse gases on the climate is greater when they are emitted high above the earth. Indeed, it may be as much as 2.7 times the warming effect of the gases when emitted closer to the ground (Harvey, 2006).

To take a techno-centric stance, advances in technology are an essential part of the solution. At present, and unlike other transport modes, there are no practical alternatives to fossil-based fuels for commercial jet aircraft (Harvey, 2006; WTO, 2007a). Kerosene is expected to remain the dominant fuel for aviation in the near term (SBAC, 2008). There is, of course, substantial research being conducted into alternative fuels for the future. The most viable alternative fuels under investigation are generally considered to be synthetic kerosene (XTL), fatty acid methyl esters (FAMEs), hydrogenated oils, liquid hydrogen, methane and ethanol/methanol (SBAC, 2008). There are many criteria that an alternative fuel needs to meet in order to make a viable and successful aviation fuel. As you can imagine, such a fuel has to operate under high temperatures and high pressure at ground level and at low temperatures and low pressure at cruise altitudes – no mean feat. In the short to medium term, such a fuel has to be a 'drop-in replacement', that is, a fuel compatible with existing aircraft, engines, and fuel delivery and storage systems (SBAC, 2008). You can also consider whether research and design into airframe and engine technology will be able to deliver a zero-emissions aircraft in the foreseeable future (WTO, 2007a). All in all, how far improvements in technology can answer the emissions problem is debatable – one line of thought is that growth in passenger demand for flights is likely to exceed technology's ability to offset the emissions contributing to global warming (Webster, 2006).

A survey by the British Air Transport Association into public attitudes towards air travel and its environmental impacts is a neat demonstration of the gap between attitudes and action – another case of 'mind the gap'. For this particular survey, 56% of people declared themselves concerned about the environmental impacts of air travel, but only 13% had changed their travel behaviour as a result of these environmental concerns (Sustainable Aviation Council, 2006).

Also among the measures being taken to improve the environmental credentials of aviation (which include charges, taxes and duties, better air traffic management and operational practices, and operating restrictions) are emissions trading and carbon offsetting. Initially aviation was excluded from the European Union's Emissions Trading Scheme (ETS), but in July 2008 it was decided that from 2012, all flights to, from and within the European Union would be subject to the ETS with its cap and trade system for carbon emissions. In the meantime, carbon offsetting is being used by airlines partly to raise awareness levels of climate change among consumers (Sustainable Aviation Council, 2006). Airline signatories to sustainable aviation (which include, among others, bmi, British Airways, easyJet, and Virgin Atlantic) have committed to

> inform passenger understanding of the climate impacts of air travel, including evaluating carbon
> offset initiatives as a practical short-term measure.
>
> (Sustainable Aviation Council, 2006, p. 12)

When British Airways launched its voluntary carbon offsetting scheme for passengers in 2005, its principal aim was to raise passenger understanding of the climate impacts of air travel (Sustainable Aviation Council, 2006). Consumers can offset the carbon dioxide emissions generated by their flight by making a contribution to an organization that invests in projects that avoid, reduce or absorb carbon dioxide emissions, using an online calculator to work out the amount of money to be donated and learning about the environmental impacts as they do so. The carbon offsetting scheme introduced in 2007 by the leisure airline of First Choice Holidays is an 'opt out' scheme (Urquhart, 2006) as opposed to the 'opt in' scheme of British Airways – for First Choice Holidays, consumers are automatically included unless they choose otherwise. So carbon offsetting schemes – in lieu of emissions trading – offer consumer awareness and education as well as some impact mitigation.[2]

---

[2] One environmental commentator – and sadly we cannot remember who, for which our apologies – most memorably highlighted carbon offsetting as the modern-day equivalent of the medieval practice of the selling of indulgences. Not everyone believes in merits of carbon offsetting.

OR ARE YOU A SLOW TOURIST?

Although not necessarily mutually exclusive, if you are among the minority of tourists who have stopped flying for environmental reasons, you may have decided to become a practising slow tourist. Slow tourism is akin to the 'slow movement' (for instance, the slow food movement or the slow cities movement in Italy). The slow movement claims back the quality of time in our increasingly harried lifestyles. Thus, slow tourists prefer to avoid flying and travel instead by train or boat, bicycle, canoe or foot. Travel is unstructured and flexible and (it is claimed) more thoughtful. Experiences evolve and exploration away from the obvious is commended. There is a letting-go of everyday speed and stress. The overall aim is not to tick down a list of key sightseeing attractions (the 'been there, done that' mentality), but rather to savour the quality of what you do and to reconnect with the people you meet and the places you visit. The pace of the holiday is slowed right down.

You do not have to be an international tourist to be a slow tourist; domestic tourists can be slow tourists too.

CRYSTAL BALL GAZING, OR NOT

In its topics and expression, this chapter has much the feel of the future. As such, our discussion around sustainability and its interactions with tourist behaviour form the first part of our offer entitled 'Gazing into the crystal ball'. Finding the best way forward may feel shrouded in metaphoric mists, but behavioural change for sustainability is a survival reality if not for our generation then for the ones that follow. Our final chapter has greater kinship with the classic use of the crystal ball analogy. It is about the future. It is about the tourist tomorrow. Some of the trends sound realistic, others sound far-fetched but have none the less been expressed by an expert body or think tank. So we now move on to consider how tourists might behave in the future, carefully entwining the strands of sustainability and pro-environmental behaviour around the stems of further ideas and insights.

REFERENCES

ABTA (2008) *Personal Communication with Media Office*, 30 September 2008.

Agrawala, S. (2007) *Climate Change in the European Alps: Executive Summary*. OECD, Paris. Available at: www.oecd.org

Benfield UCL Hazard Research Centre (2007) *Holiday 2030*. Benfield UCL Hazard Research Centre, London. Available at: www.befieldhrc.org/activities/misc_papers/Holiday.2030.pdf

Brackenbury, M. (1992) Ecotourism: introduction to ecotourism – a sustainable option? *Bulletin of the Tourism Society UK* 76, 10–12.

Burki, R., Elsasser, H. and Abegg, B. (2003) *Climate Change and Winter Sports: Environmental and Economic Threats*. UNEP, University of Zurich, Zurich, Switzerland. Available at: www.unep.org/ sport_env/Documents/torinobuerki.doc

Clarke, J. (1997) A framework of approaches to sustainable tourism. *Journal of Sustainable Tourism* 5 (3), 224–233.

Clarke, J. (2002) A synthesis of activity towards the implementation of sustainable tourism: ecotourism in a different context. *International Journal of Sustainable Development* 5 (3), 232–249.

Clarke, J. and Hawkins, R. (2008) Towards a conceptual framework for sustainable tourism management issues based on business size. *British Academy of Management BAM Conference*, Harrogate, UK, 9–11 September 2008.

Cooperative Bank (2007) *The Ethical Consumer Report 2007*. Cooperative Bank, Manchester, UK. Available at: www.co-operativebank.co.uk/ethicalconsumerismreport

First Choice (2008) Want to help? Available at: http://bookings.firstchoice.co.uk/environment/ sustainable.hmtl

Futerra (2005) *The Rules of the Game. Evidence Base for the Climate Change Communications Strategy*. Available at: www.futerra.co.uk/downloads/RulesOfTheGame.pdf

Futerra (2008) *The Greenwash Guide*. Available at: www.futerra.co.uk/revolution/leading_thinking

Goodwin, H. and Francis, J. (2003) Ethical and responsible tourism: consumer trends in the UK. *Journal of Vacation Marketing* 9(3), 271–284.

Hall, C.M. (2005) Sustainable tourism and tourism and global environmental change, e-mail 29 November, Trinet.

Harvey, F. (2006) Sins of emission. FT Magazine, November 25/26, pp. 20–22.

Icarus Foundation (2008) *The Climate Change Challenge: Implications for the Tourism Industry*. Icarus Foundation, Toronto, Canada. Available at: www.theicarusfoundation.com/Reports.hmtl

Intergovernmental Panel on Climate Change (2007a) *Climate Change 2007: The Physical Science Basis*. IPCC, Geneva. Available at: www.ipcc.ch

Intergovernmental Panel on Climate Change (2007b) *Climate Change 2007: Synthesis Report. Summary for Policymakers*. IPCC, Geneva. Available at: www.ippc.ch/pdf/assessment-report/ar4/syr/ar4_ syr_spm.pdf

International Ecotourism Society (2008) *Your Travel Choice Makes a Difference. What you can do While Travelling*. Available at: www.ecotourism.org/webmodules/webarticlesnet/templates/ eco_template_travel

International Institute for Peace through Tourism (2007) *Tourism Development and Climate Change: Understanding, Anticipating, Adapting, Participating in the Common Effort*. IIPT, Vermont Canada. Available at: www.iipt.org/pdf/TourismDevandClimateChange.pdf

International Union for the Conservation of Nature (1980) *World Conservation Strategy*. IUCN, UNEP, WWF, Geneva.

Kangun, N. and Polonsky, M.J. (1995) Regulation of environmental marketing claims: a comparative perspective. *International Journal of Advertising* 14 (1), 1–24.

Kilbourne, W.E. (1995) Green advertising: salvation or oxymoron? *Journal of Advertising* 24 (2), 7–19.

Lezard, N. (2008) A paler shade of green. *The Guardian,* 24 September 2008. Available at: www. guardian.co.uk/commentisfree/2008/sep/24/ethicalliving.recycling

Porritt, J. (2005) How capitalism can save the world. *The Independent* Extra, 4 November, 1–8.

Responsibletravel.com (2008) *Factsheet: Responsible Travel and Global Warming*. Available at: www. responsibletravel.com/copy/copy902104.htm

SBAC (2008) *Alternative Aviation Fuels. SBAC Aviation and Environment Briefing Papers*. Sustainable Aviation Council, UK. Available at: www.sustainableaviation.co.uk/pages/default/key-documents. html

Stern, N. (2006) *The Stern Review: The Economics of Climate Change. Executive Summary*. UK Government, London.

Sustainable Aviation Council (2006) *Sustainable Aviation Progress Report 2006*. Sustainable Aviation Council, UK, December 2006. Available at: www.sustainableaviation.co.uk/images/stories/key%20documents/report06final.pdf

Sustainable Development Commission (2006) *I Will if you Will: Towards Sustainable Consumption*. SDC and NCC, London. Available at: www.sd-commission.org.uk/publications/donwloads/I_Will_If_You_Will.pdf

Target Group Index (2008) *Green Values. Consumers and Branding. Global Marketing Insights from TGI*. TGI in association with The CarbonNeutral Company, London. Available at: www.tgisurveys.com

Thomson Future Holiday Forum (2004) *A Future-Gazing Study of How Holidays are Set to Change Over the Next 20 Years*. Thomson, UK. Available at: www.lexispr.com/thomson

Travel Trade Gazette (2008) Blueprint for travel's future. *Travel Trade Gazette*, Issue 2827, 25 July 2008.

Urquhart, C. (2006) From jet set to carbon offset. *The Times*, 2 December 2006, p. 19.

VisitBritain (2007) *Issue of the Month – Climate Change and What it Might Mean for UK Tourism*. VisitBritain, London.

Webster, B. (2006) For richer, not for the poorer: the great budget airline myth. *The Times*, Saturday, 11 November 2006, 3.

Wheeller, B. (1991) Tourism's troubled times: responsible tourism is not the answer. *Tourism Management* 12 (2), 91–96.

World Commission on Environment and Development (1987) *Our Common Future*. Oxford University Press, Oxford.

World Tourism Organization (2007a) *Tourism, Air Transport and Climate Change – a World Tourism Organization Discussion Paper*. UNWTO, Geneva.

World Tourism Organization (2007b) Tourism can help in global action on climate change and poverty, Media release,13 December. Available at: www.unwto.org/media/news/en/press_det.php?id=1581

World Travel and Tourism Environment Research Centre (1993) *Environment and Development. A Newsletter for International Travel and Tourism*, No.1. WTTERC, Oxford.

WWF (2008) *Weathercocks and Signposts. The Environment Movement at a Crossroads*. Available at: http://assets.panda.org/downloads/weathercocks_report2.pdf

chapter 16

THE TOURIST TOMORROW

How might your tourist behaviour change in the future? In the next 5 years? In 50 years? And to what extent will the changes be prompted by internal forces and external forces and the corresponding interplay between them? As we saw in the previous chapter, something like a shift in public consciousness towards beneficial environmental behaviour demonstrates both change in attitude within the individual (internal), government intervention and technological development (external) and – perhaps most importantly – the interaction between these internal and external forces. You may recall other ideas from earlier chapters too, for the book is infused with signposts to possible future tourist behaviours.

Tourism organizations and researchers have long been predicting the future. They have used techniques such as the systems approach (examining the interconnectedness of different elements in the system), environmental scanning (siphoning off changes in the external environment and interpreting relevance – frameworks such as political, economic, social and technological (PEST) analysis are classic tools) and scenario thinking (creating carefully crafted stories about the possible futures that provoke 'what if?' style questions) (Formica and Kothari, 2008). For example, the national tourism organization for Scotland, VisitScotland, has used scenario thinking to help inform strategic direction (e.g. Yeoman *et al.*, 2006). A recently launched project in the UK to support the tourism industry in adapting to environmental challenges – Tourism 2023 – is also using scenario thinking to guide the process (Forum for the Future, 2008).

Although not synonymous, the future for tourist behaviour has much to do with trends. A trend may be thought of as the general direction in which the object of interest is changing or developing, a movement towards the new or different (Pan *et al.*, 2008). It includes a sense of continuation from the present, the here and now, and also from the past (Pan *et al.*, 2008). Related to trends are fashions and hypes. A fashion may be thought of as a way of behaving that is popular at a particular time. A hype is something inflated by publicity and media attention to manufacture interest in it (Pan *et al.*, 2008). For example, is the practice of dining at the restaurants of celebrity television chefs a matter of trend, fashion or hype built up in the media? Different readers may take different views on this. You need to hold on to the fact that trends are of longer duration and are generally more universal than either fashions or hypes. So you can talk of a trend towards a greater number of short breaks, the shift in holiday timings to a greater spread throughout the year or the fragmentation of the tourism market. As you sift through the ideas presented in this chapter, you may think differently from the authors about whether a particular idea is a trend, fashion or hype.

Table 16.1 lists thirteen trends, fashions and hypes for you to cast your eye across. In a sense, the table acts as kind of warm-up exercise for the chapter. It is a scattering of ideas indicative of the range available. It is not comprehensive, but aims to stimulate the thought processes. Indeed, you might also like to ponder whether some of the ideas are best described as niche markets, as opposed to trends, fashions or hypes.

From the point of view of enjoying the book, shades in differences of opinion do not matter. The fun in this chapter is to be had in poking, prying and delving into different perspectives and sources – and with the more adventurous thoughts that the exercise stimulates. You are likely to have your own additional ideas, perhaps firing off what you read here. And anyway, future-spotting is not a fail-safe exercise. It is fallible. Even the experts do not get it all right all of the time. In this chapter, we do our best, both pulling out ideas expressed by credible and multiple sources, but also seeking out the more far-fetched and free-thinking – we aim to cover the 'safe' bets and the 'risky' bets (which in the final call might pay out higher rewards) in our visions for the future of tourist behaviour.

In support of our position, we draw your attention to the memorable words attributed to Dan Quayle, Vice President of the USA from 1989 to 1993, a man in high public office remembered also for his entanglement of language commonly known as 'quaylisms'. When speaking of the future, he supposedly said:

> [W]e are on an irreversible trend towards more freedom and democracy – but that could change.
> (attributed to Dan Quayle)

Leaving aside the fact that the word of web or word of mouse (online word of mouth) can distort and misappropriate words, message and sender, the quotation serves as a timely reminder that spotting a trend is one thing but that getting it right in the holistic picture of future behaviour is quite another. For the reality of any prediction, we can claim that only time will tell.

THE FUTURE PANORAMA OF TOURIST FLOWS

As the United Nations body responsible for tourism, the World Tourism Organization (WTO) published a future-orientated report called 'Tourism 2020 Vision' back in 1997. As the title suggests, one of the aims of the work was to identify the important trends in tourism demand

Table 16.1 Thirteen trends, fashions and hypes. (From World Travel Market 2007c,d,e,f; Hodson, 2004; Thomson Future Holiday Forum, 2004; Ramesh, 2005; Yeoman and McMahon-Beattie, 2006; Yeoman *et al.*, 2006; Pearson, 2008; Trendhunter Magazine, 2008.)

Trend, fashion or hype?
1. Emergence and rise of the *chaveller* (as in chavs); working class who quit poorly paid jobs or trades to travel for extended time; often young people living with parents and travelling in large groups. A nuance of gap year/backpacking?
2. Growth in holidays with pets; demand for pet-friendly holiday packages set to rise significantly over next 5 years; en suite kennel accommodation; pure organic cotton-lined cat baskets
3. Growth of halal tourism as a form of religious tourism defined as activities permissible under Islamic law; Middle East; halal food, calls for prayer, Korans in hotels and aircraft seat pockets, women-only hotels
4. By 2025 active skin technology in the form of microscopic chips printed painlessly on your hand that enable airlines to project tickets on to the back of your hand
5. Trend towards 'real' experiences such as whale watching or swimming with dolphins
6. Nudist flights, e.g. Germany
7. Tourists of the future more litigious; an offshoot of an increasing 'culture of blame'
8. By 2012 medical tourism in India forecast to be worth £1.2 billion with international medical tourist arrivals growing 15% a year; additional trend of combining medical tourism with yoga holiday or trip to Taj Mahal
9. A hippy revival set to hit about 2010; driven by increased acceptance of public emotional display, dissatisfaction with materialism and high debts, new ageism, downshifting, 21st-century piety and an anti-science undercurrent
10. Independent sources of information will become increasingly important in the tourist decision process
11. Fragmentation of the homosexual market; gay grey market; gay youth market; gay honeymoons
12. An increasingly distrustful and cynical society; criticism as the new *mood music*
13. By 2020 the first space hotels will be open for tourists

Ponder point: Fashions, hypes or are some really niche market opportunities?

in order to visualize the state of tourism by the year 2020. Part of the task included long-term forecasts for international tourist flows. As of 2008, these forecasts published in 1997 still stand (WTO, 2008).

International tourist arrivals numbered over 900 million in 2007 (WTO, 2008). Such outbound tourism is increasingly driven by emerging source (origin or generating) countries.

International tourist arrivals are forecast to reach 1 billion by 2010 and 1.6 billion by 2020. The 1.6 billion international tourist arrivals will spend over US$2 trillion (WTO, 1997). Of the 1.6 billion arrivals, 1.2 billion are forecast to be intraregional and some 378 million will be long-haul travellers.

The top three receiving regions by 2020 are predicted to be Europe with 717 million international tourist arrivals, East Asia and the Pacific with 397 million, and the Americas with 282 million (WTO, 2008). Europe is expected to hold a 45% or 46% share of the international arrivals market (WTO, 1997, 2008), a decline from its 60% share in 1995 (WTO, 2008). This decline in market share is well understood, as new and emerging destinations, including developing countries, have entered the global tourism arena (WTO, 2008). It is also, we feel, a reflection of the geographic location of emerging source markets (see Chapter 1, 'The Tourist Today', this volume, for further explanation). Thus, in 1950, the leading 15 destinations enjoyed 98% of all international tourist arrivals. By 1970, this share had fallen to 75% and by 2007 to just 57% (WTO, 2008).

Forecasts for the relative importance of domestic and international tourism suggest that typical ratios between domestic and international tourism are something like 10:1 for activity and around 3:1 or 4:1 for spending (WTO, 1997). In other words, a country might expect ten times the numbers of domestic tourist trips and perhaps three times the domestic tourist spending when contrasted with its international tourist arrivals and expenditure figures.

China is highlighted as a country of particular significance for the future. We mention something of its importance in our prologue to the book and at various other points. By 2020, China is forecast to be the leading destination in the world and the fourth most important generating country (WTO, 1997). Given its emphasis for the future of tourism, we have highlighted it as a 'country cameo' for tourist behaviour later in the chapter.

Magnifying a detail in the future panoramic

Sweeping flows of millions of tourists across the world can seem a little daunting. To grasp something more personal and story-like from this future expansion, imagine an airline in India that found out from its marketing research that as many as 40% of its passengers were flying for their very first time. Remember that we speak of a country likely to become the world's third largest economy in a generation or so. This '40% first-time fliers' was the discovery of Indian airline, SpiceJet (VisitBritain, 2006a). It is an alluring illustration of the power of the emerging source markets in tourism – and the rising power of the new middle classes – just waiting to be unleashed into the global marketplace.

BACK TO THE FUTURE

As appreciated in the introduction to the chapter, the future – or more specifically a trend – has its roots in the past and the present. So to go forward, we have to go back.

We have selected one particular author, Auliana Poon, and her influential book published in 1993 to show that some ideas expounded today about the future of tourist behaviour have much earlier roots. Many of Poon's thoughts hold strong well over a decade later. They may be expressed with different words and phrases and heralded as new – but many have been said before. Add the fact that much of Poon's research was carried out in the Caribbean, a region heavily reliant on the success of its tourism – and offering an alternative geographic perspective to much of the work we cite – and you have an attractive proposition for commencing our look at the future of tourist behaviour.

But chiefly, we use Poon's (1993) book as representative of the premise that predictions have an ancestry – our back to the future thread.

We have handpicked a selection of Poon's (1993) ideas and tried to show the relationship to current thoughts. Of course, Poon drew on the legacy of ideas available from within and outside of tourism when formulating her ideas. We would recommend reading Poon's original work – it is a fulfilling read.

Experienced, independent and flexible tourists

Poon (1993) introduced the notion of the *new* tourist as the driving force for a new or future tourism. Within the constellation of ideas, she highlighted the new tourist as being a more experienced traveller who is more flexible and more independent than the tourists of yesteryear.

In the 21st century, Tourism Australia (2006) describes the international tourist as 'more worldly than ever before' and kitted with a 'large global reference set' of experiences in different hotels, tours and attractions from which they draw comparison. Likewise, Visit-Britain (2005) describes the international tourist as having changed from the 'wide-eyed innocents' of quarter-of-a-century past to the 'sophisticated independent traveller' of today. The Thomson Future Holiday Forum (2004) refers to the 'DIY tourist' exhibiting a strong independent streak as they create their own holidays from individual purchased elements – transport, accommodation, activities and so on. A later Thomson Holidays report, Expanding Horizons, refers to this tourist as the 'self-made travel agent' (Travelmole, 2005). And a World Travel Market (2007a) piece draws attention to the recent emergence of *minipreneurs*, a form of blog-based consumer-to-consumer holiday planning – tipped as a development one step on from online dynamic packaging. Side-stepping the travel industry, consumers post their dream and imaginative holiday ideas – for example, some very unusual activity in a particular destination – on to a blog, and a minipreneur, possibly living in that destination or with inside knowledge of that dream activity, puts forward a solution. A fixing-fee is then passed from the consumer to the minipreneur. The World Travel Market (2007a) piece suggests that this tourist behaviour, a trend that has spread from the USA to Europe, is changing the online purchasing scene. So, as the collection of examples illustrates, today's ideas for the future are laced through with the notions of experience, flexibility and independence expressed in the past.

Hybrid tourists and fractional living

In talking about flexibility, Poon (1993) highlighted the rise of the *hybrid* tourist. This is the tourist who cannot be labelled in a straightforward manner as, for example, luxury or budget, because they mix up the elements from different price categories using both luxury and basic purchases during the course of a single holiday. You might, for example, stay in a youth hostel but take evening cocktails in a landmark hotel of great style and expense. You might stay in that landmark hotel, yet enjoy the experience of eating in the evening from food stalls in the street. You might decide to camp while signing on for an advanced course in an expensive water-based sport, dine out lavishly to celebrate an anniversary and fly back home using a low-cost carrier. As a hybrid tourist, your trip does not follow a standard, predictable line. You are a luxury tourist and an economy tourist within one trip – a hybrid tourist.

There is a broader parallel today in the form of *fractional living* which has produced systems of partial ownership and thereby some flexibility in lifestyle choices. You can part-own a yacht in the Caribbean, carry an expensive 'it' handbag for a period of time, drive a super car when you choose to, part-own a nightclub and join a fractional destination club to access a portfolio of luxury homes in desirable locations throughout the world. You can think of it as *luxury snacks* (Yeoman, 2008a). It is a way of living that allows an individual to dip in and out of moneyed luxury when they cannot afford full ownership or wish to spread their resources more widely to achieve a desired lifestyle. Tourism Australia (2006) indicates to its members that 'consumers have found new ways to "own" more things', and we feel that fractional living is one of them. From our borrowed perspective of Poon (1993), fractional living is a sort of cousin to the notion of the hybrid tourist.

If hybrid tourists mix and match expenditure levels within a single trip, then there is also the trend of tourists mixing and matching standards and types of holidays across a series of trips. For example, The European Travel and Tourism Action Group (2004) highlights the trend towards tourists buying luxury and simple holidays in succession. Yeoman *et al.* (2006, p. 177) refer to holiday habits having 'gradually fragmented into a pick-and-mix selection of destinations, activities, lengths of trip and times of year'. You can no longer stereotype the tourist as a luxury or economy consumer for they change mantle from one holiday to the next.

High-tech high-touch tourists

Poon (1993) stressed the 'high-tech, high-touch' phenomenon (see Naisbitt, 1984) and its repercussions for tourist behaviour. She noted 'de-personalization and computerisation' of the work environment as reinforcing people's desire for more human contact to maintain a healthy balance in their lives. Holidays can provide that compensatory human touch for the *alienation* experienced in the workplace (an alienation originally conceived as part of an *unwritten deal* pioneered by Henry Ford in return for ever-escalating material standards – Gabriel and Lang, 2006). Thus, holidays become the antidote for the computer age. High-tech, high-touch translates into a tourist desire for greater personal service as embodied in products such as boutique hotels or for more natural down-to-earth vacations.

The WTO's (1997) report 'Tourism 2020 Vision' notes that the world in the year 2020 will be characterized by the penetration of technology into all corners of life and that consequently, people will increasingly *crave* the human touch offered by tourism. VisitBritain (2005) echoes this in observing a backlash against technology and in a driving need for human contact. The Thomson Future Holiday Forum (2004) predicts a specific example in the future emergence of 'phone-free beaches' as tourists seek to escape the insistence of the mobile phone in favour of a peaceful setting. Moreover, the 'new tourist of the future' will

> use local guides, eat in local restaurants, source quality local produce, take small group cultural/ environmental excursions and be sensitive to clean and pristine environments. He/she will have a heightened appreciation of cultural differences and sensitivities.
>
> (Thomson Future Holiday Forum, 2004, p. 11)

Within this view of the future, you can clearly see the quality of human contact, more person-alized service and the expression of authenticity in a local setting shining through.

Personalized service with the human touch comes in a different form for Formica and Kothari (2008) who comment on the need for personal attention and the corresponding rise in 'pam-per me' tourism products (or 'it's all about me' – the Thomson Holiday Future Forum, 2004). A second piece from the World Travel Market (2007b) emphasizes the continuing growth in spas, health and wellness tourism across the world – products that literally sell physical human touch. The European Travel Commission (2006) uses the upward trend in volunteer tourism as an example of new tourists seeking a deeper and more meaningful experience within a local community – a way of integrating, involving or drawing closer to other people in a more life-affirming way. Pan *et al.* (2008), reviewing tourist trends in the Asia-Pacific region, also note the rise of volunteer tourism.

From addiction of having to fulfilment of being

Leading on from the idea of more meaningful experiences as discussed above, Poon (1993) wrote of the declining importance of tourism consumption as a status symbol for tourists and the corresponding shift in importance to the intrinsic qualities of holidays. In other words, a trend away from the status of *having* a holiday towards the subtler holiday that aids self-devel-opment or the art of *being* a human in the modern world. Such orientation has clear lineage to the work of Maslow and self-actualization (see Chapter 7, 'The Driving Force of Motivation', this volume). Middleton and Clarke (2001) point to the rising importance of *insight* (reflecting the intellectual curiosity of tomorrow's tourists) and of *inspiration* (reflecting spiritual, creative or similar responses to the experience in the minds of these tourists).

Yeoman *et al.* (2006) for VisitScotland underscore the point that *inconspicuous consumption* is steadily replacing the flashier, status-ridden consumption of the second half of the 20th century (although they note there is still a role for ostentatious consumption). The European

Travel Commission (2006) mentions the growth of *creative tourism* that attracts people wishing to develop their creative skills during a holiday, perhaps because of lack of time or the right environment to do so in their everyday lives. Holidays or short breaks such as photography courses, painting, cookery classes, theatre stagecraft workshops and novel writing retreats are all examples that fit the brief of creative tourism and the opportunities it offers. Such special interests may not have the same attachment to specific destinations as the traditional holidays of the past – some special interests are less reliant on borders (VisitBritain, 2005, 2007). Conversely, we feel that much creative tourism is naturally integrated with local cultures, settings and identities – improving your landscape painting in the places visited by masters of the art or learning flamenco guitar in its historical Spanish setting.

The risk you take?

Although apparently an oxymoron, Poon (1993) noted the tension between less risk taking and more risk taking within the same individual tourist. On the one hand, a trend towards everything being safer – safer food and drink, safer travel, safer airplanes – and on the other an opposing trend towards greater risk taking in white knuckle and adventure tourism where the whole excitement of the tourism experience is in the perceived (and real) risk. Some of the explanation for this tension in approach to risk lies with perceptions of personal control. 'You drive a safe car to the destination for a short-break trip – where you then compete at speed over jumps riding a young thoroughbred horse, white-water raft down a river at the edge of your abilities or sky dive for the very first time. You prepare for the next day of thrills with a carbohydrate-based meal at a restaurant where you expect no risk from eating the food presented to you and perhaps even choose from the low-cholesterol (safe) options indicated in the menu. You stay in accommodation with the same expectations of hygiene. And at the end of your short-break trip – assuming you did not fall off or out of horse, raft or parachute harness – you drive home again in your safe car with its airbags and advanced safety technology.

Allied to this, one of the major trends spotted by the WTO (1997) is the polarization between comfort-based tourists and those – as illustrated above – who seek out action and adventure. This is magnified by the corresponding trend towards elder tourists in developed countries increasingly engaging with active sports and adventures as '60 becomes the new 40' (Thomson Future Holiday Forum, 2004).

We are an increasingly anxious society that wallows in a 'culture of fear' (Yeoman *et al.*, 2006). Yet we are, in fact, richer, healthier and safer than the generations that preceded us (Yeoman *et al.*, 2006). Take one example – that of personal security. With the fear of crime, fraud and terrorism in today's society (see Chapter 13, 'Of Fear, Flight and Feistiness', this volume), personal security in the public sphere is of importance to any discussion of trends in acceptance of personal risk. You expect to be protected. There are a selection of technological developments that look to the future safety of the tourist and others (Hodson, 2004; European Travel Commission, 2006; Formica and Kothari, 2008). For example, biometric measures such as fingerprints, ePassports that incorporate an electronic image of your face or iris recognition technology at airports, other transport hubs and hotels; 'geofencing' made possible by wireless location technology which will allow mobile phone users to be tracked and security forces alerted should a suspect approach a virtual fence erected round an airport; and new electronic payments systems to better secure credit card payments online and the use of e-purses.

The counter-trend to all this risk – the trend of *cocooning* – was applied to tourism by Cooper *et al.* (1998) at the turn of the century. Cocooning embraces the notion of making the home a secure and safe base for leisure activities, a countervailing force to offset the increase in perceived risk roaming the outside world. The continued growth in second homes and *residential tourism* (European Travel Commission, 2006) may be partially attributed to the desire to cocoon while on holiday. Uncertainty in the external world boosts the desire for solid anchors and secure holds – hence the attractiveness of second home possession (European Travel and Tourism Action Group, 2004). For example, the North–South patterns in second home property buying as people in Northern Europe seek the warmth of Southern Europe, and the current growth in property purchased by British and Germans in Eastern and Central Europe (European Travel Commission, 2006). In the longer term, we believe, climate change might well exacerbate such changes in geographic patterns of second home ownership – though not necessarily restricted to Eastern and Central Europe.

Tourists with time sensitivity

The final point that we wish to extract from Poon (1993) in this section looking back to the future is the notion of tourists as increasingly sensitive to time. After all, to undertake tourism at all, one of the resources you need at your disposal is free time – blocks of it. The trend towards increasing numbers of short breaks – making use of those briefer blocks of time – is well recognized (Clark, 2000; European Travel Commission, 2006). It is to the subject of time that we now turn our attention.

TOURISTS AS TIME LORDS OR TIME SLAVES?

The time lords as understood by fans of the UK television series, Doctor Who, are able to travel in and manipulate time. Many daydream on the fantasy of time travel, but, jerked back to the real world, have to manage their time as a limited and precious resource.

Throughout our history, we have used technology to achieve faster transport modes – from foot and horse to boat, train, car and airplane and to ever-faster versions. Japan is now showcasing a prototype high-speed train – the environmentally friendly super express train or efSET – to be tested in 2010 that is expected to run at 350 km/h (Breisch, 2008). The WTO (1997) refers to our complementary desire for 'fast track travel', or to systems that surround our choice of transport to facilitate and speed up the travel process such as check-in, security controls and baggage-handling methods. For if we are to have ever-faster transport, we need ever-faster check-in and security systems to complement the effort.

Our culture today is one of *immediacy* (Yeoman *et al.*, 2006; Yeoman and McMahon-Beattie, 2006). We do not expect to wait for anything for we want it right now – the notion of 'delayed gratification' largely belongs to a bygone generation. Furthermore, for 'anything' read 'everything', for we are also a 'have it all' society (Yeoman *et al.*, 2006) and a society willing (particularly – to date – in the UK) to buy on credit. Thus, our lifestyles proceed at a rapid and accelerating pace. We operate in that media buzz-phrase, a 24/7 society. Ten years back, a piece in *USA Today* spoke of modern-day professionals as *time stackers* and *multitaskers* who juggle two or more tasks at any one time in a *time-crunched* lifestyle where people race *full throttle* through their harried lives (Hellmich, 1997). Clark (2000) refers to the phenomenon as the 'leisure time squeeze'. If you think back to Chapter 14, 'Giving Tourism: The Intangible Gift' (this volume), time invested by the donors in the planning of, and participation in, the experience gift is much prized by recipients, for they understand the scarcity and value of free time.

In our increasingly time-pressured culture, holidays provide a respite from the headlong rush of everyday life. Yeoman *et al.* (2006) label such interludes of calmness and escape as *time oases*. With our high-speed obsession, the trend is for holidays in the future to be increasingly valued as mechanisms akin to pressure valves on a cooker – a release of the head of steam. Detox diet and stress-free weekends using *spiritual* hotels in rural settings are a recent trend for Tokyo executives (Yeoman, 2008a). Chapter 15, 'Limits to Travel? The Environmental Tourist' (this volume), brings to your attention a very different yet complementary trend, that of the growth of slow tourism.

Predictions in the 1950s and 1960s suggested a future era of lives devoted to leisure and travel; after all, over a timespan of 50 years between 1900 and 1950, the number of hours the average American worked dropped by about a quarter (Surowiecki, 2005). By the end of the 20th century, so it was predicted, Americans would experience over 13 weeks of holiday and a 4-day working week (Surowiecki, 2005). An example of a fallible prediction – the reality did not match the forecast.

A WTO study (recounted in Clark, 2000) into patterns of leisure time in 18 of the world's key tourist-generating countries paints a very different picture to the forecasts of the 1950s. The study included countries with comparatively generous paid holiday as legal entitlement (such as in Europe); countries with paid holiday dependent on individual employment contracts and no statutory rights (such as the USA); and countries with strong traditions of public holidays but with relatively new legal entitlement to paid holiday (such as in many Asian Pacific countries).

In the USA, 10 days paid leave is typical. Yet one-third of Americans take no more than 50% of their holiday leave (Clark, 2000). Indeed, half of Americans today allegedly suffer from *time poverty* (European Travel Commission, 2006). In Japan, a regular 2-day weekend is still only taken by roughly half of the employees (Clark, 2000). In Western Europe, the paid-leave-blessed region of the world, average annual paid leave amounts to 24 days (plus public holidays). Yet in the UK, a quarter of employees did not take their full holiday entitlement because of work pressures. The WTO study (Clark, 2000) notes:

- The long-hours work culture and the notion that 2-week holidays might be perceived by employers as indicative of poor job commitment – both contribute to the sacrifice of paid leave entitlement by employees.
- Job insecurity and work pressures contribute to the trend of increasing numbers of short-break trips taken more frequently throughout the year – the proliferation of short-break holidays.
- Fixed-term contracts and time off between jobs help create time for longer holidays to be enjoyed. The European Travel Commission (2006) refers to the trend towards *sabbatical holidays*.
- The trend towards more people working at weekends in countries that used to have the weekend break (attributable to our 24/7 society and spread of the Anglo-Saxon work ethic) is altering the *rhythm* of leisure time. Increasingly, the weekend is not the block of free time available for participating in short-break trips.
- There is an increase in the type of short-break trips that can be characterized as time-poor and money-rich – brief holidays as intense, expensive getaways from work pressures.

In looking to the future, the WTO study (Clark, 2000) concludes that, far from the increases in leisure time predicted in the 1950s and 1960s, a decrease is more likely. Thus, the trend in shorter holidays is set to continue, with the global economy putting the break on holiday leave and longer holidays taken during employment proving harder to arrange in dual-income households requiring the coordination of busy work schedules.

As presented above, the WTO study (Clark, 2000) is best related to the world of those in work. For contrast, the reader should also remember the changing demographics towards an ageing population who – although retiring later as governments struggle with pension costs – will enjoy much longer periods of free time. Time-rich they may be but, unlike much of the current generation of retirees in the developed world, they are likely to be cash-poor. The effects of the pension crisis stretch far into the future.

Entertainingly, Surowiecki (2005) in a piece for *The New Yorker* refers to the stereotypes of the Americans as *puritan grinds* and the French as *ambitionless café-dwellers* as a vehicle to stress that, although culturally embedded beliefs and attitudes play an important role, the external factors of higher taxes, stronger unions, collectively determined contracts and regulations also shape work–leisure trends from country to country. Simply stated (Surowiecki, 2005), the upshot is that Americans trade their productivity for more wealth and the Continental Europeans trade it for more leisure time.

A nascent trend pinpointed in, among others, *The Sunday Times* (Templeton, 2004) is that of UK employees buying extra holiday time in lieu of salary. They are sacrificing part of their salary in exchange for additional paid leave entitlement, and thereby demonstrating their preference for time over money. These 'cash-for-holidays' deals offered by companies to their employees were virtually unheard before the 21st century (Templeton, 2004). At a theoretical level, the trend is a practical illustration of Zuzanek and Mannell's (1983, cited in Ryan, 1991) trade-off hypothesis between work and leisure where people choose between working more and generating greater income or working less but with reduced financial reward.

Alternatively, the Thomson Future Holiday Forum (2004) highlights the rise of *soft holidays* where work and leisure are blended, blurred and combined, a trend duly facilitated by advances in information technology. Soft holidays allow the time-poor to stay in touch with the office or with clients while on leave. The idea perhaps approaches that of Poon's (1993) new tourist who wishes to reduce the polarity between work and leisure.

TECHNOLOGY AS TOOLS AND TOYS

In this section, we consider both how tourists of the future might use technology as part of the information search and decision process (tools) and as gadgets in the tourism experience (toys).

Technology as tools

Nearly one-quarter of the world population used the Internet on a regular basis in 2008 and this figure is forecast to reach 30% (around 1.9 billion) of the world population by 2012. Approximately 40% of all Internet users worldwide have mobile Internet access and this figure is forecast to exceed 1.5 billion by 2012 (European Travel Commission, 2008a). The anticipated growth in mobile Internet technologies especially handheld communication wireless devices will become increasingly important to the tourists of tomorrow (Yeoman and McMahon-Beattie, 2006).

The advent of Internet-enabled mobile phones using 3G technology allows tourists so inclined to plan and organize components of their holiday. They will also be able to communicate with inanimate objects such as retail signs and logos. For example, tourists will be able to point their mobile phone at a car rental sign and receive details of car hire costs, models and availability (Thomson Future Holiday Forum, 2004). The World Travel Market (2007g) highlights the arrival of mobile phone blogging.

Tourists will assume yet more control over the way that they choose, receive and use information about tourism products (European Travel Commission, 2006) – this shift in control is key to the decision-making process of the future tourist. The spread of Web 2.0 technologies will further aid tourists in reviewing web sites, travel blogs, photo sharing and video sharing thus accessing and imparting information to an audience way outside their immediate circle of acquaintances and outside the control (though certainly not the concerns) of the tourism industry (Tourism Australia, 2007).

Let us look at some illustrations of this. The review web site tripadvisor.com is visited by over ten million travellers across 150 countries every week (Tourism Australia, 2007). Another source reckons that one in every ten travellers checks a hotel on this web site (Keenan and Bradt, 2007). Podcasting and blogcasting allow anyone to create an audio or visual tour of a consumer-led reality of a hotel, attraction or destination (Yeoman and McMahon-Beattie, 2006). For example, the travel section of YouTube has around 3.5 million entries for the interested tourist to scrutinize. Sharing photos or diaries on a blogging site is now normal behaviour for younger tourists; a well-established blogging site dedicated to travel, wayn.com (where are you now?), has about eight million members globally (Keenan and Bradt, 2007). The trend mentioned earlier of the minipreneur is indicative of consumers wresting control from formal tourism industry structures and the rise of adbusting web sites and blogs where consumers bite back on brands that disappoint say something about the nature of online consumer power. Although growth in new users of social networking sites in North America is beginning to level off, in other regions of the world usage is burgeoning. For example, the now market leader Facebook.com has introduced natural language interfaces in several markets to support this penetration of the non-American market (European Travel Commission, 2008b).

Tourists can communicate with each other like never before. Inundated with information, source selection and credibility have become, and will remain, crucially important. The web site, The Man in Seat 61, a personal web site based on the train-travel expertise of one man, has won awards for its efficacy and has around half a million (non-unique) visitors a month (Mark Smith, personal communication, 2008). Having first developed online credibility, The Man in Seat 61 has recently published a travel book using traditional print media. The reversal of this (i.e. offline to online) is the successful incursion of brands that build reputation and trust offline first. For example, the *Lonely Planet* now hosts online travel communities, travel blogs and podcasts, photo galleries and so forth under its brand banner.

Technology as toys

Equating technological devices to playthings is not entirely a flippant way to capture your attention. It has a serious point, for such technology can also frame and shape the tourist experience. Take the MP3 player first used and established as a portable music device. Today, there is a rapid expansion of downloadable tourist guides designed for MP3 players. These digital audio and visual guides are available either free or for purchase from different providers of tourism (from hotels to tourist information centres to attractions and museums and so on); from traditional guidebook publishers through their web sites; and from dedicated providers of the product (such as Tourist Tracks), major audio-book brands and MP3 retailers. Increasingly, you the tourist can enjoy – for example – a self-guided walking tour of the city of your choice using your MP3 player (or perhaps one borrowed from your hotel), a tour of the Normandy Beaches and the D Day landing sites or a 3-day cycling trip.

We have yet to see if the MP3 'toy' will truly change the way that tourists sightsee and experience tourism around the world.

Another trend that has been spotted is that of 'geocaching', a type of treasure hunt which uses a Global Positioning System (GPS) receiver, or other handheld electronic navigation device, to hide and seek containers (called geocaches). These geocaches are small waterproof boxes with logbooks and nominal 'treasure' and there are believed to be over 800,000 hidden in some 100 countries of the world. Undertaken as either a recreational or tourist activity, this high-tech game is shared online using geocaching web sites. These web sites allow you to create and register a geocache hunt, to use the hunts created by other, and to share photos and stories about the experience. The GPS receiver or its equivalent (coupled with the Internet) is the 'toy' that forms the basis for this tourist experience.

The MP3 player tours and geocaching could be considered as updates of existing products and experiences, namely the printed guidebook and the map and compass treasure hunt game. They are technological 'toys' that allow the tourist to do things differently. Geocaching is probably a niche product and may be more akin to a fashion too. The MP3 player tours, on the other hand, are a wider trend across the tourism market dependent on the penetration of the MP3 player (one source suggests 275 million units will be sold in the year 2011 – In-Stat, 2007) and its likely replacement by, and adoption of, the next generation of portable technology.

A third idea relates to developments in virtual reality. Right now people are creating avatars for themselves who live in interactive computer-generated worlds of which Second Life is the best known. Tour operator Synthravels is a virtual tour operator. In itself a cyberbrand, this company offers holidays in cyberspace across different virtual worlds, including Second Life (Bowes, 2007). However, real-life tourism brands, such as Starwood hotels, also create virtual presence for their products. Bowes (2007) contends that cyberspace holidays will not replace the real thing, but that the technology could be used as a sophisticated travel brochure enabling potential tourists of the future to virtually explore the destination or tourism product prior to purchase. In other words, that it could be used as a tool for decision making, as well as a 'toy'.

Gazing further into the future, active skin technology using computer chips smaller than skin cells might be able to hook up with nerve endings and electronically record the sensations for later replay (Hodson, 2004; Pearson, 2007). Thus,

> by attaching tiny transmitters to your fingertips, toes, face and lips, you could experience the sensation of a holiday – walking on a beach, feeling a warm sea breeze on your face.
>
> (Hodson, 2004 citing futurologist Ian Pearson, p. 2)

Such stay-at-home holidays would answer the call for environment-friendly holidays as no travel component would be involved. But we feel that it will not replace the urge for genuine travel. It is more likely to act as a stimulant.

THE STRUCTURAL FORCE OF DEMOGRAPHICS

In many parts of the book, you can feel the underlying tug of demographic changes in the population, for example, in the environmental concerns of a burgeoning global population; in migration patterns; and in family life cycle changes. We cannot highlight these as 'new' changes, for the roots are firmly planted in the present and the past. Over a decade ago, Poon (1993) drew our attention to the changing demographics of an ageing population, the increase in smaller households and the increasing number of single people. Do smaller households and more single people fuel a desire for a sense of connectedness? And create a need for deeper community, family, friends and expression through social occasions? The Thomson Future Holiday Forum (2004) dubs the UK a *nation of singletons*. By 2030, single females who live alone will be the largest demographic group (Yeoman, 2008b). The UK Department for Culture, Media and Sport notes a trend towards more tourists travelling alone (DCMS, 1999). On the other side of the Atlantic, nearly a quarter of US travellers choose to take a vacation on their own (Travel Industry Association cited by Yeoman, 2008b). Travel for one is on the increase.

We can see that such demographic developments might lead to an increasing demand for VFR holidays (see Chapter 12, 'The Importance of Family', this volume); for volunteer tourism; for holidays that trace family ancestry; for holidays that retrace old family haunts; for locally grounded celebrations and festivities that bring a community together and to which tourists in search of this connectedness are attracted; and for holidays designed to welcome the single tourist into a destination or special interest-based community. There is similarity between the notion of 'connectedness' and the notion of high touch.

COUNTRY CAMEO: THE FUTURE FOR CHINA?

We have taken China as an influential country for tourist behaviour in the future. As noted near the beginning of this chapter, China is forecast to be the number one destination in the world by 2020 and the fourth most important generator of tourist trips (WTO, 1997). As one member of the 'BRIC' countries (the other members being Brazil, Russia and India), China attracts attention and investment from different sectors of the tourism industry because of its expected future impact – everyone wants a share of the market. To tie into the future of technology, we find that a biometric application process for Chinese visitor visas to the UK has recently been implemented using ten-digit fingerprints and digital photographs (VisitBritain, 2008).

More than 200 million Chinese today are financially able to engage in international tourism with around 34 million doing so in 2006 (World Travel Market, 2007h). At the more extreme end of the spectrum, figures used by VisitBritain (2008) suggest that around 4% of the world's millionaires now live in China. Provisional figures for 2007 suggest that Chinese outbound tourism generated around US$29.8 billion (WTO, 2008), placing China fifth in the world rankings for outbound tourist expenditure. By 2020 or even 2015, it is estimated that the number of international tourists generated by China will reach 100 million (World

Travel Market, 2007h). International inbound tourism, that is, overseas tourists visiting China, registered around 54.7 million trips in 2007, making China the fourth most visited destination on the planet (VisitBritain, 2008). The WTO predicts that by 2020 China will be the world's top destination in the league tables, with about 137 million tourist arrivals (WTO, 1997). As we also emphasized in Chapter 2, 'Country-File: Tourist Nations' (this volume), the domestic tourism market in China is already huge and the WTO expects Chinese domestic tourism to double by 2020 (VisitBritain, 2008).

Current trends spotted in the Chinese market include:

- A growing popularity of weekend shopping breaks in Hong Kong (World Travel Market, 2007h).
- Status enhancement from international tourism trips through the purchase of luxury brands associated with the country visited – for example, Burberry in England or Gucci in Italy. These luxury brands must be brands with a strong presence in China itself, so that the message or meaning to others is not diluted (see Chapter 11, 'The Power of Brand and Celebrity', this volume). Interestingly, in a reversal of this, there are now brands emerging that are recognized in China – where the marketing effort has been focused – but largely unrecognized by non-Chinese. Ports Clothing is one such brand connected with Canada now very popular in China but lacking meaning for other international tourists (World Travel Market, 2007h).
- Outbound luxury tourism is changing towards more family-related activities and emphasis on children's pastimes, a cultural inclination towards *deep impact* sightseeing, and the development of short-break holidays in Asia such as golf, sailing, gaming and shopping excursions in countries like Thailand, Singapore and Malaysia (Graff, 2008).

THE TOURIST TOMORROW REWOUND

Looking back over this chapter, we have probed some of the possible futures for tourist behaviour. In doing so, we have recognized the array of trends, fashions, hypes and niche market products. We have looked at well-observed trends (e.g. the growth of short-break vacations and the reasons why) and the less observed (e.g. the rise of volunteer tourism and the reasons why). We hope to have triggered off your own ideas too, based on your professional or consumer experience.

We would like to finish the chapter with a few thoughts as applied to the consumer in general (and thereby encompassing you as a tourist – a consumer of tourism). Throughout this book, we have juxtaposed portraits and explanations for tourist behaviour – behaviour that often seems to lack consistency. As explained by consumer theorists, Gabriel and Lang (2006),

> [a]s consumers, we can be irrational, incoherent and inconsistent just as we can be rational, planned and organised. We can be individualist or may be driven by social norms and expectations. We can seek risk and excitement or may aim for comfort and security. We can be deeply moral

about the way we spend our money or quite unfettered by moral considerations....Such fragmentations and contradictions should be recognised as core features of contemporary consumption itself.

(Gabriel and Lang, 2006, p. 4)

As we balance on the cusp of what might be a deep economic recession, this generic book on the consumer by Gabriel and Lang published back in 2006 is prescient in talking of *consumer fatigue*, consumers being *spend-shy*, mantras of *consume less* and Western consumerism as we know it commencing 'a period of well-earned malaise' (Gabriel and Lang, 2006, p. 5), from which eventually it may re-emerge, metamorphose or collapse. The zenith of consumerism, as we know it, could enter the history books as the turn of the 20th century. The future and shape of consumerism carries an overarching influence on any future and shape of tourist behaviour.

Our final thought to leave you with is that although a sense of well-being in the life of some consumers might be engendered by consuming less (Layton and Grossbart, 2006), there are millions of people in countries across the world unable to exercise the freedom and choice to participate in tourism – whether because of poverty, illness or political exclusion. You the tourist – and indeed we the authors as tourists – remain the privileged minority in an inequitable world.

REFERENCES

Bowes, E. (2007) Virtual holidays – not as good as the real thing. *The New Zealand Herald* 30 May 2007. Available at: www.nzherald.co.nz/technology/news/article.cfm?c_id=5&objectid=10441864

Breisch, D. (2008) The race for the next high-speed train, 1 October 2008. Available at: www.gadling.com/2008/10/01/the-race-for-the-next-high-speed-train

Clark, C. (2000) Changes in leisure time: the impact on tourism. *Insights* Tourism Intelligence Papers, English Tourism Council, London.

Cooper, C., Fletcher, J., Gilbert, D. and Wanhill, S. (1998) *Tourism Principles and Practice*, 2nd edn. Addison Wesley Longman, Harlow, UK.

Department of Culture, Media and Sport (1999) *Tomorrow's Tourism*. DCMS, London.

European Travel and Tourism Action Group (2004) *Tourism in Europe – to the Year 2005 and Beyond*. ETAG, London. Available at: www.etag-euro.org/cfacts.htm

European Travel Commission (2006) *Tourism Trends for Europe*. ETC, Brussels, September 2006.

European Travel Commission (2008a) World usage patterns and demographics. Available at: www.etcnewmedia.com/review

European Travel Commission (2008b) Social networking explodes worldwide. Available at: www.etcnewmedia.com/review

Formica, S. and Kothari, T.H. (2008) Strategic destination planning: analyzing the future of tourism. *Journal of Travel Research* 46 (4), 355–367.

Forum for the Future (2008) *Tourism 2023: Vision, Scenarios and Strategy for a Sustainable UK Outbound Travel and Tourism industry*, 13 August 2008. Available at: www.forumforthefuture.org/Tourism2023

Gabriel, Y. and Lang, T. (2006) *The Unmanageable Consumer*, 2nd edn. Sage Publications, London.

Graff, R. (2008) *China Luxury Outbound Travel*. Presentation by ChinaContact. Available at: www.ccontact.com/files

Hellmich, N. (1997) Time stackers. The ultimate juggling act. Multiduties the norm for '90s professionals. *USA Today* 28 May 1997.

Hodson, M. (2004) Holiday 2010? One small step for man, seven nights self-catering for mankind. *The Sunday Times* Travel Section, 3 October 2004, 1–2.

In-Stat (2007) Worldwide demand remains strong for MP3 and Portable Media Players. Available at: www.instat.com/catalog/wcatalogue.asp?id=27

Keenan, S. and Bradt, H. (2007) Battle of the travel guides: pod or print? *The Times*, 21 July 2007. Available at: www.timesonline.co.uk/tol/travel/holiday_type/travel_and_literature

Layton, R.A. and Grossbart, S. (2006) Macromarketing: past, present and possible future. *Journal of Macromarketing* 26 (2), 193–213.

Middleton, V.T.C. and Clarke, J. (2001) *Marketing in Travel and Tourism*, 3rd edn. Butterworth-Heinemann, Oxford.

Naisbitt, J. (1984) *Megatrends: Ten New Directions Transforming Our Lives*. MacDonald, London.

Pan, S., Chon, K. and Song, H. (2008) Visualizing tourism trends: a combination of ATLAS.ti and BiPlot. *Journal of Travel Research* 46 (3), 339–348.

Pearson, I. (2007) *Towards the Virtual Economy*. Available at: http://futurizon.net/articles

Pearson, I. (2008) A 25 page guide to the future. Available at: http://futurizon.net/articles/overview.doc

Poon, A. (1993) *Tourism, Technology and Competitive Strategies*. CAB International, Wallingford, UK.

Ramesh, R. (2005) This UK patient avoided the NHS list and flew to India for a heart bypass. Is health tourism the future? *The Guardian* 1 February 2005. Available at: www.guardian.co.uk/medicine/story/0,11381,1402881,00.html

Ryan, C. (1991) *Recreational Tourism. A Social Science Perspective*. Routledge, London.

Surowiecki, J. (2005) No work and no play. *The New Yorker* 28 November. Available at: www.newyorker.com/archive/2005/11/28/051128ta_talk_surowiecki

Templeton, S.-K. (2004) Staff 'buy' extra holiday time. *The Sunday Times* 28 November, p. 8.

Thomson Future Holiday Forum (2004) *A Future-Gazing Study of How Holidays are Set to Change Over the Next 20 Years*. Thomson, UK. Available at: www.lexispr.com/thomson

Tourism Australia (2006) *Changing World – Changing Consumers. Operator Opportunities*. Available at: www.tourism.australia.com/content/Research/Factsheets/Consumer_Trends_Industry_handout_Sep_2006.pdf

Tourism Australia (2007) Word of Web. How the Internet has supercharged word of mouth recommendation, June 2007. Available at: www.tourism.australia.com/content/Research/Word%20of%20Mouth%20Word%20of%20Web%20-%20June%202007.pdf

Travelmole (2005) *Report Revels Radical Shift in Buying Habits*, 4 November 2005. Available at: www.travelmole.com/stories

Trendhunter Magazine (2008) Nudist flights – naked travel in Germany with OssiUrlaub.de. *Trendhunter Magazine*. Available at: www.trendhunter.com/trends/nudist-flights-ossiurlaubde

VisitBritain (2005) *Foresight*, Issue 26. VisitBritain, London.

VisitBritain (2006) *Foresight*, Issue 34. VisitBritain, London.

VisitBritain (2007) *Foresight*, Issue 41. VisitBritain, London.

VisitBritain (2008) *Foresight*, Issue 58. VisitBritain, London.

World Tourism Organization (1997) *Tourism 2020 Vision Executive Summary*. WTO, Madrid.

World Tourism Organization (2008) *Tourism Highlights 2008 Edition*. UNWTO, Madrid.

World Travel Market (2007a) *Minipreneurs. Potential Opportunities for Independent Agents*. The World Travel Market, London. Available at: www.wtmlondon.com/page.cfm/link=54

World Travel Market (2007b) *Health and Wellness*. The World Travel Market, London. Available at: www.wtmlondon.com/page.cfm/link=57

World Travel Market (2007c) *Chavs vs Travs. The rise and rise of the 'chaveller'*. The World Travel Market, London. Available at: www.wtmlondon.com/page.cfm/link=58

World Travel Market (2007d) *Have Pet, Will Travel*. The World Travel Market, London. Available at: www.wtmlondon.com/page.cfm/link=52

World Travel Market (2007e) *Homosexual, not Homogenous*. The World Travel Market, London. Available at: www.wtmlondon.com/page.cfm/link=233

World Travel Market (2007f) *Halal Tourism – Untapped Potential for Middle East*. The World Travel Market, London. Available at: www.wtmlondon.com/page.cfm/link=51

World Travel Market (2007g) *'Third Screen' Revolutionising Travel Marketing in Asia*. The World Travel Market, London. Available at: www.wtmlondon.com/page.cfm/link=53

World Travel Market (2007h) *China – The Final Frontier*. The World Travel Market, London. Available at: www.wtmlondon.com/page.cfm/link=60

Yeoman, I. (2008a) *The Changing Meaning of Luxury*, 22 April 2008. Available at: www.hospitalitynet.org/news/4035622.html

Yeoman, I. (2008b) *Bridget Jones Goes on Holiday*, 9 May 2008. Available at: www.hospitalitynet.org/news/4035872.html

Yeoman, I. and McMahon-Beattie, U. (2006) Practitioner Paper. Tomorrow's tourist and the information society. *Journal of Vacation Marketing* 12(3), 269–291.

Yeoman, I., Munro, C. and McMahon-Beattie, U. (2006) Practitioner paper. Tomorrow's world: consumer and tourist. *Journal of Vacation Marketing* 12(2), 174–190.

EPILOGUE

This book has taken us on a journey through contemporary tourist behaviour. We do not believe that we have captured everything – although we have tried to capture as much as we can. In truth, each chapter could rightly be expanded into a book of its own – adorned with further examples and theory.

We have addressed our book primarily to a graduate audience who is coming to the subject for the first time, or an undergraduate audience who has learned about disparate parts of the subject but wants to see how the various elements can be joined together in some sort of reasonable framework. But at the same time, we have tried to make the book accessible and easy to read (and portable) rather than a learned tome that requires full attention at all times, weighs down the rucksack and fills up the study shelf.

We decided early in the writing process that we would focus the 'Epilogue' on research methodology, given just how crucial this is to any serious study and any improvements in understanding. Moreover, in the context of tourist behaviour, it has long been apparent to us that step-developments in understanding have been generated when research problems are addressed with an appropriate methodology and resultant methods.

We believe that the interpretivist and the pragmatist approaches have much to offer.

Along with many other researchers, it appears, we were independently inspired some 15 years ago by the writings of authors such as Arnould and Price (1993) – quoted already in this book with reference to their *tour de force*, their journal article 'River Magic'. When asked to articulate what is so special about the article in a research seminar, one of the authors, who was then engaged in PhD research on tourist satisfaction on long-haul tours, generated an 11-point listing. The questions that are posed in the seminar and the notes that guided the answers are illuminating.

WHAT IS THE RESEARCH THAT IT HELPS?

All consumer behaviour research really – but specifically consumer (tourist) satisfaction and research that uses participant observation.

SO WHY IS THIS AN IMPORTANT ARTICLE?

1. It focuses attention in the field, the real world – rather than in the laboratory or in artificial settings like so much early work in consumer behaviour.

2. It uses participant observation – an innovative approach but one that is suited to much tourist behaviour research.

3. It is well written – without either mountains of theoretical literature (available elsewhere) or turgid, academic prose. It is lucid and straightforward.

4. It writes up participant observation in an attractive narrative style. It shows no shame in publishing such narrative as a core research finding – in fact quite the reverse – in a major international journal (*Journal of Consumer Research*).

5. It triangulates methods and so gives confidence in the analysis and evaluation.

6. It looks at a variety of perspectives on satisfaction – consumers ('rafters'), suppliers ('outfitters') and tourism personnel (the guide).

7. It explodes myths (e.g. on expectation) the PhD research is beginning to question – from personal experience, from (candid) interviews with a few tour operator directors and a few journal articles. Much of its detail also conforms to the day-to-day understanding of workers in the tour operator sector – like the importance of the tour guide in satisfaction and the greater influence of *fun* and *emotion* on satisfaction than cognitive elements.

8. It deals with extended experience – it attempts to gauge satisfaction through time rather than at one specific time. So, it fills a gap in knowledge.

9. It suggests avenues for future research (e.g. emotional labour).

10. It deals with a leisure/tourism context. It helps *legitimize* leisure/tourism – within the mainstream – as a subject worthy of academic study.

11. Finally, it shows a human touch – with a dedication to the authors' young son.

At the time of the seminar, other key writings that emerged to complement the work of Arnould and Price were Botterill (1987), Penaloza (1994) and Wolcott (1994). Botterill dismantled expectancy disconfirmation theory (or at least the unthinking acceptance of the theory) in a two-page commentary in *Annals of Tourism Research*. Both Penaloza and Wolcott also examined aspects of behaviour – although not tourist behaviour – with a similar methodology, innovative set of methods and real heart, a true burning commitment to the research that derived from some personal connection. This is not to say that personal connection is necessary for all good research – but it can help.

Who has held the torch for such work since 1993? We both recommend the recent study by Decrop and Snelders (2004) in which they explore the planning process followed by Belgian households as they make decisions about their summer vacation. You might expect that they would make use of a large-scale questionnaire survey of households – picked at random from, say, a government database. And certainly such a study would be entirely feasible and could match the research question set by Decrop and Snelders. But instead they have followed an interpretivist approach that seems to glean some real insight – the sort of insight that would be difficult to produce with a standard questionnaire survey. They rely on data from 25 households – a positivist might say 'just 25 households'. But the households are interviewed using a grounded theory approach (after Strauss and Corbin, 1990) – and as close to a pure grounded theory approach as we have seen. They seem not to have relied on preconceived theorizing so that the empirical data really do form the basis for the subsequent interpretation. They also engage in classic coding of data at three levels from the most descriptive to the most interpretive (open, axial and selective codes); constant comparison between the empirical material and emergent categories and so forth.

The interviews occur four times during the 1-*year-long* fieldwork and during each interview most members of the household – 'decision-making units' (DMUs) – were present. This in itself allows for triangulation although other forms of triangulation are also apparent – like a consideration of holiday pictures at the end of the second series of interviews. And so through prolonged engagement in the setting and a growing relationship of trust with informants 'who became more and more spontaneous and talkative' (Decrop and Snelders, 2004, p.1014) – as well as informant comment on their ongoing summary analysis and interpretations – the researchers are able to explicitly state that their findings are dependable and confirmable. In other words, what is said in the interpretation is worth saying and repeating because the methodology is sound – as we have already detailed in Chapter 8, 'Logical Decision or Lucky Dip?' (this volume).

A comparison of this type of detailed study with the standard large-scale questionnaire surveys completed by tourists for some academic studies – as well as for businesses and organizations at the end of customer flights and vacations throughout the world – can really reveal the limit of the *behavioural* information that some surveys produce (Bowen, 2008). Elsewhere, one of the authors has recorded how a number of tour operators even underuse the data that they gather with their questionnaires – so that after duly noting an overall score for 'satisfaction' or 'enjoyment' (both loosely defined) piles of questionnaires are then stored and forgotten. Indeed, in semi-structured interviews we have conducted with managing directors (MDs) of tourism companies, the occasional MD has placed his/her head above the parapet and confessed that sometimes that is how they act – that the collection of data and even a decent attempt at analysis is done because of an automatic assumption that such is the way research is done. Sometimes (says the occasional MD), when the data gathering is specifically targeted at a particular new innovation (such as a new baggage collection service), a week-by-week, month-by-month score – as picked up from questionnaire results – is worthwhile. But as a mechanism for deeper understanding such methods can be limited. So, we would make an appeal to tourism companies and organizations to consider some of the alternative approaches and techniques they could employ to understand paying customers.

Not that we have avoided the contribution from academics camped in the positivist field. They often provide the core concepts that the interpretivists and positivists alike can latch on to. We have also not avoided large-scale entry and exit surveys by national tourism organizations (NTOs) or the World Tourism Organization (WTO). The WTO statistics are especially good at getting a handle on tourist movements across the globe. Over the decades, much effort has been invested in the task of achieving as accurate a picture as possible – there is no substitute for WTO statistics at this point.

But we would make an appeal for university researchers to question the real value of large-scale questionnaire surveys in order to understand contemporary tourist behaviour. And especially to question the value of using students as informants – unless, as in the excellent studies by Maoz (2006), university students genuinely form part of the tourist segment. There are pressures to publish – and an interpretivist approach from conception to submission often requires a longer fuse than a positivist approach – certainly longer than the 1-year incubation period that university research allowances are commonly assigned.

One pleasure that has come from constructing this book has been the chance that it has given to reprise some classic articles from the past! And it is striking just how fluent and contemporary some of them are – free from 30 or 40 years of additional writing and references. So, apart from nudging you the reader to take a look at them for yourself we also urge you to take another look, or a first look if you are new to tourism research, at the likes of Cohen (1972, 1979) and Crompton (1979) and Mayo and Jarvis (1981) and Jafari (1987).

The study of contemporary tourist behaviour is a fascinating one. We hope that this book has enhanced your understanding of yourself and others as tourists. And that if you choose to research or work in the industry – or even just to be a tourist – your enthusiasm for knowing more about yourself and others as tourists will continue.

REFERENCES

Arnould, E.J. and Price, L. (1993) River magic: extraordinary experience and the extended service encounter. *Journal of Consumer Research* 20, 24–45.

Botterill, D.T. (1987) Dissatisfaction with a construction of satisfaction. *Annals of Tourism Research* 14, 139–140.

Bowen, D. (2008) Consumer thoughts, actions and feelings from within the service experience. *Services Industry Journal* 28 (10), 1515–1530.

Cohen, E. (1972) Toward a sociology of international tourism. *Social Research* 39 (1), 164–189.

Cohen, E. (1979) A phenomenology of tourist types. *Sociology* 13, 179–201.

Crompton, J. (1979) Motivation for pleasure travel. *Annals of Tourism Research* 4, 408–424.

Decrop, A. and Snelders, D. (2004) Planning the summer vacation. *Annals of Tourism Research* 31(4), 1008–1030.

Jafari, J. (1987) Tourism models: the socio-cultural aspects. *Tourism Management* 8(2), 151–159.

Maoz, D. (2006) The mutual gaze. *Annals of Tourism Research* 33(1), 221–239.

Mayo, E.J and Jarvis, L.P. (1981) *The Psychology of Leisure Travel*. CBI Publishing, Boston, Massachusetts.

Penaloza, L. (1994) *Atravesando Fronteras*/border crossings: a critical ethnographic exploration of the consumer acculturation of Mexican immigrants. *Journal of Consumer Research* 12, 32–54.

Strauss, A. and Corbin, J. (1990) *Basics of Qualitative Research: Grounded Theory Procedures and Techniques*. Sage, London.

Wolcott, H. (1994) *Transforming Qualitative Data – Description, Analysis and Interpretation*. Sage Publications, London.

INDEX

Page numbers in **bold** refer to tables or figures. References to information in footnotes is indicated by 'n' following the page reference.